ALSO BY RINKER BUCK

Shane Comes Home

First Job

If We Had Wings

Flight of Passage

THE
OREGON
TRAIL

A NEW AMERICAN JOURNEY

RINKER BUCK

SIMON & SCHUSTER

NEW YORK   LONDON   TORONTO   SYDNEY   NEW DELHI

Simon & Schuster
1230 Avenue of the Americas
New York, NY 10020

First Simon & Schuster hardcover edition July 2015

SIMON & SCHUSTER and colophon are registered trademarks of Simon & Schuster, Inc.

For information about special discounts for bulk purchases,
please contact Simon & Schuster Special Sales at
1-866-506-1949 or business@simonandschuster.com.

The Simon & Schuster Speakers Bureau can bring authors to your live event.
For more information or to book an event, contact the Simon & Schuster Speakers
Bureau at 1-866-248-3049 or visit our website at www.simonspeakers.com.

Interior design by Ruth Lee-Mui

Maps by Jeffrey L. Ward

Illustrations by Michael Gellatly

Manufactured in the United States of America

9   10   8

Library of Congress Cataloging-in-Publication Data

Buck, Rinker.
The Oregon Trail : a new American journey / Rinker Buck.
         pages   cm
           I. Title.
       F597.B89   2015
978—dc23   2015001159

ISBN 978-1-4516-5916-0
ISBN 978-1-4516-5918-4 (ebook)

PHOTO CREDITS

Front endpaper: Rinker Buck; Back endpaper: Vince Holtz

Sue Holtz: iv, vii; Paul Fusco: 10, 12, 80, 144; William Henry Jackson Collection;
Scotts Bluff National Monument: 52; Peter Schuttler Wagon Co. brochure: 74, 75;
Author's Collection: 90; Whitman College Collection: 101; Rufus Porter Museum: 158;
Shorpy Historic Picture Archive: 168; Nicholas Buck: 209, 224; Samuel Peery: 308

This book is for my brother, Nicholas McMahon Buck, who got us there with rare gumption and skill. Among New England horsemen, he has long been known as one of the great team drivers of his generation and he affirmed this—and more—crossing the Oregon Trail.

When I strike the open plains, something happens. I'm home.
I breathe differently. That love of great spaces, of rolling open
country like the sea, it's the grand passion of my life.

—WILLA CATHER

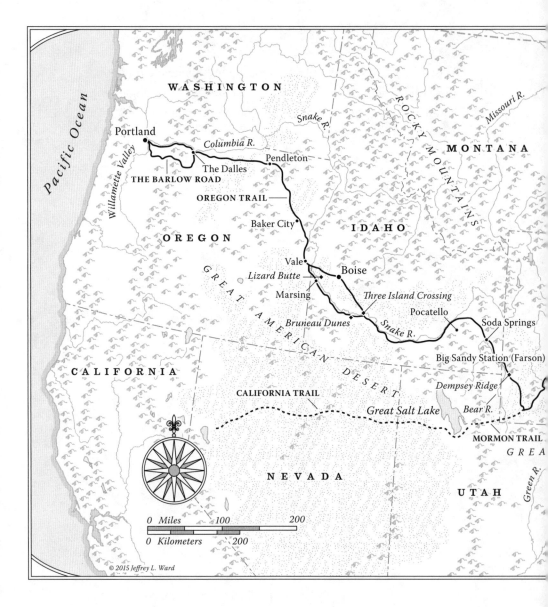

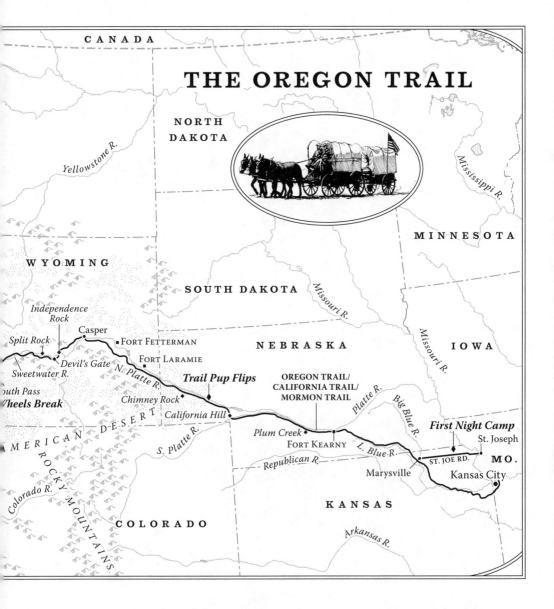

THE OREGON TRAIL

CANADA

NORTH DAKOTA

MINNESOTA

Yellowstone R.

WYOMING

SOUTH DAKOTA

Missouri R.

Independence Rock

IOWA

Split Rock · Casper

■ FORT FETTERMAN

NEBRASKA

Missouri R.

Devil's Gate

■ FORT LARAMIE

Sweetwater R.

N. Platte R.

Trail Pup Flips

OREGON TRAIL/ CALIFORNIA TRAIL/ MORMON TRAIL

Platte R.

Big Blue R.

First Night Camp

South Pass

Chimney Rock ·

Wheels Break

California Hill ·

Plum Creek ·

St. Joseph

AMERICAN DESERT

FORT KEARNY

L. Blue R.

ST. JOE RD.

MO.

ROCKY MOUNTAINS

S. Platte R.

Republican R.

Marysville

Kansas City

Colorado R.

COLORADO

KANSAS

Arkansas R.

1

I HAD KNOWN LONG BEFORE I rode a covered wagon to Oregon that naïveté was the mother of adventure. I just didn't understand how much of that I really had. Nicholas and I realized before we left Missouri with the mules that we would be the first wagon travelers in more than a century to make an authentic crossing of the Oregon Trail. But that was never the point for us. We pushed mules almost two thousand miles to learn something more important. Even more beautiful than the land that we passed, or the months spent camping on the plains, was learning to live with uncertainty.

The trip was my idea, and I fell into it in my usual barmy way. A few summers ago, while taking an afternoon off from a story I was working on in the Flint Hills of Kansas, I stopped on the road near a stout granite monument that marked a set of wheel ruts disappearing northwest across the plains.

Junction
of
Oregon Trail
with
Overland Trail
60 Rod S-E

Enchanted by the idea that I could step from a modern paved road onto the tracks of the nineteenth-century pioneers—not to mention walk all the way to Oregon—I paused just long enough to grab a water bottle and a brimmed hat from my car and set out along the ruts, heading west. It was a beautiful, breezy day, with sprays of yellow coreopsis blooming above the grasses and meadowlarks bobbing over the hills. The old ruts sloped over several gentle rises, past clumps of cottonwood trees and low shrubs at the watercourses, and handsome timber bridges that crossed two streams. The expansiveness of the landscape was hypnotic and physically exhilarating, and after the first mile I felt as if I were levitating on the plains. The distant hills of Nebraska seemed to draw my vision hundreds of miles away.

A few miles up I stopped to admire the view after climbing a steep rise. The valley below was one of those dreamy western vistas out of an Albert Bierstadt painting—a U-shaped canyon framed on one side by a large stream and on the other by green and brown hills. In the middle, a tidy group of shingled rooftops glowed orange in the sun, surrounded by browsing cattle. I walked down to the stream, where a sign announced that I had reached the old Hollenberg Ranch and Pony Express station along the Oregon Trail.

The restored ranch and Pony Express station are maintained by the Kansas State Historical Society, and at the interpretive center there, built near a modern parking lot, I learned about the place. Gerat Hollenberg was a German immigrant who had first crossed the Oregon Trail during the 1849 California Gold Rush. He made a small fortune in the northern California gold fields, then lost it in a shipwreck off Florida, and was drawn back to Kansas in 1854 by his memories of the beautiful prairie and dreams of founding a business along the busy covered wagon trail he had seen five years before. At the time, marginalized American farmers "westering" for cheap land in the Northwest, religious zealots, and just dreamers in search of adventure were flooding across the Kansas frontier, and in peak years as many as fifty thousand covered wagon immigrants spent the summer crossing the Oregon Trail and its two main tributaries, the California and Mormon trails. Entrepreneurs intent on profiting from this traffic were building a network of "road ranches" along remote stretches of the trail, providing a kind of early log-cabin convenience store for the passing wagons. Hollenberg selected a site along Cottonwood Creek to attract pioneers who needed to water their draft animals and replenish their drinking barrels at the end of their first week crossing the prairie, and apparently he chose well. The trading post and wagon-repair shop he built on the plains—later, his wife added an outdoor kitchen and sold hot meals—were quickly heralded in published trail guides as the last major layover until Fort Kearny in Nebraska, two hundred miles away.

I was intrigued by one display at the interpretive center, lying flat in a glass case. It was a facsimile reproduction of a journal entry made in May 1850 by an Oregon Trail pioneer from Indiana, Margaret Frink, describing the scene from the rise above the river that I had just left. Today, the Hollenberg Ranch sits on a lonely, deserted spot on the hilly plains, with only the green vastness of the prairie grasses, and the mosaic of yellow and purple flowers climbing the low rises, filling in the view. But Frink's 1850 journal entry described a starkly different place, a scene that could only be imagined 157 years later, looking out over the empty hills.

> In the afternoon we came to the junction of the emigrant road from St. Joseph with our road.... Both roads were thickly crowded with emigrants. It was a grand spectacle when we came, for the first time, in view of the vast migration, slowly winding its way westward over the broad plain. The country was so level we could see the long trains of white-topped wagons for many miles. It appeared to me that none of the population had been left behind. It seemed to me that I had never seen so many human beings before in all my life.

That was the moment when I first felt the rush of a dream about the Oregon Trail, but the thought quickly passed as I moved on to the other exhibits. They were mostly reproductions of paintings of the Kansas hills during the 1840s and 1850s, when dust billowing up from the wagon trains created a haze all the way to the horizon, collections of old wheel hubs and shards of harness unearthed during archeological digs, and a description of the ranch's use as a Pony Express station and stagecoach stop in the 1860s.

The site administrator from the Kansas Historical Society, an elderly man named Duane Durst, stood behind the counter as I walked through

the museum entrance. Duane was talkative and obviously lonely, glad
to have some company for the afternoon. He was a retired farmer and
feed mill manager from the nearby town of Washington, Kansas, who
had spent most of his life studying the patchwork of nineteenth-century
"feeder trails" in eastern Kansas that led to the beginning of the main Oregon Trail nearby. This network of roads was called the "junction country"
of Kansas, and in many spots near Durst's farm, the remnants of the old
wagon ruts are still visible in unplowed pastures and stream crossings. He
was exactly the kind of walking database I enjoyed meeting on such a day,
and I was quickly drawn in by the details he shared.

The feeder trails that moved northwest through Kansas and then
disappeared beyond the Flint Hills all emptied into the original Platte
River Road, as it was initially called, the main fur-trapping route to the
Rockies that passed through the Arapaho and Sioux tribal lands in western Nebraska in the 1820s and 1830s. Renamed the Oregon Trail in the
1840s, the route spanned some 2,100 miles from jumping-off towns such
as St. Joseph and Independence, Missouri, to the Willamette Valley in
Oregon, following the great river valleys of the West through five present-
day states—Kansas, Nebraska, Wyoming, Idaho, and Oregon. Unlike the
image projected in Hollywood westerns, where covered wagons are pulled
by attractive teams of matched Percheron and Belgian horses, oxen and
mules were the preferred draft animals, Duane told me. Horses require
too much forage and they couldn't take the heat and the long stretches between reliable sources of water. Many more immigrants were dispatched
by shooting accidents and wagon crashes than were killed by Indians, and
the river crossings were often treacherous in the spring, costing many
pioneers their lives. But by the fall, families regrouped. At major stopovers
like Soda Springs in Idaho, or Farewell Bend in eastern Oregon, the long
wagon trains paused while partners widowed by the rivers remarried, and
the festivities often lasted for three or four days.

My curiosity was aroused by another detail that Duane shared. Pulling from his wallet a laminated ID card, he told me that he was a twenty-
five-year member of the Oregon-California Trails Association, the main
preservationist group for the trail. Duane described himself as a "rut nut,"
and his commitment to the group was pretty typical. Over the past twenty
years he had rescued several Oregon Trail markers and monuments that

had been overrun by farming and other development, relocating them closer to traveled roads where they could be seen. He had helped design and build a visitors' center at the Hollenberg Ranch and created Oregon Trail education programs for local schools. An Oregon-California Trails Association newsletter that Duane gave me described how the group's volunteer work crews fanned out on summer weekends across broad expanses of the West, restoring mile markers along the trail, checking fence lines for land encroachments, and preserving trail grave sites in Wyoming and Nebraska.

Feelings of inadequacy overwhelmed me as I listened to Duane. I am an obsessive-compulsive reader and a history junkie. I brake by rote at every historical marker, I buy out museum bookstores, and for years my interest in colonial forts and Shaker villages so exhausted my two children that they are now permanently allergic to the past. I can tell you, right down to the hour, everything that happened at Gettysburg, Pennsylvania, during the first week of July 1863, and each setback that Franklin Roosevelt endured during World War II feels like it happened to me. Frequent summer junkets to Montana and Wyoming had convinced me that I knew a lot about the American West. But now, on a perfect Kansas day, at an exquisite historical site, I was listening to a rut nut empty his brain on the Oregon Trail, and I realized that I didn't know a thing about it. How could I have missed so much about so iconic an American experience?

And what Duane told me next seemed even more astonishing. Today, almost the entire 2,100-mile expanse of the Oregon Trail—even where it has been covered over by modern highways or railroad tracks—has been meticulously charted and marked, with long, undeveloped spaces now preserved as a National Historic Trail. Except for two bad stretches of suburban sprawl around Scottsbluff, Nebraska, and Boise, Idaho, most of the rest of the trail is still accessible along remote farm and ranch roads in the West. In western Nebraska and central Wyoming, where the trail runs through relatively undisturbed federal lands or immense private ranches, there are still more than six hundred miles of original wagon ruts, just like the path I had hiked that day. The dreamscape chain of natural landmarks and river views that the pioneers saw—Signal Bluff and Chimney Rock along the Platte, Devil's Gate on the Sweetwater, Rendezvous Point at the Green—is all still there, virtually intact.

When Duane began describing the trail, he handed me a foldout map published by the National Park Service, and I followed along as he spoke. End to end, the map stretched almost four feet across the counter, depicting an immensity of terrain, almost completely devoid of urban development, from the banks of the Missouri River at Kansas City to the end of the Columbia River gorge near the Pacific coast. The colored terrain shadings on the map looked like platters holding a giant smorgasbord of geology—plains, bluffs, high desert, and dramatic river gorges—along the route west. To me, the Oregon Trail had always been just another historic nameplate, like Manassas or Pikes Peak, but now the map in front of me was opening it up like a tableau of the enormous energy of the American experience. The visual prompt of the map was irresistible, and I formed a strong mental image as I looked out through the paned windows to the endless plains beyond the groves of cottonwood trees that curled along the floodplain of the Little Blue River. In my mind's eye, a dusty two-track trail curved northwest into the mystery of Nebraska, and then disappeared into the snowcapped rim of Wyoming's Medicine Bows.

The map, the hypnotic Flint Hills rising and falling all around me, the peaceful surroundings of the ranch, seemed an invitation to ramble. Who wouldn't, given the chance, want to ride the trail end to end? Wanderlust has always acted like amphetamine for me and I could not prevent my head from making the next leap.

St. Joe to Farewell Bend in Oregon in a covered wagon. More than two thousand miles of open country to cross. What a dream.

"So, in other words," I said to Duane, "somebody could still do it. The whole trail."

Duane looked at me quizzically, as if I were asking a question that he'd never heard before. The modern trail, he explained, mostly existed as a tourist attraction. Families driving west in their RVs—headed for Yellowstone or Glacier National Park—stopped out of curiosity when they saw signs identifying Oregon Trail sites. Most of them just wanted to quickly read a brochure and then find the next campsite with a cable TV hookup.

"But you could do it," I said. "The trail is still there."

"In theory, yeah, I suppose," Duane said. "But it isn't going to happen."

After poking around the grounds and the Pony Express station for a while, I stepped back inside to say good-bye to Duane, and then hiked back east across the rise. The words of Margaret Frink had stayed with me, and I stopped at the top to look back. It was tempting to look across the hills to Nebraska and imagine long trains of white-topped wagons for many miles, with men hollering at teams, whips cracking, and hundreds of wheels raising dust, while outriders galloped through the grasses to flush up game. At this time of day the river bottoms all the way to Nebraska would be obscured by gray clouds of smoke, as the pioneers stopped their trains for the night and cooked deer steaks and prairie chickens for their evening meal. But the plains were quiet now, the air crystalline. The cedar roofs of the Hollenberg Ranch, lit pink and amber by the falling sun, were all that I could see.

It was almost dark by the time I got back to my car. Dusk is my favorite part of the day, a time for expansive thoughts, and as I drove south my mind wandered back over the ruts and the vision of a journey that I had seen on a map at the Hollenberg Ranch. I dreamed about it all the way back to Topeka. Buy a team of mules and a covered wagon, jump off from St. Joe, and then spend an endless summer rusticating way out there, revived all day by the clangor of harness chains, the scent of mules sweating, and the vast soulful horizons of the West. I would camp at night at old pioneer stops and Pony Express corrals, soothed by the rushing waters as I fell asleep beside the Sweetwater or the Platte.

It was a completely lunatic notion. Except for the occasional faux reenactments staged for tourists by Wyoming outfitters—modern-day "pioneers" are trailed by convoys of sumptuously appointed RVs, and pampered at night with portable showers and catered meals—no one traveled more than sixty or seventy miles of the trail today. I would later read, in a history of the trail years and the subsequent homesteading period in the late nineteenth century, that "the last documented crossing of the trail occurred in 1909." Just to reach my rendezvous with dementia out along the banks of the Missouri River, I would spend two or three days driving west from my home in New England with my gear loaded into a pickup. Then I would spend four months, via covered wagon and mules, crossing what nineteenth-century travelers called the "Great American Desert." Across the high deserts of central Wyoming and Idaho, I would have to cover stretches of forty miles or more without water. And why did I think that the notorious and often fatal obstacles that the pioneers faced—mountain passes strewn with lava rock, hellacious winds and dust storms, rattlesnakes, and descents so steep that the wagons could only be lowered by ropes—would miraculously vanish from the trail for me? Only a delusional jackass, or someone seriously off his medications, would pull off the road at the Hollenberg Ranch one fine summer afternoon and concoct such a preposterous scheme.

But you can't save an addictive dreamer from himself, and that jackass happens to be me. Already, powerful forces were drawing me west. I felt an irresistible urge to forsake my life back east for a rapturous journey across the plains.

The contagion of rogue travel started early with me. I was raised during the 1950s and early 1960s on a ramshackle old horse farm in New Jersey. My father, a magazine publisher in New York City, was boundlessly energetic and inventive, devoted to what he considered the pressing entertainment needs of his eleven children. While the rest of the country raged over Pontiac tailfins or played golf, we chased around the menagerie that my father had slapped together from a nineteenth-century dairy—barns converted to horse stables, chicken houses and goat pens, a collection of more than twenty-five antique carriages and wagons, and a large stone patio and picnic area set under giant shade maples, where my father entertained the lovable drunks from his local chapter of Alcoholics Anonymous. We drove to church every Sunday in a four-seat surrey pulled by a team of matched bays, and sleighed into the toy store in town in December to pick up our Christmas presents. On lazy summer nights, my father loved nothing more than loading his children and all of our neighborhood friends—there could be twenty kids or more—into the dilapidated yellow school bus that he had purchased at a junkyard for such outings. Then we drove down to the Dairy Queen in Bernardsville and gorged on ice cream sundaes.

Over the winter of 1958, brooding in front of his fireplace one night, my father announced that he was bored with the school bus. As a family, he thought, we needed an experience that would draw us together, something that would engender in us the spirit of the American pioneers. I don't have any idea where this notion came from. But the top-rated American television show that year was NBC's *Wagon Train*, starring

Ward Bond, and we were all fans. We didn't consider it outlandish when my father told us that, for our summer vacation, we were going on a covered wagon trip to Pennsylvania. It would be a combined camping and coaching expedition, with stops along the way at historic sites like Valley Forge and Gettysburg that my father wanted his children to see.

My father had a knack for making the complex seem simple, and we were relaxed about our preparations for the trip. One January weekend that year we drove down to the Pennsylvania Dutch country in Lancaster County and made arrangements with our regular Mennonite wagon builder, Jonas Reif, to convert a large farm wagon with hoops and a canvas top. We bought our draft horses, a team of Percheron-Morgan crosses named Benny and Betty, from Jonas's son-in-law, Ivan Martin. My father, my older brother, and I spent a few delightful Saturday afternoons that spring banging around the barn with rusty hammers and saws, modifying our rig with racks for cooking pots and pans, hooks for water buckets, and a drop-down chuck wagon table for cooking meals. My father was a former barnstorming pilot and World War II flight instructor who had lost his left leg in a bad air crash in 1946. He stowed his maps for the trip in an old woolen stump sock that he placed underneath the wagon seat. With shoelaces, he hung a compass and a clock from the hoop over the front seat.

We clattered down our drive early one Saturday morning in July that year, bound for Pennsylvania, and that was a beautiful junket for a father to share with his children. I was seven years old and our covered wagon trip was the dream summer of my youth. In those days New Jersey and eastern Pennsylvania were still undeveloped, and we drove down through the green farmlands of Somerset and Hunterdon counties on quiet state highways or dirt roads, camping at dairies and state parks. In the mornings, while the waters of the Delaware or the Schuylkill river gurgled past our campsite, my father would rise at dawn and cook up a big breakfast of scrambled eggs and home fries over a wood fire, while my older brother and I fed and watered the horses. Along the cool, shaded lanes of Bucks County, Pennsylvania, we sang songs together to pass the time, and took turns learning to drive the team. On warm afternoons the bumping of the wheels over gravel roads and the rhythmic clopping of hooves made me

My father wanted his children to "see America slowly," to bond us as a family, and the journey loomed long in memory.

sleepy, and I loved stretching out in the back of the wagon and napping on a bale of hay.

The highlight of my days that summer arrived in the late afternoon. We had brought along on the trip a very gentle and safe old western cow pony, a registered quarter horse named Texas, who was trailed behind the wagon on a lead line. At four or five in the afternoon, when my father decided that we had achieved our allotted mileage for the day, he would call for either my older brother or me to throw Texas's saddle and bridle off the wagon, hitch up, and ride ahead to scout for a place to camp that night.

I am still thrilled by the sensation of those rides. As soon as I had Texas all saddled up I leaped on his back, dug in my heels, and neck-reined him around the wagon and the team, galloping ahead into the narrow aperture of light glowing between the shade trees on a Pennsylvania lane. Within a minute or two I had lost sight of the wagon. I often passed up the first two or three farms that looked good for camping, just to stretch out the ride, loping over picturesque stone bridges and past fields with browsing Herefords or tall corn. I felt so free and adventurous on those rides—loved and trusted enough to bear the responsibility of finding our camp for that night, but also completely unbounded, with the confines of family plodding along in a wagon behind me, unseen, far back on the road.

Those rides were my afternoons as an American boy, and I always returned to the wagon suffused with the thrill of spontaneous travel. The couples who owned the farms that I picked on my rides were always excited about the novelty of having a covered wagon stay for the night, and they offered us dinner, showers, or the use of their swimming pools. Sheriffs' deputies chased us down with their pickups, offering loads of grain and hay. Restaurants along the way laid out meals for us on tables in their parking lots. All of this was completely unplanned, and covered wagon travel seemed to generate its own spontaneous reality and unique bounty of rewards. *Not* having specific goals for the day seemed to be the way to live. Just harness up in the morning and go. The rest would take care of itself. Three hundred miles of green roadways down and back from Pennsylvania opened as a succession of heavens for us.

On that trip, my father gave us more than the gift of imagination.

Travel became my endorphin. In a covered wagon, while riding slowly out in the open air, every blade of grass, every fence post and farm, or the mallard ducks rising from the streams, assumes a visual and olfactory intensity that you can never feel while trapped inside a speeding car. While on a wagon seat, the land embraces you, emotionally. The rumbling wheels, the creaking top, and the pull of the driving lines in your hands multiply the pleasure of travel. A part of me would always long for that strength of feeling again, and no other form of travel could match it.

Our fifteen minutes of fame arrived in the form of a Look *magazine spread about the 1958 trip.*

The theme of escape became embedded with me—I escaped to live, I escaped to elude ennui and the boredom of everyday life, I escaped to chase off my hereditary chronic depression. By the time I was a teenager my father had lost interest in his wagons and horses for the other great love of his life, aviation, mostly because my older brother and I were now old enough to learn to fly. In 1966, when he was seventeen and I was fifteen, Kernahan and I rebuilt an old Piper Cub in our barn and flew it to California for the summer, becoming the youngest aviators ever to fly coast to coast. We navigated out past the Rockies without a radio, with just a wobbly magnetic compass and a shopping bag full of airmen's charts. In college I took long semester breaks to motorcycle out west and down south, then across Europe.

In my senior year at college, my professors discouraged me from pursuing a life of writing because they said that I would never make any money. But I was drawn to writing and journalism for a career because I knew the calling would never require me to remain very long in an office. I wanted open air, horses, or the throbbing of old cylinders hanging out in the breeze. Journey was everything for me. I learned to live for those bright, joyful intervals of travel, lasting weeks and sometimes even months, when I was liberated by my latest obsession from the grinding routine of domesticity and work—trips to Wyoming to write about cattle rustling, trips to Europe and the Middle East to cover politics and wars, trips to Arizona or California to cover wildfires and earthquakes. Even after I married, had children, and moved to the country, at least one long getaway a year was as essential as oxygen for me. There were always enough magazines or newspapers around to reward the curious and footloose like me. I felt content as long as I knew that the boy galloping ahead of the wagon could still be alive.

By the time I reached the Hollenberg Ranch, however, those wandering years were nearing their end. My life seemed to have run its course. To make the payments on my daughters' college education, I had stayed too long at my job, at America's oldest continuously published newspaper, the *Hartford Courant.* The *Courant* was now controlled by a short billionaire from Chicago whose borrowings had bankrupted the Tribune Company less than a year after he bought it. My editors had once dreamed about great writing and scoops, and they loved it when I ran out at a moment's notice and then scrambled back to the newsroom with something good about the family of a soldier just killed in Iraq, or the rude developer from New York who wanted to convert a priceless watershed into a golf course. But now my editors were ground down by the decline of print journalism, worshipping at the behest of their corporate masters the new web values of page hits, Twitter feeds, and cutting costs. They wanted stories about idiotic, "reader-driven" subjects that weren't news at all—health fads, car wrecks, and celebrity scandals. (The most coveted stories combined more than one of these elements, a celebrity health fad, say, or even better, a celebrity car wreck.) Mostly owing to my own mistakes, my marriage had ended and I had moved out of my house, and its sixteen acres of fields and woods that I loved to roam and log. I lived now in a charming barn house higher up in the mountains, but the place was lonely. Simultaneously financing a separation and college tuitions had left me nearly bankrupt, and my house was over-mortgaged to its limits. Many of my new best friends were heavy drinkers.

In short, I had become that familiar subspecies of the North American male, the divorced boozehound with a bad driving record and emerging symptoms of low self-esteem. I knew that I had to escape again—this time in a big way. It was time for me to buy some maps and a team of mules and lose myself in the West.

But I also knew that I needed a convincing rationale, a truth about history and the American experience that would justify a risky, lyrical journey across the plains.

The urge to wander west with a team of mules appeased another one of my personality defaults. As a boy, I desperately felt a need to flee the chaotic din of our house—new babies wailing downstairs, younger brothers and sisters fighting over dolls and Tonka trucks, my father's weekend asylum of Roman Catholic priests, AA buddies, and politicians streaming in and out. I often retreated upstairs to my attic room, or to a quiet corner of the barns, for bouts of reading that could last all afternoon or night. I devoured science, adventure, and especially history books, escaping my domestic reality for an alternative universe of Civil War battles or Klondike dogsled rides. My adolescent feasting on books was a protective search for privacy and self that worked for me at the time, and later became habitual and delivered other benefits. I compulsively read ahead in my course work in school and college, and as a journalist I became the newsroom idiot savant who could always be relied on to convert his vault of trivia into some useful angle on a breaking story. My modus operandi was fixed long before middle age. To escape in fact, I had to escape first into books.

That fall, after I returned from Kansas, I curled up before my fireplace in New England and binged on the trail. I began with literary classics like Francis Parkman's *The Oregon Trail*, and Bernard DeVoto's *The Year of Decision, 1846*, and then moved on to the steroidal, massively researched work of Merrill J. Mattes, author of *The Great Platte River Road*, and John D. Unruh Jr.'s *The Plains Across*. By the end of the winter my library was stacked high with piles of cardboard boxes and books, with separate archives containing maps, nineteenth-century trail guides, pioneer journals, and essays on wagon design and mules. I quickly realized that I had been missing a lot—almost the idiom of America itself—by not knowing more about the Oregon Trail.

The exodus across the plains in the fifteen years before the Civil War, when more than 400,000 pioneers made the trek between the frontier at the Missouri River and the Pacific coast, is still regarded by scholars as the largest single land migration in history. It virtually defined the American character—our plucky determination in the face of physical adversity, the joining of two coasts into one powerful country, our impetuous cycle of financial bubbles and busts, the endless, fractious clash of ethnic populations competing for the same jobs and space. Before the Oregon Trail, America was a loosely coordinated land of emerging industrial centers in the Northeast, and a plantation South, with a frontier of hotly contested soil mutating west. Post–Oregon Trail—with a big assist from the Civil War—America was a continental dynamo connected by railroads and the telegraph from the Atlantic to the Pacific, with certain precedents for settlement, statehood, and quickly establishing large commercial cities. For another generation the West would be destabilized, and our folklore made, by Indian fighters and gunslingers, mining and railroad plunderers, and range wars over cattle. But the trail experience had clarified our destiny and national character. Americans were those folks who loved to profess peace-loving values, but who fought about everything. Allegedly America was founded in part to promote religious freedom and harmony, but in fact we were a cauldron of denominational spats, prejudice, and even homicidal church wars. This created a lot of conflict, and for millions of Americans, the solution for problems where they were was to quickly sell out, pack their belongings, and move somewhere else, preferably west. Our economic affairs were chaotically mismanaged by government and exploited by cabals of stock swindlers and banks. But the huge national bounty was too considerable to destroy and America would quickly assemble a wealth and an élan unrivaled anywhere else in the world.

But you couldn't get to the bottom of that without first knowing the Oregon Trail. The ruts crossing the plains had not only physically connected a finished continental space, but spiritually cohered a young country's first principles into a national psyche. For most Americans, the time line between the American Revolution and the Civil War is a seventy-year black hole, as if nothing had happened in between. But now I saw in the Oregon Trail the big event that filled the void and explained what we came to be.

And the details of the prairie migration were wonderful, crying out for renewed attention. Historian Richard Slotkin has shown how the myth of Indian savagery was required to justify the subjugation of the tribes so that their prairie kingdoms could be seized by the Americans crossing the frontier after 1843. But that image, faithfully passed down by purple-sage novels and Hollywood westerns, is wildly inaccurate. The initial encounters between the first covered wagon trains and the tribes were extraordinarily friendly, and the pioneers would never have made it past Kansas without their Pawnee and Shoshone guides. The pioneers and their new Indian partners amply displayed the American penchant for technological prowess, developing shore-to-shore windlasses and flatboat ferries to cross the rivers, innovations as vital to the country's progress as the steam engine and the telegraph. America's default toward massive waste and environmental havoc was also, and hilariously, perfected along the trail. Scammed by the merchants of Independence and St. Joe into overloading their wagons, the pioneers jettisoned thousands of tons of excess gear, food, and even pianos along the ruts, turning vast riverfront regions of the West into America's first and largest Superfund sites. On issue after issue—disease, religious strife, the fierce competition for water—the trail served as an incubator for conflicts that would continue to reverberate through American culture until our own day.

Another compelling detail emerged from my research that winter. Along the Oregon Trail—unlike such embalmed historic places as Independence Hall in Philadelphia or the Custer Battlefield in Montana—the continuum of history is still very much alive. After the Civil War, the rush to build a transcontinental railroad made the familiar and mapped wagon train path the preferred route, and the Union Pacific and Burlington Northern lines were quickly laid down within yards of the original trail. The Pony Express, the telegraph lines, and the stagecoach routes followed, usually right along the original ruts, and then the big ranches, cities, and beef packing yards followed. Early in the twentieth century, the nation's first coast-to-coast motorway, the Lincoln Highway, was built along six hundred miles of the trail in Nebraska and eastern Wyoming. The western reaches of the interstate highway system—Route 80 through Nebraska and Wyoming, routes 86 and 84 through Idaho and Oregon—closely follow the old ruts. In the U.S. highway system, the marked "auto trail" following the emigrant road between Independence, Missouri, and Astoria, Oregon is now called the "Old Oregon Trail Highway," and includes more than a dozen interstates and two-lane highways.

Today, at some of the loveliest and most historic spots along the trail, O'Fallon's Bluff in Nebraska, or Register Rocks in Idaho, you can sit and watch a landscape that still hums with western movement. The whistles of the big yellow Union Pacific engines wail day and night at the track crossings, along what is now the busiest freight corridor in the world. Just a football field away, often even closer, the semitrailers race down the interstates in packs, their metal sides glaring under the sun like the white-tops of the pioneers.

And now there is a new scrum along the trail. Over the past fifteen years, from the Missouri to the Columbia, the old emigrant road has become dotted with innumerable energy projects—ethanol plants, massive wind farms, high-speed transmission lines, hydrofracked gas fields, and huge data centers for Google and Microsoft. The Oregon Trail could aptly be renamed the "Energy Trail." All of this passes by an environmental treasure, a proud legacy of Teddy Roosevelt's Progressive Era—nearly a dozen national forests, millions of acres of preserved land, that stretch 1,500 miles from the Medicine Bows in Wyoming to the Cascades in Oregon. The trail today, far from being a historic artifact, reverberates with the modern echoes of America's most eternal struggle—the battle between those who would preserve the plains and the mountain forests, and those who gaze across the same pristine landscape and say, "Drill, baby, drill."

A sensible plan seemed to have emerged from my winter of reading. A long ride across the plains would allow me to experience the incomparable joys and physical rigors of wagon travel, and I would be seeing the country slowly, with plenty of time for reflecting on how a fabled landscape had matured and still bore spiritual meaning today. All the bombast and bravery of the overland years in the 1840s and 1850s, the religious strife, the scams at the jumping-off cities, the wonder the pioneers felt about the unfolding vistas of the West, could be conveyed, adequately enough, from the safe remove of a library. But actually *riding* the trail would deliver me to so much more, tangibly connecting me to the history I now felt so passionate about.

Roaming west would also embrace a very old American theme. Henry David Thoreau immortalized this urge with his poetic "Eastward I go only by force; but westward I go free." A century later, beat writer Jack Kerouac was still exploring this motif in his road books. Kerouac, as his friend John Clellon Holmes wrote, "hankered for the West, for Western health and openness of spirit, for the immemorial dream of freedom [and] joy." The pioneers had found this too. William Barlow of Indiana, who crossed the trail in 1845 when he was twenty-three years old, was in many respects an emblematic American. His father, S. K. Barlow, led a company of fifty wagons across the trail, carrying several hundred pounds of tobacco for trading with the Indians. In Oregon, the Barlows were dissatisfied with the existing trail around the Cascades, so they built a new one, which became the famous Barlow Road. Later, the Barlows helped found Oregon City, a bustling lumber and industrial center along the Willamette River south of Portland. As an old man, William Barlow vividly recalled his five months on the plains. "I will now say again, for myself and our company, that I never passed a more pleasant, cheerful and happy summer in my whole life."

One of my favorite pioneer journalists is George Law Curry, perhaps because his life story so reminded me of my own grandfather and father. A Pennsylvanian who couldn't afford an education, Curry started his career as a printer's apprentice and worked his way up to becoming a newspaper publisher. He crossed the trail in 1846 and later followed a career track common to many overland emigrants, becoming a prominent newspaperman and politician in Oregon, and briefly served as the state's acting governor. In May 1846, Curry wrote back to the paper he had founded in St. Louis, *The Reveille*, from the banks of the Wakarusa River in Kansas.

> Life on the plains far surpasses my expectation; there is a freedom and
> a nobleness about it that tend to bring forth the full manhood. A man
> upon the horizon-bound prairie feels his own strength and estimates
> his own weakness. He is alive to every thing around him. For him there

is a joy in the "lone elm" grandeur on the mounds, beauty in the grassy and flower-besprinkled couch on which he rests, and a glory forever round him, stretching his spirit to its fullest tension.

In the trail journals, I often came across the phrase "seeing the elephant," a term that the pioneers used to describe their anticipation about striking out across the unknowable wilderness of the plains. The origins of the phrase are not certain, but it seems to have been a popular nineteenth-century colloquialism that referred to the rare thrill that families felt when leaving their isolated farms to see the elephants marching through town when a traveling circus arrived. The term was a kind of destroyer-preserver image that changed in meaning over time, and depending on the circumstances.

Initially, the pioneers jubilantly expected to "see the elephant" in the endlessly scenic plains that they would encounter after embarking across the Missouri River. "All hands early up anxious to see the path that leads to the Elephant," wrote gold seeker John Clark of Virginia in 1852, the day he left for the trail on the St. Joseph Road. But a mythic, baleful elephant also came to represent the many hazards of the trail—disease, drowning, or stampeding buffalo that carried off a wagon train's cattle. Pioneer Lucy Cooke made a difficult early-season crossing of the trail in April 1851, when the waterways of Kansas were perilously swollen from heavy rains. The wagons of her train had to be tediously unloaded and then pulled across even small streams by chains. "Oh, surely we are seeing the elephant," Cooke wrote in her journal. "From the tip of his trunk to the end of his tail!"

Seeing the elephant, as historian Merrill Mattes put it, "was the popular symbol of the Great Adventure, all the wonder and the glory and the shivering thrill of the plunge into the ocean of prairie and plains, and the brave assault upon mountains and deserts that were gigantic barriers to California gold. It was the poetic imagery of all the deadly perils that threatened a westering emigrant."

In the early 1850s, during the frantic California Gold Rush, another popular phrase gained circulation among the mostly young, urban eastern men and Europeans who were rushing west on the trail. "The cowards never started," they said. In a 1962 article on the covered wagon, a writer for *American Heritage* offered his own amendment for the old saying. "Only the madmen started!" he wrote. As I made my final preparations to depart for the West, I knew that many people would consider me unhinged for wanting to see the elephant. I was a madman for becoming a twenty-first-century traveler along the ruts. But I was cheerful about that. I would live for the summer according to my own personal creed.

I do not believe in organized religion, herbal remedies, yoga, Reiki, kabbalah, deep massage, slow food, or chicken soup for the soul. The nostrums of Deepak Chopra and Barbara De Angelis cannot rescue people like me.

I believe in crazyass passion. It was crazyass passion that dug America's canals, flung the wagons west, built the railroads, and propelled the God-fearing to their deaths at Cold Harbor and Shiloh. My father's generation gave great crazyass passion surviving the Depression and then fighting a noble world war. Brandy and words mixed with Winston Churchill became the crazyass passion that saved the last free country in Europe. Crazyass passion threw Herman Melville to the seas, Jack Kerouac on the road, and Wilfred Thesiger across the sands. My corporeal self would be driving mules across the plains, but it was crazyass passion that would deliver me to the trail.

2

MY DREAMS OF CROSSING MORE than two thousand miles of western terrain were fortified by two gloriously farcical delusions. I would cross the trail alone. And, in addition to the mules and a covered wagon, I would be taking along a riding horse. I knew that I would enjoy exploring on horseback the distant canyons and river bottoms that I could see from the wagon seat, especially after I reached the dramatic bluff country of western Nebraska, and my childhood memories required me to think of myself galloping across the sage every evening to scout for a camp. I pictured myself high atop my horse under a cowboy hat, cheerfully taking notes about my poetic surroundings as I simultaneously juggled the reins, a lead line for the mules, my canteens, a compass, and maps. I would be the happiest multitasker in the history of the Oregon Trail.

To accomplish this, however, I would need my old riding saddle, bought twenty years earlier on a Wyoming cattle drive. In a transaction typical of the arrangements between members of my family, I had lent the saddle many years ago to my younger brother Nicholas, in return for his help when I was renovating my house. The saddle had sat all those years, mostly unused, in a dusty corner of Nick's barn in Maine. Early one morning in April, just a few weeks before I was scheduled to leave on the trip, I emailed Nick and asked him to ship me the saddle.

I wasn't surprised when Nick's reply arrived a few minutes later. He had plenty of time on his hands. The summer before, he had taken a bad fall from a neighbor's roof and shattered the bones in his right foot into dozens of fragments. The injury had not healed quickly, and for the past eight months he had been confined to either the postoperative ward of the Veterans Administration hospital in Augusta or his living room couch. Nick's postcards and emails have always been a tonic for me, evoking the literacy standards of the nineteenth century, when Civil War soldiers and stagecoach drivers were too busy leading interesting lives to bother much about punctuation or spelling. Hearing from Nick instantly put me in the mood for pioneer travel.

"I can send you the sadle just tell me were and when and listen hear you ashol why didn't you tell me you were making the Oregin trip this year Im comin."

Some of you are already familiar with my brother Nick. Last summer, while you were touring the beautiful seacoast of Maine, Nick Buck was that rather generously proportioned, gregarious fellow with the Fu Manchu mustache and a NAPA Auto Parts cap, rumbling north on U.S. Route 1 near Damariscotta in a battered old farm wagon pulled by a team of mismatched draft horses. Stopping traffic in both directions on the busy coastal highway, Nick wheeled into the parking lot of the Hannaford Supermarket and then trotted over to the handicapped parking space, where he tied up his team. ("Whadya mean *why* do I park in handicapped?" Nick said to me once, when I was along for his Saturday-morning ride. "That's the only place where they put a sign so I can tie my horses.") It takes Nick a long time to shop at Hannaford's, and not simply because he is an ambitious eater. Nick is a much beloved figure along the mid-coast of Maine, and everyone wants to stop and talk when they see him. At the supermarket, Nick's whereabouts are rarely a mystery. His booming baritone voice carries everywhere, even through hardened walls.

"OH, YEAH! Did you see that team of mine jump the ditch? I thought I was going to lose that whole frickin load of kids off the back of the sleigh!"

Nick is our family's Renaissance man. He volunteers his wagon and team every year for free kiddie rides at local fund-raisers, he's a popular actor in community theaters, a mainstay of several local self-help groups, and his lectures about horses, stagecoaches, and the old Boston Post Road have been some of the most highly attended events in the history of several Maine libraries and museums. Nick is also well known for being able to build or repair anything, a kind of local handyman and global Robin Hood rolled into one. If your grandmother in Waldoboro is complaining about her leaky water heater, Nick will generously offer to drive up there and install a new one, probably forgetting to send her a bill, but he's just as likely to be found rebuilding homes for hurricane or earthquake victims in New Orleans or Peru.

Many people, after they have met Nick and spoken with him for a while, drool over his curriculum vitae. He epitomizes the personality type that down-easters call the Mainiac—a person so completely devoid of practicality, yet so devoted to fun, that his life can only be considered utterly romantic. He is also something of a prototype for the middle sons in large families. By the time Nick arrived, there were already seven Buck children. My father and mother devoted a lot of care to raising children properly, but they can be classified only as burned-out parents by the time number eight was born. This led to a curious phenomenon that I saw in other families. The older sons and daughters received an extraordinary amount of attention and contributed to my father's personal bankruptcy scheme by attending the best private schools. But the middle boys were just surplus carnal results, afterthoughts, and no one cared how they dressed or what they did in school. Then the parents of these large Catholic clans gathered a second wind and showered the youngest children with affection. But the middle boys were neglected truants who could do whatever they wanted.

During his senior year in high school, Nick was suspended for a minor smoking violation—he says that he was taking the rap for a friend—and never went back, finding that he enjoyed jacking up barns and working in a gas station a lot more than classes in algebra and European history. A few months later he enlisted in the U.S. Coast Guard. Nick became certified as a marine engineer and was assigned to work on icebreakers along the Penobscot and Kennebec rivers in Maine. He crewed boats that performed several dramatic sea rescues, and then he became the last lighthouse keeper in Maine when he took over the windswept, historic Whitehead Light Station, on an island south of Rockland, running it for eighteen months before it was automated and abandoned as a manned station. The trajectory of Nick's life was celebrated twenty years later, when he returned to Whitehead to lovingly restore the light keeper's house for the wealthy family who bought the island after it was sold at a government auction.

After the Coast Guard, Nick converted the love of horses and antique rigs that he picked up on our old farm in New Jersey into a successful sleigh-ride business at New Hampshire ski resorts. He spent the next ten winters up there, building huge, thirty-passenger sleighs from scratch. By day he pranced his big, dappled teams of Percheron and Belgian draft horses across icy parking lots and through the porte cocheres of fancy inns, building a considerable reputation as a horseman, and by night he partied with the ski bunnies that he met in the bars. Every summer he decamped for Dutch Harbor in Alaska, where he ran the engine room of the largest American fish processing boat in the Bering Sea. When he was in his thirties, a girlfriend persuaded him to stop drinking and settle down in Maine. Nick bought a run-down farm in Newcastle and—sort of—fixed it up. The next fifteen years were devoted to building and restoring trophy mansions along the Maine coast, and collecting carriages and sleighs, and Nick imaginatively treated his ferocious attention deficit disorder with a busy weekend schedule of team driving, acting in plays, and Habitat for Humanity projects.

But the recession of 2008 had wiped out mansion-building in Maine, and then Nick had fallen off his neighbor's roof. He was now unemployed, and an invalid, so financially desperate that his family and friends had to throw fund-raisers to help him catch up on his mortgage payments and credit card bills. I hadn't considered Nick for the Oregon trip, because he was so immobilized by pain and recurrent infections in his foot that he couldn't even rise from his couch to cook his own meals. My sisters in Boston had been running up to Maine on weekends, housekeeping and caring for Nick as best as they could.

Now, on the eve of my departure, Nick was flooding me with emails, insisting that he could make the trip. His doctors were promising to give him a clean bill of health soon. He was passionate about going not only because, as an experienced horseman—arguably one of the best team drivers of his generation—Nick knew that I couldn't possibly make it from

Missouri to Oregon alone. He also knew that an Oregon run with mules was the dream opportunity of a lifetime.

My sister Ferriss says that Nick was "born at the wrong time." There is even an informal psychiatric term for people like him: "born out of century." His knowledge about old wagons is encyclopedic and adamant. When I was with him once at a museum outside Boston, Nick saw a restored Civil War escort wagon and said, loudly enough to be heard by the museum director a floor away, "Oh, Christ, look at that. Those are World War I artillery hubs on an 1863 wagon. Why would anyone do somethin so frickin stupid like that?" If it is an Albany cutter, and you call it a sleigh, he will remind you. It becomes frightening to be around him when you realize that he can do the same thing across a broad spectrum of artifacts—airplanes, ships, steam engines, antique pickups, churches, breakwaters, and Victorian houses. Nick is a gorgeous cluster of autodidacticism, and you can't believe that this guy standing next to you with hydraulic fluid all over his shirt is more erudite than the curators at the Smithsonian Institution.

There are a few other contradictions, glaring but charming. Nick is well known in Maine as a fastidious builder, and none of his multimillion-dollar projects is done until every balustrade and vaulted ceiling has been approved by the architect as perfect. His standards for personal possessions—his pickup, his farm, his furniture—are a great deal more proletarian than that. An avid reader, Nick often surprises me with his recall of history books, even classic novels. But a lack of performance in school and the general addled nature of the brain through which information must be processed results in a pronounced verbal dyslexia, which Nick calls his "lysdexia." During December one year, Nick and I decided that we wanted to watch a Christmas video together.

"Okay, so Rink," Nick said. "Let's watch Jimmy Stewart in *It's a Wonderful Wife.*"

But it's easy to ignore these oddities because Nick's outlook is so endlessly jolly. Recently, he faced a problem with his elderly cat, Poopy, who was not well. One night after work, he rushed Poopy to the vet. Via our family email tree, Nick delivered the news about what happened there.

"My cat Poopy passed away this evening about six o'clock at the vet's office were I had taken him to be passed on. Because he passed away while the paper work was being filled out I got out of there with out a bill. I feel terribly guilty to be filled with joy over the fact that I got out with a dead cat and no bill. I think I may be on a paved road to you Know were."

I called Nick to commiserate about Poopy. But it was one of those weeks when he had lost his cell phone and he wasn't receiving messages. Eventually, he got back to me via email.

"Rinker Sorry I Missed your calls. The Cat Poopy has left the Planet. It was a sad day but he had lived a long life and died at the last moment of it, as most all of us do."

My email exchanges with Nick about the Oregon Trail trip became a study of our divergent personalities, the amazing wealth of possibilities contained within shared DNA. I would write Nick long, learned dissertations on my plans, with links to maps, and typically overresearched histories of the places along the trail where I planned to camp. Nick emailed back about wheel grease and tools.

"I have two horse anchors a wheel wrench my wheel jack actually two if one brakes dad's old leather tool kit from the covered wagon trip '58 and my buddy Alan can get some High tech grease that will prolong times between greasing the wheels. Blankets for the Mules we'l need for cold nights and equine aspiran lots of every bolt on the wagon all perpose tools I have a Coleman stove and a Keroseen lantern as well. O and PS no matter what any jerkof waggonmaker says we'l have to Rebild the brakes evry 100 miles."

I was torn about Nick coming along. Clearly, his nonpareil knowledge about wagons and teams would be a big asset on the trail. But there were compatibility issues—massive, oceanic, hemispheric compatibility issues—that I had to consider. I had difficulty picturing myself, on a narrow wagon seat, crossing two thousand miles of Oregon Trail with a 250-pound brother whose calling of the mules would be heard several canyons away. I am bookish and neat, with a fondness for antique furniture, good wine, and clean cars. If I am depressed or have writer's block, I spend the afternoon logging in the woods or ironing my Brooks Brothers shirts. Nick buys a new Carhartt shirt at Reny's Discount in Damariscotta and breaks it in by using it as an oil rag on the way home. For Nick, a good afternoon of logging with his brother in the Maine woods usually includes dropping a tree inches from my head, destroying my chain saw, and then ripping out the transaxle on his truck while dragging an immense oak out to the cleared field.

"Rink, it's just a frickin chain saw, okay?" Nick would say to me as I carried my prize Husqvarna back to my truck in pieces. "A glide bar, some sprockets, and a plastic housing. If you break it, you get to fix it!"

Over the years I had devised an elaborate syllabus of coping techniques for spending time with Nick. I double-wrap my gear in plastic garbage bags as a prophylaxis against the grime in his truck, and I look away at meals while he speaks with an open mouth full of cole slaw, scalloped potatoes, and lobster au gratin. I've mentally trained myself to consider it charmingly down-market when Nick mangles clichés, drops the g's at the end of "ing" words, and uses the F bomb as frequently as most English speakers use "and" or "the." In the rural, blue-collar ghettos of Maine and neighboring New England, "frickin," "freakin," and "fuckin" are pause-fillers, a verbal tick that can indicate either wickedly good or bad.

"Rink, I've spent my life in barnyards and bilges, okay?" Nick told me once. "How'm I supposed to fuckin sound?"

Long ago I had decided that two days with Nick was my limit. Now he was proposing months together on the Oregon Trail.

Nick was particularly avid about bringing his Jack Russell terrier, Olive Oyl, which gave me a nervous twitch. With her beguiling cocked head, her cheery bark, and the brown patch on her right ear, Olive Oyl is unquestionably the most adorable canine since the Little Rascals' mascot, Petey. She is an amazing dog, able to leap onto the roof of a minivan while fetching a stick. But Olive is also incurably filthy, porcine filthy. Her favorite activity when I arrive at Nick's place in Maine is to sprint out the door for a long, strenuous roll in the patch of driveway where he changes the oil in his trucks. Then she burrows for rats in the manure pile before racing back to the porch to make a giant parabola leap onto my lap. Usually, I have stopped at the L.L. Bean outlet store on my way north and I am already wearing my new Allaghash twill chinos. I feel like taking a shower every time I see Olive Oyl.

In his emails, Nick was now discussing Olive Oyl as an indispensable addition to "our" covered wagon trip.

"Rink the thing to do is to creat as happy an enviremint for Olive Oyl as posible. She will remember this trip and talk about it for the rest of her life and I wudnt deny it to her for anythin I promis to wash her at the end of the day the same time with the same hos we wash the mules."

When this didn't seem to convince me, Nick tried another approach.

"Rink ther are prayeri dogs and ciotes and probly in wyomin even mtn lions and Olive Oyl will never stand for them being anywere near r camp shel be good with the mules and if it's a cold nite she can sleep with you in the wagon and beleve me shes toasty."

Eventually I realized that it would be madness not to bring Nick. He is an incomparable horseman, and I needed him for such an ambitious trip. There would be wagon breakdowns, and it wasn't wise to travel without a skilled mechanic. I tried to have positive thoughts about this. Nick and Olive Oyl were a package deal, but this was an opportunity for me. I could use the Oregon Trail trip to cure myself of my neatness fetish. I could abandon the English language as a work of art. Nick is a recovering alcoholic, and I could emulate his sobriety. Call the mules two thousand miles across the West with your brother and his squalid Jack Russell terrier. Return home a new man, no longer a boozer, a clotheshorse, or a control freak.

So, we agreed. Nick's final appointment with the VA doctor was slated for the first Friday in May, and he would reschedule it for early in the morning. Then he would drive down to my place in the Berkshires with a truck full of wagon jacks and tools, and we would depart the same day for the West.

There was just one hitch. Anticipating his recovery, Nick had agreed to perform the difficult lead role in an Irish play, *Stones in His Pockets*, which was scheduled to begin its Damariscotta run in late June. In the production, Nick's role was hermaphroditic. He would assume the voices and personalities of seven different characters, both male and female. "Rink, there just isn't another actor in Maine who can do that," Nick told me, insisting that he couldn't back out of the commitment. So, after a month with me on the trail, Nick would take an acting hiatus and return to Maine.

After consulting my maps, I didn't think that this would be a problem. By the time Nick departed for his play, we would probably have reached

North Platte, Nebraska, along a lovely stretch of the trail where the pioneers were hemmed in by the Platte River to the north, and on the south by a chain of elevated terrain called the South Hills. This natural corridor curves northwest toward Scotts Bluff and the Wyoming line, and all I had to do was follow the old Platte River Road that hugs the river. I was reasonably confident that I would have mastered the mules and the wagon by then. In early July, once he was done with *Stones in His Pockets*, Nick would return for the most epic portion of the trail—350 miles of undisturbed ruts that crossed the high desert of Wyoming, from Casper to Cokeville, in the cutoff country out near the Idaho line.

Through the marvelous accident of family, I now had a sidekick for the trail, which I realized I had desperately needed all along. But what did this say about the adequacy of my planning, and how many other important things had I ignored? Several times, sitting up late at night or early in the morning, obsessively brooding over my maps, I realized that I still didn't have a plan for navigating around the modern obstacles of the trail—interstate highways from Nebraska to Oregon, or the tangle of housing subdivisions and malls around Scottsbluff and Boise. There was no trail to speak of after Baker City, Oregon, where the old ruts were paved over by the interstate that ran the rest of the way to Portland. All of this would have to be explained to Nick who, given his hyperactive sarcasm gene, would remind me every time I erred on the trail.

Still, there was a pleasing verisimilitude about Nick joining me for the junket out west. Two brothers uprooting themselves to seek adventure or a better life together was a pretty typical Oregon Trail pairing, and our resemblance to the nineteenth-century pioneers was significant. Nick was an injured, unemployed construction worker in the midst of a deep recession in home building in Maine. As a print journalist I typified an American character type that had been familiar since the industrial revolution—the worker with redundant, antiquated skills displaced by technological change. We were going to see the elephant because there wasn't much else going on for us at home.

The theme of personal and financial desperation—that most of the pioneers left for the frontier because they literally had nowhere else to go—was popular with historians from the earliest days of the trail. Francis

Parkman, a notoriously snobbish Boston Brahmin, went too far when he called the emigrants he met during his 1846 crossing "some of the vilest outcasts in the country." But he was probably correct in concluding that most of the wagon travelers were motivated either by "an insane hope of a better condition in life, or a desire of shaking off restraints of law and society, or mere restlessness."

The 1840s and 1850s were tumultuous decades in American life, and the chronic instability of the young republic had a broad impact, especially on the farmers and rural tradesmen who made up the majority of the population. Families were disrupted and lives destroyed by the financial panics and bank failures that recurred every decade, towns were divided by bitter religious squabbling and labor strife, and the biggest political issue of the day—the spread of slavery—had degenerated into guerrilla warfare on the Kansas and Missouri frontier. Frequently, to be an American then was to be periodically unmoored, transient, so bereft of options that moving on was the only choice. Settling the frontier wasn't simply America's "manifest destiny." It was a safety valve that prevented a calamitous society from imploding.

Nick and I were certainly among the unmoored of the twenty-first century, and that was our joint advantage. Nothing prevented us from risking everything to take on the obsession of crossing the Oregon Trail. But escaping our personal problems to become wagon tramps for the summer didn't mean that we possessed the know-how and skills to cross the trail. While I waited for Nick to arrive, I woke early most mornings to brood over my maps, spending what I called my "dread hour" at my kitchen table, drinking coffee while I agonized over the long, cluttered spaces out west where the trail had been subsumed by the suburbs of Scottsbluff or Boise, or blocked by the interstate highways. As a modern wagon traveler, I also faced another small problem. Before I could launch, I had to learn as much as I could about nineteenth-century prairie schooners and mules.

3

MULES OCCUPY A WONDERFULLY ANOMALOUS place in the American mind. Although the hybrid product of breeding a female horse with a male "jack" donkey was indispensable toward creating the America we know, most of us have very little idea what mules really are. Beyond associating them with long, floppy ears, ornery behavior, and loud, long braying—a noise that they can't actually make—we regard mules as a quaint, mysterious anachronism about which knowing more is quite useless.

In my own case, ignorance about mules was particularly pathetic. I had spent a lifetime around draft horses and mules, driving sleighs on weekends, skidding out logs in the woods, whiling away whole weeks on the farms of my Amish and Mennonite friends, watching mules work during planting and harvesting seasons. Now I had made the rash decision to drive a mule team two thousand miles across some of the most punishing terrain my country had to offer. It was as vital to me as it had been to the overland pioneers to find a team that could get me there. Still, I knew almost nothing about the animals.

I was intrigued, as I began researching mules, to learn that no less a figure than George Washington was America's original maharaja of mules. Historians have long been squeamish about acknowledging that General Washington, like many of the American founders, was a voracious land speculator. Few academics and high school history teachers want to risk their careers by suggesting to their students that the father of their country worked the same day job as Donald Trump. Washington was a land developer, often described as the richest of his generation. By the end of the American Revolution, General Washington controlled about sixty thousand acres of land, more than half of it in the promising frontier country west of the Alleghenies, in what we today call West Virginia, Ohio, and western Pennsylvania. Wresting clear title to this rich bounty of soil from the English crown may not have been a principal motive for fighting the Revolutionary War, but Washington knew that he would profit mightily if independence was achieved. In the 1780s, after the Revolution was over, Washington suffered the woes of all land developers. As he toured his vast frontier holdings—relentlessly collecting rents from tenant farmers and attempting to evict squatters—Washington envisioned a busy new commercial era during which the value of his lands would be enhanced by extensive forest clearing, road construction, and canal building. But the common beast for accomplishing such work, the horse, would never do.

The traditional draft horses imported from Europe or bred on colonial plantations were magnificent equine specimens, weighing up to a ton apiece, their marbled thighs glistening under the sun as they pulled plows and farm wagons over the flat corn and tobacco fields of eastern Virginia or Pennsylvania. But these agrarian mastodons were enormously hungry at the end of the day, and, like so many "purebred" species, suffered the common defects of animals mated too often within the same bloodlines. The big, beautiful drafts were prone to lameness and chipped hooves, they lacked stamina, and essentially they could perform only one job—yanking a plow or a wagon across level cropland. Heavy draft horses were notoriously ungainly on the kind of steep slopes and rocky ground that would be encountered while conquering the Alleghenies.

Washington and his fellow Virginia planters had long known about the plucky, kick-ass little mules developed for pack trains and for pulling light freight wagons in the Spanish territories of the lower Mississippi and Texas. These "crosses" were bred from horses and small Mexican donkeys, usually producing a mule that stood only four feet at the withers, the part of a horse or mule where the neck joins the body. What the young republic needed now was something much bigger—sturdier, draft-quality mules that stood at five or six feet. In Spain and France, where farming required pulling loads up the steep paths of terraced vineyards and wheat fields, mules of this size had been bred for centuries out of tall donkey sires called "Mammoth Jacks." Mammoth jacks were any of several long-legged, large-boned studs selectively developed for draftlike qualities, probably from Middle Eastern donkeys brought back from the Crusades. The mammoth jacks had eventually branched off into several discrete European breeds: the Andalusian, Catalonian, Majorcan, and Maltese lines. But the courts of France and Spain, reluctant to share such prize breeding stock with the colonies of their rival Britain, had always banned the export of mammoth jacks to America.

After the American Revolution, however, Washington was a global hero, and the Europeans were glad to help the man who had trounced their old British foes. In 1785 the king of Spain, Charles III, dispatched to Mount Vernon a shipment of mammoth breeding stock that included an Andalusian jack named Royal Gift. The shipment included two "jennies," or female donkeys, suitable for mating with Royal Gift to create more mammoth studs. In the meantime, Washington's old fighting companion during the Revolution, the Marquis de Lafayette, had shipped from France his own gift, a Maltese jack named Knight of Malta and four jennies.

An experienced animal breeder like Washington—he is also credited with developing the American foxhound—knew what to do now. The new jacks had to be bred like bunnies in two directions at once. First, to create a new crop of mammoth donkey sires, the jacks had to mate with the jennies. The jacks produced from these unions in turn would be bred to as many draft-horse mares as possible—there were plenty in America—to complete the finished genetic product called mules.

There were problems at first. Royal Gift was an inexperienced four-year-old who initially seems to have been intimidated by Washington's tall draft-horse mares, and he wouldn't fornicate with horses. But after a year or two of conjugal training with the friendly jennies, Royal Gift emerged. At his main estate in Mount Vernon, Washington built new barns and fenced in nearby pastures to create what he called "the compound," ambitiously interbreeding his new Andalusian and Maltese stock for the best conformation and temperament. By the time he died in 1799, there were sixty working draft mules at Mount Vernon alone.

But that was only the beginning. A single jack could service several horse mares a day, twenty or more a week, up to a thousand a year, and Malthusian growth just took over from there. Washington either sold his jacks outright to other breeders, or advertised in the Pennsylvania and Virginia newspapers the "at fee" services of his jacks, who made long breeding tours throughout the old colonies and the new frontier states every year. The new draft mules proved wildly popular. Many other Virginia planters, seeing a good thing, began importing the European mammoths themselves, and before long the Old Dominion had essentially become a mule bordello. By 1810 the region's initial breeding stock had yielded an estimated 800,000 mules distributed throughout the South and beyond the Allegheny frontier.

The early descendants of the Mount Vernon stock—tall, drafty, and weighing between a thousand and 1,200 pounds—were initially called "American Mammoth" mules, but the breed name gradually changed as the frontier moved west. In the 1820s, the most prized farm animals were called "Tennessee" and then "Kentucky" mules, because the frontier of Tennessee and Kentucky were where most of them were working and the best breeding lines were being established. By the 1840s the frontier had moved to Missouri and it was the "Missouri Mule" that became the American archetype. Thousands of these tall, reliable draft animals— mostly bred from black Percheron mares—were produced every year to supply the burgeoning overland trail traffic. The rapid spread of the Missouri mule and the success of farmers at breeding them to meet each new demand were signature American achievements. But it was government spending—so often a factor in developing a new industry—that proved decisive after the 1850s.

More than a million mules were used by the Quartermaster Corps and the sutler trains that supplied the Union forces during the Civil War, a vital contribution when you consider that provisioning, as much as anything else, helped win the war for the North. After the Civil War, the same bloodlines were used to produce thousands of mules every year for the U.S. Army's supply convoys, which traveled all summer along the many tributaries of the Oregon Trail to military forts in the West. During the great stagecoach era of the American West in the 1860s and 1870s, mules did most of the work, even if, later, in Hollywood westerns, horses got all of the credit. Perhaps as many as 800,000 distinctive, black Missouri mules—branded with a large "U.S." on their rumps—were sent to Europe during World War I. In World War II, roughly 35,000 Missouri mules were deployed to mountainous or jungle theaters where Jeeps and trucks couldn't get through, mostly for hauling light artillery, ammunition, and soldiers' rations. The animals played valiant roles in two of the most important actions of the war—the 10th Mountain Division's storming of the Italian Alps, and with the fabled Merrill's Marauders along the Burma Road to China. After the terrorist attacks on New York and Washington in 2001, the U.S. Marines and the U.S. Army's Special Forces Command quickly reactivated the mule programs, and thousands of distant descendants of Washington's jacks have been deployed in Afghanistan and other mountainous countries around the world. The marines and the army maintain their herds at bases in North Carolina and California, where mountain warfare troops are trained in mule handling, packing, and veterinary care.

The advantages of mules have been known since ancient times. Fully grown mules tend to have the height and musculature of their mother, while inheriting the leaner physique and more nimble legs of their jack father. This produces a hybrid with the strength, but nowhere near the weight, of the mother. The two most common draft-mule crosses today are mammoth jacks bred to black or gray Percheron mares, and the sorrel and dun mules produced by mating with Belgian mares. When mature, the hybrid offspring weigh as much as seven hundred pounds less than their mother, giving the finished mule an extraordinary strength-to-weight ratio and agility far beyond its roots in the horse. In the equine world, the most common adjective applied to mules is "athletic."

The hybridization of closely related but not exactly matched species, like horses and donkeys, produces sterile offspring, and mules cannot reproduce themselves. (Donkeys have sixty-two chromosomes; horses have sixty-four. This creates a mule with sixty-three chromosomes, preventing a full "chain" of matches that can produce an embryo.) But the contributions from the more feral side of the donkey sire more than make up for the mule's inability to reproduce itself. Mules endure heat much better than horses and can travel long distances without water. They require about half the feed of horses and don't gorge on grain. The legs and hooves of a mule are stronger and tend not to "founder," or go lame, on rocky ground or with hard use. Mules live and continue to work until they are thirty years old, while most horses have finished their working lives at twenty. Another critical advantage is contributed by the donkey's large eyes. Because mules' eyes are set farther back on the head and are more D-shaped than a horse's, their peripheral vision includes their hind feet, making them exceptionally sure-footed and confident in rough terrain.

The mule's reputation for difficult behavior derives, ironically, from its superior instincts. Mules have a slightly larger cranial cavity than horses, and thus larger brains, and are more intelligent and judgmental. Mules also possess, from their donkey side, a more feral, self-preservationist nature, and intensely dislike putting themselves in danger. At a water crossing or a steep ravine, the highly domesticated and more pliant horse will usually behave much like a dog, cheerfully obeying its master. Spur the horse and urge it forward and it will jump into the creek. A mule won't do that until it considers the next step safe, or through experience has seen the same situation a few times. The placid, saturnine faces of mules indicate a lot about their personalities. Mules ponder matters a lot more.

Two related feral traits of mules—a keen sense of smell and acute hearing—made them legendary on frontier farms and the overland trails, at least to men sensitive enough to understand them. At the approach of predators, like a pack of coyotes or a herd of buffalo, mules would lift their heads and throw their ears forward, gazing intently toward the threat. This might happen long before the perceived hazard was visible—a mule's sense of smell extends a mile or more, even beyond nearby hills or forests. Once they are sure of the approach of an unfamiliar or dangerous object, mules stop and refuse to be driven toward it, a kind of early-warning function that eventually came to be appreciated on the desolate plains. (When a wagon train's mules indicated the approach of a buffalo herd, hunting parties would quickly mount and rush off for fresh meat, galloping in the direction indicated by the mule ears.) Pioneer Dexter Tiffany, who crossed the Oregon Trail during the busy Gold Rush year of 1849, commented on this while approaching the Green River ford in southern Wyoming. "My mules know whether they are safe long before I do, & I can not whip or spur them on to one [situation] which is dangerous."

The superior instincts of mules require special handling. A good team driver steps off his wagon at a creek and lets his mules watch him cross the water with his arms held in the air, demonstrating to them that the water is only waist-high. Or he can ride a horse across first and let the mules watch. Best, he can appreciate that mules suspicious of a threat feel vulnerable about being hitched to a heavy, cumbersome wagon that prevents them from exercising their deepest instinct—fleeing from danger. This led to the common practice during the overland era, especially on the first two hundred miles of trail, of unhitching mules at even a shallow stream, leading them across individually, and then ferrying the wagon over by hand or by using chains and ropes.

Mules are also acutely sensitive to voices and establish trust over time with a familiar driver. At a steep downhill, the naturally cautious mules are terrified that the heavy rig they are attached to will overrun them from behind. By repetition a driver displays to his team that, on steep grades, he always brakes securely, with a perceptible jerk of the wheels that the mules can feel through their harness. The better drivers "call" their mules properly with reassuring, soothing words. Mules like to be addressed with familiar, one-syllable words that they can readily understand and inform them that their driver is aware of the dangers they face. Loud, jubilant calling is appropriate on an open road or during a steep uphill climb, when the mules can see for themselves that they are not in danger and are simply being urged to pull hard or step lively. But at a tricky gate or a perilous descent, soft, confidence-building talk tells the team that the driver will protect them.

Of course, over the years, the human side of the mule world has been populated with as many blockheads as you would find at a muffler shop or golf course. At the bank of a rushing stream, or the top of a steep hill, when the mules stop to look the situation over, the dolt on the wagon seat gets annoyed at his team and decides to whip them. In unfamiliar terrain, a plastic bag impaled on barbed wire is snapping in the breeze. Mules are skittish about that because they haven't seen it before, and it reminds them of a predator. So the "muleteer" beats them there too. Eventually, when the mules tire of getting beaten, or are just fed up dealing with a less intelligent species, they use the tremendous power of their hind legs to kick out the tug chains and run away. For this, mules are known as "ornery." In English we use the common phrase "stubborn as a mule," a classic example of man ascribing stupidity to the beast instead of to himself.

America's bent toward overproduction also contributed to the unfavorable reputation of mules. During the peak mule-breeding years, from
the 1840s to the 1920s, hundreds of thousands of mules were indiscrimi-
nately bred every year to supply the expanding frontier, the booming farm
economy, and the military. Mules were considered less valuable than
purebred horses, and many farmers saved their best mares for breeding
with male horses. Too often, the mammoth jacks were "put" instead to
inferior mares, just about any old hag around the farm. This undesirable
practice tended to concentrate a lot of bad DNA in mules. Then, after
rudimentary training, the mules were quickly shipped off to auctions that
catered to the kind of agricultural rube who couldn't tell the difference
between a "green" or a "well broke" animal. Mules were like used cars, or
high school athletic directors, swapped around the land according to a
system that guaranteed mediocrity and disappointment.

Over the last thirty years, however, mules have become hot, expensive
trophy purchases, much prized by Connecticut rich girls and California dentists. Considerable care is now devoted to making good matches
of jacks and mares. Today, a variety of high-quality mules—Paint and
Thoroughbred crosses for dressage and jumping, Morgan and Tennessee
Walker mules for driving, really fine Percheron draft mules—are being
produced.

The overland pioneers of the 1840s and 1850s, whose experience
contributed mightily to the formation of American attitudes, were legendary victims of the chiselers who ran the mule business. No one actually
planned the Oregon and California trails. They were created by an explo-
sion of travel that happened after 1843, when thousands of needy or adventurous farm families and gold seekers began flocking every summer to
the frontier along the Missouri River around Kansas City. By then, there
had been settlement in Missouri for almost thirty years, enough time for
the establishment of mule lines and big breeding farms. To service the
sudden burst in demand for draft animals created by the overland trails,
Missouri mule breeders put their jacks to anything in sight, imported
large herds of Mexican mules from Louisiana and Texas, and generally
thrived in the carnival atmosphere that now surrounded the mule business along the frontier. In the autumn, Missouri farms echoed with the
whinnies and groans of jacks and horse mares coupling. In the spring the

cleared lands chimed with trace chains and iron tires as two- and three-year-old colt mules were slapped into harness with a big gang team, run around for a few miles, and then pronounced "fit" to sell to the pioneers. It wasn't unusual for one farm or breeding operation to have a hundred or more mules penned in a single large corral. In late April or early May, the mules were herded up and run over to Independence or St. Joseph to be quickly sold off as "dead-ass broke" teams ready for the overland trails.

Missouri mule breeders didn't consider themselves dishonest. They considered themselves Americans, obligated by birth to accumulate not quality but cash. They knew that the bustling tent cities and outfitting depots mushrooming around the jumping-off towns created market conditions favorable to them. The pioneers who bought their mules would never be seen again. Once safely ferried across the Missouri, the wagon trains disappeared beyond the bluffs into a prairie wilderness that was, literally, a no-man's-land, a vaguely mapped "Northwest Territory," or "Indian Country," large parts of which were disputed by Mexico, Great Britain, and the United States. Few returned from this foreign abyss, waving a lemon law in your face, demanding their money back for deficient, green mules.

Fortunes were made. The shorter, less attractive Mexican mules were best used as pack animals, or for pulling light buggies, and brought only $50 a head, or $100 a team. Prices shot up from there for taller, stronger Missouri mules, anywhere between $125 to $250 for a choice team. Pioneer families buying for their wagon might want either a four-mule or a six-mule hitch. Depending on the year and the supplies of mules that season, the price of a team could reach $1,000 or more per wagon, a large capital investment for the time. The owners of even a relatively small breeding operation could travel to the Missouri River in the spring with just a dozen or more mules, realizing profits of $700 or so, and then return home with enough cash to pay off their bank loans and maybe invest for next year in more mares, or to branch off into wagon dealerships or dry goods. Larger operations of "mule jockeys" made thousands of dollars in profits every spring.

The enormous economic impact of the mule trade and how Oregon Trail traffic stimulated the American economy have been frequently ignored by historians, mostly because it is a lot more prestigious for professional academics to sound learned about Senator Thomas Hart Benton or the Missouri Compromise than to actually know something about America's basic means of transportation for a century—wagons and mules. Yes, the Oregon and California trails delivered thousands of hearty pioneers every year to the Pacific, developing America's west coast and its interior plains. But the convergence of an extensive trail system and a ready supply of mules at embarkation points along the Missouri River effected a historic transfer of wealth that left most of the capital back in Missouri. America's "westering" urge after 1843 was a mobile banking network. Cash for mules, cash for mules. After a season or two selling mules to pioneers, farmers morphed into mule brokers, then big outfitters and bankers, then land speculators and the owners of paddle-wheel steamers. The transaction was as American as apple pie. You risk losing your life to cholera or to a runaway team just over that bluff there; I get possession of your family savings for bigger, safer things. Every year more pioneers came. Missouri, a critical frontier state, prospered for many reasons—good soil, river access, fast-growing hardwood forests—but mostly because of mules.

Boom cycles are notoriously cruel to the economically vulnerable, and there is no question that the pioneers were fleeced by the mule brokers. After buying green mules from the Missouri River brokers, the pioneers endured brutal shakedown runs across the plains. Throughout the 1840s and 1850s, there were ravines along the Wakarusa and Little Blue rivers in Kansas, just a hundred miles from the jumping-off cities, that became vast boneyards littered with wagon wrecks, most of them the result of runaway mules. The 1849 Gold Rush introduced a particularly hazardous character to the West—the urban, nonfarming dreamer who couldn't drive teams. The combination of green mules with inexperienced drivers from back east was only occasionally fatal, but hundreds of gold bugs and pioneer families were forced to cut their mangled wagons in half and continue west with carts, abandon their possessions and join up with other wagons, or, in rare cases, return to Missouri to be resupplied. Wrangling difficult mules became an inseparable part of Oregon Trail lore.

John Clark, the Virginia pioneer who caught gold fever in 1852, traveled the Mississippi River system from Cincinnati to St. Joe, and disembarked for the plains in early May that year. Historian Merrill Mattes

quotes from Clark's journal, which describes the scene when Clark selected his mules at "a large coroll full of stock, many of them young and
unbroken. We had to . . . risk our lives in roping them. After being kicked
across the pen some half dozen times & run over as often, we at last suc-
ceeded in leading them out. . . . It was laughable . . . to see the wild devils
run with all hands hanging on to the ropes to keep them in check." Other
arrivals at St. Joe that year reported being forced to choose among emaci-
ated Mexican mules that had just been run up from Texas in a stock drive,
or spending most of April training their green teams before they felt it
was safe to cross the Missouri. The pioneer journals occasionally recorded
instances of untamed Mexican mules kicking men to death. Henry Coke,
a pioneer who crossed the trail in 1850 with a string of pack mules, spoke
for many when he wrote, "What perverse brutes these mules are. . . . Eh,
the beasts! How I hate 'em."

Another pioneer, John Nevin King, was a Mexican War veteran who
decided to cross the trail in 1850 in a relatively unusual way. He paid an
everything-included fare to an "express train" company, Alexander & Hall,
that carried commercial passengers across the trail in wagons with bench
seats. The service included meals, sleeping tents, and clean laundry once a
week. While still waiting to depart from the jumping-off town of Weston,
Missouri, King wrote to his mother back in Illinois.

> Soon after arriving in town a Team came in, the Teamsters reporting
> to Alexander that another Teamster had harnessed his 4 mules and
> hitched them to a Timber wagon and when ready to start the mules
> became frightened, ran off with the wagon smashing everything—one
> of the lead mules running against a tree & killing himself instantly the
> other ran against a sapling and stunned himself badly.

Apparently the situation never improved. In 1861, a young Missouri
native whose career as a Mississippi River steamboat pilot had been
briefly interrupted by the Civil War, Samuel Clemens, rode west from
St. Joseph on the Oregon Trail, which now also served as a stagecoach
route. Clemens, of course, would eventually adopt the name Mark Twain,
and his journey west across the trail became one of the most defining in
American history, beginning the development of both a persona and a

style of literature that continues to be felt today. Twain initially traveled west on a lark, to accompany his brother Orion, who had been appointed secretary of the Nevada Territory, and he worked as a miner and a journalist in Nevada and California before finding his voice as a writer. In 1872, Twain published a remembered and highly embellished account of his western adventures, the nonfiction classic *Roughing It*. Twain describes how, at a stage stop in southern Nebraska, the horses pulling his stagecoach were changed out for the sturdier mules that would be used the rest of the way west.

> We left our six fine horses and took six mules in their place. But they were wild Mexican fellows, and a man had to stand at the head of each of them and hold him fast while the driver gloved and got himself ready. And when at last he grasped the reins and gave the word, the men sprung suddenly away from the mules' heads and the coach shot from the station as if it had issued from a cannon. How the frantic animals did scamper! It was a fierce and furious gallop—and the gait never altered for a moment till we reeled off ten or twelve miles and swept up to the next collection of little station-huts and stables.

But mules never occupied a consistent place in American mythology. If, by some, they were considered difficult and unpredictable, many Americans also considered the mule a symbol of durability and reliability. The modern image of the mule has always had a decidedly southern spin—probably a legacy of the "forty acres and a mule" policy of the Lincoln administration during the Civil War, for settling freed slaves on southern plantations, or the familiarity of Depression-era photographs of poor southern sharecroppers with their tired-looking, long-eared draft animals. Mules suggested the South, Tobacco Road, the backwardness of Alabama's or Mississippi's agrarian economy left behind by a wealthier and more progressive North.

This would have surprised nineteenth-century northerners, for whom the mule evoked progress, achievement, and Yankee economic drive. Thousands of northern draft mules, from Pennsylvania to the Great Lakes, were a familiar and deeply beloved fixture along the towpaths of the barge canals that served as critical transportation arteries after the

Civil War, carrying passengers and freight between major cities and the outlying country. Towpath mules pulling barges along the extensive Erie canal system through New York's Finger Lakes, or from Easton to Philadelphia along the Delaware canal system, were an American motif, and up until World War II millions of American schoolchildren were required to memorize the lyrics of a popular Tin Pan Alley tune, "Low Bridge, Everybody Down," which was also known as the "Erie Canal Song." In the opening lines of the song, "fifteen miles" refers to the distance a mule usually towed a barge before being replaced by another, rested mule.

I've got a mule, and her name is Sal
Fifteen miles on the Erie Canal
She's a good old worker and a good old pal,
Fifteen miles on the Erie Canal.

The marvelous dichotomy of the American mule endures to this day. Stubborn yet reliable, less attractive than a horse but somehow more adorable, mules evoke America's past, particularly the challenges of the overland years. Mules were infinitely more desirable for covered wagon travelers as a draft animal, considering the other choices. Horses were too heavy, couldn't take the heat, and required too much grain. Oxen were cheaper but painfully slow. "I should unquestionably give the preference to mules," wrote Captain Randolph B. Marcy of the U.S. Army, the author of *The Prairie Traveler*, a handbook for pioneers that became a bestseller in the 1850s. "They travel much faster, and endure the heat of the summer much better than oxen."

A westering American needed mules. Now that I was planning on becoming one myself, I needed a team of big Percheron draft mules, but I couldn't rely on simply arriving at Independence or St. Joe and picking out my team from the spring herds delivered to the jumping-off corrals. Instead, I spent a fitful winter combing equine websites and phoning mule brokers from Alabama to Idaho, usually coming up short. But finally by pulling every connection I had in the Old Order horse world I located what sounded like a promising team at Ropp's Mule Farm in Jamesport, Missouri, run by a legendary Amish mule trainer named Philip Ropp, who agreed to begin driving the three mules I had bought to get them in shape for a two-thousand-mile run across the plains, and to order the correct draft harness at the local harness shop run by his father-in-law, Elmer Beechy. Meanwhile an acquaintance of mine from earlier trips west, Don Werner of the Werner Wagon Works in Horton, Kansas, sold me a restored nineteenth-century Peter Schuttler wagon and began making the modifications I needed for an Oregon Trail run. Werner also began building, out of an old set of wagon wheels and an axle lying in his back pasture, a two-wheel "Trail Pup" provision cart that we would tow behind the main wagon, liberating us from the annoyance of motorized support by a fleet of pickup trucks. I had designed the Trail Pup myself, modeling it after the Spanish "carreta" donkey-carts, also called "Red River carts," which were used to cross the Rockies during the fur-trapping era, and the military commissary carts towed behind escort wagons during the Civil War. I had outfitted myself by telephone and email, but now I had a real team of Missouri mules and an authentic prairie schooner and cart. I felt as ready—and as fearful—about going as a nineteenth-century pioneer.

4

NICK ARRIVED IN HIS PICKUP on the first Friday in May. I was overwhelmed with joy to see him but also stabbed by pangs of worry. He had put on a lot of weight during his winter of inactivity and he walked with a noticeable limp. But he looked buoyant and happy, finally liberated from his invalid's bed for a ride across the Oregon Trail. He had driven hard from Maine as soon as the appointment with his doctor was over, making the trip from Augusta in under five hours. This was one trail hand raring to go.

Nick and I immediately addressed the serious matter of how much equipment we could carry. We knew beforehand that we would have duplicates of a lot of items, and that we should eliminate as much gear as possible to avoid overloading the wagon. Still, my attitude about a covered wagon trip was that we were about to shove off for four or five months of living out of a twelve- by three-foot wagon box. Everything that was dear to me would have to be wedged inside my new wheeled abode on the plains.

Nick's attitude toward me has always been that I am too acquisitive and fussy. In his mind, a college education ruins people and he associates my fondness for worldly goods with that. But our differences were a lot worse than I thought. It all came to a head when Nick saw my piles of gear on the porch of my house.

"Rink, what the frig is this?" he said, holding up my wheel wrench.

I was proud of my wheel wrench. I had found it at an antique store in Vermont over the winter, and I even checked that it was the right size for our Schuttler wheel hubs.

"Nick," I said. "That's my wheel wrench. It fits the wagon."

"Rink, this is not a wheel wrench. It's a frickin piece of crap. It's cheap alloy from Korea or China or somewhere. It will break on the first wheel. I've already got two good ones in my tool kit."

Nick tossed the wheel wrench a few feet away onto the lawn, indicating that he was starting a reject pile, and began poking through the rest of the gear on my porch.

"Oh, I am not fuckin believing this," he said, holding up one piece of gear that I had carefully stacked into a waterproof Tupperware container. "Rink, what *is* this?"

"It's a shoe shine kit," I said. "C'mon, Nick. Somebody might invite us in for dinner at the ranch house, you know? We might want to look neat."

Nick tossed the shoe shine kit toward the rejected wheel wrench, and our provisioning session proceeded from there.

The rejects on my lawn quickly grew into a large, pyramid-shaped pile, a vertical yard sale depicting the vanities of life. Nick didn't want to bring my CD player, my salad spinner and mixing bowls, or my boccie ball set, and on top of that he tossed extra pillows, my garment bag for wet-weather gear, my pasta colander, and several L.L. Bean bags loaded with Oregon Trail books. He had his own container of harness oil and a leather punch, so we didn't need mine. By the time he was done, the pile of my gear that Nick had rejected would have filled about half the bed of a pickup truck.

I was deliberately meek about all of this, and Nick seemed surprised that I didn't put up a bigger fight. But I had known this was coming. To cross the Oregon Trail, my job would be to suppress as much of myself as possible, to manage the trip by never appearing to be a manager. In exchange for having Nick along, I would evaporate as a person.

Nick was so disgusted with the chore of confronting my gear, and so tired after his long drive from Maine, that he decided he needed a long restroom stop inside the house, on top of my toilet. Grabbing an illustrated history of tugboats from my library, he disappeared inside the bathroom.

Realizing that this was my last opportunity, I quickly sorted through the reject pile and pulled out the stuff that I still wanted—the boccie set, the kitchen gear, the shoe shine kit, and a lot more. Racing back and forth to Nick's pickup truck, I stowed all of it way up front by the cab, hiding it in the cavities underneath Nick's wheel jacks and tool kits. When we got to Missouri, I would have to figure out a way to secretly transfer my contraband stash to the covered wagon. I would buy hay in advance, I decided, and load it into the Trail Pup. You can hide a lot of shoe shine kits under bales of hay.

While Nick was still on the toilet, I clunked up the stairs next to the bathroom as loudly as I could. Up in the attic, which was just above Nick's head in the bathroom, I dropped some boxes full of heavy books, and kicked my snowshoes around a little, simulating the sounds of a dejected brother returning a lot of gear to storage. I sighed and moaned a lot when I got back to the bottom of the stairs, just beside the bathroom door.

"Jeez," I said out loud. "My boccie balls. Nick doesn't like them. I can't even bring my shoe shine kit."

One of Nick's better qualities is that his short attention span does not permit him to hold a grudge for more than five minutes. When he emerged from the bathroom, he seemed refreshed, jubilant about leaving.

"Yo, are we going now, or what?"

As we left my drive I habitually reached into my jeans pocket to make sure that I had my keys. But there were no keys, and I suddenly realized the enormity of this leap. I looked back over my shoulder to my tidy barn house, with its neat board sides, clipped lawns, and flower beds. I didn't need a key for the door there now. My home was sublet until November. My car keys had been left at my other house, with the car, so that my daughter could use it for the summer. I had also left behind the key to my post office box—the friendly postmistress in town would keep my mail. I had no keys, nothing to open, and nowhere to live, except in a covered wagon. I had never felt departure as strongly as this, as if I were leaving one form of existence for another.

A few miles west of my home, the purple-black rim of the Appalachian chain rises steeply from the banks of the Blackberry River. It is a purposeful landscape, still bearing the relics of America's nineteenth-century iron-making district. There are snowy-white lime pits dug into the hills, old stone furnaces beside the road, and a long chain of picturesque dairies in the valley. I drove that route several times a week, on my way to the supermarket, or to the library.

Now I was leaving this familiar prospect behind to go forth and live my dream. But as I looked back one last time on the mountains of New England, I was racked by self-doubt, and my stomach and chest swirled with panic attacks. Being romantic, always effecting a new escape, wasn't liberating at all. I didn't even know if I could push mules a mere fifty miles on the Oregon Trail, and the challenge I had taken on seemed terrifying. As we followed the back roads out over the Catskills and then picked up the interstates to drive west, my spasms of fear returned intermittently, especially early in the morning. I was departing on a crazyass errand into the wilderness and had no idea how it would end.

In northern Missouri, as we pulled off the highway and entered the large Old Order community in Jamesport, I could see right away that we had found a great jumping-off town. It was early afternoon during planting season and Amish and Mennonite farmers were clattering past the brick facades on Locust Street in their spring wagons, carrying furniture and potted flowers to sell to the tourists out on the highway. The two-lane highway north toward Ropp's Mule Farm was crowded with big draft teams pulling harrows and corn planters to the fields.

The Ropp farm was the classic Amish place, a zone of fecundity busy with new life up against low green hills. Mule colts were kicking up their heels and galloping in circles in the pastures and spring puppies scampered across the lawns. In the barnyard, Ropp's teenage son was training an attractive riding mule by standing on top of the saddle and running a long rope over the mule's ears and rump.

Philip Ropp is short and wiry, with a lean Abe Lincoln visage and beard, a bundle of nervous, cheerful energy. He was just about to run off on an errand and was working on the broken engine of his horse-drawn brush hog. But Ropp told me that my mules were in the large walk-in pen at the rear of the stables of the main barn below. Nick grabbed his tool kit from the pickup and jumped onto the brush hog to figure out the engine problems.

I had expected this to be an emotional moment but, still, I wasn't quite prepared for the heartthrob I felt when I first saw that team. The mules were enormously tall—the big gelding, Jake, had to be over seventeen hands—and looked at me with those beautiful, imperturbable faces that mules have. The sunlight reaching the pen shone off their broad black backs, and it was set off by the mushroom-colored markings on their muzzles and the inside of their legs. I was smitten right away and couldn't believe that I had purchased such an attractive team so casually, almost by accident, over the phone.

When I opened the gate of the pen and stepped in, the taller of the two female mules wheeled on her rear legs, leaped off the sawdust bedding, and vaulted outside, showing me her new shoes when she kicked out going through the doorway. That would have to be Beck, and I could see why Ropp had warned me about her skittishness when we first talked about the team six weeks before. Bute, a little shorter, with a small, adorable head and almost Morgan horse good looks, placidly trotted off to join Beck outside.

Crazy Beck (left), *Steady Jake, and Prom Queen Bute.*

But Jake, a gentle giant, immediately walked over to me with a curious look in his eyes, his immense long ears pushed forward. When I reached out my hand to pat his muzzle and gently grab him by the halter, he buried his face in my armpit, nuzzling affectionately to say hello. I reached up to scratch behind his ears and he rubbed his head up and down along my ribs, lifting me to my toes with his strong head. God, did I love that mule right away and, right there, I understood something important about him.

He was so strong and self-confident that he didn't fear a stranger. He could afford to be outgoing and friendly. No beast on earth was a threat to Jake.

Ropp had told me that Jake drove single and that I should try him out. I found a single harness hanging in the barn and decided to drive back up the county highway to pick up our new team harness. Jake was classically Amish-trained and stood calmly while I threw on the harness, and his only fault seemed to be that he pawed the ground impatiently when I had him hooked to the wagon—he was that anxious to go. I was eager myself to get him on the road and see how he handled and moved because I had laid such plans in having a single-driving mule to hitch to the Trail Pup when we made one- or two-day stops.

When I reached the brush hog up by the house, Nick was standing over the engine, parts distributed all around him, his hands and face smudged with grease.

"Nick, c'mon. Let's try Jake out on the road. You can finish the engine later."

At the road, when I slapped the reins on Jake's rump for a trot, he gamely bowed his head and neck, vaulting forward with an attractive, willing leap toward work. His stride was effortless and very long, and he naturally curled his hooves high, Percheron-proud, and then pounded back for the pavement, never breaking his trot. He was a gorgeously moving animal, unbelievably nimble for his size.

It was a delight to be on a new Missouri road in a wagon pulled by a good mule, with my brother beside me on the seat. Olive Oyl sat between us, cocking her head sideways with curiosity about this new land. Every blade of spring grass and dandelion seemed to reach up to us from the fields, and the freshening breeze carried Jake's dandruffy smell back over our faces. The harness and the shafts rumbled as they bounced together and the iron tires sang. Jake rhythmically pounded the road on new shoes. The cows and the horses in the fields ran to the fence lines, galloping beside us, to see the big black mule.

"God, this is one fine fuckin mule," Nick said. "If the other two are this nice we're home free. I can't believe you picked so well."

"Nick, sometimes you're just so idiotically naive that you get lucky."

"Right," Nick said. "Then, the next time? You're as dumb as a stump post."

• • •

The next day was sunny and bright, with high cumulus clouds resting in a big western sky as we made the Highway 36 crossing west from St. Joe to see our wagon. The bridge over the broad Missouri River crosses right where the ferry services bearing the wagons ran in the 1840s and 1850s. I asked Nick to drive slowly on the bridge so that we could see the high bluffs on the western side of the river that the pioneers described in their trail journals.

From there, stretching more than a hundred miles southeast in a series of giant horseshoe bends, the Missouri's course had defined the edge of the frontier. For twenty years before the Civil War the jumping-off towns along the river—Independence, Kansas City, Westport, St. Joe, and the Mormon crossing from Iowa, Council Bluffs—had bustled with departing trail traffic. Mule brokers, wagon dealers, and outfitters selling flour and sides of cured bacon competed fiercely for the new business that arrived every spring. Most of these towns were founded expressly to serve the Oregon Trail pioneers or the military forts, and every year their civic boosters sent thousands of printed pamphlets east to advertise their advantages. St. Joseph, which after its founding in 1843 quickly overtook Independence as the most popular jumping-off town, mushroomed from a population of just five hundred people in the early 1840s to almost nine thousand in 1860. The sudden boost in economic activity along the frontier helped the country recover from the devastating impact of the Panic of 1837. On a busy spring day, when everyone seemed to be launching for the trails at once, there were dozens of ferries and barges crossing with wagons at each spot, so thick on the river that it was said someone could step from barge to barge and get across to the far bank.

As we entered the rolling farm country of Brown County and then drove up the shore of Mission Lake in Horton, where the Werner Wagon Works sits on a small plateau above town, my heart raced again. There, on the mowed lawn outside Werner's shop, stood my covered wagon rig. The Peter Schuttler wagon and its matching Trail Pup were perched alone on the prairie, and from the bottom of the hill near the lake they were framed by the clouds and a distant fence line, lovely and idealized, like a monument reaching for the sky. The fresh canvas tops glowed bleach white under the sun, and the light glinted off the green wagon box and the matte red wheels. The smell of fresh wheel paint and the sound of the wind buffeting through the new wagon top filled me with the romance of travel, and all of my worries about the trip evaporated in an endorphin rush.

The jumping-off towns along the Missouri River frontier (here, Westport, Missouri, depicted by William Henry Jackson) boomed with overland traffic and became a major stimulus for the nineteenth-century American economy.

Don Werner was glad to see us, and came out of his shop in worn dungarees, a plaid shirt, and an old pair of lace-up packer's boots. He had grown up in the 1940s on a small Kansas farm, where his father still used horses, and retained as a favorite memory riding the family's farm wagons as a boy. He spent his young adult years working as a union electrician on big construction projects in Kansas City, spending his weekends restoring covered wagons for friends. In 1989, Werner was awarded a dream contract, an order to build eight historically correct covered wagons for the displays at the National Oregon-California Trail Center in Montpelier, Idaho. Werner quit his union job and used the museum contract to establish his business, eventually emerging as one of the most respected wagon builders and wheelwrights in the West.

Werner showed us the modifications he had made to the wagon according to my specifications, including the wooden platform bed with foam mattress that was installed inside the wagon box.

When Don briefly left us to take a phone call in his office, Nick scrambled underneath the wagon on his shoulders and rump as he inspected the running gear and axles. We had agreed on a plan as we drove out that morning. We weren't going to raise with Don any issues that were either ornamental or easy to fix back in Jamesport. But if Nick found anything mechanically wrong with the wagon, he would take his NAPA Auto Parts cap off and stow it in his back pocket. That would be our signal to quietly discuss the subject and decide what to do. Nick never took off his hat. But he did find a few things that he thought we should do. The oak brake shoes did not have rubber pads, and Nick didn't think that the naked wood would last very long with the constant abrasion against the iron tire rims, especially after we started hitting a lot of hills. Nick thought that we should take along extra brake shoes.

"Did you happen to make extra brake shoes?" he asked Don when he returned from his shop. "Or can I take along some uncut oak stock? I'm not sure these oak shoes are going to last very long."

Werner frowned and sniffed at the thought. He was obviously very sensitive to any criticism about his wagon restoration.

"Oh, that won't be necessary, Nick," Werner said. "Those brake shoes will last you all the way to Oregon. I guarantee it."

Nick was working hard at being polite, but his Fu Manchu mustache dropped. I quickly looked at him, shook my head, and then spoke up and changed the subject with Don.

What Werner had just said was ludicrous to me. Wooden brake shoes without pads—rubbing against iron tire rims through the first stretch of the Flint Hills—wouldn't last even a hundred miles. But it wasn't Werner's fault. Like most wagon makers today, he restores pristine, "period-accurate" vehicles for museum displays, or for collectors who might run horse-drawn vehicles ten or fifteen miles a year in parades. He doesn't know working hitches, and few wagon makers today would understand the problems we would have with wooden brakes over two thousand miles. And it wasn't worth an argument now, because I had Nick, who could rebuild a set of brake shoes in less than an afternoon.

There was one thing that happened in Horton that I wouldn't fully appreciate until hundreds of miles later. When Nick tested the Trail Pup wheels by grabbing the spokes just above the hub and giving them a strong shake, he grimaced. When he ran his hands over the front wheels of the main wagon, I could tell that he was unhappy. But he never mentioned anything, and he didn't take off his NAPA cap.

In the jumping-off commotion of our next few days, and then the elation of travel after we left, I completely forgot about this. And it was typical of our different personalities that I failed to pick up on what Nick was seeing in the wheels. He knows mechanics, wood, and hubs that pass or fail the shake test. I am incurably aesthetic, and the wagon looked beautiful. Silence often results from incompatibilities like that. So, the question of the wheels didn't come up.

That afternoon, the trucker we'd hired in Kansas, Doyle Prawl, rolled in to pull the wagon and Trail Pup back to Ropp's place in Missouri. There, at an Amish welding shop near Ropp's farm, we would install a number of additional modifications—a rearview mirror, safety lights, brackets and hangers for our ropes and buckets—that Werner wasn't interested in doing because they were not "period-accurate." When we had all the fixes on the wagon made, the trucker would haul our mules and the wagons across the Missouri for his farm along the St. Joe Road, where we'd launch for the junction with the Oregon Trail farther west in Kansas.

That night, crickets screeched and spring peepers peeped from the wetlands as we rode east in the dark toward the Missouri River. At the river the great horseshoe bend where the pioneers had crossed glowed neon purple and blue from the lights of the riverfront casinos. I was exhausted and unsettled, still worried about all of the fixes we had to make to the wagon, realizing that in the morning I would be dealing with so much uncertainty. But after we cleared the lights of St. Joe the Missouri farmland outside the truck was moody and quiet, with just a few lit houses widely spaced along the road. The cool air racing in through the pickup windows, and my fatigue, whittled my thoughts down to a satisfying, narrow clarity.

We were jumping off. Uncertainty was my life now and I had to learn to improvise day to day.

•   •   •

The conflict between the reenactor-collector mentality that Werner represented and my own determination to make a modern crossing of the Oregon Trail went to the heart of what I was doing with this trip. There is no such thing anymore as *the* Oregon Trail. There never was a single Oregon Trail. After Fort Kearny on the Platte in eastern Nebraska, some wagon trains hugged the north side of the Platte along the edge of the Sand Hills, and some took the south banks. To avoid each other's dust and to hunt for game, the wagons fanned out widely across the prairie all day. The trains generally followed a set of central "ruts," or the rivers, for navigation, but the trail west was often five miles wide on either side of the river, or as much as twelve miles total, including both banks. By the 1850s, western Wyoming was a sprawling network of wagon tracks and shortcuts—the Lander Cutoff, the Farson Cutoff, the Sublette Cutoff, the Hams Fork Cutoff—that extended more than a hundred miles north and south, all of it considered the Oregon Trail. By some counts there are as many as forty cutoffs and alternate branches from the main ruts along the 2,100-mile route. The "trail" was really just an aggregated landscape that the pioneers followed across the plains and then the high deserts.

With the trail being that broad, innumerable paved roads, rail lines, irrigation ditches, and equipment sheds now interrupt it in many places. The Oregon Trail is what historic space always becomes—a landscape blending modernity with the past. The original emigrant road runs through modern downtown Lawrence and Topeka, Kansas. In Oregon, the last two hundred miles of the trail hugging the Columbia River are now Interstate Highway 84.

The reenactors, the self-appointed protectors of our past, hate this. They don't want to run their shiny Schuttler or Studebaker wagons on asphalt, down past the Dairy Queen or the Sinclair convenience store. They want ruts, dust, verisimilitude, the geographic equivalent of their button and holster fetishes. Fine, chucklehead, be a reenactor reenactoring in a wagon, but I just want to ride the old route and see what's out there today. The real world doesn't frighten me. I knew that I would be enjoying many long, dreamy afternoons following undisturbed old trail ruts through the lonely bluff country of Nebraska and Wyoming. But because the trail naturally morphed over time into county roads and state highways, I would be riding on a lot of asphalt too. That's the challenge, the fun, the point, of crossing the Oregon Trail today. Flashing safety lights and a rearview mirror are required to cross what the modern trail has become.

I rejected the dogmatic "authenticity" fetish of the reenacting mentality for another reason. The reasons the trail has changed are the story of my country. In Kansas, the old St. Joe Road that fed into the Oregon Trail between St. Joseph and Marysville is now State Highway 36. In Nebraska, the Oregon Trail between North Platte and the Wyoming line—a mythic stretch along pink desert soil that includes Chimney Rock—is now Highway 30 and Highway 26. The paving of these particularly scenic stretches of the old trail wasn't a crime against the past. It was something called American history, economic history, to be more exact. The original trail went where people wanted to go, west toward free lands, forming the roadbed of the largest land migration in history, and then it continued going in the direction that people wanted to go. Even before the flood of pioneers and homesteaders crossing the frontier ended in the 1890s, farmers and ranchers in the West used the old Oregon Trail route, which followed the rivers and the best, level terrain, to run their cattle east into the big slaughter yards and railroad terminals in Omaha and Kansas City. Those cities grew and became major economic engines of the Midwest because the Oregon Trail was gradually converted from a wagon road into a cattle-driving route. Later, during World War I, long stretches of the trail in Nebraska were paved over to truck cattle to the slaughter yards of Omaha, so that canned beef could more quickly be shipped to the more than three million American doughboys serving in Europe. The Nebraska beef industry boomed. That's the trail. That is our history and what it means today. That's the trail I wanted to see. Often, it's a paved road, requiring safety lights on a slow-moving wagon.

But by refusing to add features like this because they weren't "authentic," Werner was teaching me one of the most valuable lessons of the trip. Modern wagon making is determined to remain locked in the past, and putting real people and a real team across the trail today is a lost art. I would have to figure that out for myself. In that way, there was something very authentic about the experience I was having. Now I knew a little bit more about how the pioneers felt as they embarked for the West. It was my jumping-off time and I was getting jacked around by the outfitters.

•   •   •

Back in Jamesport, Nick and I spent three happy days inside the large welding and machine shop run by Ropp's Amish neighbor, Ivan Schrock, fabricating parts for our wagon and equipment for our camp. Schrock's shop was busy with planting season work, but he carved off a corner of the barn near the doors for us to work, strolling over every hour to offer suggestions about the parts we were making for the wagon. I reached a nice jumping-off moment there in Schrock's barn. Hammering away at an anvil on one of our projects, Nick would frequently interrupt his progress to step over and help someone else fix a hydraulic line, or to shitrig a cultivator with an old windmill part. Keeping Nick focused can be a full-time job, and it was frustrating to watch him wander off to help someone else every hour or so. But everyone racing through Schrock's shop for spring repairs adored Nick for this, or they simply adored him because of his laughter and fun. People would do anything for him. This would become a major asset during our crossing of the trail, and in Jamesport I became more relaxed, less obsessive about meeting deadlines, and enjoyed letting Nick just be Nick.

While Nick worked on his projects, Philip and I addressed the most important challenge of our hitch—the tongue-reliever to lift the heavy weight of the tongue, also called the pole, off the mule collars. Knowledge about tongue-relievers is almost completely lost today, even in the team-driving community. Heavy wagons don't travel long distances anymore, and the era of tongue-relievers essentially ended in the 1890s when the blue military escort wagons of the western plains were phased out and replaced by rail transport. I had seen only two tongue-relievers in my life, and both were mounted differently. But they came down to the same thing—a long chain and spring assembly that ran from the front of the wagon box, attached to a hitch point midway along the pole. The chain provided heft, lifting the pole to the right height to take the weight off the mule collars. The strong, industrial-strength spring provided flexibility, allowing the pole to gently rock up and down with the movement of the team.

Ropp and I spent an entire day, standing at the metal presses and welding stands in Schrock's shop, fabricating the mounts for our tongue-reliever, and then mounting it on the Schuttler wagon. When we were done, the heavy tongue was suspended almost perfectly at the chest-height of the mule team, and even Nick was impressed.

"Rink, when you first told me about this tongue-reliever idea, I couldn't even find one in my wagon books. But this solution works. The weight of the pole is off the mule collars. I never thought a jerk like you could do this."

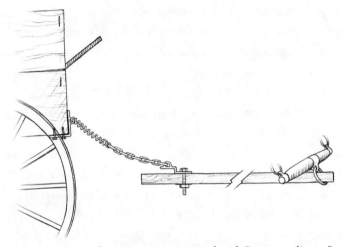

Nineteenth-century covered wagons were equipped with "tongue-relievers" to take the weight of the heavy pole, or tongue, off the collars of the mules.

My parole from mechanical idiocy, however, didn't last very long. On our last day in Jamesport, when I drove into the Ropp farm after running errands in town, Philip and Nick were standing by the barn near the Trail Pup, the commissary cart I had designed and asked Don Werner to build, which we would tow behind the wagon to carry the bulk of our supplies. The Trail Pup was vital to our crossing, because it would liberate us from the fuss and obnoxious presence of the pickup trucks and canteen rigs that provide the "motorized support" of modern covered wagon trips staged by reenactors. I had asked Werner to build the Trail Pup with a detachable towing tongue, so that single-mule shafts could be installed when we were camping somewhere and the cart could be used as a run-about to make shorter trips into towns for supplies.

Nick and Philip had detached the Trail Pup from the main wagon, taken the towing tongue off, and replaced it with my single-mule driving shafts. The Trail Pup sat on the grass, looking forlorn and all alone, resting forward on the shafts.

I walked over and Nick spoke first.

"Rink, pick up the Trail Pup."

When I grabbed the shafts, the Trail Pup was so heavy to lift that I could barely get the cart level, and there was no center of gravity to be found. The bed was set so far forward on the axle that the weight was all in the front, and even just a single passenger would add greatly to that. The cart had no resting moment where it should be—level on the wheels. No mule, even one as strong as Jake, could handle that load. As a passenger cart, my half-wagon was a flop.

I dropped the shafts back down.

"Fucked again," Nick said. "You bought a cart that isn't a cart. There's no resting moment."

There wasn't time to dwell on my design failure. My mind instantly moved to the next problem. The Trail Pup was also my emergency backup plan. If we broke a wheel out in western Nebraska and Wyoming, where we'd often be fifty miles from the closest town, I was counting on being able to hook Jake to the Trail Pup, tying the other mules behind, and riding to safety with Nick and just the provisions we needed for a day or two. But now I didn't have that.

"Philip," I said, "does Jake really ride okay?"

"He rides fine," Ropp said. "It's like being on a truck, but he rides."

Jake became my new backup plan. If we got stranded in the Wyoming wilderness, Nick and I could ride him out together, or I could leave Nick behind with enough provisions and water for a day or two and ride alone for help. This would require a return trip to the Amish harness shop where I could trade in my old Wyoming saddle for a larger saddle that would fit Jake's broad back.

I walked down to the barn, harnessed and hooked Jake to the spring wagon, and threw my saddle into the back for a run down the county highway to the harness shop. It was a lonely drive and I felt dejected about my failed design for the Trail Pup, and also pressed for time. I was determined to jump off by May 15, now just two days away, but there were still so many details to nail down.

When I arrived at the harness shop, carrying my saddle on my shoulder, Elmer Beechy was standing at the front counter. Elmer is a slender middle-aged man with a scraggly white beard, glasses, and a plain old straw hat—not the flattops that most Amish wear. He is more western than Pennsylvania Dutch. I liked him right away because he is such an American character type, and classic Amish. There is a reason that he's the biggest harness dealer in the West. Elmer is a born salesman who maneuvers you toward a deal by trying to make you feel that he really cares deeply about your needs.

I explained to Elmer that I needed a draft saddle built on a wider frame for Jake's broad back. I would trade in my old high-quality handmade saddle for a used one, which we would then build out with the extra tack—a breastplate and breeching straps for the rumps—that traditionally is used on mules. I figured that these modifications would cost me about $200. But my Wyoming saddle was so valuable—I had originally paid $800 for it—that I would probably be able to make an even trade for everything and not spend any more money.

Holding it up with one hand, Elmer briefly inspected my saddle and then dropped it onto the floor by the sales counter.

"This saddle you want to trade is worthless," he said. "It's got a slick seat. Everybody wants padded saddles these days. That thing will sit in my shop for months and I'll end up having to wholesale it out at a loss."

"Elmer, this is a handmade Wyoming saddle. Look at this thing. I bought it at the best shop in Rock Springs."

"I'll do you a favor, seeing as you already spent money on harness here," Elmer said. "I'll take the saddle off your hands so you don't have to worry. I'll be losing money, but I am willing to do that, just for you."

"How much for the trade-in?"

"I'll give you $150. And it ain't worth even half of that."

It was the classic jumping-off hustle and Amish cash burn, rolled into one. Elmer knew that I was in a hurry to get on the trail and that there wasn't another harness shop within hundreds of miles that could build out a mule saddle. I didn't have any choice.

"Okay, Elmer," I said. "Can you help me pick out the right saddle for Jake? Then we can get started on the breeching."

We ended up finding a used padded saddle on the sales floor that Elmer said he would "let go" for $350. He was making $200 before he sold me all of the extra tack.

While Elmer and I were saddle-trading, a middle-aged, obviously well-heeled horse fancier from the Kansas City suburbs had come in. He drove a shiny cream-white SuperCrew Ford pickup with the expensive King Ranch options package, and he wore a ridiculously large rodeo buckle and lizard-skin boots. His daughter had just married and the new son-in-law wanted to join the family weekends by learning to ride. The indulgent father-in-law was buying everything in sight for the new family brat—chaps, spurs, a fancy breastplate, a Navaho-pattern saddle blanket, the whole nine yards of cowboy pimp.

When the man carried this pile of loot up to the front of the shop, he saw my old saddle sitting on the floor by the counter. He walked over and picked it up.

"Elmer, what's this?" he said. "It's a nice saddle."

"That's handmade in Wyoming," Elmer said. "And it's got the slick seat. You sure don't see many of them anymore. Tell me, is your new son-in-law a he-man?"

"Oh yeah. He's big. He's tough."

"Well, we ain't going to sell any padded saddle to him."

"Nope. Padded is for dressage girls. So, what do you want for it?"

"Well, I'll tell you," Elmer said. "Seeing as you're buying so much stuff here today, I am going to do you a favor. I'll give it away to you for my absolute, Amish Wal-Mart, everyday low price, okay? $350."

"Done," the man said. "Thanks, Elmer. Wayland is going to love this baby."

I was not believing this. It was as if my old saddle were a leopard that could erase its spots. One minute a slick saddle seat was antiquated, utterly out of fashion, and unsalable. The next minute it was studmuffin testosterone additive. Elmer Beechy had made $200 on that saddle in less than five minutes, not to mention all of the other expensive gear he was selling both of us.

The tab for everything the man was buying, including my saddle, came to more than $1,000, and he paid in cash.

I was still standing there, stupefied.

"Say, Rinker," Elmer said. "You wanna help this gentleman carry this gear out to his pickup? I wanna get someone out back started on your mule saddle."

Jesus. Now I am even Elmer Beechy's errand boy. I was in such a staggered state that I did it, carrying my old Wyoming saddle, and all of its memories, out to the man's shiny pickup, throwing it on, and then watching him drive away.

When I got back inside, Elmer was amiably smiling, not at all concerned about what I thought.

"Elmer, you just screwed me," I said. "That guy would have paid $500 for that saddle. You could have paid me so much more. You said it would sit here for months. It was gone in five minutes, at a $200 profit."

Elmer sighed.

"Rinker," he said. "You are looking at a humble Amish businessman. First I did you a favor by taking the saddle off your hands. Then I did him a favor, letting it go cheap because he was already spending so much money here. Everybody's happy. But let me ask you something. Did you watch me do that?"

"Yeah, Elmer," I said. "I watched you do that."

"Good," he said. "Because now you're honorary Amish."

When my saddle was ready I unharnessed Jake, and Elmer helped me throw on my new mule saddle. I rode Jake out across the hilly meadows for half an hour. Ropp was right. Jake rode like a big old Boeing Stratocruiser—the same gentle, sweet Jake, but a freighter. However, I could steer him, and he would trot if I urged him hard. In Elmer's hands, I had become the classic pioneer rube. But now I had a plausible worst-case scenario plan. Jake could carry me out of the wilderness if we broke a wheel.

When I got back to Ropp's farm with Jake, Nick was working in the barnyard behind the Schuttler making last-minute tweaks to our modifications and checking the axels for grease. One of the additions he had made to the wagon while I was gone filled me with nostalgia.

After my father died in 1975, there was a great dispersion of his fabulous loot, according to a family pecking order that made sense only to us. His wagon collection had already been sold off, but my sisters managed to get all of the valuable dry sinks and the best antique furniture. One of my brothers ran off with my father's leather flight jackets and helmets. Nick, of course, secured most of the contents of my father's shop, a mechanic's booty of antique tools, anvils, hydraulic jack stands, piles of wagon parts, and four hubcaps for a 1967 Oldsmobile 88. I got a cardboard box filled with dog-eared reference books and a worn shearling coat.

But the jewel in the family crown was a simple wooden sign, which Nick had hung for many years above his fireplace in Maine.

On our 1958 covered wagon trip, my father wanted the automobile drivers backed up behind us to know that we appreciated their patience. They deserved to understand, he thought, why a covered wagon was running down the roads of New Jersey and Pennsylvania in the middle of an otherwise normal summer in the late 1950s. So he had a sign maker in New York City paint a simple explanation in black and red letters on a white background, across a four-foot pine board that hung from leather straps behind the wagon. It read:

We're Sorry For The Delay—But We Want The Children To
SEE AMERICA SLOWLY
New Vernon, New Jersey to Valley Forge, Lancaster, Gettysburg, Penna

The sign was a big hit everywhere we went that summer and when the local newspapers printed photographs of our wagon trip, SEE AMERICA SLOWLY was always prominently featured.

The back of the sign had never been painted, and over the years the pine had aged to a smooth surface. Nick had painted that white, and then taken the board to a sign painter in Maine for the similar messaging he considered appropriate for our trip.

We Are Sorry For The Delay, But We Want To
SEE AMERICA SLOWLY
St. Joseph, Ft. Kearny, Scotts Bluff, South Pass, Farewell Bend

While I was away at the harness shop, Nick had hung the reverse side of the sign, with its new lettering, on the back of the Trail Pup, where it would be clearly visible to drivers following us on the highways west. I was charmed by the idea of recycling my father's old sign. Our tailgate motto, fifty-three years after it had been created for my childhood covered wagon trip, would still be SEE AMERICA SLOWLY.

The sight of our wagon rig finished off with the SEE AMERICA SLOWLY sign possessed me with jumping-off fever. We still had a long punch list of minor fixes that we wanted to make—extra harness rings for the driving lines, better attachments for our hoses and water barrels, a staff for the American flag we wanted to hang from the wagon. But, fuck it. Perfectionism was my enemy now. We would be dicking around Missouri for days if we continued to noodle with these fixes, most of which could be made after we launched on the trail.

"Nick," I said. "I'm calling the trucker in a few minutes. I'm going to ask him to get here tomorrow, as early in the day as possible. We'll haul the mules and the wagons across the river tomorrow, spend the afternoon making any last-minute fixes, and launch the next morning. It's time to leave."

"Yeah, but I still have more fixes," Nick said. "And have we shopped for food? Rinker, we need food. We need hay and oats."

"No more fixes, Nick. Screw food for now. We'll buy that at the first Wal-Mart. Do you want to hit the trail?"

"Do *you* want to hit the trail?"

"I want to hit the trail."

"Okay, boss. Let's head 'em up and move 'em out."

5

THE ERA OF THE CANVAS-TOPPED wagons crossing the American plains lasted about fifty years. During the peak migration years of the 1840s and 1850s, more than 400,000 pioneers crossed, in about sixty thousand wagons, but there were still remnant wagon trains rumbling across the prairie with homesteaders well into the 1890s. A giant wave of economic destiny rolled west with the red wheels. But history is often nonlinear and event followed event with unpredictable charm.

With time, of course, the covered wagon became one of our most enduring cultural symbols, expressing both the wandering urge and the go-getter spirit of a society that had stumbled upon mobility as an engine of growth. But unlike the railroads or the clipper ships that propelled America's growth as an industrial power and a global trading giant, the green wagons crossing Nebraska en masse after 1843 were not a result of planning or deliberation. Happenstance and local experimentation, more than anything else, created the distinctive American covered wagon, and its exact provenance is unknown for a very good reason. By the 1820s, covered wagon prototypes had become so common, and their design features were so democratically shared, that no one thought it useful to record their history. But to understand the rough ambit of wagon development is to understand America itself.

One particularly strong misconception still persists. During the spring before I left, as I began to tell a few friends that I was headed for the plains for a covered wagon trip, they universally assumed that I would be taking a Conestoga wagon. There was even an interesting gender break about it. "Oh, so you're taking a Conestoga across," one male friend said. "Tell me, how much does that baby weigh? It looks big." A woman friend said, "Oh, the Conestoga. I've seen these lovely pictures of them with couches and carpets inside. So comfy. Can I come along for a week?"

In fact, the Conestoga wagon was an eighteenth-century behemoth, essentially a brigantine on wheels, and it had very little to do with the overland migration before the Civil War. The Conestoga was an eastern wagon and saw only limited use out west on the big commercial roads like the Santa Fe Trail between Missouri and New Mexico, or along the military trails that conveyed munitions and hardtack from Fort Riley and Fort Leavenworth in Kansas to the distant, outlying forts up in the Indian country of Nebraska and Wyoming. But there was a connection between the Conestoga and the lighter, fleeter prairie schooners of the pioneers.

In the 1730s, the sturdy forebears of today's Lancaster County Amish and Mennonites had made a significant step forward on the ground they farmed along the rich bottomlands of the Conestoga River in eastern Pennsylvania. Briskly efficient at farming, very commercial in outlook, the Swiss-Germans were producing surplus grain on their farms within a generation of reaching America. The growing cities of Philadelphia and New York offered a ready market for these cash crops and were only a week or so away by wagon. But which vehicle to use? The Mennonite farmers along the Conestoga, many of whom built their own wagons, simply adopted a design that they knew well from Europe, and which probably dated back to medieval times.

The Conestoga certainly looked medieval. The big hardwood wagons, up to twenty feet long, were built with floors that sloped sharply upward from the middle, with a tall front and back, to keep the load of grain or barrels pressed toward the center of gravity. The sides flared out dramatically like those on a coastal dory, also to stabilize the load, so that the finished vehicle looked nautical, capable of floating across the rivers it encountered nearby. (In fact, empty Conestoga wagon beds, their seams caulked with tar, could be floated across rivers and streams.) The Conestogas were massively overbuilt, weighing up to 3,500 pounds, and could carry four times their weight—eight tons of grain or cordwood, bound for Philadelphia.

Conestogas had clunky, four-foot wheels with up to six-inch iron tire rims. The wagon body holding the cargo, and the axle undercarriage, later called the "running gear," were connected as one structure, secured together with bolts or iron strapping on the axles. The distinctive-looking covered top, called the "bonnet," was developed to protect the cargo against bad weather. Heavy-grade linen or cotton sheets, soaked in linseed oil to make them water-resistant, were stretched across a series of semi-circular hickory or oak hoops, or "bows," fitted to the side of the wagon. (Later, an even thicker cotton-linen blend made with hemp—canvas—was deemed more durable.) Heavy chains lashed to the sides prevented the bulging load from breaking the structure. This ungainly vehicle, hitched to long gang-teams of eight to twelve oxen or horses, squeaked and lurched over the bumpy colonial roads, complaining like the rigging on a four-master. Thousands of Conestogas were built, and they were usually organized into long cargo convoys of a dozen or more, which could be heard miles away. The professional teamsters who ran these caravans manned America's earliest inland transportation routes, spurring trade, road building, and the development of urban markets, and also helping to build a sense of continental unity by linking the disparate colonies with reliable deliveries of food and other supplies. After the American Revolution, the groaning leviathans were hauled over the steep, muddy reaches of the Alleghenies, to connect the old colonies back east with the new settlements in the Ohio River valley. The Conestoga was the semitruck of young America.

The Conestogas were legendary for their durability and load-bearing capacity, but they were also notorious for breakdowns. Because the wagon vessel and running gear were usually connected, essentially secured together as a single unit, the bearing weight of the load was applied directly to the hickory axle, and from there to the wheels. Eight tons of downward and sideways force were applied every time the wheels hit a bump or some Allegheny bedrock. Often, shortcuts had been taken while making wagons, and the wooden axles or running gear parts were not always made from the best, cured wood. Everyone overloaded their wagons, to make as much money as possible on a western Pennsylvania or Ohio run.

Bump, axle break. Bump, axle break. The cursing of the teamsters echoed across the Allegheny hollows.

Obsolescence overtook the Conestoga for other reasons. By the 1830s, two dynamics were roiling the young nation. The availability of cheap or even free land on the frontier west of the Appalachians had made America a very mobile society. Americans had always been absolute beavers about clearing forest land, but they were not very good at conserving soil by rotating crops, contour plowing, or providing fertilizer to keep their ground productive. The dispositive feature of the American character was impatience, and every few years families just moved on to fresh, fertile ground, leapfrogging hundreds of miles at a time. (By the time he was twenty-one, in 1830, Abraham Lincoln had lived with his family on at least five farms, moving from his birthplace in Kentucky to Indiana, then Illinois. George Donner, the leader of the famously unlucky Donner Party wagon train that was trapped by snow in the Sierra Nevadas in 1846, had lived in North Carolina, Kentucky, and Illinois before migrating west.) To facilitate these moves, and to meet the diverse needs of America's briefly tenanted farms, a new wagon design emerged, more or less by accident.

The "mover's wagon" that began to appear on American farms in the 1820s—so called, we think, because farmers used them to move a lot—introduced several major improvements. The new, boxier wagons were much shorter than Conestogas, about ten to twelve feet long, and lighter, with an empty weight of about 1,200 pounds. But they could still carry a great deal, up to two tons. Tall, four-foot wheels in the back distributed the load over bumps, and smaller, three-foot wheels in the front enhanced maneuverability and turning radius. The wheel base was wide—up to five feet—but the wagon box itself was narrow, usually just a few inches more than three feet. This design concentrated most of the weight toward the center of a wide platform of wheels, giving the new wagons more stability than the old, swaying Conestogas.

But one seemingly small advance changed everything. It was a transportation tweak akin to the conversion from propeller airliners to jets in the late 1950s, or the widespread introduction of automatic transmissions in cars in the 1960s. By the early nineteenth century, wagon makers began perfecting a U-shaped assembly on top of the axles that acted as a cradle for the wagon box. This part was called the "bolster." Gradually, the bolster was improved to provide a tighter, more engineered support for the wagon box, called "fitted bolsters." The rectangular wagon box now *rested* on the axles, kept in place by gravity and the tight framing of the bolster. This eliminated the need for bolting the assembly to the axle as one unit. The empty weight of the box was just heavy enough, and the bolster so perfectly formed, that the wagon and running gear remained together without being attached.

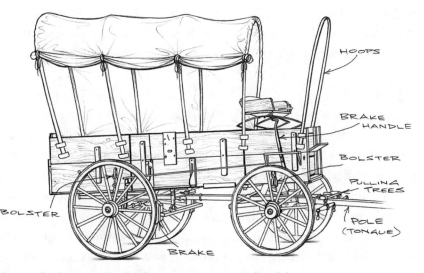

The standard Peter Schuttler farm wagon, converted with hoops and a canvas top at the frontier, was the minivan of the plains before the Civil War.

It was a baby step, and it probably didn't happen all at once. But, once the bolts or straps connecting the wagon box to the axle were removed, the physics were hugely advantageous. The wagon box now floated free, no longer rigidly bound to the axles. At a bad turn or bump, at least half of the load stresses were bounced back up into the load in the box, or dissipated into the air. This greatly reduced the bearing stresses on the axle. The wagon boxes bounced and jostled a lot, but that represented energy that wasn't being transferred to the running gear. Bump, the harvested corn absorbs the shock. Bump, the cordwood rearranges itself. At the end of a long day on the wagon seat, a farmer's butt felt like roadkill. But the running gear and axles were intact.

By the mid-1820s, America had commenced its glorious but now forgotten Canal Age. Canals were being built everywhere to carry coal, grain, firewood, and whiskey from the hinterlands to the cities—along the Raritan and Delaware watersheds in New Jersey, across all of the Pennsylvania river basins, and throughout the new frontier country in Ohio and Indiana. The grandest of these was the Erie Canal, which opened for use in 1825, "wedding the waters" of the Great Lakes and the Atlantic with a 363-mile ditch that crossed from Buffalo on Lake Erie to the Hudson River at Albany, New York. The Erie Canal was forty feet wide, had thirty-six locks, and had an elaborate system of towpaths and intersections with major wagon roads. Thousands of Irish laborers were dispatched to upstate New York to work under subhuman conditions with wheelbarrows and shovels.

Nobody in his right mind would excavate a 363-mile canal that is forty feet across by running a big old Conestoga onto the crowded and dangerous construction sites. The Irish were dying like flies already and in terms of labor efficiency it made no sense to kill a lot more with capsizing wagons. Historians have long been frustrated by a lack of accurate record-keeping during the canal-building era, but we do know that farmers along the western New York frontier began selling their mover's wagons to the builder of the canal, the Niagara Canal Company, which in turn hired wheelwrights and mechanics to improve these wagons for canal work. The lower front wheels of the wagons made them easier to maneuver around the obstacle course of dirt piles and rocks at the canal's edge, and they were used primarily at lock sites and road connections, to haul away and relocate the construction debris. Overloading was a frequent problem, but the relative ease with which broken wagon boxes could be replaced was an advantage. It was probably along the Erie Canal that the practice of stock-piling extra wagon boxes and wheels was introduced.

The riddles of history are always more interesting than the proven facts. Did the farmers, seeing an opportunity to make extra money over the winter, modify and strengthen their wagons specifically for canal building? Or did the canal builders make most of the design enhancements themselves? At some point, the wrought iron braces and pins that were used to assemble the running gear were improved. Wheel brakes for steep downhill grades were added during the 1830s, but where? On the farms or on the canals? Who built the first reinforced cast steel skeins to connect the axle to the wheel hubs? In the end, there are no specific answers to these questions, but a larger truth obtains. Two great impulses of the American experience—moving from farm to farm along the frontier, and building canals—resulted in the mythic prairie wagon that opened the West.

Within a few years, business-minded visionaries saw an opportunity to transform a cottage industry into manufacturing enterprises. After 1850, when the Oregon Trail traffic took off because of the Gold Rush and the exodus of the Mormons to Utah, wagon manufacturing became big business, a major engine that drove an expanding economy. Many companies that would become enduring American brand names—John Deere, Studebaker, Sears, Roebuck—began by manufacturing wagons, adopting the common design of the farm-built mover's wagon and mass-producing it for a growing market. Distinctive designs and wagon features were introduced by competition in the wagon business, which encouraged endless experimentation. By the late 1850s, a nautical-looking wagon with flared sides and tongue-and-groove flooring, to improve flotation, was developed in response to pioneer demand for a better vehicle for crossing rivers. To advertise their superior marine handling, these designs became known as "prairie schooners," a term that stuck and eventually referred to almost any wagon that crossed the plains. Overlanders who expected to establish dry goods companies or lumber mills on the frontier, and wanted to be already set up for business, knew they could rely on the sturdy designs of the J. Murphy Wagon Company of St. Louis, which supplied many of the military escort wagons used during the Civil War, or the Turnbull Wagon Company of Defiance, Ohio. Most of these names have faded from history. But they were great wagons, built to withstand a lot of abuse and to last forever. You can still see restored Murphys and Turnbulls rolling along in July Fourth parades today.

These new companies did what nascent manufacturers always do—they transformed a dispersed cottage industry of handcrafted products into one that was organized according to factory practices. Wagon assembly lines (no, Henry Ford did *not* invent that), standardized and interchangeable parts, and stronger pieces of cast iron and steel were introduced. Water power and steam engine technology made it possible to quickly and precisely cut axles, bolsters, and other parts of the running gear. Improvements in metal forging helped develop iron and later steel "skeins," thimble-shaped structures that connected the axle to the wheel hub, replacing the wooden parts of the eighteenth century. Kilns were built to cure wooden parts uniformly so they wouldn't crack when exposed to seasonal changes in humidity. Wheel hubs and spokes were precisely engineered and then fitted together at wheelwright stations located where they were needed—near the spot on the factory floor where the finished running gears were completed.

By the mid-1850s wagon prices had stabilized at about $75 apiece, and replacing broken parts no longer required a long day in the barn with wood planes, ball-peen hammers, and an anvil. Because wagon making had been standardized, parts could be ordered by mail. Later, a telegraphic code of dedicated shorthand words—to save money on telegraph costs—was devoted just to ordering wagon parts. If a homesteader or his distant wagon dealer out west needed the board for a nine-inch top box, he telegraphed for a "Becalm." The thirteen-inch tip top box was a "Bray." A cast-iron axle skein was an "Apollo." The tougher steel skein was an "Ape."

Eventually the wagon-making business became concentrated in the emerging manufacturing centers of the Midwest—John Deere in Moline, Illinois, Studebaker and Sears, Roebuck in South Bend, Indiana, and Murphy and Weber & Damme in St. Louis. Fortunes were made manufacturing wagons, first for the overland trail traffic, and then during the huge government stimulus provided by the Civil War, and more than thirty wagon companies exhibited their models at the 1876 Centennial Exposition in Philadelphia. The business was exemplified by an enterprising German-American whose name became virtually synonymous with the Oregon Trail.

Peter Schuttler was a German immigrant who arrived in New York in 1834, when he was twenty-two years old. He bounced around at the edge of the frontier for several years, learning wagon building in western New York and wheelwrighting in Ohio, gaining a reputation as an innovator who could figure out how to make parts with saws instead of axes, and who designed his own machinery and lathes. After his first two wagon shops in Ohio failed, Schuttler rode a buggy across the plains to Chicago, where he briefly dabbled with brewing beer because he considered the wagon-building field too crowded. (At the time, Chicago had about four thousand adult citizens, and thirteen wagon shops.) But in 1843, after he soured on brewing, Schuttler opened up a wagon works at the corner of Randolph and Franklin streets, living with his family in a wooden shanty behind his shop.

Schuttler's timing was fortuitous. In the early 1840s, travel along the Oregon Trail had been just a trickle—no more than two hundred pioneers a year. But the reverberations of the Panic of 1837, which had virtually destroyed American farming, were still being felt, and this had sent an army of essentially homeless families west in search of new opportunities and cheap land. In 1843, a missionary and an experienced western wagon traveler, Marcus Whitman, led an exodus of about a thousand pioneers across the plains, and after that Oregon Trail traffic grew dramatically every year, culminating in the estimated forty thousand wagon travelers who flocked to the trail in the Gold Rush year of 1849.

Schuttler, who would eventually gather one of the great Chicago fortunes, just grew with the trail from there. He was as disciplined and methodical as a Shaker, and early on he saw the need to build parts that were prone to breakage with stouter grades of iron, and that carefully machined wheel spokes and hubs were essential for the reputation of a wagon company. He also understood the need to specialize, and soon scuttled the less lucrative lines of small buggies and carriages that were dragging other wagon makers down, concentrating instead on the design and parts of the standard farm wagon. Schuttler also profited from disaster. In 1850 his original wooden shop burned to the ground, but he used this as an opportunity to build a new, fireproof brick factory that incorporated everything he had learned about building wagons over the past fifteen years. The Peter Schuttler works, which eventually covered more than ten acres, became one of Chicago's biggest factories, turning out 1,800 wagons a year.

Schuttler and the other large wagon manufacturers played a critical role in accelerating America's industrial revolution. Their metalworking, in particular, became a principal reason that America began overtaking Britain as an industrial power by the end of the nineteenth century. The demands of producing thousands of wagons every year for the overland trails forced the wagon makers to efficiently mass-produce iron and steel parts—wheel hubs, running gear braces, brakes—that had once been made by hand. The clunky and complex old Conestoga, with dozens of handmade parts for each wagon, was gradually replaced by a more elegant, simpler box wagon that was now the product of a briskly moving factory operation.

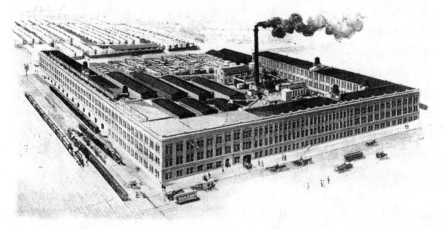

The ten-acre Peter Schuttler works was the largest factory in Chicago, and supplying the overland trails with wagons created one of the great nineteenth-century fortunes.

The major wagon manufacturers were located in river towns, with good access to the Mississippi River transportation system, which proved decisive for delivering their products. As the Oregon Trail traffic picked up in the 1840s, outfitters along the Missouri river above Kansas City were ordering hundreds of wagons a year in anticipation of a new and larger emigration every spring, and Schuttler's big works near the Illinois River, and his ability to meet the demand, placed him in a strong position. Shipping efficiency was key. Most of the wagons Schuttler dispatched to the West were not completely assembled at the factory. The running gear and wheels were bundled together and stacked on top of each other on big flatboats and, later, barges pulled by steamboats. The wagon boxes were loaded with all of the remaining parts—tongues, seats, barrels, roof bows—and stacked neatly beside the running gear. The load of wagon boxes then rode the Mississippi downstream to its confluence with the

Missouri at St. Louis, looking very much like modern container ships. The 350-mile run to the Missouri took about three weeks. By the end of April every year, the wharves and cleared fields of Missouri River towns like St. Joseph, Weston, and Independence gleamed with tall columns of green wagons, and over time an efficient dealership network was established.

A Peter Schuttler advertisement from the 1850s. Aggressive marketing and a strong dealership network gave Schuttler an advantage over competitors like Studebaker and John Deere.

The Schuttler wagons were strong and durable, but not really much better than a Springfield or a Studebaker. The company thrived because Schuttler was a lively marketer who understood that word of mouth and appearances meant a great deal. Schuttler flooded the frontier with attractive pamphlets advertising his wagons and dispensed from Chicago the kind of pious commercial mottoes that Americans have always liked to consume. ("The Old Reliable Peter Schuttler," "Peter Schuttler Wagons Spell QUALITY.") In 1855, when the Mormons placed an order for thirty-five wagons to support their next wagon train to Utah, Schuttler made sure that the market knew why. He had guaranteed the Mormon elders that each wagon could hold 3,500 pounds. The Mormons were not liked in America, but their achievements on the Oregon Trail couldn't be denied and this undoubtedly helped Schuttler. The Saints continued to be his best customer. Schuttler was dubbed "The Wagon King of Chicago," and it is thought that the popular nineteenth-century pioneer phrase for their vehicles, "The Chicago Wagon," derived from the popularity of the Schuttler wagon on the western trails. The Peter Schuttler wagon was the minivan of the plains, and by the 1880s at least thirty thousand Schuttler wagons had crossed the frontier.

The wagon king of Chicago forged the industrialist style later perfected by Andrew Carnegie, John D. Rockefeller, and Henry Ford. While pretending to be modest, he was ludicrously self-indulgent. At his factory in Chicago, Schuttler loved to entertain visitors with tales about his humble origins and lifestyle, and he told stories about working eighteen-hour days in the factory and then retiring to his family in the wood shack behind the plant. But by middle age, selling upwards of sixty thousand wagons and owning Chicago's largest factory had turned him into a rote tycoon. The 1860 census showed that Schuttler was one of three millionaires in Chicago; it had taken him just seventeen years, building wagons at his scale, to achieve that status. The other two millionaires were the Marshall Field department store barons, Potter Palmer and John V. Farwell. The Schuttlers, the Palmers, and the Farwells were soon engaged in one of America's great mansion-building frenzies, throwing up estates for themselves and their children all over Chicago. Schuttler outdid them all. The new Schuttler shack occupied a whole city block bounded by Adams and Monroe streets, took three years to build, and is variously estimated to have cost between $250,000 and $500,000, or more than $15 million today.

We tend to associate the creation of the great family fortunes of America with the bloated, monopolistic trusts of such Gilded Age figures as Andrew Carnegie, John D. Rockefeller, or E. H. Harriman. But Schuttler predated them by almost forty years, never felt that he had to corner the market to succeed, and built his entire fortune out of a single factory that made just one product—wagons.

And for at least the next century, the American style of transportation—crucial for the nation's growth—had been defined. The ride was never good, and your spine ached after a day's run up to North Platte. But your wheels usually got you there because the chassis and box were way overbuilt for the job. And there was another American trait imparted by the covered wagon: spontaneity. Yeah, let's do it, there is free land out in Oregon. Let's buy this rig for $75, throw on the top, and find some mules. The covered wagon delivered western dreams, in a hurry. The improvised and rushed wanderlust of the American character—celebrated by observers from Walt Whitman to Ken Kesey—was symbolized by the vehicle that initially crossed the plains.

The covered wagon's Erector Set quality also helped the Americans. At the Missouri River jumping-off towns on the frontier, the manufactured pieces could be fitted together into a finished wagon in a single morning. Only a few simple tools were needed—an iron wheel wrench, which usually came with the wagon, a screwdriver for attaching brackets for the bows, a hammer, and maybe a darning needle and thread, for making roll-up windows cut into the canvas. Here the German influence continued. The pioneers called their wagon bonnets "Osnaburgs," after the town in Germany, Osnabrück, where the stout cotton-hemp canvas, treated with linseed oil, originated. Many pioneers added false bottoms to the wagon bed to store equipment like harness kits or furniture parts that wouldn't be used every day. Water barrels were attached by building a cantilever platform off the sides, and held in place by leather straps. For her water, Margaret Frink carried india-rubber bottles. It was not generally true that the pioneers painted "Oregon or Bust!" on their canvas tops, as American lore would have it. They usually painted their surnames and their originating town or county on the canvas, in large block letters that could be seen from far away. That way, after an evening spent hunting for game or searching for water, the pioneers could return to the crowded encampments and walk straight to their own wagon.

The pioneers' practice of painting names and geographic origins on wagon covers led to an interesting American colloquialism that still exists today. In the early days of the trail, a large number of wagon travelers

originated from Pike County in eastern Missouri, an area that was originally settled by backwoodsmen from Kentucky in the 1820s. Many of
these painted "From Pike Co., Mo." on their wagon covers, or just "Pike
County" or "Pike," to make it easier to assemble as a train in the crowded
covered wagon camps. Naturally, they began to be called "Pikers." But
because there were so many Pike counties across the country that generated overland emigrants—Pennsylvania, Ohio, Kentucky, Indiana, and
Illinois all have Pike counties—"Pikers" became a broad, generalized term
that could refer to any number of wagon companies that crossed in the
1840s and 1850s. The original Pikers from Kentucky and Missouri, in the
words of pioneer diarist William Audley Maxwell, were considered "of a
'backwoods' class, rather short in culture, and in personal makeup and
language, bearing a general air of the extremely rural." Over time "Pikers" became accepted as a term that referred to people who were slow of
speech, plodding, and not ambitious in business. When I was a boy, and
I told my father that I had a difficult exam in school the next day, he would
say, "Don't be a Piker, son. Go upstairs and study." But I'm sure he had no
idea that the term originated along the Oregon Trail.

In *The Americans*, historian Daniel Boorstin described another important trait of the covered wagon. "The wagon was plainly a community
vehicle: everything about it required traveling in groups. To cross deep
streams or climb steep slopes the ox teams had to be doubled and the
wagons managed one at a time. Many ways were found to use the group's
total resources to conquer obstacles and reduce risk."

Indeed, at places like California Hill near Brule, Nebraska, one of the
sharpest ascents of the trail, or at the steep descent at Windlass Hill above
Ash Hollow, Nebraska, a multitude of hands in the covered wagon trains
were available to help. Everything in the wagons was off-loaded and carried uphill by brigades of children and wives. Some men led most of the
teams up to the top of the hill and watched them, while others remained
below to hook up and drive the doubled teams that towed the wagons
over the obstacle. Conversely, at a downhill, the wagons were lightened
by brigades of pioneers carrying furniture and cooking utensils to the
valley floor. Some men led the teams down, while others remained at the
summit to hold the heavy ropes and the prairie-crafted windlasses that
lowered the wagons down.

I've always thought that this is why the sight of a covered wagon going by, or a group of them, arouses such primordial emotions. Perhaps we possess a dimly repressed but nevertheless accessible memory of how much community was formed by the necessities and sheer obstacle-climbing along the trail. That's what the covered wagon represents. Families would never forget the powerful friendships they formed along the trail, or what pioneering did for their own nuclear unit. We have always called this the "pioneering spirit."

"Pioneering spirit" is a phrase that was used a lot in my family while I was growing up in the 1950s, and it probably explains, too, why I was so drawn to covered wagon travel. I am emotionally connected to my past as a covered wagon traveler—a time when my father was so strapping and young, fun-loving and emotive, a man so wonderful to love. He was a nonconformist in a rigidly conformist age, but I've often felt since then that there was a logic behind his eccentricity.

On our 1958 covered wagon trip, in the evenings in our camp, my father would hold me with one hand by the scruff of my neck and wash my face with his other hand, using a washcloth dipped into a bucket of cold, soapy water. I didn't particularly like that, but this might have been because my father used the time to remind me of my obligations.

"Rinker," my father said during washing one night, "you fought with your brother today. Why do you keep doing that?"

"Dad. It wasn't my fault. It was my turn to ride Texas when we got into camp, but Kern stole the horse. So I kicked him when he got off Texas. Big deal."

"Well, okay, son," my father said. "But don't fight. Next time, come and ask me first, all right? Fighting with your brother is not in the pioneering spirit."

On the other hand, there were chores required on a covered wagon trip that I loved to perform.

I was this squirrely little Irish pipsqueak boy who seemed to understand that I had too much energy. My psychiatrists would later diagnose a mild disorder called hypomania, or the hyperthymic personality, a kind of diluted bipolarism. I am manic, but not necessarily depressive. I cannot enjoy life unless I am overactive, or find a challenge that makes me ebullient. When I travel to visit friends, I can't relax unless I am clearing fallen limbs in their yard or rebuilding their fence. The related symptoms are insomnia, obsessive-compulsive reading disorder, alcoholism, satyriasis, and fastidiously ironed shirts. Extrapolated backward into the life of a boy, this meant someone who loved to carry water for horses.

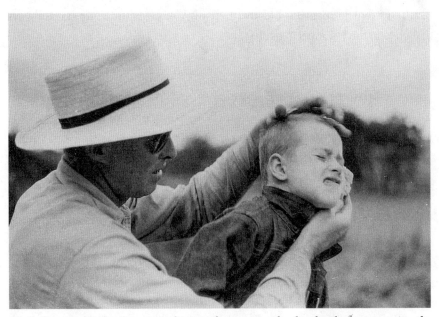

My father scrubbed me every night out of a watering bucket for the horses, using the occasion to lecture me about the "pioneering spirit."

God, did I love carrying water for the horses on the covered wagon trip. Down to the river with the buckets, dip them in while the water riffled over the rocks, and then clamber up the banks with the water splashing on my legs and the galvanized handles digging into my palms. I used a short stepladder to hold up the buckets while the horses drank. Our Belgian shepherd, Midnight, lapped from the bottom of the bucket when the horses were done. I was always up at dawn, running down to the river with the buckets so that none of my siblings could beat me to it.

"That's the pioneering spirit, son," my father would call out as I ran back and forth to the river. "Children, look at Rinker. He's so lickety-split!"

Childhood competition dies hard. I am still a dawn-riser, outside well before breakfast, attacking the garden weeds or spreading crabgrass preventer on the lawns, mildly annoyed that everyone else in the family remains in bed.

Now I would be using a covered wagon to escape one life and replace it with another, pursuing my dream of being on the plains for a whole summer. I have the pioneering spirit for many reasons. But surely the most important is that I still miss my father so, and those days when we crossed Pennsylvania together in the wagon seem like the last time that we were really good for each other.

6

I SLEPT IN THE WAGON for the first time the night before we left, and I loved my new womb on red wheels. Nick and I had followed in his pickup while our trucker, Doyle Prawl, hauled the mules and the wagons over the Missouri River into Kansas, and after it started to rain we pushed the wagons into the implement barn at Doyle's small farm. I left the barn doors open so that I would feel as if I were really camping. It was a beautiful Kansas night with light rain pattering on the tin roof and, far off, I could hear dogs barking and the traffic on the St. Joe Road.

The next morning I woke at dawn and immediately was gripped by one last paroxysm of dread. Inside my wagon womb, I lay on the pillow with my hands clasped behind my head, brooding, staring up at the oak bows, unable to chase away my fears. Oh, Rinker, what have you done to yourself here? It is two thousand miles to the end of the trail. There are so many details to be on top of every day, and Nick will be looking to you for answers, for a daily plan. The maps, finding supplies, finding water. Harnessing every day. Bute is probably a defective mule, Beck shies more than any equine you have ever driven. Why do you have to be such a crazyass? You could be back in your house in New England, writing a nice, safe book about clipper ships.

But I felt better after a while, mostly by schooling myself with the basics, the alluring simplicity of wagon travel. My assignment for the day was straightforward. Just follow the back roads up through the old junction country to Hiawatha, twenty-five miles away. It would just be a long hayride northwest through Kansas, and the next day would just be another hayride due west along the St. Joe Road. This would be my mantra now: Navigate—and live—day by day. I couldn't default to my personality as a born worrier, and looking at the big picture of the journey would only rattle me with the enormity of the challenge we had taken on. I could succeed only by piecing together a series of small-picture days.

Nick had slept in the guest room at Doyle's and came down to the barn early, while I was making coffee on our Coleman cookstove. He stood on the concrete floor of the implement shed, freshly showered and in clean clothes, with his L.L. Bean backpack at his feet. His booming voice echoed off the corrugated aluminum walls.

"Yo, Trail Boss! Let's get rollin!"

Nick had been doing this strange thing for the last couple of days, always calling me "Boss." He had always had this inexplicable quirk of character. When he visited my place and I took him to parties at the homes of my friends, he became very deferential, not at all his cheerful, brash self. Often, he called me "sir," as if some bizarre British class system applied when he was visiting my world. At the time, he was supervising elaborate $3 million mansion projects on exclusive islands off the coast of Maine, but Nick would tell my friends, "Oh, I'm just a carpenter from Maine." This made me feel uncomfortable and I hated it when he was implying that his status was beneath mine, that our different lives implied superiority on my part, inferiority on his.

"Nick," I said. "What is this 'Boss' shit? I am not your boss. We're doing this trip together."

"I think it's better to define the relationship," Nick said. "I'm the Trail Hand. You're the Boss. So just call me Trail Hand, okay?"

Nick had spent a long time the night before on a cell phone call to his best friend in Maine, Ripley Swan, and he explained that he and Rip were worried about his brash personality. Nick knows a lot more about teams and wagons than I do, he is not exactly meek, and if he asserted himself too strongly we might develop conflicts and fight. There were decisions to be made every day. We might have emergencies. Somebody had to be in charge for the trip to be successful. Rip was also aware that Nick rarely paces himself, throwing himself into projects so frantically that he's exhausted before they are even half done. Rip had advised Nick not to "take ownership" of the trip. The Boss title for me, they both thought, would help Nick police himself and find a sustainable level of energy for the trip.

I didn't feel that the denotation of titles was necessary, but I was touched that Nick and Rip had devoted so much thought to the question. This was obviously something that was important to Nick. It would be good management to buy into his plan.

I handed Nick a cup of coffee.

"All right, Trail Hand, go out and grain the mules," I said. "We're harnessing in half an hour."

The biggest single danger on our trip was something that is both familiar to and greatly feared by horsemen—the "hitch runaway." A hitch runaway happens when horses or mules, while being hooked to a wagon, suddenly take off because they have been spooked by a deer bounding into camp or by children riding past on bicycles. When one unhooked mule on a team decides to run, the other two will often try to join it, and in the muling chaos that follows poles get snapped and wagons are overturned. Hitch runaways injure people and wreck a lot of wagons.

Runaway teams and getting run over by the wheels were frequent causes of injury and death along the Oregon Trail, dreaded almost as much as disease and hunting accidents. In peak migration years like 1849 or 1852, when literally thousands of wagons were being hitched every morning, there were dozens of runaway accidents, and many trail journals I read described how a team spooked by buffalo, or by a boy getting careless, led to sudden death under the wheels.

After hitching several times in Jamesport, I appreciated the enormous power of our draft mules and was naturally concerned about this. Nick's tendency to focus so intently on a job that he runs out of circuits to process language, communicating instead by a crude pantomime of grunts, shrugs, and nods of his head, could be fatal during hitching. Now the designation that Nick had conferred on me, Trail Boss, gave me the authority to establish the procedure that we would follow every day. During harnessing, I told him, the mules would always be chained "short" to a hitching post or the wagon wheels, and I would always hold the mules by their bridles at the pole while Nick attached the yoke and then walked behind to hook the trace chains. When all was ready with the hitch, Nick would climb onto the wagon seat, take the lines, and check the manual brake, making one last inspection to be sure that the harness, tugs, and lines were hooked right. I wouldn't let go of the team until he said, "The wagon is mine. The brake is on."

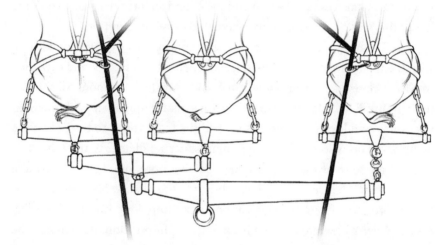

The standard "triple-tree" design for a three-mule hitch, with the evener bar that keeps the team pulling the wagon in a consistent direction.

"Nick," I said. "Procedure. Communication. You've got to *talk* to me. We've got $30,000 worth of wagon and mules here. One dumbass mistake and it all ends up in a ditch."

"Copy, Boss. Just don't get mad at me if my ADD kicks in and I forget to talk."

"I won't get mad at you. I'll just tell you, 'Trail Hand, speak up. Talk. Be specific.' "

When we were done establishing these procedures, Nick thanked me and said one other thing that surprised me.

"Hitching is such an intense time, Boss. I never want to talk because I'm afraid every time I hitch a team."

"What? You, afraid? You never told me that."

"You didn't ask. I don't relax until I'm on the seat and have the lines in my hands."

This was fascinating to me because I had assumed that I was the only one afraid, but we didn't have time to explore the issue. Doyle was calling from the porch of his house that breakfast was ready.

Nick was so fastidious about hitching the mules that morning that he sounded like a prisoner in a chain gang. He was Paul Newman in *Cool Hand Luke.* "Boss, Jake coming out of pasture, chained," he said. "Boss, three mules harnessed, let's rein and yoke," and so forth. He was overdoing it, but this was good because we needed to develop a routine.

The hitch that day revealed the behavioral issues that we would have with the team. Sweet little Bute regarded herself as a Hollywood diva. She was Kate Hudson, visiting friends in Malibu for the afternoon. All she had to do to fulfill her life purpose was lie on a chaise longue in a bikini, looking skinny and lovely. As soon as we had the team yoked to the pole, Bute would sway out wide with her hips, almost perpendicular to the other two mules, and stare at me with a look of divine boredom. "Oh, like, you're hitching *me*?" Before he could attach Bute's tug chains, Nick would have to take the trace from its keeper up on her rump, loop it around her leg, and then yank her cute diva ass back to the right position. Bute pulled the same act every morning. Jake, anxious to go, would paw his front hoof just inches from my foot until I told him to stop, and then give me feral love bites on my arm. Interestingly, Beck, who Nick and I thought was going to be our problem mule, would stand patiently during hitching. She was saving all of her craziness for later.

When everything was ready, Nick stepped onto the wheel hub, hefted his weight into the wagon by holding on to the seat, and then plopped down and took the lines.

"It's my wagon, Boss. The brake is on."

While Nick held the team, I made one last inspection tour around the wagon, switched on our hazard lights, and then cradled Olive Oyl in my arms and handed her up to Nick. Stepping onto the right wheel hub and then laddering myself up by standing on the wheel rim and holding on to the edge of the seat produced an immensely satisfying feeling. We were mounted now, ready to go. The stress of the hitch-up was over.

I had taken the right side of the wagon seat, the traditional position for the main driver. The brake is on the right-hand side, but there was another reason that the principal driver sat there. In the eighteenth and nineteenth centuries, wagon roads were little more than crude earthen pathways worn down by traffic, a boggy morass when it rained, and a bumpy grid of hardened ruts when it was dry. The shoulders of the roads were indefinite and often contained deep crevices or creek ditches hidden in the grass. The safest way for a driver to pass a wagon coming from the other direction was to pull right as far as he could, concentrating on the ground just beside him to see obstacles and potholes.

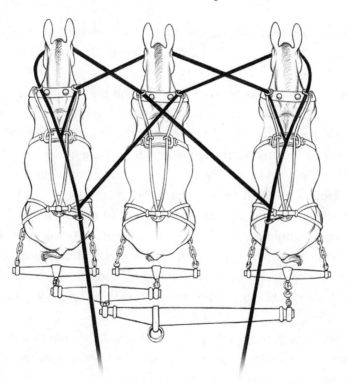

Our three-mule driving lines arrangement allowed us to "rein in" the entire team, a traditional but largely forgotten nineteenth-century hookup.

But Nick and I had always been pretty good "transition drivers," sitting on either side of the seat, and if we reached a difficult point in the road, our seating arrangement had the advantage that he was able to hold the team while I worked the brakes.

When I had settled in the seat, Nick handed me the driving lines, but I handed them back.

"Nick, it's only right that you drive this wagon the first few miles. You've earned it. And that's an order, Trail Hand."

"Cool. You're asking me to launch."

"Call the mules, Trail Hand. We're taking this rig to Oregon."

Doyle's place has two cleared fields on either side of the road, but the area is heavily wooded and we were surrounded by a tunnel of green forest ahead. When Nick called the mules, his bellow briefly shot skyward but then the sound was caught and muffled by the thick cover of spring leaves.

"Jake, Bute, Beck. Big Team! Big Team! C'mon, Big Team! Get on there you odd buggers! Big Team! We're going to Oregon with this rig, Big Team!"

Nick slapped the lines twice for a trot and the mules picked up their feet nicely, in the mood for a morning run. The pole bounced and the tug chains jingled. The iron tires sang on the road. Twelve hooves were moving in unison and pounding the asphalt. Behind us the new oak bows creaked and swayed at every bump and the wagon box jumped.

In Troy, Kansas, there is a stately brick courthouse at the highest elevation in town, and we could see it from the top of the first rise. The Doniphan County courthouse is a magnificent Victorian pile of brick, listed on the National Register of Historic Places, with a unique, octagonal belfry with large clerestory windows. Beside it on the lawn is a tall flagpole with a large American flag, which was billowing brightly in the stiff winds aloft.

As we trotted the team up the hill toward the courthouse and the American flag, there was a sensation from the wagon of sharply climbing toward the clouds to go out and see our country.

The team was running up the hill and my heart was singing now. We were climbing toward sky inside a tunnel of green to go see the elephant. I wasn't going to give up until we got there. We would never stop trying. I would walk the last five hundred miles if I had to. All I wanted to do for the next summer of my life was work hard to put mule shoes in Oregon.

♦   ♦   ♦

I was in heaven out there on the plains. I had spent many long winter nights studying maps of the fabled "junction country" of eastern Kansas, so named because it was littered by the junctions of many early-nineteenth-century trails that eventually fed into the main Oregon Trail along the Platte River in Nebraska, 250 miles away. There were old fur-trading trails, military freighter routes that ran up from Fort Riley and Fort Leavenworth, and the ruts of the Independence Road and the St. Joseph Road. The prairie was wide open then and the wagon trains, depending on which rivers were high or where the grazing was good, followed a variety of routes to reach the Platte. In the 1860s, the Pony Express trail, the stagecoach lines, and then the telegraph lines and railroad tracks cut new fissures on the plains. These routes generally followed the main junction trails, diverting here and there for several miles for more favorable terrain, endlessly intersecting on their way up to the Platte.

Understanding this had fundamentally changed my view of the overland emigration. The pioneers didn't follow a single set of ruts worn into the prairie. They meandered along a collection of trails, requiring many choices. Each turn in the road involved considerable freedom, but also the peril of not knowing what was ahead. Now I was passing the junctions where these decisions had been made, picking my way along the dirt section roads with my detailed *DeLorme Atlas & Gazetteer* and a full set of geodetic maps of the Oregon Trail.

During our first three days out, we were mostly paralleling Route 36, which had been paved over the original St. Joseph Road early in the twentieth century. We also passed markers for the Independence Road and many old military trails. The country we were crossing was a kind of universal American landscape, level farm ground in some spots, pale green from recent planting, and then wetlands and fringes of forest, with small housing developments climbing the Flint Hills. From the wagon seat, with a team of mules in front of me, I could easily eliminate the modern, visual obstructions—paved roads, farm silos, pivot irrigators slowly circling the crop fields—and stare across the plains, imagining what each choice along the trail felt like. The landscape reaching up to me was a diorama of the wagon routes that had defined the history of the West.

Many sections of the old Oregon Trail were paved over in the early twentieth century to create two-lane blacktops. Here we travel along U.S. Highway 36, "The Pony Express Highway," west of Seneca, Kansas.

It was a lovely day as we ambled along with our new mules. The harness chains jingled, the wheels drummed along the roads, and the prospect of the Kansas farm country from the high wagon seat was panoramic. The weather was uneven, typical for Kansas in the spring. For half an hour or so we would be in sunlight, and we would throw back the canvas cover directly on top of us to let in more sun. Then it suddenly turned blustery and cold, occasionally spitting light rain. Wiggling around on the narrow wagon seat, we pulled on jackets and spread a blanket between our legs. Olive Oyl snuggled tightly in the space between us and napped, a welcome source of warmth.

Calling mules is not just something theatrical that mule skinners do. The calls are purposeful, specific. Mules respond to the sound of their simple, monosyllabic names. They respond to directions like "Get Up," "Easy Now," or "Whoa" for stop. For a faster pace, a slap of the reins and "Trot, Team, Trot" will do. "Walk Lively Now!" is the preferred call for the brisk walk that allows a wagon to cover ground at about four miles per hour.

In Jamesport, I had listened carefully to the commands that Philip Ropp used, as well as his pronunciation. To slow a team for challenging terrain, but not to stop them, the command is "Easy, Team," or "Easy, Now, Team." But in Ropp's thick Pennsylvania Dutch accent, this came out "Eas-A, Eas-A." We would have to pronounce it that way or the mules would be confused.

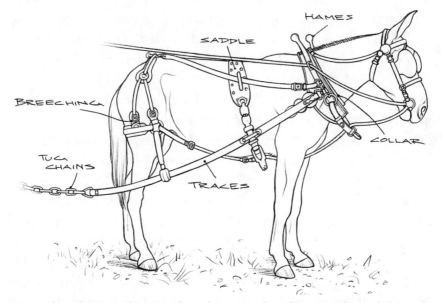

We used modern, BioThane synthetic harnesses, based on a traditional design for leather draft-mule harnesses, as a hedge against breakage along the two-thousand-mile trail.

But calling mules well goes beyond that. Mule-calling expresses a feeling about life, a passion for the land that is being crossed, and a love of the animals in front of you. Mules actually have a great deal of emotional complexity. Except for the occasional laggard like Bute, they love to work, and they can sense when they are headed off for a long ride and not just a brief run up to the cornfields. Mule-calling developed because the trips—along the nine-hundred-mile Sante Fe Trail, the 2,100-mile Oregon Trail—were so long. The driver shared his loneliness with his team, expressing his thoughts about the lengthy road ahead, warding off boredom, and trying to stay awake. The particular timbre of the caller's voice tells the mules who is driving and conveys to them a mood. That is why so many mule-callers speak to their animals with an animated, sing-song style.

In nineteenth-century America, team-calling was a familiar sound of everyday life. Walt Whitman was legendary for walking from place to place, and he often heard the mule-callers along the busy roads that he followed on his rambles up and down the Eastern Seaboard and out west. "I hear the chirp of the Mexican muleteer, and the bells of the mule," Whitman wrote in "Salut au Monde!" ("The bells of the mule" is a reference to the bells that teamsters would attach to the collars of their draft animals, to warn another driver of the approach of a wagon from the opposite direction, on days when rain or fog reduced visibility.) From the 1840s to the 1880s, the country that Nick and I were passing through was thick with mule teamsters and covered freight wagons. The worn military roads that ran through the Flint Hills curved northwest to the two main forts along the Platte—Fort Kearny in Nebraska and Fort Laramie in eastern Wyoming, and later, after the Indian wars began in the 1860s, there were a dozen new forts just in Wyoming to supply. Most of these forts were founded specifically to protect the covered wagon trains of the pioneers along the Oregon Trail, and the freighting teamsters and the pioneers often commingled on the trails. One of the largest and most recognizable companies in the country then—the FedEx of its day—was Russell, Majors and Waddell, which ran freight, supplied the military forts, and carried mail on the West's intricate system of trails. In the Kansas junction country, the freighting season stretched from May to early November. As the long wagon caravans moved north toward the Platte, the hills echoed with the mule skinners' calls.

Often, learning why a teamster uses a particular call tells you something about his or her personality. I asked Nick once why he called his teams "odd buggers." That sounded like a derisive term to me, but I knew that Nick loved his horses.

"It's from the James Herriot book *All Creatures Great and Small*," Nick said. "Odd buggers is a Yorkshire Dales term for all animals. My horses aren't insulted by it. They know I'm paying them a compliment."

To understand mule-calling, you have to imagine yourself in a place that you love, and what you would sing, say, to your favorite canoe or cross-country skiing trail. Alone on a hiking trail, people sing to their dogs. When I am working in my woods at home, I sing into the trees as I split logs. Now Nick and I were in the comely junction country of eastern Kansas, surrounded by green hills, kids at the housing developments circling on small bikes, and pheasants flushing as we rumbled the wagon over the creeks. I was on the dream journey of my life and I longed to sing to my new mules.

When I could see the town of Highland, Kansas, coming up, and knew that we were safely established on a westward course for Hiawatha, I decided that it was time for me to drive the team myself and learn the proper calling of mules. Thinking about it, I decided that I should emphasize a feminine theme. Beck and Bute, the base team that had worked together for years at the Ropp farm, were mollies. And Jake is a big, self-confident guy, obviously the sort of friend to whom I could say, "Well, Jake, just between us girls, you know?" I would call in a style that acknowledged the feminine nature of our team.

When Nick handed me the lines, I took a deep breath, reassured myself that this wasn't going to be as difficult as I had imagined, and inaugurated my calling career.

"Girls! Let's Go, Girls! Yo, Step Lively Now. Girls! Beck! Bute! Jake! Girls, Girls, Girls! Rah, Rah, Rah! Go! Go! Go! Oh, Girls, We're Going to Hiawatha! Don't be Sissy, Girls! Go! Go! Go!"

The mules stopped. The wagon lurched to a halt. As soon as I started calling them, the mules planted their feet on the dirt road as firmly as a runner reaching second base and stamping his cleats on the bag. WTF? Boy, I am really developing into a unique badass mule skinner here.

Nick's Fu Manchu mustache dropped, and he looked disgusted.

"Jesus, Rink," he said. "These are well-trained mules. Amish mules. If you say 'Go,' it sounds just like 'Whoa.' So they stop. Do I fuckin have to tell you everything? You fuckin said 'Go' to a mule."

"Give me a break here, Nick," I said. "I'm just learning."

"And what is this 'Girls, Girls, Girls' shit?" Nick said. "You sound like the fuckin lacrosse coach at Miss Porter's School."

"Nick, c'mon, they're females, mollie mules. Right? I addressed them with the proper respect that you show all women."

"Oh, God. I am not believing this."

Nick picked up Olive Oyl and placed her in his lap, scratching beneath her chin, as if she were the only comfort left for him now.

"It's all right, Olive," he said. "The Trail Boss is just learning. He's such a fuckin idiot he said 'Go' to a mule. But don't worry, Olive. He'll get better."

I decided to revert to a calling style that I knew would work. I slapped the lines on the mules and tried again.

"Team! Big Team! Big Team! Jake! Beck! Bute! Get Up There Now! Team, Get Up!"

The mules picked up their feet and briskly trotted west on the section road. We clattered over the narrow concrete bridge that crossed Mission Creek, flushing up some wood ducks that became silhouetted in the sky against a red barn up the hill.

The Peter Schuttler was a memory wheel too. By the middle of the afternoon, Nick and I were both fighting sleep, the need to get off the seat for an hour or two and escape the effects of wagon travel. The metronomic clopping of hooves, the exposure to sunlight and wind, and the bouncing of the wagon were powerfully soporific. We both had sore backs for the first two weeks, until our bodies adjusted to the hard seat and constant jostling. But neither of us wanted to give up valuable time, which would be translated as miles not elapsed, by stopping to take a rest.

We began to realize just how much persistence would be required to make twenty miles a day, and the experience of trying not to nod off on the wagon seat was actually frightening. Up on our tall seat, above the wagon box, there was nothing holding us in—no seat belts or sides. If we fell asleep at the lines and rolled off the wagon, we would either be caught in the whippletrees up front or crushed by the wheels.

"This is just a whole lot of work," Nick said that afternoon. "It's not at all like our Saturday-morning rides with Dad."

The image of our Saturday-morning rides with my father surprised me, because it returned so powerfully and reminded me of how much work in the barn I had done with Nick when we were boys. I had completely forgotten about this period in our lives and was amused that a covered wagon trip across the plains, almost fifty years later, prompted a memory so potent.

In the early 1960s, my father was the associate publisher of *Look* magazine, second only to *Life* as America's big picture title. He actually ran the entire operation—Mike Cowles, the owner, kept the title of publisher for himself but he was in the office only once or twice a month. Tom Buck was a very inspiring man who perceived his role as promoting the career of everyone who worked for him, and his staff adored him. "I supply the charisma," he used to say. "They do all the work." He was enormous fun, a quirky high school dropout and autodidact who sold advertising space by taking clients out to lunch and quoting Winston Churchill and Pierre Teilhard de Chardin. He worked hard for *Look* in the morning and then, after lunch, manned the phones for his "causes"—getting friends elected to Congress or as governor, raising money for an Alcoholics Anonymous clinic that he had cofounded, civil rights. We never saw him during the week because most evenings he was either at an AA meeting or giving a political speech. His weekends were often devoted to entertaining clients or his AA friends, and the only free time he had was on Saturday morning.

We all knew that my father needed time alone on Saturday mornings, just to goof off with a horse. Nicky and I were the two horsemen in the family who liked to rise early, and most weekends we walked down the long hill outside our house together to spend the hours after dawn in the barn, doing chores and harnessing a horse for my father.

Nicky was this fun little belly laugh of a kid. He was enormously tough and energetic one minute, then bawling his shorts off the next. He loved wagons and horses. When we came down into the barn through the large space where my father's wagon collection sat, Nicky would caress the patent-leather fenders of every carriage he passed. Then we descended an ancient set of oak stairs into our boy cave, the stone-foundation stable and tack room area. The stable cellar smelled heavily of moist foundation rock, manure, and harness oil, and Nicky and I puttered around down there for hours. We taught ourselves to harness the horses by using step ladders to reach their withers and heads.

Many Saturday mornings, my father took us along with him in a surrey or a buckboard, and we enjoyed long, dreamy rides across the New

Jersey horse country or trotted into town and ordered fried egg sandwiches at the village store. But usually we could see that our father was brooding and distracted, overwhelmed by the details of his dense-packed life, and he just wanted to drive alone. When Nicky ran up to the house to check, my father would tell him to hitch one of his favorite mares, Maxine or Boots, to one of his single-seat racing sulkies.

When we were all done with the hitch, Nicky would hold the reins and ride the sulky up to the top of the drive with his feet dangling off the seat while I led the horse by the bridle. The window at the head of the kitchen table was right there, and my father could look out and see that his sulky was ready.

On cool mornings in the summer, my father would take his buggy ride in an Irish cardigan sweater with leather buttons and a tweed cap. In the fall, he wore a scarf and one of the tweed jackets from his tailor in Dublin. He would step out from the house, cross the patio, and mount the sulky by grabbing his trousers with a hand to heave his bad leg past the tall wheel. Once he sat down and took the reins, he stuffed and lit his corncob pipe, blew out a smoke ring, and thanked us for bringing up his horse.

"Nice job, boys," he said. "You guys are lickety-split."

Then he trotted off with his mare, slapping the reins for a fast trot as soon as he hit the road. The buggy whip in his right hand was perched at an angle over the rump of the horse, and the smoke from his pipe billowed out over his shoulder. He was an endlessly fascinating and contradictory man—enormously social yet in need of solitude, gifted but demanding with children, superbly organized for business but always broke. Nick and I would stand there and watch him disappear in his sulky down the road, the pounding of the horse hooves slowly dissipating as he got a quarter mile out.

I had completely forgotten this image from my childhood, but there was probably a good reason that I repressed a memory this poignant. I had spent my early adulthood terrified that I would turn out like my father—his eccentricities, his financial disorganization, and his wild scattered energy weren't an example I wanted to emulate. But in recent years I had come to accept, even embrace, his paternal stamp. The him in me wasn't frightening anymore. I couldn't change myself anyway, and my obvious similarities with my father—escapes from reality in covered wagons and planes, obsessive reading, a devil-may-care attitude toward social proprieties—were not embarrassments, but the skill set that propelled me out on the Oregon Trail.

Nick's mental jolt about my father's Saturday-morning rides also forced me to reconsider what memories are. I sat on the wagon seat brooding about it. Why are some cameos from our past always there, while other, important ones are repressed and require a prompt to revive them? Certainly memory isn't completely random. An invisible hand of logic and need, even self-protection, rules our recollections, and memory is an expression of character. I had told myself that I was out on the trail seeking adventure, knowledge of an epic era of American history, proof that a modern crossing could still be done. But now, as Kansas slowly passed by, with the clopping of hooves and the ringing of harness acting as a neuroenhancer, I knew that I was also out here seeking my past.

We camped that night at the Brown County Agricultural Museum south of Hiawatha, a hokey, agrarian Louvre on the plains. Beside a small village of restored barns, antique tractors and rusting farm equipment were haphazardly displayed in long rows across several acres of cleared fields. The gem of this collection was Windmill Lane, a large display of historic windmills gathered from farms throughout Kansas and Nebraska. We stabled the mules for the night on a grassy area behind an old Union Pacific caboose. While Nick walked off with Olive Oyl to explore the barns, I hauled water for the mules, lugging the heavy buckets forty yards from a water hydrant. I lit a barbecue fire to cook dinner, and then Nick and I strolled down Windmill Lane.

You have not really lived until you've sampled a classic American hodgepodge like Windmill Lane with Nick Buck. Nick didn't really know much about windmills, but he could instantly figure out the mechanics of the old Dempsters, Aeromotors, and thirty-two-volt Windmeters that we stopped to look at. From Nick that night, I learned all about ninety-degree gear reductions, what a sucker rod is, and how you can tell, just by looking at a windmill, whether it's intended for livestock feeding, or to supply water to a house. I was in love with our trip that first night. As we traveled west, I had expected to be trapped in Oregon Trail interpretive centers or at cowboys-and-Indians farces at the big rodeo shows. But Windmill Lane in Hiawatha seemed to promise that I would be seeing so much more.

As we returned toward the wagon at dusk, I realized that we had already learned something important. Elaborate travel planning and careful logistics weren't required here. We had reached Jamesport on a Monday and launched today, the following Saturday. We had spent only five days jumping off.

One thing about Nick would endlessly impress me on our trip. He can sleep anywhere. His only requirements for bedding are enough space for his wide girth and oxygen in the air. When we were planning the trip, I told Nick that I would be bringing along a spacious four-person tent to erect for him every night as we made camp. I would also pack a double-wide foam cushion to provide more comfort against concrete slabs or the hard desert floor. But Nick wasn't interested. "Tents are for pussies," he said. "I never use them, and we don't want to clutter the wagon with that much gear." For the entire trip, while I slept in my wagon bed, he bedded down in barns, horse stalls full of manure, sagebrush plains, and abandoned log cabins. He never complained and only once got a bad night's sleep. Traveling with him for the summer changed my mind about a lot of things, and the need for expensive accommodations is one of them. If you are as tough and as spontaneous as Nick Buck, tents and Comfort Inns don't need to exist.

When Nick and Olive walked off to sleep in a barn, I fussed around the wagon for a while, cleaning up after dinner, and then I walked over to the mules at their red caboose, making sure that they had enough water. Jake nuzzled me hard when I scratched him behind his ears.

After the occasional rains that day, the sky had finally cleared. The sun was setting against high cirrus clouds, with fleecy Winslow Homer yellows and pinks softening the sky. As I fell asleep in my wagon bed, the view through the narrow canvas opening concentrated and fused pastel sky to pastel plains. The mules contentedly munched on their hay over at the caboose and I heard my first wail of a Union Pacific whistle, a certain reminder that I was on the Oregon Trail.

7

THE EMIGRATION TO OREGON AND California was epic adventure and social history, but I was intrigued by the overland years for another reason. The cast of characters along the western trails yielded many surprises, revealing a past more nuanced than I had thought was there. The vaudeville of American life was acted out on the trail and, in particular, religion and conquering gender stereotypes played a formative role in developing the route to the Pacific. The very idea of wagon travel across the plains might have been indefinitely delayed had it not been for Narcissa Prentiss Whitman, a dreamy but persistent evangelist from the Finger Lakes of New York, who in 1836 became the first white woman to cross the Rockies. Narcissa Whitman is largely forgotten today, but her impact on American history was enormous, and for a time she was one of the most famous women in antebellum America.

Narcissa Prentiss was a product of the "Burned-Over District" of upstate New York. The term was coined when religious fervor swept Appalachian America in the 1820s and evangelization became so intense in western New York that the area was considered "burned out" of new souls to convert. A natural beauty with a frizzy mane of auburn hair and a pretty, symmetrically oval face, Narcissa was the third of nine children in a devoutly Presbyterian family from Prattsburgh, New York. At the age of sixteen, during a "born again" experience, Narcissa decided to devote her life to converting American Indians to Christianity. But she had spent most of her adult life in utter frustration. As a traveling schoolteacher and busy organizer of missionary fund-raising events, she remained single, and her applications to the American Board of Commissioners for Foreign Missions were consistently rejected because she was unmarried. (The board considered missionary work beyond the Missouri River "foreign" because the uncharted plains included lands disputed by Mexico, Great Britain, and the United States.) Narcissa solved this problem by abruptly deciding to marry a man she hardly knew, a medical doctor and fellow missionary zealot, Marcus Whitman. After a hastily arranged wedding ceremony at the Presbyterian church in Angelica, New York, Narcissa and Marcus left for the Missouri frontier the next day, arranging to travel with another missionary couple, Henry and Eliza Spalding. The importance of the Whitmans' speedy marriage for American history can hardly be overestimated. The 1836 Whitman-Spalding covered wagon train was the first to go beyond the Rockies and complete the Oregon Trail.

The year before, during an epic four-thousand-mile round-trip on horseback between western New York and Wyoming to explore routes west to the Indian tribes, Marcus Whitman had already made a discovery that revolutionized western travel. While camping at the sprawling Green River fur-trapper rendezvous in Wyoming, he learned that an earlier expedition by Captain Benjamin Bonneville of the U.S. Army had traveled a thousand miles from the Missouri to western Wyoming with twenty heavily loaded covered wagons—the first known crossing by wagons along what would become the Oregon Trail route. Discussions with chiefs from the Shoshone and Nez Perce tribes convinced Whitman that wagons could cross the remaining thousand miles to the Pacific by following the Bear and Snake rivers through Idaho to Oregon.

To reach the rich agricultural lands of the Pacific Northwest, wagons were considered vital. The trek of two thousand miles across the Rockies was so time-consuming and arduous that it would never be practical for farmers to push oxen or mules all the way to Oregon, stake a claim, clear some land, and then spend two additional summers traveling back for their families and bringing them out west. The first trip west would be the only journey. Farming was a family enterprise, and a completed family would be needed in the first year to clear land for crops and harvest trees for a house and barn.

Missionary Narcissa Whitman, the first white woman to cross the Rockies, is largely forgotten today, but she had an immense impact on the development of the trail.

By Narcissa Whitman's day, the very concept of "pioneer" was associated with wagon travel, though at first the term implied traveling by foot. The derivation of the word is significant, a linguistic trace of America's influences from Europe changing over time. The word began appearing in English in the sixteenth century, originating from a medieval Latin root, *pedonem*, meaning one who "goes on foot," or foot soldier, which slightly changed meaning in the European Romance languages to become *peon*, a person of humble social status who was an infantry soldier, day laborer, or agricultural worker. In French, the word evolved into *paonier* and then *pionnier*, gradually acquiring new connotations as "one who clears land" and "one who goes first."

The Europeans spent most of the seventeenth and eighteenth centuries in nonstop wars (the Thirty Years' War, the Eighty Years' War), and the word *pionnier* naturally acquired a military connotation. During the pan-European Seven Years' War between 1756 and 1763, and later the

Napoleonic Wars of the early nineteenth century, the *pionnier* (in English *pioneer*) units were small, highly mobile groups of sappers and engineers who occupied challenged ground first, to build roads, trenches, and fortifications, preparing the way for occupation by a larger army. On the American frontier, the term "pioneer" gradually assumed a civilian meaning for those who first explored new lands for farming development. The noun was probably introduced with the help of French Canadian trappers, many of whom were veterans of the Napoleonic Wars. In the Great Lakes region, and then the far West, the French trappers often returned east from their winter fur expeditions to find new settlers clearing forests in what they once considered wilderness, and they began calling these settlers *pionniers*.

In the American context, pioneers became coupled with wagons because the distances that had to be covered were so vast, and forging into new country so far from civilization and settlement (pretty much an unknown experience in Europe) required material too bulky and heavy to carry on foot—furniture, farm implements, a full kitchen and wood shop. The perceived need for wagons was also driven by nineteenth-century gender attitudes, and real necessity. Because settling a wilderness farm without women and children was considered unrealistic, wagons were required so that the family could spend at least part of the day as passengers, reducing the agony of the journey. Backwoodsmen like Daniel Boone and Ethan Allen could disappear into the great forests for months alone, carrying just a small haversack, a musket, and a long knife. But bringing the family along required a mobile home away from home, both for the journey itself and for camping on a claim until a log cabin was built.

But wagons were not yet a proven vehicle. Trips of five hundred or six hundred miles from Virginia or Pennsylvania to the frontier in Ohio or Indiana offered the challenge of crossing the Alleghenies over established freight routes, but this was relatively mild compared with two thousand miles clear across the Rockies. No one knew if the common farm wagon could sustain the trip across the blistering West without constant rebuilding.

As the newlywed Marcus and Narcissa Whitman sleighed from western New York to Pittsburgh, where they would pick up a steamer to travel to Missouri, they had assigned themselves a mythic mission, something that had not been accomplished before. They would have to cross the arid plains and then the Rockies in a wagon capable of carrying females.

In 1836, there was still enormous prejudice against this. The "hea-thenish" and dry far West beyond the Missouri River was not considered a fit place for white women, and to date the fur-trapping caravans had used only simple two-wheel carts pulled by donkeys. They carried supplies and pelts, not passengers. There was something suspicious, and even morally offensive to American values, about a man who would propose exposing delicate females to such risk. "Only parties of men could undergo the vi-cissitudes of the journey; none who ever made the trip would assert that a woman could have accompanied them," said a writer for the influential *New England Magazine* in 1832. When he heard about the Whitmans' plans, one of the most experienced western travelers, the explorer and Indian painter George Catlin, said that he would not take a "white female into that country for the whole continent of America." *New York Tribune* editor Horace Greeley would later be credited with coining the motto of manifest destiny, "Go west, young man." But initially Greeley was viru-lently opposed to western expansion and attacked trail leaders like Whit-man. "For what, then, do they brave the desert, the wilderness, the savage, the snowy precipices of the Rocky Mountains, the weary summer march, the storm-drenched bivouac, and the gnawings of famine?" Greeley asked his *Tribune* readers in 1843. "Only to fulfill their destiny! There is probably not one among them whose outward circumstances will be improved by this perilous pilgrimage."

But the Whitmans defied this conventional wisdom, leaving Liberty, Missouri, in early April 1836 to rush across the Kansas plains with two wag-ons and catch up with a fur caravan that they would follow west along the Platte. What later became known as the First Whitman Crossing was one of the great American adventure tales, but the Whitmans' prowess as travelers isn't what made them famous or changed the course of history. It was Nar-cissa's writing that popularized the idea of crossing the trail. In early June, when the Whitmans and their party were well along the Platte, they were met by an eastern-bound fur caravan and Marcus halted the wagons for an hour so that Narcissa could hastily pen an addendum to a letter back home to her family describing her trip. In the nineteenth century, personal letters were often shared with extended families and reprinted in both rural and large urban newspapers, and Narcissa had given her family permission to do this as a means of encouraging other missionaries to follow her path west.

Whitman's letters created a sensation when they were published back east, and even as far away as London. Her writing style about the "moving village" of the caravan and its trailing wagons was highly visual and charmingly self-effacing, and she confronted with telling detail American stereotypes about the West. The Whitman party suffered when the mules gave out, and occasionally had difficulty finding water and shade, but Narcissa clearly was thriving on the trail. She and Marcus learned to cook outdoors every night with buffalo dung for fuel, they loved elk and salmon steaks, and Narcissa rejoiced about having been liberated from a woman's weekly chore of having to do the wash. She had made her cotton-ticking tent herself, and her description of bundling up inside it at night under woolen blankets made it sound like a cozy home on the plains. In her letters, Narcissa also gradually revealed her growing affection for Marcus, whom she referred to as "husband," lending a romantic patina to her journey. At night, in camp, Marcus sat on the prairie with his legs crossed so that Narcissa could use them as a chair while they ate their elk steaks. Later, readers would learn that Narcissa had conceived on the trail.

Narcissa was a new woman out there on the plains. In Missouri, she had insisted on buying a riding horse and sidesaddle so that she could ride part of the day. That image was a potent one for nineteenth-century Americans. Women were not expected to ride astride a horse like men, except for members of the aristocracy for whom "equitation sport" was acceptable, so long as they rode the ungainly sidesaddle with both legs on the left side of the horse, to protect their skirts. (In foxhunting England, these equestriennes were called "amazones.") But non-elite women like Narcissa Whitman were expected to travel by coach or buggy, or walk. Why Narcissa Whitman decided to ignore this social convention is unknown, but as a traveling schoolteacher she was probably already an accomplished rider. Her persona as a trailblazer who was a rider, not a sedentary wagon traveler, helped establish her unique appeal as an adventurous woman bent on proving that other American women could also brave the West.

On cool mornings, Narcissa loved galloping sidesaddle ahead of the wagons on her new horse and even briefly losing sight of the party. Her practical observations about the plains had an immense impact on an American public that still considered wagon travel in the West impossible. The hard, arid soil of the prairie, for example, rutted evenly under wagon wheels—not at all like the sloppy, treacherous mud of the East. Two sentences of Narcissa's from Nebraska, endlessly repeated in newspaper accounts of her crossing, probably contributed more than any other words to the westward migration: "It is astonishing how well we get along with our wagons where there are no roads. I think I may say that it is easier traveling here than on any turnpike in the States."

Americans were already wanderers by nature, and they didn't need much prompting to dream of following Narcissa out beyond the Missouri. Another widely quoted passage made Americans feel that, by crossing the trail, they would be as free as a prairie lark.

> I wish I could discribe to you how we live so that you can realize it. Our manner of living is far preferable to any in the States. I never was so contented and happy before. Neither have I enjoyed such health for years. In the morn as soon as the day breaks the first that we hear is the word—arise, arise. Then the mules set up such noise as you never heard which puts the whole camp in motion.

Whitman drew thousands of American families to consider emigrating across the frontier by frankly confronting their greatest fears, particularly about the Indian tribes. In Nebraska and Wyoming, the Pawnee and Shoshone hunting parties that the Whitman party met were invariably friendly and, in the evening, the braves lined up outside Narcissa's tent and opened up the flap, just to see their first white woman. At remote military forts and trading posts, where the tribes gathered in the early summer to trade furs, Narcissa and Eliza were mobbed by squaws who were overjoyed to meet their first white women, and embraced them and kissed them on the cheeks.

"After we had been seated awhile in the midst of the gazing throng," Narcissa wrote, "one of the chiefs, whom we had seen before, came with his wife and very politely introduced her to us. They say they all like us very much, and thank God that they have seen us, and that we have come to live with them."

Nineteenth-century Americans were also terrified of rivers, and most families had either relatives or friends who had been carried away when bridges collapsed or coaches overturned at the river fords. But Whitman's descriptions of the western rivers defied this image. In fact, the Platte and the Sweetwater were narrower and usually shallower than eastern rivers, with natural strata of sand and bottom rocks that made wagon crossings safe, though bumpy, in normal water conditions. Her rapturous accounts made the river crossings seem appealing, almost like a modern American weekend rafting adventure.

As her party approached each river, throngs of Indian boys gathered on the banks, stripped to their loincloths, and dived into the current to swim the livestock and mules across. Then they swam back over in groups, laughing and amphibious, to steer the wagons across by lashing them to logs. Young braves competed fiercely to be on the team that carried the white women across to the far banks. Newspaper readers in America and Europe learned that Narcissa and Eliza rode the rivers in crafts of every conceivable description—stick baskets wrapped in buffalo hides called bull boats, dugouts, cottonwood rafts, and canoes made of animal skins and bark—with their saddles and trunks piled high around them.

"O! if father and mother and the girls could have seen us in our snug little canoe, floating on the water," Narcissa wrote from the Snake River in Idaho. "I once thought that crossing streams would be the most dreadful part of the journey. I can now cross the most difficult stream without the least fear."

Popular apprehension about the Indian tribes and the rivers, in short, was resolved by Narcissa Whitman's letters back east. But Whitman provided even more for an American public deeply in need of new space but anxious about traveling beyond the western frontier. Liberated from a fixed house, the routine of chores, and village life back home, covered wagon travelers could discover an entirely new self out on the open plains. Living and foraging day by day under hooped canvas, amid spectacular scenery, was almost heaven on earth. One sentiment that Whitman introduced about the far West—that she was healthier and happier there than at any other time of her life—would be endlessly repeated in the hundreds of trail journals written by the pioneers over the next twenty years, and indeed presaged the sense of freedom on the plains that Willa Cather wrote about a century later.

But the fame of the Whitman crossing also derived from the powerful, gender-breaking imagery that occurred three weeks after the wagons reached Fort Laramie in eastern Wyoming in mid-June. There, Marcus Whitman sensibly abandoned his heavier wagon, transferring supplies to a lighter Dearborn wagon and pack animals, to continue on through the rougher terrain of the Rocky foothills with a more maneuverable set of wheels. Narcissa Whitman and Eliza Spalding no longer had a wagon to ride when they tired of their sidesaddles, and would make the rest of the journey either on horseback or walking. Near present-day Casper, Wyoming, the Whitmans and the caravan they were still following made a difficult high-water crossing of the Platte by stretching buffalo hides under their wagons for better flotation. The party then continued down through the dramatic channel of landmarks—Red Buttes, Avenue of the Rocks, and the Rattlesnake Hills—toward Independence Rock.

A few days later, Narcissa Whitman and Eliza Spalding galloped sidesaddle up a broad, slightly inclined plain high above the winding Sweetwater River. They were surrounded by dimpled hills and dramatic rock formations that climbed to 7,500 feet and then leveled for about a quarter of a mile to form a rounded summit. This was the fabled South Pass that the fur trappers had used since the 1820s. The pass, the benign opening in the Rockies that made the trail west possible, marks the Continental Divide, separating the drainages of the Atlantic and Pacific oceans. The views west from South Pass are spectacular. Vast sagebrush lands, rimmed by the foothills along the western face of the Rockies, stretch toward the rendezvous country along the Green River. Narcissa and Eliza paused at the top to rest their horses and wait for the wagon and the pack train, staring off toward the capacious vistas of the Green.

It was an epochal moment for western migration, and few Americans who read about the women summiting South Pass failed to grasp the symbolism of their timing. It was July 4, 1836. The first white women had crossed the Rockies on Independence Day.

Marcus Whitman was fiercely determined to continue with his Dearborn wagon to Oregon, to disprove the skeptics who said it couldn't be done. The Idaho extension of the trail along the Snake River that the Whitmans blazed that summer is strewn with lava-rock boulder fields, dramatic climbs up through the buttes, and difficult downhill slides, a terrain that battered a Dearborn never designed for such abuse. When his front axle broke, Whitman cut the wagon in half and continued on with the wagon rebuilt as a cart—a considerable feat of high-desert mechanics. When the mules started to give out farther along the Snake, he jettisoned Narcissa's heavy traveling trunk, one of her last possessions from back east.

"Farewell little Trunk," Narcissa wrote. "I thank thee for thy faithful services & that I have been cheered by thy presence so long. Thus we scatter as we go along."

Near present-day Glenns Ferry, Idaho, when the Whitmans decided to risk a dangerous crossing to the north side of the Snake across a series of islands in the river, the cart capsized in the fiercely churning whirlpools between the islands, nearly drowning the mules. The Whitmans finally staggered into the old Hudson's Bay Company trading post at Fort Boise, just a few miles from the border with Oregon, with exhausted mules and a cart hardly worthy of the name. Marcus finally conceded that it was time to abandon his prized wheeled transport and have the party walk and ride the rest of the way to the Cayuse country on the Walla Walla River.

But he had done it. He had "made" Oregon with a set of wheels, traveling 1,600 miles from the banks of the Missouri with a wagon—six hundred miles farther west than the Bonneville expedition with wagons in 1832. Oregon Trail experts still marvel at Whitman's determination and the resourcefulness of his small party. Whitman's clarity of purpose and his ability to sense the mood of the country were most significant. He knew that the news that a wagon had reached the mythical Oregon country—a wagon, in Oregon!—would electrify a nation poised to jump off for the next phase of its expansion, and it did. Two years earlier he had been a hardworking but largely unknown doctor in the Bible-thumping, canal-boating, Burned-Over lands, 3,500 miles away. Now he was famous for doing this crazyass thing. He had put mule hooves and wagon wheels into Oregon.

After several adventures in wilderness Oregon, the Whitmans settled and began building their mission to the Cayuse tribe at a beautiful spot along the Walla Walla River called Waiilatpu. Marcus built a log-and-adobe house in the style of a New England saltbox and it was there, in March 1837, that Narcissa Whitman established another milestone, delivering a daughter who was named Alice Clarissa, the first white child conceived on the trail and born in the far West. This news was considered particularly important in an age when birth control was all but nonexistent and married women, already overburdened with several children, knew that they could conceive at almost any time. Women could quickly calculate back from Narcissa's published diary and realize that she had been on the Platte, in June, when she conceived. After that, she had crossed the dry country past Chimney Rock, made a difficult ford of the Platte, galloped up South Pass, and then made the hellish passage along the Snake River in Idaho—all while pregnant. Her safe delivery of a healthy girl the next spring proved that even the likely prospect of pregnancy shouldn't prevent women from crossing the trail.

Marcus Whitman would make one last—and invaluable—contribution to the western migration. Over the winter of 1842–1843 he abruptly decided to make a dangerous crossing eastward along the trail, to return to Boston and persuade the American missionary board to continue supporting his missionary project at Waiilatpu, even though it was clearly failing. After reaching Boston, he arrived back on the Missouri in the spring of 1843, and was alarmed to discover a spontaneous gathering of more than a thousand pioneers near Independence, Missouri. The group had organized into a train of about 120 wagons that was about to jump off for Oregon. The pioneers had hired Captain John Gantt, a former army officer and fur trader, to lead them across as far as the remote Fort Hall on the Snake River in eastern Idaho, where they planned to abandon their wagons and walk the rest of the way to the Pacific, trailing a pack train. Whitman considered the idea of scuttling wagons in Idaho disastrous and agreed to lead the expedition jointly with Gantt.

A few smaller wagon trains and military exploration parties had crossed to Oregon and California in 1840 and 1841. But the 1843 wagon train—called both the "Gantt-Whitman Train" and the "Great Migration"—is considered the first mass crossing of the Oregon Trail, and historians now date the beginning of the overland trail migration to 1843. Interestingly, there is no single explanation for the haphazard gathering of pioneers outside Independence in 1843. The tide of desperate and essentially homeless farming families had begun to build in late winter, probably because after the Panic of 1837 almost half of the banks in America had failed. During the deep economic depression that followed, farmers deprived of both markets and credit realized that they couldn't afford to buy planting seed that year, and they were forced to either abandon their land or quickly cash out at fire-sale prices. Meanwhile, considerable and well-publicized sentiment was building in Congress to flood the Oregon country with American pioneers, to overwhelm Britain's thinly staffed fur-trading empire, managed by the Hudson's Bay Company. American citizens would effectively seize control of the Pacific Northwest by squatting on the land—the same practice that had worked in the Alleghenies during the American Revolution. The tactic worked brilliantly in the Pacific Northwest, where there were about five hundred English agents and trappers allied with them in the early 1840s. By 1845, there were already five thousand Americans.

The pioneer years are often depicted as a single, deliberate moment of history, when thousands of emigrants decided together to move west to find new lands and fulfill America's continental destiny. In fact, the movement was more accidental. It was also a default toward traditional patterns of settlement. Americans were simply doing what they had always done, outfitting their mover's wagons with hickory bows and a canvas top, loading up, and pushing west, hopeful that they would find a solution and a new situation for themselves when they reached the frontier, but, really, having no finished plan. Many pioneer trains were also formed by breakaway groups of Baptists and Methodists eager to escape bitter denominational fighting at home. Departing for the trail was an adventure forced on them by economic necessity and dreams of more religious elbow room. There was no certainty about the outcome and most families didn't really know where they would end up.

Settlement on the old "Northwest" frontier—Kentucky, Ohio, and Indiana—had established this rootless American style. Each new stage of frontier development was a rolling infrastructure supporting the next stage moving farther west. Americans who decided to become pioneers knew that they could count on the hospitality of the small settlements and rugged farms—populated by recent pioneers like themselves—that stood between them and the Missouri. Meanwhile, the rapid development of the Mississippi River steamboat business had led to the growth of small towns in Ohio, Iowa, and Illinois, conveniently placing a string of supply depots along the roads to the Missouri frontier. As the homeless families moved west, they formed into "companies" that picked up new members as they passed new towns.

Suddenly pulling up stakes and becoming a "westering" family wasn't considered unusual, and a kind of national ethos formed around the idea. In 1843, a new American term, "Oregon fever," was coined. "The Oregon fever is raging in almost every part of the Union," the *Ohio Statesman* reported in April that year. "Companies are forming in the East, and in several parts of Ohio, which added to those of Illinois, Iowa, and Missouri, will make a pretty formidable army." In May, the *Telegraph* in Painesville, Ohio, reported, "From ten to fifteen teams [with wagons] have passed through this town every day for the last three weeks." Oregon fever was contagious and soon even families with relatively prosperous farms, and no apparent reason for picking up and leaving, were deciding to sell out and join the adventurous train of white-tops moving west.

Whitman's experience and natural talents made him an ideal leader for the 1843 wagon train. A relentless but inspiring taskmaster, he goaded families to rise early and hitch their teams, without stopping more than one night at a camp. Whitman's biographer, Clifford M. Drury, describes how he would exhort the 1843 pioneers with the motto, "Travel, travel, travel!" Whitman rode far ahead of the wagons to scout the route every day, and he delivered the first baby born on the Oregon Trail. On his riding mule, he was an engaging figure, tall and rugged, dressed in fringed buckskin pants and a mangy fur cap.

"The Doctor spent much of his time in hunting out the best route for the wagons, and would plunge into streams in search of practical fords, regardless of the depth or the temperature of the water," wrote one of the 1843 emigrants, J. W. Nesmith. "Sometimes after the fatigue of a hard day's march, [he] would spend much of the night in going from one party to another to minister to the sick." (Wagon masters soon learned that attracting doctors to their "company" would help recruit families, and thus increase their guide fees.) When the pioneers reached Fort Hall, Whitman's insistence on continuing with wagons is credited with saving the expedition and delivering the first big wagon train to Oregon.

By the spring of 1844, accounts of the Gantt-Whitman Train—the letters and journals of the pioneers—had been published in many eastern and midwestern newspapers. Whitman epitomized a new American character type, the benevolent but driven wagon master. The first mass crossing had positioned the trail for rapid growth. By 1845, trail traffic had picked up to 2,500 people crossing in a single summer, and then with the Mormon hegira that began in 1847, and the crazed Gold Rush of 1849, as many as fifty thousand were crossing in a year. America's insatiable drive west would have happened anyway, but the Whitmans' contributions—especially trailblazing the five-hundred-mile leg along the Snake River in Idaho—had been pivotal, defining the style and the élan of a new age of travel.

Over the winter that I read about the Whitmans, New England was blanketed by record snows. The powdery vortices swirling past my windows at night provided a romantic stimulant that helped me realize something important about the Whitmans before my dread hours of planning began in the spring. Before entering the wilderness west of the Missouri in 1836, Marcus Whitman was an unknown country doctor in western New York, and Narcissa was a schoolmarm, neither of them possessing the specific "hard" skills required for cutting a wagon road west. The experts scoffed at their inexperience, and they had to overcome a deep cultural skepticism that wagons could be pushed to the Pacific Northwest. Their only real endowments were soft skills such as a willingness to accept the help of strangers, stubborn practicality, and the ability to live with uncertainty. But they became the first married couple to "make" Oregon with a covered wagon, inviting the multitude that followed.

Starting out, my own dreams of western adventure were just as unrealistic. The only advantages I could count on were the soft ones—luck, maybe, and persistence, as well as an enthusiasm for learning what I needed to know as I went along. More or less impulsively, I had bought a covered wagon and a cranky team of mules, and enough canned chili and lantern fuel to last me for several months. Maybe that would be enough. In Kansas, in my wagon womb at night, exhausted after a day of splashing across swollen creeks and carrying water for the mules, I was comforted by the spunky image of American womanhood that Narcissa Whitman presented, galloping sidesaddle up to South Pass. I often fell asleep thinking of her as my guardian angel of the trail.

8

NARCISSA WHITMAN'S LITTLE TRUNK ABANDONED on the Snake was symbolic for me. My own comedy of discarding began that first morning, when I woke at the agricultural museum in Hiawatha. I had slept peaceably enough, but across the thirty-eight-inch span of the wagon my head was wedged between a barbecue cooker on one side and a stack of books on the other. My feet had rattled all night on a pile of kitchenware and boots mounded in the back of the wagon. I felt like an Egyptian pharaoh, buried in his crypt with all the possessions needed for the journey into the hereafter.

It's amazing how transformative twenty-four hours in a covered wagon can be. I had left St. Joe the day before obsessed with the fear that I was forgetting something. Everything I needed for four months of travel to Oregon *had* to be in that wagon. Now, as I gingerly fanny-walked past the barbecue cooker, and then fell through the wobbly pile of kitchenware and boots to get out of the wagon, I was gripped by the opposite obsession. Deep-six this shit.

It was dawn, with weak tendrils of light filtering in over the prairie, making the distant silos and barns glow pink. I pulled on my boots and rummaged around in the pile of gear in the Trail Pup for the Coleman cookstove, propane, and coffee, got that started, and began sorting through my redundant gear.

Creating a new discard pile of my possessions was a useful exercise in self-analysis. First of all, the assortment of kitchenware that I had assembled for the trip—glass casserole cookers, extra Revere Ware pans, a pasta cooker, and a vegetable steamer—was patently ridiculous, the prissy collection of a cable-TV chef. Oh, and Rinker, isn't it useful, you ludicrous fop, to have retained the shoe shine kit for this long? Underneath the bales of hay in the Trail Pup I retrieved the contraband that I had smuggled past Nick in Jamesport—the CD player, the boccie balls, and the backgammon set. Another item, I thought, truly burnished my image as a pioneer. I had packed my Brooks Brothers bathrobe. Walking back and forth in camp every morning to carry hay to the mules, I would look so fetching in a Brooks Brothers bathrobe. And look at this! A can of Niagara Spray Starch! For ironing shirts! Rinker, from the beginning of all time to the end of all eternity there certainly have been and will continue to be a great number of imbeciles, but you are rising pretty quickly here to the top of the dickhead heap.

When I was done, I had four large garbage bags stuffed with excess barn jackets, boots, saucepans, and the rest of the yard sale that I had packed. I tossed the garbage bags beside a wagon wheel, walked over to the caboose to feed and water the mules, and then enjoyed what would become my most pleasurable time on the trip—the first hour after dawn, before Nick and Olive Oyl woke up. While the windmills across the field whirled in the morning breeze, I tidied up camp and then stood at the tailgate of the wagon, preparing breakfast. I loved being alone in camp on the plains. The smell of sizzling bacon and the expanse of prairie, bright green and fresh with dew, gave me an expectant feeling about the day.

On the way out of Hiawatha that morning, we couldn't find a Salvation Army or a Goodwill store. I asked Nick to stop the wagon on Kickapoo Street, near the door of the social hall at the First Presbyterian Church. It is strange how people behave when they fear they are being watched. Kickapoo Street was a quintessentially placid and sensible residential neighborhood in a small Kansas town. Nearby, children circled on bikes in the driveways of lovely Victorians and prairie-style bungalows, and people walked their dogs. Lifting the large bags of my discarded possessions out of the wagon, I tiptoed over to the Presbyterian social hall and discreetly placed them on the steps. Then I tiptoed back to the wagon and we headed north for the junction country along the old St. Joseph Road.

My contributions to the next attic sale at the First Presbyterian Church reminded me that, no matter how much I had studied the overland journals and tried to learn from them, I was condemned to repeat the pioneers' mistakes. My choice of conveyance—a covered wagon—determined my behavior and had turned me into a twenty-first-century retread. The westbound travelers who crossed the plains before the Civil War were, in the words of one historian, "the greatest litterbugs of American history." By the late 1840s, a vast solid landfill of wrecked wagons, ox and mule carcasses, bacon barrels, and discarded sinks had replaced the charming waypoints of Chimney Rock or Lizard Butte. Dozens of pioneers would report in their journals that they had simply followed the debris field all the way to the Columbia River.

In peak migration years like 1850 and 1852, the crush of wagon travelers converging at the Missouri every spring created tent cities around Independence or St. Joseph that were sometimes as large as three square miles. The burgeoning merchant class of these towns knew what this jumping-off economy meant. The outfitters had a month, at most six weeks, to extract from the overlanders as much income as they could get, and they told lurid tales about wagon travelers who had starved before they even reached Fort Kearny in Nebraska.

The scare tactics of the Missouri River outfitters were abetted by a lively secondary market generated by the trail, guidebooks like Randolph Marcy's *The Prairie Traveler* and Lansford Hastings's *Emigrant Guide* that began to be published as early as 1845. These Baedekers contained elaborate lists of the camping gear, guns and ammunition, and dry provisions that a typical family should pack and were available at every jumping-off town and even sold in bookstores in New York and Chicago. In addition to advising pioneers to carry a broad assortment of tents, poles, axes, and tools, Hastings suggested packing at least sixty feet of rope for each draft animal. One of the most popular of these guides, *Journal of Travels over the Rocky Mountains to the Mouth of the Columbia River*, was written by an enterprising Indiana Quaker named Joel Palmer, who recommended that covered wagon travelers amass, for each adult, two hundred pounds of flour, seventy-five pounds of salted bacon, twenty pounds of sugar, ten pounds of rice, and casks of vinegar, salt, dried beans, and coffee.

The pioneers quickly learned that they didn't need all of this loot. In the early years, game was still plentiful along the trail, and during several dry years in the late 1850s the buffalo and antelope grazed near the rivers to be near water. Meanwhile, the draft teams were struggling up the steep slopes of California Hill in Nebraska or Register Cliff in Wyoming, and unloading and then reloading the wagons at the river fords was becoming tedious.

The result was a historic American dumping. "This jettisoning process began in a mild way a few miles out of Independence or St. Joe," historian Merrill J. Mattes writes in *The Great Platte River Road*. "It began in a serious way at Fort Kearny and continued to its climax at Fort Laramie."

One of my favorite trail diarists is Franklin Langworthy, a Universalist minister and scientist from Illinois who crossed the trail in 1850. Langworthy should be credited with being America's first recycler, a Goodwill Industries sort of man. On the trail, when he tired of the chore of washing his clothes, Langworthy simply threw them out and replaced them with the long johns and suits of his size that he found on the shoulders of the ruts. When he was done reading a volume of Cicero or Voltaire, he tossed it overboard for another pioneer to find and soon replaced it with another book from the vast prairie library at his feet.

In his delightful and ironic *Scenery of the Plains, Mountains and Mines*, published in 1855, Langworthy pointed out that the pioneer dump zone stretched all the way to the Pacific. Langworthy traveled the California Trail, the branch of the overland trail system through the deserts of Utah and Nevada that was developed during the 1849 Gold Rush. It departed southwest for California at Fort Bridger in western Wyoming, after following the main ruts of the Oregon Trail for a thousand miles. In the deserts of Utah, Langworthy stopped to rest at places that were littered with emigrant graves, or where a man ate his lunch "gravely sitting upon the carcass of a dead horse." He described another desert scene, a few days' travel beyond Salt Lake.

The destruction of property upon this part of the road, is beyond all computation. Abandoned wagons literally crowded the way for twenty miles, and dead animals are so numerous, that I have counted fifty carcasses within a distance of forty rods.

The Desert from side to side, is strewn with goods of every name. The following articles however, are peculiarly abundant; log chains, wagons, and wagon irons, iron bound water-casks, cooking implements, all kinds of dishes and hollow ware, cooking stoves and utensils, boots and shoes, and clothing of all kinds, even life preservers, trunks and boxes, tin-bakers, books, guns, pistols, gunlocks and barrels. Edged tools, planes, augurs and chisels, mill and cross-cut saws, good geese feathers in heaps, or blowing over the Desert, feather beds, canvas tents, and wagon covers.

An adaptive swap-meet mentality soon prevailed on the plains. Having been cheated by the Missouri outfitters with poor-quality flour or bacon, the pioneers quickly learned to just exchange their inferior barrels for better-quality supplies discarded by someone else along the way. The Missouri River outfitters, and traders at the forts, were adept at multiplying their chicanery. As soon as a covered wagon train disappeared over the bluffs, the merchants dispatched wagons of their own to recover the tons of flour and dried beef that they knew would be thrown overboard. The recovered goods were then hauled back to the post to be resold to the next train of suckers.

The American traveler's remarkable penchant for oversupplying was a theme that played out in many other ways. Pioneer journals recorded how, when a wagon train arrived at a frequently used camp at night, the men happily plugged away at the confused, thirsty steers abandoned just that morning by the preceding wagon train. Then they cooked steaks on the cast-iron and tin stoves also left behind by earlier wagons. In this way, each hundred-wagon train became a sort of dusty logistical support system for the train just behind it, a mobile convenience store that consumed some of its inventory itself but left plenty behind for others.

It's impressive how, even then, America was so superlatively organized for producing waste. The Gold Rush of 1849 was one of the great boom years in American history, and the butchers of Missouri and the steamboat lines had worked overtime the winter before, preparing for what they expected to be a record invasion along the trail. The documented tally of 49ers and pioneers who crossed that year is 25,000, but historians believe it could have been as high as 32,000. The overloading that spring of wagons, carriages, and wheeled vehicles of every description—some 49ers crossed the trail pushing wheelbarrows and dogcarts—was epic. After Fort Kearny along the Platte in Nebraska, Fort Laramie in eastern Wyoming, about 350 miles down the trail, was the second big stop. It was located near a pleasant grove of cottonwoods at the junction of the North Platte and Laramie rivers and was a popular resting place where the pioneers camped for a day or two to trade with the Indians and reassess their loads. By May 30 that year—still early in the travel season—twenty thousand pounds of bacon lay abandoned on the plains outside the fort.

As we harnessed and hitched the team in Hiawatha, I began to realize how much work was required every day to get a covered wagon rolling again. Feeding and carrying water for the mules, breaking camp and reloading the wagon, and then harnessing and hitching took at least an hour. The dust flew from the mules while I curried them, the harnesses dug into my back as I carried them across to the team, and the wagon pole creaked as I raised it to hook to the yoke. Nick and I worked briskly and efficiently together and the last few minutes of our morning routine—while I held the mules up front, Nick attached the chain tugs—were tense. Even in the cool morning air, as I climbed the wheel to mount the wagon seat, the back of my shirt was spongy with sweat. Still, every morning I felt the wonderful endorphin rush of the Ultimate Equine Vacation.

We headed due west, diverting a mile or two above the paved Route 36 to follow the quiet dirt section roads that paralleled the highway. The mules were fresh and wanted to trot. It was a brisk and clear Kansas morning, with cattle bounding over to the fence lines to stare at us as we passed, meadowlarks bobbing above the grasslands, and low, creamy sun on our backs. I kept track of our progress on my maps and was pleased to see that we could make the important waypoint of Marysville, Kansas, an old trail and Pony Express stop, after just a few days of pleasant camping.

We quickly noticed all of the problems we would have with the team. Bute was actually quite game for work and struggled to keep up whenever Beck trotted ahead of her, but Bute's hooves were splayed sideways and too small for her body weight, and she had an awkward, short stride that made it hard for her to keep up with the more athletic Jake and Beck. We had planned to trot at least an hour or two every morning to make good time when the air was cool. At a trot, mules can make seven miles per hour. They walk at four miles per hour. I was already mile-obsessed and wanted to gain at least fifteen miles of trail before noon, so we could enjoy leisurely afternoons of walking in the warmer temperatures and be guaranteed our twenty or twenty-five miles per day by the evening.

But Bute just couldn't do this. She was a walker. After fifteen or twenty minutes of trotting, she would stumble and start to favor her right leg—not limping, just shambling along with an ungainly, obviously uncomfortable gait. I tensed up with stomach spasms every time Bute stumbled, especially when we were on paved roads. If she fell to her knees, the other two mules would probably drag her for several yards before we could get them stopped. An injured Bute would then have to be replaced, a time-consuming setback this early in the trip.

Beck presented her own cluster of issues. She was an immensely attractive mule, jet-black, tall and leggy, with a naturally long, athletic stride. She loved to pull and perform as the "lead" mule of the team, and her trace chains were always tight. But she was an unpredictable, crazy girl who shied at everything—strange-looking culverts, a piece of farm machinery beside the road, cows chasing up behind us in a field—leaping sideways in her harness and pushing hard left against the other mules, momentarily breaking into a gallop and frothing at the mouth as she bolted away.

Beck is very strong, and several times, when she suddenly veered sideways, the whole team would be pushed toward the center of the road and even over the painted line, which was dangerous if there was traffic. Instantly, even when Nick was driving, I would grab the right line and seesaw it back and forth, grinding the bit into her molars to get her back in line. Whenever Beck shied, Nick and I would pull the team back that way, both of us gripping with all our strength on a single line.

But Nick loved our twisted sister mule. She appealed to his thrill for danger and his natural empathy for tortured souls.

"Okay, so Beck is just Tonya Harding on steroids," Nick said, as we pulled her back toward the shoulder of the road one day. "Big fuckin deal. That just makes me like her more. She's the smartest of the three."

I was careful after that not to denigrate Beck, but this was difficult after she made it clear that she despised me. She would act up in harness as soon as she could tell that I had taken the driving lines from Nick. In the morning, if I approached her with the harness, she spooked sideways and looked at me angrily, promising to kick my brains to a spongiform pulp.

Beck was Nick's mule, Nick's project. In the pastures at night, he cooed to her and caressed her with brushes and gall ointment, while I carried apples to Jake and let him bury his head in my arms.

Nick and I discussed the team and what it meant for our trip several times those first few days. We expected the mules to settle quite a bit after a week or two of work and after losing their winter fat. Perhaps Bute and Beck would improve. Still, understanding what had happened and what we faced with the mules led to one of the first big revelations of the trip.

I didn't believe that Philip Ropp had deliberately sold us a bad base team of mules. Beck would not have been shying very regularly on a farm that was familiar to her. So Ropp wouldn't have known how bad she was that way. Bute's poor feet, which made it impossible for her to trot, might not have shown up on Ropp's farm either, because he rarely ran the team while working his fields. A mule man of Ropp's experience should have known about these limitations of Beck and Bute. But I was the one who made the bigger mistake, buying a team as quickly as I did.

"We're just as naive as the pioneers," I said to Nick as we bumped along on the wagon seat. "Don Werner wouldn't make the changes we wanted on the wagon, and Phillip Ropp sold us some bozo mules."

"But it's not their fault," Nick said. "Nobody really knows what it takes to drive a team a thousand miles anymore. The art of horsemanship has been lost. We've got to reinvent that ourselves."

"I'm not going to live this whole trip blaming our outfitters for our mules and rig," I said. "This is *our* trip, our responsibility. If we'd known about these problems before?"

"We never would have left," Nick said.

"Nobody knows," I said. "We're just going to have to fix our problems ourselves as we go along."

This became our creed, almost a religious faith. Nobody knows and we would have to figure everything out ourselves.

Nick and I were also adjusting to our very different driving styles. Even when I am relaxed and enjoying myself out there, I hold a team with the lines gathered tightly on my lap, always ready for a mule to shy or for the team to decide to bolt. Fear is my retentive personality. I consider it my great weakness and could spend hours ruminating on where it came from. Had I simply been born this way—cautious, skittish, cerebral—or did the chaos of my upbringing force me toward a need to control? When I was a boy, my father had scared the hell out of me on horses and in wagons, and stunting in planes, and terrified me with his temper. I was convinced that a hideous death, or at least injury, lurked everywhere for me, and my fatalism extended to virtually every other aspect of my life. I turned in my best work as a journalist convinced that my editors would reject it. Logging, I could take the better part of an hour roping, notching, and then felling a tree. Now I sat on the seat of a Peter Schuttler wagon, climbing the hills and crossing the creek beds of eastern Kansas, gritting my teeth and trying not to confess to Nick that I was gripped by images of disaster every time he trotted the team.

Nick had developed his bold style of driving over the past twenty years in New Hampshire and Maine, lunging his teams through drifts and over streams to get his sleighs through. If there's a challenge to face— inching a wagon through a narrow space, backing to get out of a parking lot—Nick is all driver, intensely focused and just about the best there is. But the rest of the time he sits cross-legged with the lines loosely gripped in one hand, daydreaming. He enjoys a rough ride and doesn't carefully plan a turn, skittering the wagon over at the next road.

It was a style driven by Nick's psychology. If you ignore a problem long enough, things will build to a crisis. The mules will shy wide, kicking at their tug chains, nearly toppling the wagon. Then Nick could rescue the situation and prove his mettle as a driver. The normal precautions of life don't occur to Nick. One of my brothers describes him as "proud to be careless."

But we were adjusting. During those first few days in Kansas, if I didn't like the look of an intersection ahead or saw some farm machinery coming over a hill that would probably spook Beck, I reached over and took the lines myself or spoke up to Nick.

"Nick, gather your lines now. Hold this team back. I don't like the looks of this."

It was a frequent refrain and I hated correcting Nick. But I was constantly aware that one mistake could cost us the trip. Each time, I apologized to Nick as soon as we were clear of the danger.

"You don't have to apologize," Nick said. "It's not your fault that you grew up to be such an old lady."

The other big problem we had out along the St. Joe Road in Kansas, and then later in Nebraska, were the recreational vehicles. Someday, when historians perform their "why the Mayans declined" necropsy on American society, they will marvel at the way that, at a time of high anxiety about energy resources and costs, millions of elderly people took to the road in the clumsiest, most inefficient vehicles ever devised by man. The lunacy of America is all right there, in the RVs.

Highway 36 through Kansas is, essentially, a motorized ghetto for the massive Winnebago and Gulf Stream motor homes that American seniors drive themselves around in these days. As they head out toward Yellowstone Park or to visit their grandchildren in Seattle, these road geriatrics follow the advice of their guidebooks and motor along the "Pony Express Highway" between St. Joe and Marysville, and then lumber up to highways 30 and 26 in Nebraska to follow the Oregon Trail country along the Platte. Spending six figures for a McMansion mounted on a bus chassis is truly an adventure in bad taste. At a few state parks and Sinclair convenience stores where we stopped along the Pony Express Highway, the proud owners of a Winnebago Adventurer or a Newmar Mountain Aire would occasionally insist that we step inside their rig for an inspection tour. Everything desired by America's gaudiest consumers is inside these things—immense flat-screen TVs in the kitchen and living room, microwaves big enough to stew a whole cow in, whirlpool baths, extra dens and porches that extend off the sides by activating humming motors. The designers at Winnebago and Gulf Stream seem to understand the Walter Mitty fantasies of American seniors. In most of these RVs, the driver's seat is called the "pilot's cockpit." The passenger side, which includes a laptop stand on the dashboard, is called the "copilot" seat.

Of course, the RVers were *thrilled* to see a covered wagon moving down the St. Joe Road. Opportunities to create traffic hazards are much coveted by RV couples, and they loved us. They were relentlessly bad drivers and would sway their big Gulf Streams around the back of the wagon, rumble alongside at four miles per hour, just inches from the mules, and then open their windows and flash away with a cell phone camera for several minutes as traffic backed up behind them.

Several times a day, packs of RVs would pass us on the highway, and then the drivers would stop a half mile ahead, positioning themselves to take better pictures. They parked with about two feet of the Gulf Stream girth on the shoulder of the road, with the remaining eight feet blocking our westbound lane. The driver of an eastbound RV, curious about why the Sun Sport with Wisconsin plates had stopped, of course had to stop too, allegedly parking on the shoulder of his side of the highway. There was just enough room in between for us to squeeze the wagon through this RV gauntlet.

RV occupants, however, have fine, salient minds. True erudition rides behind those windshields. As we inched our way through the behemoth Venture-Ride and Endura-Maxes blocking our way, the RVers stood to take pictures and asked us questions.

"Hey, how come their ears are so long?"

"Where's your police escort? I don't see escort cars."

"Who cooks? How do you cook?"

As we traveled the St. Joe Road, we found that the Sinclair convenience stores were a comfortable place to stop. The large roofs built over the gas pumps provided shade for the mules, we could water them there, and then run in for a coffee for me and a Diet Pepsi for Nick. The Sinclairs were our road ranches in Kansas. We ran into a lot of RVers there.

Apparently, there is a considerable gassing off of formaldehydes and vinyl parts inside a moving RV that causes aggressively boring men to consider themselves wildly funny. They would come bobbing out of the

Sinclair shops in their veterans' ball caps and baggy cargo shorts *with suspenders*, see the covered wagon at the gas pumps, and then knock off a one-liner that they were convinced was hilarious.

"Hey, whad'y'a put into this baby, hunh? Regular or High-Test? Ha, ha, ha, ha! Doris, did you hear what I just said? Regular or High-Test! Aren't I funny? What a gas!"

One afternoon, outside Seneca, Kansas, another one of these himbos strolled toward us across the Sinclair ramp. His humor was more highly refined than your average RVer. Any mere reference to High-Test or Regular was too hackneyed for him.

"Hey, how many pounds per square inch do you pump into them tires, hunh? Ha, ha, ha, ha! PSI thirty-five or thirty-six? Ha, ha, ha, ha!"

As the man walked by toward his green RV, Beck followed him with her eyes, turning her ears slightly in his direction. Then she abruptly spread her rear legs, squatted down with her rump, and let off a riverine piss that splashed onto the pavement. The bladder capacity of these big draft mules is legendary, and Beck is clearly a best of breed. Her Nile of urine ran downhill and formed a shiny yellow moat around the man's Winnebago Adventurer.

As he tiptoed in his Naugahyde sandals through the urine pool, the man craned his head backward and yelled.

"Hey! Hey! This is . . . That mule of yours . . . That's public urination!"

Nick was up on the wagon seat, sharing some fried chicken with Olive Oyl. His Fu Manchu dropped and he looked over, expressionless, at the fatboy standing in the urine pool.

"Thanks for the information, bubba," Nick said. "But don't blame my mule, okay? We trained her to do that."

The man stepped inside his Winnebago, angrily slamming the door with a metallic bang. Through the tinted windows of the RV we watched him delicately remove his sandals with his fingertips, and then wash them in the RV sink and drop them into the dish strainer. Then he plunked himself down into his pilot's seat, the Winnebago muffler roared with life, and the RV departed the Sinclair, its rear dual tires leaving sparkling tread marks of mule urine on the highway.

After that, for the rest of Kansas, we diverted north or south of the Pony Express Highway whenever we could and stayed on the parallel dirt section roads. Modern covered wagon travel requires a strict policy of Winnebago avoidance. Waste is the eternal American by-product, and along today's Oregon Trail, RVs have replaced the dead mules and discarded bedposts.

As we entered the Big Blue River country and slowly crossed the attractive farmland around Axtell, Beattie, and Home, Kansas, I was delighted by one aspect of the trip. The May wildflowers of Kansas, growing in the depressions of the tall prairie grass country, are rapturously beautiful. On either side of the wagon there was a profusion of prairie flox, purple vervains, and riotously yellow coreopsis, an ocean of petals and tall grass stems extending to the tree lines. In a covered wagon it takes so long to cross this garden on the plains, and the fragrances are so abundant, that all of life and its possibilities seemed arrayed forever, sky to sky, Flint Hill to Flint Hill. The kaleidoscope of naturally lit color going past the wagon seat was almost exhausting, too visually rich.

The surprising wealth of wildflowers on the plains was something the pioneers noticed, and wildflowers played an important role in forming a national consciousness about the desirability of settling the near West. The rich native growth this close to the Missouri River suggested fertile soil and spring rains—land that eventually could be tilled. For now, the pioneers were passing through this country to reach the Shangri-la of Oregon. By the late 1850s, however, the frequent references to wildflowers in pioneer journals had convinced many American farmers that land in eastern Kansas and Nebraska could be settled and tilled. I also enjoyed the description of wildflowers in the journals because it showed that, despite the hardships of their crossing, the pioneers were capable of pausing to admire the abundant natural beauty they passed.

On May 14, 1852, Abigail Jane Scott had reached a point on the plains about sixty miles from the Big Blue, and had camped the night before within sight of forty other wagons.

> The country as we pass along, looks more and more level; and the *plains* certainly wear a charm which I little expected to see. . . . We roll along, level roads for the most of the time, and those who are walking, or on horseback by going off the main road a little can see a sight

which looks fit for angels to admire; The little hollows which at a short distance from the road we can see at almost any time are generally filled with flowers and variegated with ten thousand tints which are almost sufficient to perfectly enchant the mind of every lover of nature.

But within two days, as she approached the Big Blue, Abigail discovered another side of Kansas. "The cold wind blows very hard and very disagreeably, and the atmosphere is cold enough for a drear November morning." The winds didn't abate for two more days and Abigail was clearly quite miserable.

The brisk and incessant prairie winds of Kansas and Nebraska were one of the most persistent obstacles to travel that the pioneers complained about in their journals. Men chased their hats a quarter of a mile down through the hollows and couldn't catch them. Mules spooked at blowing dust and tumbleweed, raw meat was eaten for dinner because fires couldn't be lit, and wagon covers and tents blew away in the middle of the night. The wind exhausted children and turned them into crying brats. "The wind blew so hard I could not get out of the wagon for fear of being blown away," wrote pioneer Martha Moore, a member of a particularly enterprising family that drove five thousand sheep across the trail in 1852, to sell at the trading posts. "The wind so rocked the wagons [at night] that in vain I wooed the goddess Sleep."

For Nick and me, mornings spent pleasantly driving the mules through attractive farmlands and the long wildflower patches merged into afternoons with leaden skies, temperatures in the forties, and winds so brisk that there was no way to stay warm. We huddled together on the wagon seat with blankets spread across our laps and Olive Oyl wedged between our legs. Our hats blew off and had to be restrained with chin straps we made from shoelaces and rawhide strips, and there were gusts that shook the canvas top of the wagon so hard we were afraid that the bows would crack.

The constant battering by the wind had a curious, counterintuitive effect on me. I found myself even more stubborn and self-confident than before, and very dreamy and romantic. I had never realized before just how tiring and dehydrating long exposure to the wind can be, but this made me feel closer to nature. In modern life we move from one insulated igloo to another—air-conditioned buildings, plush cars, glut-tonously overbuilt homes—serially abstracting ourselves from nature and its impacts. But now I had to get somewhere in a more primitive form of transportation, a covered wagon, that instead of protecting me immersed me in the elements.

There were other miseries of the trail. Five days would go by when neither Nick nor I took a shower, and a filmy residue of dust, axle grease, mule hair, and hayseeds covered everything in the wagon, including the plates we ate on every night. Coleman lanterns and flashlights, jostled by the constant bumping of the wagon, refused to work, so we started just living sunup to sundown, without any artificial light. Before harnessing, we had to chase mules every morning. Our backs ached from sitting on a hard wooden seat for eight or ten hours every day, holding back mules.

But we adored the simplicity of life out there and pushing hard every day toward our twenty-mile goal. The fragrances of the wildflower fields sedated me and, when my brother called the mules, I felt that I was living a stanza of Walt Whitman.

9

THE NINETEENTH-CENTURY PIONEERS CROSSING THE Big Blue
River country in Kansas to the lower Platte in Nebraska faced a gauntlet
of topography and weather unlike anything most of them had ever seen.
The wagon trains generally left the Missouri jumping-off grounds no
later than mid-May. By then the spring rains had turned the prairie into
a natural if unevenly green pasture, providing critical forage for the draft
animals during the first few weeks of travel. But this schedule exposed
the overlanders and their vulnerable white-tops to a collateral problem—
the notoriously violent thunderstorms that rattled down the Platte and the
Big Blue in late May and June. Humorist Alonzo Delano, a 49er, called the
Nebraska storms "King Lear in the height of his madness," and in 1851
pioneer Daniel Bacon wrote home to his mother, "You may think it rains
in Indiana but if you want to see it storm come to the Platte."

Nick and I found this treacherous reality impossible to avoid as we
pushed on for Marysville. That spring was one of the wettest on record for
eastern Kansas and Nebraska, and there were several days during which
more than two inches of rain fell in twenty-four hours, raising the Big Blue
and Little Blue rivers to flood stage. The situation was the same throughout the West. The winter before, record storms in the western mountains
had laid down a Himalayan snowpack, and this was emptying millions of

acre-feet of spring melt into the Platte River reservoirs, which could not contain the flow. From Grand Island, Nebraska, to Casper, Wyoming, the Platte was cresting over bridges and paved roads, turning campgrounds and crop fields into vast inland lakes. Along our riverine Oregon Trail route—the Platte, the Sweetwater, the Bear, and the Snake—we would not see a river at less than full stage all summer.

On our fourth day out, just west of Axtell, Kansas, a monster downpour that lasted for two hours dropped from the angry, black clouds festering to the west. When I could see the leaves of the trees a half mile ahead flattened by the rain, I pulled up the wagon, handed the lines to Nick, and stood up on the seat to pull the front of the canvas cover over our heads. But the wagon top wouldn't stay down in the stiff breeze pushing ahead of the rain and I jumped off to pull the pucker ropes tight. I was drenched by the time I got back into the wagon and within minutes everything on our rig—the mules, the sides of the wagon, our faces and jackets—was splattered with a pudding of wet, sandy mud. Pummeled by the heavy rain, we couldn't see far enough ahead of the wagon to navigate very well and we were almost on top of an inundated bridge at Wolf Creek before we realized the hazard, which forced us to divert two miles north on muddy roads to find a route west.

The experience was claustrophobic. With the canvas top pulled tight over our heads, our field of vision ahead was restricted to about sixty degrees—just the mules and what was directly ahead of them. Our hats bumped up against the canvas, and the woolen blanket spread over our laps was saturated with rain. The rain lashed sideways under the wagon cover, freezing our faces and our hands. The strong quartering winds from the northwest buffeted the wagon top and box, almost nautically rocking us back and forth against the running gear. Beside us, the plains disappeared and now we were sailors experiencing the narrow aperture of storm—punishing rain and wind, rigging struggling against the elements, the fear that we would be overturned by the next gale-force blast. As we slogged through the mud past Beattie and Home, Kansas, I could feel my socks and the skin of my feet congealing together, a pulpy, putrid mass that disintegrated against the leather inside my boots. I wouldn't feel dry again for two days.

•   •   •

For the pioneers, water—how to avoid it when it was too abundant, and how to find it when it was scarce—was the great destroyer-preserver on the trail. The prairie monsoons in the Kansas-Nebraska junction country were only the beginning of the problem. Waterways like the Kansas and the Big Blue rivers were relatively stable, with defined channels and high, established banks, and they ebbed and flowed predictably with the rains. But the Platte just to the north was both a hydrologic wonder and a true monster—serene and enticingly fordable one hour, and then a raging, turbulent killer an hour or two later. The largest land migration in history took place along seven hundred miles of a river valley that was one of the most capricious travel environments in the world.

With its two tributaries, the North and South Platte rivers, the Platte River network runs more than a thousand miles from its headwaters along the east face of the Rockies in central Wyoming and Colorado. For most of its course through Colorado and Wyoming, the Platte is a relatively predictable river. After a heavy winter, the river rages bank to bank as it accepts the snowmelt from eleven-thousand-foot peaks, or peaceably runs over exposed river rock after a mild snowfall year. But by the time it loops southeast to the plains of western Nebraska, the Platte spills wide across flat bottomlands, expanding and contracting according to the delayed impact of snowmelt and rains hundreds of miles away. This created a drainage with an indefinite main channel and several continually shifting, parallel streams, more a delta of water than a river, a formation called a "braided stream" or "braided flow."

Braided flow rivers like the Platte distribute silt deposits across a broad area, creating a diverse riparian landscape—wooded islands toward the center of the channel, sandbars, river rock flats, and abrupt pothole depressions. The resulting variegation is scenic but deadly. Eddying currents form whirlpools as the water races past islands and sandbars, and the flow is destabilized by running past so many contrasting surfaces and shapes. The Platte is famous for its lovely sandbars, but these are deceptive. The subterranean water flow can often rise unseen to just a foot or two below the surface, undermining the apparently dry sand above and converting it into a porridge of quicksand that can swallow a man or a draft animal in less than a minute.

Except during particularly intense high-water years, this hazardous environment is mostly forgotten today. In the twentieth century, the Platte was dammed in eight separate spots for large hydroelectric, irrigation, and water-containment projects, shrinking its drainage area and diminishing the old braided stream character of the river. But in the nineteenth century, the Platte and its adjacent mudflats were often a mile or more across. This required not so much a single fording of the river but what wagon masters had to organize as a staged fording, with the wagons and teams first crossing deep pools in the channel, then sandbars and low valleys of river rock. Chaos was often the norm as two or three wagon companies crowded down the banks to cross at once.

The impetuosity of the river was maddening. The wagon trains would stop to "noon" or camp overnight at popular riverside resting places like Elm Island or Plum Creek, and children frolicked and draft animals were watered at the river's edge. An hour later, snowmelt and rains that had gathered momentum the day before, hundreds of miles away, would flow around the bend and flood the wagon camp. The sudden surges of water could happen while a forty-wagon train was in the middle of fording the river, or become a silent menace when the water unexpectedly rose at night. Frequently, heavy local rains combined with snowmelt from the Rockies to expand the river drainage so dramatically that the Platte wasn't really a river any longer but instead a series of interconnected lakes. The wagon companies had to wait for days before the water dropped to fordable levels.

Margaret Frink, the Indiana pioneer woman who crossed to California in 1850, was a kind of iterated Narcissa Whitman. Unusually for a woman in a covered wagon train, Frink rode sidesaddle all the way across the country, and later attracted attention for her spirited and detailed published diary, *Journal of the Adventures of a Party of California Gold Seekers*. She must have struck quite a figure, galloping sidesaddle across the prairie and then plunging into the rivers, and the Sioux along the Platte so marveled at her appearance that they called her the "white squaw." Frink witnessed a variety of river crossings—by commercial ferry across the Missouri, by ropes lowering the wagons down the steep banks of the Green River in Wyoming, and traditional fords along the Platte.

Here is her description of crossing the South Platte at "The Forks," near present-day North Platte, Nebraska, where the North and South Platte curving in from the Rockies join to form a single, wide channel.

> The stream we had now reached was fearful to look at, rushing and boiling and yellow with mud, a mile wide, and in many places of unknown depth. The bed was of quicksand—this was the worst difficulty. But there was no way to do but to ford it. . . .
>
> Of all the excitement that I ever experienced or thought of, the crossing of that river was the greatest. A great many other wagons and people were crossing at the same time—mule teams, horse teams, ox teams, men on horseback, men wading and struggling against the quicksand and current, many of them with long poles in their hands, feeling their way. Sometimes they would be in shallow water only up to their knees; then, all at once, some unlucky one would plunge in where it was three or four feet deep.
>
> The deafening noise and halloing that this army of people kept up, made the alarm in the river more intense. The quicksand and the uncertainty of depth of water kept all in a state of anxiety. Our horses would sometimes be in water no more than a foot deep; then, in a moment they would go down up to their collars. On one occasion I was considerably alarmed. Several other wagons, in their haste, had crowded in ahead of us on both sides, and we were compelled to stop for several minutes. Our wagon at once began to settle in the quicksand, and it required the assistance of three or four men lifting at the wheels to enable the horses to pull out.
>
> Where we crossed, the river was a mile wide, and we were just three-quarters of an hour in getting over. I here date one of the happiest and most thankful moments of my life to have been when we landed safe on the north side. The danger in the crossing consisted of the continual shifting of the sandy bed, so that a safe ford to-day might be a dangerous one to-morrow.

Frink was not overestimating the danger. That year, at least ninety people drowned in the rivers along the trail, forty of them in the Platte. In his monumental *The Plains Across*, historian John D. Unruh Jr.

meticulously toted up trail deaths by category. He concluded that at least three hundred pioneers drowned in the 1840s and 1850s, and he points out that almost every overland diary records drownings or near misses along the rivers. The victims were not just impatient pioneers, attempting an unsafe crossing when the fords ahead of them were jammed with other wagons, or mounted riders pushing cattle across the raging rivers for better grass. "One inebriated 1853 emigrant," Unruh writes, "misjudged rain-swollen Buffalo Creek for a slough, drove his wagon in, and was never seen again."

As we moved west with the wagon through northeastern Kansas, word started to circulate about our progress via an informal cell phone and internet grapevine. The old St. Joe Road between Seneca and Beattie was mostly rural, but between the towns there were occasional clusters of housing developments built along the agricultural frontage. The modest ranch and colonial houses were well kept and their driveways and yards contained the usual totems of American contentment—vinyl gazebos facing the open plains, boats on trailers, piles of children's bikes left by the corner of the garage.

Everyone loves the sight of a covered wagon going by and, in Kansas, you can see the traffic coming from miles away. Often, as we approached the next group of houses, children and their parents had gathered near the mailboxes out on the road, with wheelbarrows and little red wagons filled with water buckets, apples, and carrots for the mules. There were bottles of Gatorade and ham-salad sandwiches for us. Families who saw us coming from a distance hopped into their minivans and drove into the supermarket in town for bags of apples for the mules.

I began to notice something interesting about the families. At several homes, the parents, or the people who appeared to be the parents, weren't the right age. They were in their late fifties or early sixties, sometimes even older, and the children called them "Mom-Mom" or "Pappy." There seemed to be a lot of grandparents caring for their grandchildren out here in Kansas.

I was so curious that I asked one of the grandparents about it. The family lived in a pleasant green Cape-style house with a matching green garage and a white picket fence around the front lawn, about two miles outside Marysville. When we stopped the wagon near the end of the driveway, Nick stepped down to stand at the front of the team and show the children how to snack mules by holding an apple upright in the palm of their hands. The man of the house, who I guessed was in his mid-sixties, was wearing a white T-shirt, Dickies khakis, and fashionable Keen shoes. He had stepped back by the wagon seat to ask me about our trip.

When I asked him if the kids at the front of the wagon were his grandchildren, he smiled patiently and seemed eager to talk about it.

"Right, they're our grandchildren," he said. "You're going to see a lot of families like ours out here, and anywhere in the Midwest. It's meth. Meth and the recession."

The man explained that his son, who was now almost thirty, had not wanted to go to college or join the military when he finished high school. He knew that he wanted to work with his hands and dreamed of eventually owning his own welding shop. So he took a six-month welding course at the local community college, then worked in a muffler shop for a year until he found a better job at a factory outside St. Joseph that fabricated pickup trailers. But he was furloughed after three years when orders for the trailers dried up, mostly due to the national recession after 2008.

Meanwhile, an epidemic of methamphetamine abuse—the underground drug is made from a mixture of acidic chemicals and over-the-counter pharmaceuticals—had swept the country, hitting particularly hard in small towns and rural communities in the Midwest. Meth dealers and what to do about them is a big problem from Indiana to Arizona. The dealers prey particularly hard in high schools and community colleges.

"We had always known he did a little meth," the man said. "But he was basically a good kid. He had a decent job, a live-in girlfriend, he went water-skiing on weekends with his friends. But after he lost his job he started dealing in meth. It broke our hearts."

After his son and his girlfriend had two children, their lives spun out of control, and the man and his wife went to court to obtain custody of their grandchildren. The son was now in a long-term treatment facility run by the state of Kansas, and the family had not seen his former girlfriend, the mother of the children they were now raising, for more than two years.

"It completely changed our lives, but we're actually real happy to be raising children again," the man said.

The man decided against retiring from his job as a supervisor at a local sewage treatment plant, but his wife, a schoolteacher, retired early, despite losing a few hundred dollars a month in pension payments. She had worked all through the childhood of her own kids, regretted it, and wanted someone home every day when her grandchildren returned on the school bus.

I saw this later in the towns of central Nebraska and all through Wyoming and Idaho. On Sunday mornings, the cafés of towns like North Platte, Nebraska, and Douglas, Wyoming, were full of grandparents who take their grandchildren out for pancake breakfasts. The grandparents are raising the children because the biological parents have skipped off—for whatever reason, not always meth. The demands of the wars in Iraq and Afghanistan have often meant that both parents in a military family get deployed at once, and they leave their children with their grandparents. Layoffs of single working mothers lead a lot of families to decide to become multigenerational again. A wave of bipolar disorders and addiction to video games and gambling has also taken a toll on families.

Later, when I researched the subject, I was surprised to learn that what I saw from my covered wagon was confirmed by census data—a demographic change so dramatic that the U.S. Census Bureau highlighted it in its 2010 population reports. Today, roughly seven million American children live in households that include their grandparents. Almost half of these children are being raised primarily by their grandparents, a 16 percent increase over the numbers for the 2000 census. That's a huge statistical spike for such a small subset of families. In many western states now, efforts are under way to change the laws affecting health care, so that grandchildren can qualify for their grandparents' medical plans. There are large, active support groups in many western towns for grandparents raising their grandchildren, and the churches have also jumped right in, scheduling evening play groups and extended hours for Sunday schools that allow grandparents to spend time alone at home or go out for dinner with their friends while the kids are cared for at church.

Before we rumbled off in the wagon, the grandfather beside the road near Marysville said one other thing that I would hear again and again from his peers in the West.

"I wish every couple had a chance to do this," he said. "You do a lot better job raising grandkids than you did with your kids, and we're too busy to be lonely. I'm volunteering as a Little League coach next year."

Children, of course, rarely yearn to stand at the end of their drives offering buckets of water and bags of apples to passing traffic, and I never would have seen this from a speeding car. I began to think of my Peter Schuttler as a plodding social observatory, and the contradiction of being able to see the modern world more clearly from the vantage of a nineteenth-century wagon appealed to me. Seeing America slowly was, in a way, like eating slow food—I wasn't covering much ground in a single day, but I was digesting a lot more.

At Marysville, Kansas, I decided to stop for an extra day to rest the mules and see the Oregon Trail sites, which had always been my plan. A mile or two outside town, the skies cleared and we decided to stop at a veterinary supply store to buy some gall ointment and food supplements for the mules, and I also needed to find hay. While I went inside, Nick held the mules from the wagon seat, talking to some tourists who wanted to take pictures of the wagon and the team.

Northeast Kansas is big horse country, and the thirtyish woman behind the counter inside was dressed in a western shirt, blue jeans, and lace-up packer's boots. She was a rodeo performer and told me that she barrel-raced and competed at dressage meets out as far as western Nebraska and Wyoming. She was very knowledgeable and helpful and wanted to know where we were headed with the wagon and team.

"All the way," I said. "We're hoping that we can make Oregon."

"Oh, God, I would kill to do what you're doing," she said. "Kill. Okay, so where are you sleeping tonight? Where's your camp?"

I told her that we were planning on crossing the Big Blue River, and then finding a farm nearby to rest the mules for a day. We could either walk or hitch rides into Marysville.

"No," she said. "Go to the corrals right here. Just take a right at the Hardee's. You'll see the ball field, the public park, and the rodeo grounds.

There's water there, a big corral for the mules, and you'll be right in town. Just roll the wagon right in there and enjoy yourselves."

"Nobody cares?"

"Nobody cares. Look, those corrals are for *you*. Every town in this country out here has public campgrounds and corrals. It'll be that way all the way out to Wyoming. When we go barrel racing? We camp at the corrals. Just hit the public corrals every night."

When I asked about hay for the mules, she pulled out her cell phone and called her boyfriend, a local rancher, talked for a few minutes, and then told me that a stack of 30 percent alfalfa hay would be waiting for us at the public corrals.

"Should I pay you for the hay?" I said. "I might miss him."

"You're not paying anybody for that hay," she said. "And I'm giving you the ranch discount on what you're buying here. Everybody is going to be so into this, all the way out. Your biggest problem is going to be dealing with all of the people who want to help you."

We enjoyed Marysville and had a great camp there. At the public corrals, we pulled the wagon out of the wind in a depression below a large barn, ran our hose down from the water hydrant, and washed the mules. They kicked up their heels and galloped off when we turned them lose in the corrals, happy just to be wild equines again.

Everybody in town, grandparents with their grandchildren, policemen on their patrols, a group of German tourists, came to visit us in camp, and Nick entertained these visitors by showing how Olive Oyl could retrieve a stick from the top of a pickup cab. Sitting on our camp chairs down off left field at the baseball diamond, we watched some of the best softball I've ever seen—ladies' fast-pitch, Marysville versus Riley County. (In the fourth inning, the Marysville shortstop caught an impossible pop fly behind third and whipped it to the third baseman, who tagged the runner and then whipped it to second for another tag, an astonishing triple-play.) When we turned up for the wagon to cook dinner, I discovered that the constant jostling of the axles had broken the gas line on our cookstove, so I walked a mile up to the Wal-Mart to buy a new one.

On the way back, while I was walking along the highway with a new Coleman stove under my arm, a pickup stopped on the shoulder beside me. The driver was a fun-looking, studmuffin cowboy, and his girlfriend, also wearing a cowboy hat, sat close to him in the middle seat. They rolled down the window, offered me a ride back to camp, and then ran home for steaks and beer to join us for dinner. There was a beautiful sunset that night in Marysville, with a low deck of cottony cumulus, lit blue and yellow by the falling sun, and we sat up until after dark talking, enjoying ourselves, and going over the maps of the routes we would follow into Nebraska.

By our second night in Marysville, everyone in town seemed to know that a covered wagon was parked at the rodeo corrals. The young couples and the grandparents brought their children down and, while Nick and I showed the mules and the wagon to the adults, the children chased around the ball field with Olive Oyl, throwing her sticks, squealing with delight when she made fox leaps out of the tall prairie grasses to catch bugs, and sitting around in a circle and coaxing her onto her back so they could scratch her belly.

Nick was convinced that the children had come into our camp to learn about covered wagons and the Oregon Trail. After he had exhausted all of the adults with his grand blarney about wheel hubs and draft teams, he called all of the children over and sat them down for a lecture too. This is the wagon tongue, this is a whippletree, and, children, let me show you how the braking system works. The kids fidgeted a lot and looked anxiously back toward their parents. But Nick has no summary function. He palavered on to the kids for another ten minutes about cast-iron skeins and oak wheels.

When he was finally done, Nick grandiloquently held out his arms and smiled at the children.

"Okay, kids. Do you have any questions about the wagon or the Oregon Trail?"

A bright young girl in a pink tank top raised her hand.

"Yes, honey," Nick said. "What would you like to know about the wagon?"

"Can we play with Olive Oyl now?"

Everyone laughed and the kids chased down to the ball field with Olive Oyl. Nick shrugged and turned for the corrals to feed and water the mules while I stepped up to the wagon to cook dinner.

"See, what did I tell you?" Nick said. "It would have been a mistake, big-time, to come out here without that dog."

We loved the gypsy life in Kansas. After dinner, we sat on our camp chairs facing the corrals, watching the sun fall over the junction country. At the fairgrounds above the wagon, Nick had found a corner in the sheep barn filled with fresh straw, and slept there. As I dozed off in the wagon, the distant barking of dogs, teenagers squealing off from the Hardee's in their pickups, and the Union Pacific trains rumbling through bathed me in the familiar night sounds of a midwestern town. I was excited about the next day, when we would cross an important milestone along the trail, the Big Blue River just west of town.

10

IN THE MORNING, LIGHT RAIN fell through low clouds, obscuring the new concrete bridge that gracefully arches skyward over the old pioneer ford at Marshall's Ferry. Descending the hill in Marysville for the bridge, we passed St. Gregory's Roman Catholic School, where the students knew that we were coming. Smiling, attractive Anglo and Mexican faces filled the windows, and the children were pumping their hands over their heads to urge us on. A few of them were waving small American flags and one boy held up a sign that he had handwritten on a piece of school paper. JESUS LOVES MULES.

I was cautious about and even afraid of making our first crossing of the trip over a tall bridge, especially with a team of mules that we really didn't know well yet. Bridges are notorious runaway zones for teams. A mule or a horse can get a third of the way across a bridge, look sideways and realize that it is suspended high over water, panic, and then bolt from side to side in an attempt to escape, overturning the wagon or crashing into oncoming cars. The covered bridges of the nineteenth century, which prevented horses from seeing out the side, solved this problem, but modern open-air spans can grip them with agoraphobic terror. I've nearly lost a horse several times crossing long bridges and, once, I dragged my wheel hubs all the way down the side of a school bus.

My dread of taking horses across bridges is an echo from the nineteenth century that was embedded early in life. On our 1958 covered wagon trip, during our fifth or sixth day out, we were approaching the old rickety span that crossed the Delaware River between Lambertville, New Jersey, and New Hope, Pennsylvania. With traffic behind us, my father trotted our team, Benny and Betty, up the inclined approach to the bridge. When the horses saw the grated metal roadway of the bridge, through which they could see the water below, they balked and reared, lunging backward and sideways so that the wheels of the wagon banged against the metal stops on the wagon box.

My father was clearly overwhelmed by this sudden crisis at the bridge and, with a load of children in the wagon, worried, but he managed to calm the team and then called out to the motorists behind us to back their cars away from the bridge. By inching the team backward, then turning, he shoehorned the wagon off the bridge entrance and then, throwing home the brake, he drove us down an embankment near the bridge entrance to a safe patch of grass. My brother and I scrambled off the wagon and unhitched the team, tying them to the wheels.

My father walked back up the embankment to survey the bridge. I still remember the way he was silhouetted in the harsh sunlight against the bridge structure high above me and how, with a worried look, he pulled off his Amish straw hat and wiped his forehead with a red bandanna handkerchief taken from his back pocket. This was one of the few times that I remember feeling that this man whom I revered and trusted to guide me didn't know what to do. Maybe he couldn't protect us here.

When he came back down the embankment, my father wiped his forehead again with his bandanna and told us what he wanted to do.

With a length of rope, he said, he was going to lash the pole of the wagon to his shoulders and pull the rig across the bridge by hand. To the right of the automobile span there was a pedestrian walkway with flooring made from wooden planks. The horses would walk on that, he thought, and my brother and I would lead them one by one across the bridge. There was a short metal grating entrance to the walkway that would spook the horses at first. But my father said that my older brother would lead the more sensible and willing horse, Benny, by a long line, and I would be positioned next to the grating with the buggy whip. When Benny balked at the grating, I would surprise him from behind with a lash on his rump, and he would probably jump to the wooden planking, and the other horses would follow.

"Boys," my father told us, "when you get up on the walkway, if the horses start to fuss or run away, just let them go. Let them go. When a horse is afraid it just wants to be free to take care of themselves. So just let them go if they rear and balk."

"Dad," I said. "That's crazy. They'll run away and we'll never catch them."

"Just listen to me," my father said. "Let them go. A horse will never go far. Once they're past what they're afraid of, they stop. Get the team and Texas onto the planks and then let them go if you have to. We'll catch them on the other side."

I felt queasy and uncertain inside because I didn't think my father was right, and I wasn't comfortable following the directions of someone who was making things up as we went along. I was suddenly filled with doubt about this trip. Why were we traveling by covered wagon if we didn't know what we were doing? My father should have known about this bridge. The whole trip was a bad idea.

Up near the bridge, while my brother led Benny to the walkway, I stood back with the buggy whip hidden behind my back, holding the other horse, Betty, with a line. When Benny balked at the metal grating, I surprised him from behind with a good crack on the ass and he vaulted to the wooden planking, galloping a few strides before he calmed down, but my brother ran several strides ahead of him and then had no trouble leading him across. Betty had been teamed with Benny for her entire life and didn't like being left behind, so she leaped over the metal grate too, pulling the lead line out of my hands. But my father had said just to let her go. So I followed on the wooden planking, leading our riding horse Texas, more or less herding Betty from behind.

It was an eerie, incongruous feeling, being suspended seventy or eighty feet above the Delaware River, herding horses across a narrow wooden walkway that seemed to stretch forever to the distant bank. I had crossed this bridge several times by car, but on foot I noticed things that I hadn't seen before. Up close, the steel structure of the bridge was unbelievably rusty and corroded, with large, scabrous flakes hanging out from the beams and blowing in the wind. On the river below us, teenage girls were laughing and screaming as they jumped off a houseboat to swim. I was frightened by the way the bridge shook and rattled underfoot every time a car passed.

It was a long walk to the other side of the river. I was gripped by a long, gray depression while my heart raced with panic attacks. I was often overwhelmed as a boy by feelings of anxiety, and by profound embarrassment about the kind of family that I came from, my fears made worse by my inability to share them with anyone else or even to comprehend what they meant. These pangs struck particularly hard when we all had to file into Mass together and then sit in front of the other families at Christ the King Church. I believed in God then, and didn't understand why He was being so unfair to me. God, why did you have to give me this crazy family? Why did you give me this crazy father? When I prayed, I begged God to suddenly and miraculously make my family normal.

On the Pennsylvania side, I was surprised by how many trees along the banks were emerging into my vision, and that we were above them. I looped and knotted Texas's reins around his neck, let him go free, and then stepped forward with my buggy whip to get Betty across the metal grating at the end of the wooden walkway. When she balked at the grating, I gripped the whip handle and reached high with both hands and swung down hard, like trying to hit a pitch for a home run, cracking her hard on the rump. When Betty jumped, I leaped right behind her across the grate and dived for the lead line attached to her bridle.

I just managed to grab the line and then quickly rolled over and held on for dear life, sitting down on the grass as Betty cantered downhill off the bridge embankment. That was my arrival in Pennsylvania. It was all one fluid motion: leap, grab the line, flip over to a sitting position, and then get hauled on my ass by a big draft mare for the Nantucket sleigh ride into New Hope. But I had her, and after she got to the bottom Betty stopped, walked over to a tall green patch, and began browsing on grass.

We still have a wonderful photograph of my father, in a simple denim work shirt with sweat laving off his face, pulling the wagon across the Lambertville–New Hope bridge as my younger brother Bryan contentedly sucked his thumb up on the wagon seat. By this time a state trooper

The image of my father pulling the wagon by hand across the Delaware still resonates more than fifty years later.

had arrived and held the traffic up behind the wagon. My father was tall and strong, six feet four inches with big, tabletop shoulders, so keeping the wagon moving after he got it started was not much for him. The iron wagon wheels bumped and sang across the metal grating, and my father wore the mien of a man struggling without complaint against a heavy load. I was so elated about getting the team and the wagon across that I forgot my embarrassment about my family, and of course I admired how strapping a man my father was. He could do all of these things despite his amputation, on a wooden left leg.

New Hope, a busy tourist town, was festive that day. The tourists and the residents poured out of the ice cream shops and antique stores and crowded around the covered wagon, asking us what we were doing. We carried some water and oats over for the team and then relaxed in town. My father bought us all ice cream cones and we sat on benches in a small, shaded park that overlooked the river and watched the motorboats race by. It was pleasant to be out of the sun and we all felt a sense of accomplishment about getting our rig across the Delaware River.

We camped that night in a park built beside the old towpath of the Delaware Canal. In camp, I loved to rest in the evening the way that I had seen Ward Bond and his trail hands do it on *Wagon Train*. They would make a semicircle of saddles around the campfire, put their saddle blankets on top of the saddles, and then recline with their heads on the saddles, with pieces of straw clasped in their teeth. That's how I did it. With our campfire burning, I was resting against my saddle staring at the flames when my father walked over with his camp stool, sat beside me, and squeezed my knee.

"Hey, you and your brother did a good job with the team today, son. You were a big help getting across the river."

"Dad. I didn't do anything. I let the horses go."

"Nope. I saw you from the bridge. Betty dragged you all the way down the hill."

"Big deal, Dad. I didn't do anything. First I let the horses go, and then Betty dragged me down the hill."

"All right, son. You're not listening to me, but it's okay."

"Dad. I'm listening. You keep saying that I'm not listening, but I'm listening."

My father lit his pipe and blew out a smoke ring. He stared at the flames of the campfire for a while.

"Okay, son. All I am saying is that sometimes you're doing quite a lot by not doing anything. You're not quitting. You just keep going. That's the pioneer spirit."

The idea that I could be doing quite a lot by not doing anything at all, just by not quitting, was quite beyond me at the time, but I did feel that night that I had the pioneer spirit. With the embers of the fire glowing at my feet, I dozed off with my head resting on my saddle. My father let me sleep there all night and I woke in the morning draped in the blanket he had placed over me before he went to bed.

I was momentarily relieved when we got to the bridge over the Big Blue. The mules looked ahead on the road, saw the uphill climb to the span, and pushed their ears forward. They bowed into their collars with determination to pull hard for the incline. Jake had this enormously attractive habit of skipping a stride, swinging his head from side to side, and then bending low for the work ahead. The mules didn't seem to mind the river. Still, I kept my lines gathered in case we had trouble.

"These mules have been over water before," I said to Nick. "They seem fine with the bridge."

"It looks that way," he said. "We'll see."

As we climbed the bridge a wide black line of heavy metal, bisecting the pavement, began to emerge in front of us. Beck threw her ears forward, turned her head sideways to look at the ominous black line, and then began pulling hard on her bit, trotting sideways and then even cantering in her harness, kicking with her rear legs. She was spooking the other two mules, who began to fuss and try to break away too. It's the herd instinct in mules. One mule running and starting to break away is very dangerous because the other members of the team don't want to be left behind. I held back the mules as hard as I could, but they were threatening now to run away.

"Oh, fuck," Nick said. "That's an expansion joint. The mules don't like that."

It was the runaway approach. Beck was kicking up an enormous fuss now, frothing at the mouth and jumping sideways, trying to break into a gallop by launching off her hind legs. Bute, who would imitate anything Beck was doing, started to fuss too. We were about to lose the team. Nick is a much better driver than me, and much stronger, and I gave the lines to him and reached over with both hands for the brake.

"Hold them back, Nick!" I said. "But we can't turn around. We have to get them over the joint."

Expansion joints are intersecting sections of heavy-gauge steel, fitting like a huge zipper, that allow a bridge to flex with changes in humidity and heat, and to vibrate gently under the stress of heavy traffic. They are just the kind of heavy man-made shape, like manhole covers, that provoke the fiendish imagination of mules. There's a bogeyman there, crouching on the road, just waiting to leap up and bite you in the belly when you get close to it. Big, dark, man-made shapes. To a mule, they're the devil.

Beck and Bute were fussing terribly in their harness now, breaking into short gallops and pushing off their hind legs, dancing against the pole, wanting to run away but knowing that they wouldn't cross the expansion joint ahead. As we got closer they began to rear, leaping up and down off the concrete pavement.

Only Jake was being sensible. He pushed his ears forward and looked at the joint. Then he swayed his head from side to side with a grim expression. His body language said, "C'mon, girls. It's just another bogeyman out there. We're going to get to the joint and then we're going to jump it. Cut the crap."

We were at the joint now and Beck and Bute were panicked, rearing and refusing to cross. Desperate to escape the joint, they swayed violently sideways, pushing the pole from one side to the other, all the way to the wheel stops. I could feel the wagon tipping almost up on two wheels.

"Nick, it's Jake! Jake is key here. Jake will jump the joint. Jake! Jake! Jump the joint, Jake!"

"Get the whip, Boss," Nick yelled. "When I say so, give Beck a good crack on the ass."

It was madness now at the joint. The oncoming traffic from the other side of the bridge raced past us as the team shied into their lane. The driver of a white minivan *stopped* right beside us, rolled down her window, and began spooking the team even more by taking pictures with a strobe flash. More minivan morons came on after this. These drivers were crazy, pulling even closer to the team to get pictures, completely oblivious of the danger. It was a circus show for them, even as the mules spooked sideways and were now rearing just inches from their front fenders.

I had the whip in my hands but I knew that I wasn't going to lash Beck. We were about to lose the team and any moment now they were going to rear backward and bolt sideways, snapping the pole and over-turning the wagon. Fuck it, I thought, we'll rebuild the wagon somehow. We'll walk the mules across. It will be a mess up here. I knew that we'd have problems at bridges—it was a big dread hour fear. I had handled this all wrong.

Nick was expertly holding the team back and still calling for the mules to cross the joint, but Beck was crazy now, rearing, kicking her tug chains, frothing at the bit. But I knew that if I lashed her, this early in the trip, she would expect it every time and run away at every bridge.

Jake was swaying back and forth, ready to jump. The morons in their minivans kept stopping right beside the rearing team. But this was good, I realized. The line of idle cars on our left was herding the team from that side, and there were guardrails to the right. We might just gallop through this chute and get the mules stopped later. But, Christ, I would have to hold the right line for Nick. But how could I do that and manage the brake? We had only a second or two left before a runaway.

I held the whip high so the mules could see it and yelled to Jake.

"Jake! It's coming, Jake. I'll tap you and then you jump! Lead these mollies over the joint! Here it comes, Jake."

I reached down from the seat and tapped Jake gently but firmly on his right rump.

Oh, that was one great Andalusian spawn right there. Royal Gift left behind such dignity and strength. As soon as I tapped him on the rump Jake swung his head down, curled his massive neck, leaned back on his powerful rear legs, and crouched to jump.

Beck is crazy. Her psychology is fantastically neurotic. The bogeyman was waiting there under the joint to jump up and bite her, but there was no way, now that she saw Jake crouching to jump, that she would let him get ahead of her in harness. Now the second Andalusian was back on her rear legs too, rearing. Jake and Beck were bodies in unison, crouching, getting ready to vault.

The moment when Jake and Beck vaulted the joint together showed me why mules are now winning jumping competitions all over the country.

The power and athleticism of a big draft mule are extraordinary. Just before the mules jumped, Nick screamed at them in his booming voice—"Beck, you odd bugger, JUMP, you crazy mule!"—and then he released the lines and slapped the mules on the rear at just the right moment, when their rumps were way low and their front knees were bent, poised to jump. Whaboom, with little Bute in the middle yanked upward, just along for the ride, with a glorious rattle and bang of the harness chains and the pole, and all the whippletrees straining, we were airborne over the Big Blue River in Kansas and catapulting over the joint.

The touch-and-go that we made over the joint on the Marysville bridge lasted longer than I believed possible. For a second or two, I could see space between the front wheels and the concrete floor of the bridge.

The wagon landed with a loud bang on the other side of the joint, jolting us, and we both had to brace our legs against the footrest to stay on the seat. Nick managed the team adroitly after that, loosening the lines for a second or two so that Beck could race forward against her harness and release her need to flee, but then he pulled the mules back to an anxious walk, constantly releasing and then restraining the team with his strong, brawny arms.

We were in runaway deacceleration mode now, putting out the spoilers and reversing thrust to slow the big jet down on the runway. I slammed the brake home every time the mules threatened to gallop away, then released it when they slowed down again. The rear wheels skidded sideways on the wet concrete every time I applied the brake. This was a moment when Nick's supreme comfort in the face of danger, his calm during chaos, saved us. Build to a crisis, enjoy it. Each time Beck turned sideways and threatened to gallop, he pulled her in the other direction, to distract her attention from running away. He didn't yell at the mules—which would just spook them more. He merged his personality with theirs. His voice—calling them gently, but firmly—was their brain now.

At this moment, loving forgiveness of your mules and the ability to calm them were key. Nick worked at genius level on that.

"Oh, Big Team. Goooooood Team. Goooooood Team. It's all right,

Beck. Beck, it's all right. We just won the National Steeplechase, girls. You won the steeplechase, team. Jake, you're a pisser. You did well, Jake."

There were two more expansion joints on the bridge, and both times Beck and Bute reared again on their hind legs, refused to cross, and swayed sideways against the pole. Nick handled this by steering the team against the right guardrails on the bridge, with our wheel hubs just an inch or two from the heavy metal rails, which prevented Beck from jumping in that direction. He held his right line rock hard against Beck's bit, so that she had no leeway and could rear only straight ahead.

I got into Nick's head and tried to time my next move with his. Tap Jake's rump, and he led the team over the joint. It was all one choreographed moment. Mules, taxi into position and jump. We were gold medalists at jumping mules by the third joint.

As we trotted down the western portal of the bridge, Nick calmed the mules by calling them in a low voice, while I worked the brake in and out.

We stopped the mules below the bridge, after turning north along the Big Blue. My arms and stomach muscles were trembling and my chest was heaving in and out. I felt desperate for air.

"Rink, you handled that just right," Nick said. "It was a good idea not to whip Beck. I was wrong and you were right."

"Yeah, but I planned this poorly," I said. "I should have walked ahead and shown the mules that the joints were safe. That way, I could have stopped the traffic."

"Oh, see? That's so *you*, Rinker. We've just had a big success here, gettin across our first long bridge, but Rinker says he blew it. Why do you have to blame yourself like that?"

"Nick, I am not the horseman you are. I'm a standardbred driver."

"Boss, no," Nick said. "When we get to Oregon?"

"What?"

"You're not goin to believe how good you are at drivin team. I will make you better."

The sun occasionally came out as we headed north on the section roads and I was jubilant, late that afternoon, when we crossed the Nebraska line, in mixed scrub country and mowed fields a few miles below Steele City. By dead reckoning, and carefully consulting my geodetic maps, we managed to find two markers for the old Independence Road and then our first marker for the Oregon Trail. We were making what the pioneers called the Big Blue–Little Blue transit, up through a choke point on the trail called The Narrows. The Flint Hills were receding behind us.

"Trail Hand," I said, looking at my maps. "We've made one hundred twenty-five miles in five days."

Still, we were in Oregon Trail purgatory for the next several days. At Steele City, the same storm system that would level Joplin, Missouri, a few hours later passed directly over our heads, forcing us into an emergency camp in the equipment shed of an abandoned farm. The Little Blue reached flood stage over the local roads, and we had to remain in our soggy bivouac for an extra day, and then more rains forced us into a quick camp in Strang, Nebraska, where we lost our Coleman lantern and gave up on using any artificial light. At night, the local farmers would drive over to our camps, splashing through the puddles in their pickups. They begged us to stay at their places for a few days. This was the worst high-water year in a century, they told us, and all of the creek crossings would be flooded. Across southern Nebraska, there were roads closed all the way up past Aurora and Grand Island.

But I wanted to make more miles across what I was now calling the lake district of southern Nebraska. Several times, along a lovely stretch of rolling hills called the Little Sandy Creek country, we slid the wagon down a muddy hill to find, along the creek bottoms, a bridge that was flooded with almost two feet of rushing water, with no way to get the rig turned around on the narrow road. But by walking over the submerged bridge with my arms outstretched—my boots sank above the ankles in the mud and gravel, and the water splashed up past my knees—I was able to show the mules that crossing the swollen creeks was safe. Bute was the only mule who balked at the water. But by goading the much stronger Jake and Beck at the water's edge, we yanked her across.

We pushed on through several fords a day like that, and through a series of miserable, wet camps. At our squalid, swampy camp on the abandoned farm in Steele City, I cooked our meals on top of a John Deere rotary mower in the equipment shed, tenting myself with a blanket to keep the flies and the cinder dust off our food. At night, I could at least retreat outside to the wagon, but Nick and Olive Oyl were trapped inside the implement shed, coughing and heaving all night from the dust stirred up by the mules.

But there were compensations, at least for me. At Steele City, I spent my first night sleeping in the covered wagon during a thunderstorm, and it was surprisingly comfortable and warm in there. Purple bursts of light flashed through the wagon cover as lightning landed on the plains. The constant, rolling thunder nearby shook the ground, passing up through the wheels and gently rocking the wagon. The rain pounding hard on the canvas top sounded like a timpani drum, but I was always dry. I realized that the pioneers had fashioned an almost perfect roof design against the rain, with the semicircular top preventing the moisture from ever gaining purchase on a flat surface.

The Schuttler was an outdoor pavilion exposing me to the intensity of the storm but protecting me from its dangers. The views of the black clouds and lightning rolling over the prairie, and the rivulets of rain trickling down the canvas cover, filled me with contentment, a kind of melancholy loneliness of the plains. We were living so simply and haphazardly now, cobbling together an existence from what we carried in the wagon or could find on abandoned homesteads. It felt incomparably romantic to be there and I wanted this trip to last forever.

11

A BIG THUNDER CELL FINALLY landed right on top of us just east of Shickley, Nebraska. We were pushing northwest on paved roads out past Fairbury, trying to make our transit from the Little Blue to the Platte, surrounded by storms so violent that the mules were beginning to spook. Mules are actually quite comfortable in a storm, as long as they are left free in an open field or corral. Then they bunch together for protection, point their rumps toward the storm, and patiently wait out the weather while the rain pummels their backs. But when a storm arrives overhead, they are terrified of being restrained by harness and a wagon, because that deprives them of their feral ability to protect themselves. Now we were on the open plains, with thunderbolts fusing off purple and orange auras as they landed all around us, and a menacing black cloud swirling low directly ahead. At most, we had ten minutes to get the mules to shelter.

At an attractive farm ahead, we saw a woman chasing around her lawn on a riding mower, trying to get the last of her grass cut before the storm hit. Behind the tree line along the road I could see an extensive compound of barn roofs and grain bins. There would have to be a feedlot corral somewhere in there. With the mules jumping sideways and beginning to panic every time another lightning bolt landed, we ran the wagon up to the farm and I jumped off.

"Ah, ma'am, we need to get these mules unhitched before that cell lands on us. Can we use your corrals?"

The woman looked confused and uncertain and bit her lip. Her hair was blown up past her ears by the wind and she glanced hurriedly around, as if looking for help.

"Oh, I don't know. I wish my husband was here. He's still in the fields."

"Well, ma'am, if we could just get in there . . ."

"Oh, no! Did I just say that? I didn't mean it that way. Of course, go in, go in. I just don't know where he'd want you."

"Is there a corral?"

"All around the barns."

"Okay, we'll find one. I'm sorry, I can't talk. We have to rush."

"Rush. Go. My husband will be back after the storm hits."

I waved to Nick and then ran ahead of the wagon into the farmyard, found a corral, and decided that it would be best to run the team around a long gray barn on the left. There wasn't any time now. Lightning was touching down on the plains on three sides of us, and the wind had picked up so strongly it blew my hat off.

"Nick! Don't stop the wagon. Just get around the barn facing out. Quick! We *have* to be unhitched."

I hadn't checked the barn, but there wasn't any reason I would have thought of that. As soon as the mules approached the low pens on the ground floor, a grotesque roar of grunts, squeals, and the sound of dozens of feet sloshing through wet manure rose from the barn. Damn. Hogs. There must have been hundreds of them in there. The roar was deafening, and the mules immediately began to leap away from the sound, with Beck rearing in her harness and refusing to walk ahead, and then Bute rearing and acting out because that's what Beck was doing. Somehow, Nick got the team moving forward again and disappeared around the far end of the barn.

I will never forget the image of Nick and the wagon reemerging around the corner of the barn underneath the storm clouds. The mules were rearing away from the sound of the hogs on one side, and bolting sideways from the lightning on the other side. It was a complete spectacle of chaos.

Nick's display of horsemanship was extraordinary. Every time the team reared and balked he screamed at the mules above the wind to move forward again. Hogs, lightning. Hogs, lightning, with Nick in the middle lashed by the rain and wind, absolutely fearless and incapable of giving up, holding back a team that would have defeated almost any other driver.

When Nick finally got the team past the hog pens I knew what I had to do. Beck and Bute were still rearing and turning sideways against the pole and I was terrified about scrumming in there beside them, but I didn't have any choice. *Don't think. Just do it.* I splashed across the wet grass with an armful of lead chains and leaped up for Beck's bridle, managing to get her lead chain attached before I went for Bute.

Holding on to two rearing mules like that, I was just one of those jerky little lifeless marionettes in a Pinocchio show, suspended between the bridles of two leaping mules, bobbing up on one arm and off my feet when Beck reared, then yanked sideways again and up to the other side when Bute pulled high. Now I knew what it felt like to be a condemned man in medieval times who got quartered by horses. There was one spectral moment when a thunderclap boomed right on top of us and both mules reared together. I was launched high between Beck and Bute and reached my zenith over black mule ears just as a thunderbolt hit nearby, sparking off a purple spear of light on the misty plain.

It was just one madass dysfunction of rearing mules after that. The rain was pounding now. Nick managed to stumble off the wagon and with his pudgy, stiff hands rip the tug chains away. Fearlessly, he pushed up through the rearing team, grabbed a lead chain, and walked Jake over to the corrals, and then came back for Bute.

I was left alone with crazy Beck, pinned between the pole of the wagon and a rusty corral fence, holding on to her lead chain as she reared a few more times and her front shoes passed right by my face. I found I could almost bear the fear if I closed my eyes, and that is probably why I didn't sense Nick coming up from behind me to take Beck. Then I heard myself spontaneously calling out against the wind.

"Oh, God. I am never going to be able to do this alone. God, I can't do this alone."

Nick shouldered past me in the rain and grabbed Beck by the bridle, leading her off to the corrals.

I was humiliated by my admission of vulnerability in front of Nick, but there wasn't any time to dwell on my feelings now. I ran over behind Nick and Beck to help strip the harness off the mules. Once we had the harness off and the team safely behind the corral gate, the mules stood together near the center and turned their backs west into the storm, waiting placidly while the wind and the rain lashed their backs.

Nick and I stood in the rain with our arms resting on the iron corral railings, looking over to the mules. My shoulders were sore from holding back Beck and Bute, and the lead chains had turned my hands into cube steak. Underneath my shirt, the rain ran over my back, past my belt line, and down my legs into my boots.

I was upset with myself for my spontaneous wailing in the rain. I didn't want Nick to interpret what I said as an indirect request for him to abandon his plans to return to Maine and act in his play. We had discussed the problem a few times already and I had always reassured him that I would find a way to continue alone for the five weeks when he would be gone. But now my true worries had burst out in the most embarrassing way, and I felt guilty about that.

"Nick," I said. "I'm sorry for what I said back there. It just came out. I'm not trying to talk you into staying after North Platte."

For once, Nick didn't have a sarcastic reply. The rain had matted his graying hair against his ears and he just stared straight ahead at the mules.

At Shickley, Nick and I established our road ranch layover style. The couple who owned the farm, Don and Shirley Kempf, were exceptionally hospitable and excited to have a covered wagon running through Nebraska, and they were the beginning of a long run of happy Nebraskans who welcomed us onto their farms, fed us, gave us hay for the mules, and even drove us ahead on the trail to scout our routes. At the Kempfs', we took our first showers of the trip, pulled the wagon into their large implement shed for repairs, and even went off one night to their church supper. Nick, who bored too easily just sitting around with nothing to do, acted as a mechanical ambassador for the expedition, helping Don and his brother-in-law rebuild their field cultivator.

I am a master at self-deception, and at first I refused to use my time at Shickley torturing myself with worry about what I would do after Nick left me in North Platte. I didn't blame myself, either, for exposing us to a runaway by driving the team through storms. We were making impressive time across eastern Nebraska, and not stopping for bad weather was one of the reasons why. One advantage of having spent the prior winter reading pioneer journals was the knowledge that everything that had happened to us so far was predictable.

Perhaps the best account of the dangers of traveling in stormy weather with mules was written by Niles Searls, a 49er from Albany, New York, whose *Diary of a Pioneer* was a Gold Rush classic. Searls paid $200 to be carried to California with Turner and Allen's thirty-eight-wagon "Pioneer Line," a transportation experiment that drew an excited response when it was announced in St. Louis in the spring of 1849. The passengers would be spared the bother of buying their own wagons and draft teams, and instead would be carried to California in the six-passenger mule wagons of the commercial line, with all of their provisions and sleeping essentials provided as part of the fee.

Turner and Allen enticed gold seekers to their line with a beaut of a boast. They promised to deliver their passengers to the gold fields two thousand miles away in only sixty days—half the traveling time of a conventional covered wagon train. To live up to their advertising, Turner and Allen amassed a large herd of three hundred mules that would have to perform the considerable feat of traveling almost thirty-five miles per day. A gullible, pro-trail, pro-development western press helped promote the scheme. The *Daily Missouri Republican* pronounced the plan a "magnificent enterprise" and wrote approvingly of the elegant wagons and "the finest mules" that Turner and Allen would deploy. By May, more than 250 gold seekers had subscribed for the trip, and demand was so high that Turner and Allen planned a second wagon train later in the spring.

This was 1849, a year when the frenzy to reach California gold was so intense that all wisdom had percolated from the American brain. Speed in reaching northern California was everything, and Turner and Allen were actually pikers in that department. The craziest westering scheme of all was devised by a head case New Yorker named Rufus Porter, an inventor and balloon enthusiast who was the founder of *Scientific American* magazine. Like many Americans, Porter was swept up by the visionary possibilities of a mass crossing to plunder the gold fields of the Pacific West. Porter became convinced that giant balloons, powered by twin steam engines borrowed from a paddle-wheeler, could loft as many as two hundred Gold Rush miners to California at once.

The rush to reach the California gold fields created many crackpot schemes, like Rufus Porter's steam-powered dirigible "Air Ship to California."

Porter's aerial palace, complete with twenty-six windows, a long exhaust pipe for steam sticking out the rear, and a giant American flag fluttering over the rudders, was designed to ride beneath an immense cigar-shaped dirigible. The engineering was lunacy, but Porter's marketing was brilliant. He proposed dispensing entirely with the notorious jumping-off hassles along the Missouri River by launching his "aerial locomotive" from New York. The coast-to-coast trip, Porter's calculations showed, could be made in just three days—five days if the prevailing headwinds were particularly bad that week. Porter aggressively advertised his "Air Line to California" in eastern newspapers and magazines. Amazingly, over two hundred suckers paid a subscription price of $50, which included three-course meals and wine, for the inaugural balloon hop to the gold fields. That winter, a large crowd gathered in a Long Island cornfield to watch Porter test a model of his airship. But the craft never left the ground because the steam engines were far too heavy for the balloon.

The would-be Porter aeronauts, however, were the lucky ones—they never had to leave in the first place. The 125 paying passengers on the first Turner and Allen Pioneer Train were not so fortunate.

The Turner and Allen expedition of 1849 was the Edsel of wagon trains. Moses "Black" Harris, the mountain man hired to guide the thirty-eight wagons of the Pioneer Line across the ruts, died of cholera before the expedition left Independence. Many of the teamsters hired by Turner and Allen deserted along the Platte, forcing the passengers to drive the mules themselves, a difficult task considering that most of the mules were not "the finest" at all but wild and green, and few of the passengers had any experience beyond driving one-horse rigs in the city. At least twenty passengers died of disease, and violent free-for-alls for discarded provisions broke out when the overloaded wagons were progressively lightened at river crossings. A ton of cured meats was left at one campsite in Nebraska, fifty gallons of liquor were poured into a Wyoming stream, and the last of the coffee and sugar was depleted by Soda Springs in Idaho. Fleeing mules and wrecked wagons forced most of the "passengers" to walk the final seven hundred miles into California. The survivors of the Pioneer Line ended up reaching California after more than five months of suffering, and founders Turner and Allen barely escaped being lynched. In Oregon Trail lore, the term "Turner and Allen" became synonymous with disaster and advertising hype.

Most of the problems faced by Turner and Allen's train derived from a simple fact of life that I had just faced: mules and thunderstorms do not mix. Of the three hundred mules that the Pioneer Line departed with, only half were left by the time the train had emerged from the thunderstorm belt in central Nebraska. Most of them had run away, harness and all, during thunderstorms and hailstorms and vanished on the plains.

Niles Searls's published diary described the difficulties of introducing skittish green mules to the stormy springtime climate of Nebraska. After 1849, accounts like his would persuade many pioneers to choose the more plodding but less excitable oxen.

We have several times in this trip experienced heavy showers and once or twice have had hail. The rain fell in torrents accompanied by a whirlwind and hail the size of hickory nuts. Two of our carriages were overset by the gale and one of them crushed to atoms. Mules and loose stock were stampeded and ran for hours. Captain Turner, who was on horseback, was struck in the finger by a hailstone, which dislocated the joint. In the short space of ten minutes no less than three inches of hail and rain fell. Our only course was to turn our teams to the leeward and, in the language of the seaman, scud before the gale.

At Shickley, scudding before the gale seemed to have become our permanent challenge—we were delayed two days there by more storms rolling over the plains from the Rockies. I chided myself for being unrealistic in my planning and despaired that we would ever reach the Platte. Maybe living with this much uncertainty was beyond me. But what was most interesting about the trail experience so far was that it was also making me *more* unrealistic. The dream of pushing mules to Oregon still acted so powerfully on me that I could imagine any number of contingencies that would allow me to continue once Nick was gone. At North Platte, I would hire a cowboy to ride with me for a month and help handle the mules. I could carefully stage the team every night at corral fences, where the mules could be chained while I unhitched alone. I could find a ranch and hole up for a month, studying trail journals and ironing my shirts until Nick was back, even if this would delay our arrival in Oregon until October.

But speculations like these were just distractions that prevented me from facing a deeper problem. I hated asking Nick for help. This was still the big, unresolved legacy of my childhood and Catholic upbringing—an obdurate guilt complex about asking for what I needed, which only exposed me as vulnerable and weak. My father had drilled this into all of us, but especially the older boys. We were the ones who helped someone else and never asked for help ourselves, especially from a younger brother. When we drove into town to shop for food or visit the Sears, Roebuck store, if my father saw an old woman struggling across the green with her shopping bags, he hustled the boys out of the car to help her cross the street. We got bonus points if she was a nun, or blind. This was a huge pain in the ass because the Seeing Eye Foundation for blind people had headquarters nearby, and the hills around our place were dotted with convents for retired nuns. Every time we drove into town my brothers and I were jumping into an out of the car like circus clowns.

Never ask for help—provide it. Now I was on the dream journey of my life and surrounded every day with a surfeit of help. Receiving help, not providing it, made me feel guilty. I couldn't possibly ask one more favor of Nick.

And I certainly understood Nick's problem. He is ferociously loyal to friends and to his commitments, whether it's building a house or a long-standing promise to act in a play. If he stayed on the Oregon Trail with me, he would disappoint everyone who was counting on him for *Stones in His Pockets*.

Nothing is ever very private with Nick, and I could tell that he was mulling things over. Between the storms at Shickley he was spending a lot of time on his cell phone talking with friends back in Maine, his booming voice echoing over the soybean fields as he walked out to the edges of the barnyard. I heard just snippets of his conversations—"Well, Rinker, you know," or "North Platte." If I looked toward him, Nick pressed his finger deeper into his ear and walked farther out into the fields.

During our second afternoon at Shickley, I took a long, relaxing pickup ride out over the Nebraska plains to scout the trail ahead, while Nick spent a few hours in town. When I returned to the Kempf farm, Nick was sitting quietly near the wagon in the implement shed, changing the batteries in the hazard lights on the rear of the Trail Pup. When I stepped toward the back of the wagon for one of our camp chairs, I found a neat pile of my clothes—blue jeans, several shirts, my underwear and socks, all meticulously folded. I grabbed my travel bag from the wagon and placed the pile of clothes inside, amazed.

"Jesus, Nick. I can't believe this. You did my laundry."

"I found a laundromat in town. Does that surprise you?"

"Well, sure. You *folded* my shirts."

"You seem to forget that we have the same mother."

Clutching the hazard lights in one hand, Nick carried his chair over to the wagon to sit beside me. When he spoke, his voice was low, not his usual baritone foghorn, and he seemed very relaxed about something.

"Listen, I've made my decision," he said. "I'm not going back to Maine. I'm going to stay with you for the whole trail."

I was too grateful and flabbergasted to respond right away.

"But, Nick, what about your play?"

"Don't worry about my play. I talked to all of my theater friends about it. They all agree it's a no-brainer. Why would I start the Oregon Trail and not finish it? I want to be out here. Every horseman in New England will be jealous of me for this."

It was hard for me to be humble and say what I really felt then, but I knew that I had to.

"I do need you, Nick. I can't get across the trail without you."

"We need each other," he said. "When you sent me that email about the saddle, I knew that this was my ticket out. I needed to get the fuck out of Maine."

"Okay. But I appreciate that you are sacrificing a lot here."

"Rink, no. Don't pull a guilt trip on yourself. I hate it when you do that. It's our trip. We're doing this together."

We talked for a while longer sitting beside the wagon, and then I realized that I was immensely tired. A great burden had been lifted from me. Ever since the bridge at Marysville I'd been waking at three o'clock in the morning to brood, turning from shoulder to shoulder for two hours before first light, trying to reassure myself that I could survive without Nick. Now I felt exhausted. I stood up, gripped Nick by the shoulder, squeezed hard, and then climbed into the wagon for some sleep—my first afternoon nap of the trip. While King Lear at the height of his madness raged outside, I slept soundly for several hours.

Along the Little Blue, I discovered walking. The monotonous rumbling of the iron wheels and the plodding of twelve hooves on the dusty section roads, hour after hour, became a prairie lullaby, and by noon or one o'clock every day I was drowsy on the wagon seat, nodding off sideways and then frantically grabbing on to the brake handle as I swayed above the rotating spokes.

For me, falling off the wagon and then getting crushed by the wheels was one of the most frightening dangers of the trip. As a boy, I snared my leg once in the moving spokes of one of my father's buggies, and was flipped upside down and dragged along a gravel driveway. I lost most of the skin on one cheek and my head ached for days. I knew from the trail journals that few wagon trains reached Oregon without fatalities underneath the wheels, and the casualty rate was particularly high among children.

One of the most poignant accounts of death under the wheels appears in the journal written by Lucia Loraine Williams, an Ohio pioneer who made a speedy but perilous crossing in a seventy-wagon train in 1851. Along the Platte, while Lucia and her three-year-old daughter Helen were in their wagon, it was blown over by a windstorm. Later, Helen almost died of scarlet fever. At the large Ash Hollow pioneer encampment in central Nebraska, the Williamses' train met a party of Sioux raiders who were carrying Pawnee scalps still wet with blood. A month later, just after crossing the Green River in western Wyoming, Williams and her husband, Elijah, decided to let their ten-year-old son, Johnny, a popular boy on the train, ride for the day with a baggage wagon far behind them. But the driver fell asleep, probably from the heat and the monotony of the ride, and his team ran away. Johnny fell off and was crushed by the wheels. Riders were sent ahead to alert the Williamses about the accident, and they rushed back for their son.

"Poor little fellow, we could do nothing for him," Lucia wrote in a letter to her mother that fall. "He was beyond our reach and Oh, how suddenly, one half hour before we had left him in health as lively as a lark, and then to find him breathless so soon was awful. I cannot describe to you our feelings."

Johnny was buried in the high desert, a half mile east of Fontenelle Creek. Many years later, Lucia's closest friend in the train, Esther Lockhart, described the impact of Johnny's death on the other pioneers.

The entire train was immediately stopped. We were the first to reach poor little Johnny, and we saw at once that he was beyond earthly aid. The heavy wagon wheels had passed directly over his forehead and face, and death must have been instantaneous. The innocent victim never knew what happened to him and when Mr. Williams, who was an extraordinarily devoted father, saw the lifeless form of his child he was beside himself with grief and anger. He ran for his gun and was about to shoot the unfortunate driver when four men overpowered him and took his weapon away. Later, when reason and calm judgment returned to the distraught father, he was thankful he had been restrained from committing a heinous crime.

The driver was broken-hearted over the tragedy. He did not

recover from the effects of this deplorable accident during the remainder of the journey. A rude casket was improvised from a large trunk belonging to Mrs. Williams, and the body of the dear little lad who had been a merry companion a few hours before, and loved by everybody, was tenderly buried near the scene of the accident. After some hymns had been sung and a few prayers said, a wooden marker was placed at the head of the grave. His parents wished this to be done, as they felt that we were now in a neighborhood where the Indians would not disturb such places. On the headstone was written the little lad's name, his age and the brief circumstances attending his death. Then, with many regretful tears for the promising young life so suddenly and cruelly cut short, we drove sadly away, leaving him alone in the wilderness, in his last long sleep. For many days we could not forget this agonizing experience. It hung over us like a black shadow. It took all the joy out of our lives, it had been so sudden, so unnecessary, so full of all that was sad and tragic.

My drowsiness now also had a lot to do with the weather. By the middle of the day the flatlands of Nebraska were hot, and beside us the mixed fields and scrub prairie were luminously green under a cloudless sky, with sleepy, vapory mirages rising over the tree line of the Little Blue. The heat didn't seem to affect Nick at all and I asked him to pull the wagon up while I changed into canvas hiking boots. A long, brisk walk would improve my circulation and wake me.

"You'll be all right?" I said.

"I love drivin team alone. Enjoy yourself out there."

I knew that the faster-walking mules would quickly outpace me, and that Nick would daydream off and forget about me. I asked him to wait if I fell out of sight.

"Sure," Nick said. "Here, take Olive Oyl. She'll enjoy the run."

It was rhapsodic out there. As the wagon slowly pulled ahead of me our American flag snapped in the breeze, six bright red wheels turned up contrails of dust, and the sun high in the southeast sky cast a long, cock-eyed shadow—a silhouette of mule ears, canvas tops, and churning wheels slanting across the scrub brush. On foot, the prairie seemed even more wide open, and once more I was levitating on plains. I felt better, wide awake, right away.

Nick, of course, daydreamed and forgot about me. The wagon disappeared off the far rise and I wouldn't see it again for two hours. But it was refreshing to feel so abandoned, wrapped in solitude. Narcissa Whitman had galloped ahead of the fur caravan, losing sight of the wagons. I was walking alone on plains that I had dreamed about for years, our transit to the Platte was nearly complete, and my brother was staying with me on the trail.

12

IN 1906 THE HOMESTEADERS WHO lived along the watery draws of
the abandoned Oregon Trail witnessed the spectacle of a thin, very old
man, incongruously dressed in a three-piece gabardine suit, walking eastward across the old emigrant road. He was leading a team of oxen pulling
a covered wagon decorated with patriotic mottoes and an American flag.
The prairie schooner hobo was living simply off the land, camping at old
trail stops like Farewell Bend and Independence Rock, supporting himself
by selling five-cent postcards to schoolchildren. His idea was simple, but
so idealistic that no one had thought to articulate it before. Before the
Oregon Trail was obliterated by progress—the farmer's plow, irrigation
ditches, new railroad sidings—he wanted to mark it for posterity.

Ezra Meeker was a geriatric burst of energy, the John Muir of the
Oregon Trail, who reinvented himself for lasting fame after a life of spectacular success and failure. Born in Ohio in 1830, Meeker first crossed the
trail as a pioneer in the peak migration year of 1852, settling in Puyallup,
Washington, and quickly establishing himself as a prototypical western
achiever. He made a fortune growing hops for breweries, indulged a grand
tour of Europe and returned to build his wife a fabulous Italianate mansion in Puyallup, then lost it all when a plague of aphids destroyed his
crops in the 1890s. Meeker dabbled in many businesses after that, briefly

entered politics, and was involved in several unseemly squabbles over efforts to promote the business prospects of the Pacific Northwest. But he didn't become a household name until 1906 when, at the age of seventy-six, he began his covered wagon journey across the trail, stopping along the way to harangue crowds about the importance of preserving trail history and installing granite "Meeker Markers" at important trail junctions.

Meeker was rakishly handsome and had matured into elfin old age. With his long white beard, floppy brim hat, and gimpy team of oxen—"Twist" and "Dave"—Meeker made an improbable hero, but America soon fell in love with the geezer adventurer bent on saving the Oregon Trail. Oddsmakers in Chicago and New York took bets on where Meeker would die on the plains, but he astonished everyone by making it past the Missouri River by the end of the summer and then continuing on to Indianapolis, where he wintered over and printed a journal about his walk, *Ox-Team Days*. In the spring, finding that he enjoyed trail life, Meeker continued on to New York, where he scuffled with police who wouldn't allow him to run his oxen down Fifth Avenue. In Washington, D.C., he ran his rig onto the White House lawn and enlisted President Theodore Roosevelt to help him preserve the trail.

Meeker was a big, visionary thinker. Not content with merely preserving the trail, he advocated the creation of a national commercial and military road across the West, linking growing cities like Denver and Salt Lake with the East, and spur roads that would connect with the vast national parks that had been created during the Progressive Era. Swimming and fishing facilities, hotels, and even towers with navigational beacons for passing airmail planes were all part of Meeker's plan. None of this was built during his lifetime, and Meeker would receive no credit for his elaborate transportation dreams. But the national parks system built during the New Deal, and the interstate highways paved in the 1950s, eventually created a network of concrete and open spaces remarkably similar to Meeker's original scheme.

Meeker showed no sign of slowing down in old age. In 1910, at the age of eighty, he made another crossing of the trail by covered wagon, and then progressed through transportation technology by making several more crossings by train, automobile, and—at the age of ninety-four—

open-cockpit biplane. He died in 1928, just two years shy of his hundredth birthday, while working with Henry Ford on still another rig, a stretched Model A outfitted with a covered wagon top. Meeker called it the "Ox-Mobile" and was planning to use it that summer to make a new crossing of the trail.

Ezra Meeker was a geriatric dynamo and visionary whose frequent recrossings of the overland route were critical to preserving the trail.

After Meeker's death, the organizations that he founded or inspired—the Oregon Trail Memorial Association and the American Pioneer Trails Association—managed to stage a few commemorative events at major trail stops like Independence Rock. Workers from the Works Progress Administration and the Civilian Conservation Corps built an Oregon Trail Museum at Scotts Bluff National Monument in western Nebraska. But it wasn't until 1982 that a group of trail enthusiasts and historians founded the Oregon-California Trails Association (OCTA), which has carried on the mostly thankless work of marking remote stretches of the trail, preventing encroachment by housing developments and energy projects, and identifying pioneer graves.

But Meeker did leave behind one vital legacy. During his 1906 trip, he installed more than thirty inscribed monuments along the trail, and a hundred temporary wooden tablets awaiting permanent fixtures, a rudimentary chain that eventually became the basis for marking the trail. On his subsequent trips, Meeker lobbied state government officials to follow his example, and his popularity made him hard to resist. After World War I, several state governments along the trail—Kansas, Nebraska, Oregon—installed hundreds of granite markers along the original ruts, and these were supplemented by U.S. Department of the Interior markers across more than four hundred miles of the trail on public lands in Wyoming. The relatively few stone markers that Meeker installed himself, and the government granite markers, collectively came to be known as Meeker Markers and dozens of them still exist on the trail today. Every year, the state chapters of OCTA regularly replace worn or vandalized markers with metal stakes.

Though relatively simple, Meeker's contribution had lasting effects. The trail route was now staked, known. Without the markers, hundreds of miles of trail would have been overrun by irrigation projects and new roads and lost to history. In 1982, OCTA's founder Gregory M. Franzwa published a three-hundred-page bound edition of geodetic maps covering the whole trail, and it is now possible to pick up the trail in the suburbs of Kansas City and follow the original route more than two thousand miles to Portland, Oregon.

By early June, with the Meeker markers and the Franzwa maps as our guides, Nick and I had completed the first big leg of the trip—the 250-mile transit from St. Joe to the Platte. Now, at Minden, Nebraska, just below the Platte, we would rest the mules for a few days and make some needed repairs to the wagon. But surely the biggest delight of laying over once we reached the Platte was meeting a latter-day Ezra Meeker who embodied his spirit of preserving the trail.

In 1997 the former police chief of Minden, Nebraska, Bill Petersen, had just retired from the National Guard after a thirty-one-year weekend career. Worried that he would not have enough to do on weekends, he went down to a hardware store on a Saturday morning to buy some angling equipment and purchase a fishing license. In a state guidebook containing suggestions about popular fishing spots along the Platte, he noticed several notations for the Oregon Trail, which ran right through prime fishing country. As he began to dabble with fishing on weekends, Petersen became interested in the trail markers and commemorative plaques marking the trail, and then became concerned that a marking system meant to preserve a treasured history really wasn't being maintained very well. He began immersing himself in trail journals and histories, joined OCTA, enrolled in a Rut-Swale Identification Certification Course, and assigned himself the job of meticulously restoring the markers, or adding new ones, along a 250-mile stretch of the trail east of Gothenburg. Intrigued, he quit fishing and began spending most of his time marking the trail.

I had first heard about Petersen, now the president of the trail association's Nebraska chapter, when we stopped off at the OCTA national headquarters in Independence, Missouri, as we drove west to pick up our mules. After we left with the wagon, I contacted Petersen by cell phone from Kansas. He sounded skeptical about what we were trying to accomplish and told me he did not believe that anyone had made an unassisted crossing of the trail since Ezra Meeker's last run in 1910. But, at sixty-eight, Petersen is computer-savvy, and he began following our progress on his laptop map of the trail, which he overlaid with weather maps. He was impressed that we had pushed through the rains past Marysville and Shickley, and that we were pretty much tracking the typical daily mileage of the pioneers. He offered us the use of a small vacation trailer parked behind his house in Minden if we made it that far.

It was raining again when we pulled into Minden over the Memorial Day weekend. Minden is a popular tourist town and farming center just south of the main Oregon Trail junction with the Platte, and it stands honestly on the plains, classically midwestern, with very little of the suburban creep that mars other American towns. The railroad tracks intersect with large grain elevators at the edge of town and the restored opera house faces a lovely town square. We found Petersen's modest ranch house on Blaine Avenue, a few blocks west of the tidy, shaded mansion district.

Petersen is a thin, energetic man in cowboy boots, blue jeans, and an Indian-print shirt, with thinning white hair and a gravelly voice. He is effortlessly gregarious and helpful. When we pulled up with the wagon, he came out from his house and offered to help us find a farm with corrals for the mules. We settled into the comparative luxury of the backyard trailer behind Petersen's house, feeling almost guilty about accepting the comforts of civilization again. Every morning we stepped across the dewy patch of lawn behind Bill's house and entered the small dining nook beside the kitchen, dawdling over coffee and breakfast prepared by Bill's cheerful wife, Nancy.

Nick called the instant bonding we were making on the trip "trail family." In Nebraska, we never lacked for trail family.

Petersen patrols the Platte River valley in a purple and red Dodge pickup equipped with a dashboard Compaq laptop that, with GPS software, constantly updates his position on or near the trail. His pickup bed is filled with metal stakes, Oregon Trail signs, and equipment for upgrading trail markers. His personal disc storage of data about the trail and trail sites, not simply in Nebraska, but from Independence to Mount Hood, is up there in the gigabytes. He soon proved to be an invaluable source of information about the trail and, in between running errands to hardware stores for Nick, while he was repairing the wagon, and buying supplies for our leg across central Nebraska, I spent several afternoons with Petersen learning more about the trail.

Petersen has spent the past few years studying a forgotten but important spur of the trail, the Fort Kearny Cutoff, which was originally developed in the late 1860s as a military freight corridor between Nebraska City on the Missouri and the Platte, and was later used by remnant wagon trains carrying homesteaders looking for a shortcut west. He uses old pioneer journals, newly unearthed maps, and local land records to establish the original route. Documenting the innumerable cutoffs in the west, Petersen believes, tells an important story about how the trail was really used by the pioneers.

"The single biggest error newcomers to the trail make is believing that it was this single set of ruts crossing the plains," Petersen told me one day as we drove toward The Narrows, a choke point on the trail near Oak, Nebraska, where the pioneers were forced by high terrain down to the banks of the Little Blue. "The trail went all over the place. There's an enormous amount of country between here and Independence, Missouri, or St. Joe, and whenever people thought that they had invented a shortcut to get to the Platte quicker, they tried it. When they got to the Platte and, yes, had to follow those banks, they were still all over the place looking for forage or better camping spots. Some days they were right on the river, some days four miles away. Our trail markers are just indicators. There's an immense swath of land on either side of them that was all really the Oregon Trail."

A few miles north, near a muddy crop field filled with wild turkeys and yellow iris, Petersen stopped beside a monument dedicated to Robert Emery, a stagecoach driver who in August 1864 wheeled his wagon around near The Narrows after being chased by Indians and raced back to the protection of a wagon train, saving his nine passengers. The monument is one of several in the area dedicated to the Indian wars that ignited throughout the West after the late 1860s, mostly because the tribes had concluded that the U.S. government had no intention of enforcing treaties that guaranteed them protection from settlers and buffalo hunters, and had now turned on the wagon trains they once welcomed. But Petersen said that the meaning of the Emery monument goes beyond this.

"It's significant that this stage driver galloped back for the protection of the wagon train, because it shows the overlapping traffic that was always on the trail," he says. "The pioneers cut what would eventually also be the stage routes, the telegraph lines, the Burlington Northern and Union Pacific tracks, and even today's Route 80. The Oregon Trail was an economic catalyst for a lot of history since then, even today."

But continued economic development in the West remains the biggest threat to preserving the trail. Advances in irrigation technology and a spike in commodity farm prices since 2008—mostly a result of the ethanol boom—have made it financially desirable for farmers to develop the gullied fields and wetlands along the bottomlands of rivers that were unplowed until a few years ago. There's a new sod-busting rush in America today. The big new effort is the expansion of center-pivot irrigators. These are the large, gantry-like structures of sprayer bars, mounted on all-terrain tires, that rotate in a circle around a crop field from a central source of water. (This is the method of irrigation that gives the Midwest, from the window of an airliner, the appearance of being a matrix of bright green circles.) Corn prices that shot up from $105 per metric ton in 2002 to more than $250 per ton in 2011 have driven farmers to sod-bust hilly, virgin ground that they used to ignore. Across the Midwest, there is a brisk entrepreneurial business in building bridges for the pivot-irrigator wheels, so that creeks and sharp gullies in the fields can be crossed by the circling irrigators. All the way out from St. Joe, whenever we reached a paved highway, we saw dozens of long-body pickups and flatbeds speeding by, carrying these welded structures to expanding farms.

McMansions built by retired couples, wind farms, and oil and gas fields in Wyoming are increasingly crisscrossing sections of the trail that were pristine landscapes with visible ruts ten years ago. As we approached the hamlet of Oak, Nebraska, from the north, Petersen pointed out an eight-section pivot that was slowly moving across a hilly cornfield. As we watched, the pivot irrigator inched up a mounded rise in the middle of the field. Later, when we returned along the same road, the pivot irrigator had completely disappeared down the far side of the same rise. The land being irrigated today is that hilly.

"There's a prime example right there of the biggest threat to the trail today," Petersen said. "The trail came through on the top of that saddle of land you see there. When the Little Blue was high, the wagons had to keep to the high ground to avoid the marshy areas. But that new pivot has annihilated the old ruts. We are losing more and more trail every year, and you lose the trail experience as you lose the authentic visual environment that it once had."

But Petersen also reassured me that long stretches of the trail just ahead remained intact. At his kitchen table, with a large coffeepot between us, we sat up for two nights and mapped out our route across the south banks of the Platte through Nebraska, carefully marking, with a blue highlighter, every road we would follow. The map work was exciting. In many places the trail route wove back and forth across the asphalt for several miles. But once we reached the Platte below Kearney, just half a day's ride by mule, we would enjoy long stretches of dirt roads along the river that were the original trail. The countryside along the Platte was remote and undeveloped, Petersen said, and the two main features of the trail that the pioneers saw—the river itself and the gullied South Hills that kept them along the banks—are unchanged.

Along other sections of the trail, especially a particularly scenic stretch through the bluffs of private ranches after Ash Hollow, we would be riding the original dirt ruts. Every twenty-five miles or so there were small rodeo corrals, private ranches, and public campgrounds in small towns where we could stay overnight. Many of these overnight spots were former pioneer camps or Pony Express stops. We would be seeing a great deal of original trail.

Bill was also concerned that we would take the challenge of following the "original trail" too seriously. There were many obstacles of terrain ahead that the pioneers had conquered only because they were traveling in large trains of wagons that offered them a generous pool of labor. Teenagers and children helped unload the wagons and carried the flour casks and bedposts up to the summits of sharp hills. At steep downhill grades, the wagons were lowered by teams of men with chains and ropes.

Petersen knew that we wouldn't have this advantage. He pointed out a few problem areas on the map, like the sharply rising hills after O'Fallon's Bluff, or the first big ascent of the trail where the wagons were unloaded, California Hill. The Platte was running exceptionally high this year, he said, and there were plenty of other places where we'd find the trail submerged in lakes. With his blue highlighter, he carefully marked routes around these barriers.

"Don't overdo it," he said. "I'm no mule man, but I do know grades. By my book, if you follow Route 30 and then Day Road around California Hill, you've still done the trail."

Minden was also an important mechanical reckoning for me. I had dreamed about this trip for years, and planned and planned. But now that I'd come the first 250 shakedown miles, I was confronting my many errors of foresight. The bare wooden brakes that Don Werner had assured us would "last all the way to Oregon" were already shot from slowing down the wagon over the low, gentle grades of the junction country. Two hundred miles ahead, we would face the perilous canyons and downhill plunges around California Hill and Ash Hollow, Nebraska. When we removed the oak shoes from the brake assembly to inspect them, the right brake fell apart in our hands. One of Bill Petersen's friends, a woodworking hobbyist, completely rebuilt the brake out of fresh oak. In a farmer's barn north of town, I found a coil of thresher belt—a durable rubber, reinforced with nylon, used to convey power from an engine to a thresher or combine—which Nick cut into enough brake pads to last us for the rest of the trip, protecting the wooden brakes from the worst abuse of the hills ahead.

I had also concluded that the fifty gallons of water we were carrying would never do once we got past the forks of the Platte, where the towns and ranches thinned out and we would need to carry more than a one-day supply. Scrounging around another farm, I found a blue fifty-five-gallon plastic drum that had been used to deliver corn syrup to bakeries. Nick spent a day and a half building a cantilever extension to the Trail Pup to mount the barrel and plumb it with a spigot and hose, while I ran back and forth to hardware stores or dumpster-dived for the lumber and parts that we needed. We added racks beside the plastic barrel for our food coolers and pots and pans. My pretty, exquisitely restored Peter Schuttler now looked like a hobo rig, with a thick coating of matted wheel grease, dust, and prairie grass on the sides.

The Minden layover just made us hungrier for more trail. We were acclimated now to movement, freedom, the languor and sweet exhaustion of long days behind the mules. Sitting up late at night with my maps and a pot of coffee separating me from a white-haired, reincarnated Ezra Meeker, was dreamy. The long, serpentine line of our planned route along the Platte, with the braided flow of the river marked on the Franzwa and DeLorme maps, and triangle hatches for the wetlands, was beguiling. Nick and I were impatient to launch for the Platte, and after dinner with Bill and Nancy on our third night we drove out to the wagon and carefully reloaded our supplies, using bungee cords to secure our food coolers on the new Trail Pup extension. Afterward, we sat on our camp chairs beside the wagon and stared up at the stars.

"Rink, I just want to get back on the trail," Nick said. "Life is simple out there."

The next day, as we fell in along the Platte, I could instantly see why the pioneers found the river valley so seductive and navigable. To our right the silvery chain of the river stretched northwest until it disappeared over the horizon, its waters at full stage skimming by so swiftly that the wagon seemed to be racing beside it. Within a half day's ride from Kearney, the South Hills appeared on the left. They were low and rounded at first but after Cozad they broke into a series of sharply rising, jagged bluffs, with mesmerizing beige and green badlands falling in between. Together, the river and the parallel hills formed the natural shoulders of the avenue where the covered wagons had fanned wide, searching for the best forage or clear air away from the dust created by the trains ahead.

Historian Merrill Mattes has written that the pioneers were "welding a continent together with wagon wheels" as they followed this highway across the plains. "If God smiled on America's credo of Manifest Destiny," Mattes wrote, "He showed it most clearly in providing a geographically central corridor up the Platte." For the next hundred miles, until The Forks at North Platte, we hugged the same course along the river on narrow paved roads and dirt tracks.

The trail on the south side of the river was uninhabited and desolate. But through the misty condensation rising off the river we could see the grain elevators and shiny silos of the farm hamlets on the north side. Alfalfa Center went by, then Odessa and Elm Creek. By the middle of the afternoon the jingling of the harness and the rumbling of the wheels had put me to sleep again, and once more I caught myself from falling off the wagon by grabbing the brake handle. I got off to hike, and enjoyed the way that the Schuttler white-top disappeared into the green vastness ahead as the mules outpaced me. It didn't matter to me if the wagon got too far ahead, or if Nick daydreamed and forgot about me. I was bounded by the South Hills off my left shoulder, and the river flowed past to my right. Everything I could see along the funnel of land in between was the Oregon Trail.

13

OUR DAYS OF ENDLESS BEAUTY along the Platte made it difficult to believe that we were traveling through a great valley of death. After the late 1840s, however, the Platte River valley was just that, an avenue through the bluffs that led to an epidemiological cul-de-sac. Even before the wagon trains left Independence or St. Joe, the massing in the camps of so many disparate groups virtually guaranteed outbreaks of infectious diseases like measles and smallpox, but the great killer was Asiatic cholera. After an outbreak in Calcutta in the 1820s, the *Vibrio cholerae* bacteria were carried across trade routes by rats on ships, exploded across Europe in the 1830s, and reached New Orleans in 1849, just in time to travel up the Mississippi River in the spring steamboats to meet the swelling Gold Rush migration.

The swampy drainage of the Platte extended several hundred yards from the main river channels. The expanse of standing pools of brackish water and salty, alkaline mudflats often began just a few steps from the wagon ruts. This created a natural petri dish for the microorganism responsible for causing cholera, and the pioneers were adding fresh host material for bacteria—human waste, animal manure, the carcasses and offal of slaughtered animals—every day. Biologists now know that the alkaline deposits that occurred naturally along the Platte River flats mimicked the salty delta conditions of the bacteria's native India, encouraging the growth of *Vibrio cholerae* in the squalid waste piles of the camps. The anarchy of latrines in the camps festered overnight, becoming killers for the next arriving train. When the river rose after storms, cholera traveled downstream several miles in a single night.

Viewed in this way, the largest land migration in history created a fascinating intersection between human need and biological self-destruction. For 450 miles the Platte offered the pioneers everything they required in an otherwise arid, hostile environment—clear navigation points west, water, fresh game, and timber for cooking fires. But the Platte also provided ideal conditions for disease: warm temperatures, alkali soil, and mud holes that acted as stewpots for organic waste.

Throughout May and June every year there were dozens of covered wagon trains along a single fifty-mile stretch of the Platte, and every one of them functioned as an ad hoc disease transmission system for the wagons downstream. Cholera, which attacks the digestive system and intestines with acute diarrhea, followed by convulsions and vomiting, can turn victims purple and blue in the face and cause an agonizing death within hours. Illinois pioneer John Nevin King rode a paid "express train" to California in 1850, similar to the Turner and Allen experiment of 1849, and saw four men in his group die before reaching the forks of the Platte. "Tis awful when you see an acquaintance at noon well and in the enjoyment of health and learn in the evening that he is a corpse."

The cholera outbreaks on the Platte have to be considered an economic indicator, not just a matter of health. Families suddenly dispossessed of their farms by financial panics, or young easterners overwhelmed by the irrational exuberance of gold fever, either had no choice about traveling west or were too crazed by greed to read the warning signs. In peak migration years like 1849 and 1852 as many as 2,500 pioneers died every year between the jumping-off cities and Fort Laramie in Wyoming, making for an average of four graves per mile all the way across from Independence or St. Joe. Historians now estimate that the toll from cholera was between twenty thousand and thirty thousand deaths between 1849 and the Civil War.

The problem, mainly, was ignorance, and the long delays in communicating scientific knowledge in the nineteenth century. Doctors who had treated patients during earlier outbreaks in Paris and in the teeming industrial cities of England suspected that the source of cholera was contaminated water, particularly brackish water mixed with sewage in the low-lying dockside areas inhabited by the working class. In 1854 an English doctor, John Snow, identified a polluted London well as the source of a cholera outbreak, a discovery now thought to be the beginning of modern germ theory. Snow's work was not widely known outside England, and most Americans continued to believe in the medieval "miasma theory" of disease transmission—that noxious vapors from swamps and bad air carried disease. Snow's research finally reached North America in the 1860s, but this was too late to save the emigrants during the peak travel years along the Oregon Trail. This invasion of humanity, implanted on this ecosystem, was killing the participants every day.

The pioneers seemed to understand the threat posed by the imperfect water supply, but did very little about it. Abigail Jane Scott's 1852 journal aptly describes the infectious trap posed by the Platte. After her train "struck" the Platte in late May, Scott reported seeing as many as ten "fresh graves" every day along the shoulders of the trail, complained about sickness in her own train, and passed a wagon company from Springfield, Illinois, that had turned back for the Missouri after burying one member of its party in the afternoon and another the next morning. But like the rest of the wagon companies, Abigail's train was desperately dependent on the water that was killing its members. A single covered wagon carrying five or six pioneers, drawn by thirsty oxen or mules, required up to seventy gallons of water a day.

But decent water was hard to find. Scott found the water from the main channels of the Platte—roiling with mud, sticks, and sand brought down by the spring rains—distasteful. "The water of the Platte being so mudy and warm that it was impossible to drink it." Instead, the pioneers were forced to root around in the mud holes and swamps along the edges of the river drainage, even though they knew these sources of water were unhealthy. "The great cause of dierrehea which has proved to be so fatal on the road," Scott wrote on June 8, "has been occasioned in most instances by drinking water from holes dug in the river banks and along marshes." She *knew*. Still, Scott and her party continued drawing water from the brackish and cholera-infested mud holes, a practice they would continue until they reached the cleaner banks and natural springs after crossing into the higher elevations of Wyoming.

Virginian John Clark also crossed in the busy emigration year of 1852 and, as early as St. Joe, observed the impact of cholera on the crowded jumping-off camps. A shortage of spades meant that many cholera victims were buried so poorly that their toes protruded from their graves, and shady volunteers lingering on the edges of the camps cheerfully offered to help dig graves, only to run off with the flour casks and cooking pots of the deceased, which were quickly resold to incoming pioneers. Clark described another scene when his train camped one afternoon between the Big Blue and the Platte.

> We pitched our tents but soon found we were in a distressed crowd. Many Oregon families. One woman and two men lay dead on the grass & some more ready to die of cholra, measles & small pocks. A few men were digging graves, others tending the sick. Women & children crying, some hunting medicine & none to be found scarcely; those that had were loathe to spare. With heartfelt sorrow we looked around for some time until I felt unwell myself. Ordered the teams got up & move forward one mile so as to be out of hearing of crying & suffering.

The rote burials along the trail numbed many of the pioneers. There is rarely any mention of a religious service before the dead were interred, and pioneers already inured to death by passing a dozen or more graves a day seemed more intent on keeping the wagons moving. After hastily hacking away at the hard prairie soil, the survivors buried the latest cholera victims in graves so shallow that the outline of the body could still be clearly seen. Many families worried that a new grave would be disturbed by coyotes and deliberately buried their dead on the shoulder of the trail, or even in the middle of the ruts. Then, thirty or forty teams and wagons were run directly over the grave to hide its existence from predators.

Trail scholars are particularly grateful to Micajah Littleton, a native of Georgia who quit his job on a Mississippi River steamboat to cross to California in 1850. Littleton became a sort of professional grave-spotter, meticulously recording the names of over three hundred of the dead, carved on headboards, that he saw between St. Joe and South Pass. He often wandered far off the main ruts in search of additional burials and found dozens of unmarked graves hundreds of yards from the main ruts. Littleton's precise notes helped historians to make estimates of the complete death toll in a bad cholera year. An accurate grid of burial sites has also helped trail experts establish how far the wagon trains traveled away from the main path.

During just two days in the third week of June 1850, Littleton found thirty-one graves along the Platte. One grave he described depicts a common sight along the trail and demonstrated the hastiness of the burials. His tender sadness yet resignation about the scene must have been typical for pioneers who, by the time they reached Fort Laramie, regarded another new grave as no more noteworthy than a passing antelope.

> I passed one today what appeared to be a woman poor creature. Her skirts and dress lay some 15 feet from her grave as though She had dropped them. . . . Her bed a few yards further and her pillows and blankets with some other clothing lay around like it had been only a few hours Since she was buried, a sad spectacle. It caused deep emotions to thrill in my bosom to look on the Sad Sight but Sooner or later we all have to render up an account to our God.

There seems to have been a supreme irony, however, about being surrounded by so much misery and death. Bodies stacked five and six deep in the camps did not diminish the aesthetic appeal of the Platte Valley landscape, and in many journals there was a prevailing sense of charmed travel. One afternoon in early June 1852, Abigail Scott saddled her horse and left the "very sandy" road beside the Platte for a ride up through the nearby hills. Scott's journal entry that day is significant because it challenges the traditional depiction of pioneer women as either passengers in the wagons or weary walkers hurrying the children along on foot, while the men galloped off to hunt buffalo. Like Narcissa Whitman and Margaret Frink, Scott was an avid equestrienne.

> In one place the bluffs came up very near to the river, and I ascended on horseback to the top of the highest one that we could see from the road, and there saw, indeed a romantic spectacle. The Platte below me

flowing on in peaceful music, intersected with numerous islands covered with timber. . . . The emigrants wagons cattle and horses on the
road in either direction [stretched] as far as the eye could reach.

Over the next two weeks, hardly a day went by without Scott's re-
marking on the majestic terrain. She found the "columns above columns
of sand and sand stone" that the wagon trains used as navigation points—
Courthouse Rock, Jail House Rock, Chimney Rock—aesthetically irresistible. On June 15 her train reached Scotts Bluff in western Nebraska, the
gateway to the Rockies. To the west, she could see the purple dome of
Laramie Peak, seventy miles away.

"The hills have a truly grand romantic appearance," Abigail wrote,
"calculated to fill the mind with indescribeble amazement approaching
almost to sublimity."

Over those same two weeks, the Scott train had covered more than
two hundred miles and passed fifty-two fresh graves.

The theme of beauty intimately mingling with death occurred to me, too,
at the end of our first day out from Minden, when we rested and watered
the mules on the site of a popular pioneer wagon camp that we reached
by crossing a small bridge, now the location of the Plum Creek Cemetery.

Nick and I had spent the day running the mules west along roads that
hugged the river, following Bill Petersen's trail markers, so that we reached
Plum Creek with a wonderful feeling of having "struck" the Platte in the
morning to follow the old ruts for the rest of the day. Yellow coneflowers
and bitterweed glowed in the untilled fields, and the wind from the river
blew a summer snow of cottonwood seeds across us on the wagon seat.
The mules picked up their feet and wanted to trot when we reached the
long, cool tunnels of shade beneath the occasional groves of cottonwoods
along the trail.

The Plum Creek Cemetery stands on a level patch of open prairie
with a breathtaking view to the South Hills. The burial ground is primarily known for its memorial to the thirteen victims of an attack on a wagon
train by a Cheyenne and Arapaho war party in 1864. But I was particularly
intrigued by an intricately carved marble headstone that stood near the
entrance to the graveyard and dates to one year later.

Sarepta Gore Fly, a Missouri native, had originally traveled across the trail with her husband, William, in 1859, to join the Colorado Gold Rush. The Flys decided to return to Missouri in 1865 and were traveling eastbound on the trail when Sarepta suddenly died—probably of cholera—in early June. In the early twentieth century, her headstone was found by children playing in a field near Plum Creek, and it was moved to the cemetery in 1930. The professional carving on the headstone and the impressive use of type fonts made it obvious that the marker couldn't have been made locally in 1865. Over time a legend grew about how the stone reached this lonely stretch of the Platte. Sarepta's husband, William Fly, it was said, was so disconsolate about losing his wife that he traveled east to Kearney, supervised the carving of the headstone by a stonemason, and then pushed the two-hundred-pound stone all the way back along the Platte in a wheelbarrow.

The story is almost certainly apocryphal. William Fly was a practical man who had participated in both the California and the Colorado gold rushes and would move on to a successful career as a Montana rancher. It's far more likely that he hauled the headstone back to Plum Creek on the family wagon, or caught a ride on one of the many freight wagon trains that by the 1860s were passing through Kearney every day.

But for more than a century the wheelbarrow story has been retold as if it were historic truth, and variants of it are a persistent western myth. I had already encountered it at the grave of Susan Haile near Kenesaw, Nebraska—her husband, Richard Haile, is said to have pushed her heavy marble headstone all the way from St. Joe. (This version of the legend is usually told with an O. Henry twist, that Richard Haile was forced to resort to a wheelbarrow because he had sold his team and wagon to pay for the headstone.) Over the summer I would encounter four more versions of the wheelbarrow story at trail graves farther west, and there are any number of stories like it on other overland trails. Randy Brown, a Wyoming historian and preservationist who has exhaustively studied trail burials, concludes that "the wheelbarrow aspect is probably an embellishment added in later years by local people."

I was fascinated by this. The serial legend of a mourning widower pushing a gravestone for his wife across the plains in a wheelbarrow seemed to be an ineluctable narrative of the Oregon Trail. Standing alone before Sarepta Fly's headstone, I wondered how shared stories like this get started, why they are so contagious, and what they mean. Perhaps the early homesteaders, whose field plows often turned up bones from shallow pioneer graves, felt a need to atone for the haphazard placement of so many bodies across the plains. Maybe the desolation of the early homesteads, the sadness of the constant howling wind, naturally conjured up an image of a lonely man pushing a wheelbarrow. Pioneer widowers were well known for hasty remarriages, often before they had even finished the trail, and the journals are full of examples of thirty-year-old men with several children wooing and winning teenage girls. William Fly was known to be different, however, and did not remarry for seven years. The image of a disconsolate but determined husband pushing a heavy wheelbarrow across the trail certainly implied true love.

We pushed on and that evening made the six-thousand-acre Robb Ranch, which stands on the south banks of the Platte, across from a large island in the river with timber stands and cleared pastures. The proprietor there, Joe Jeffrey, is a joyful, round-faced veterinarian in his seventies, a self-described "cowboy poet" who delivers humorous lectures across the country on the history of outhouses and fence posts. A sign on his barn reads POST HOLES FOR SALE. Jeffrey took us down to the southern portion of his ranch and showed us the old pioneer ford across Plum Creek and the deep swales cut by the wagons that still remain in a few of his unplowed pastures. We ate home-raised Angus steaks in the ranch house with Joe and his wife, Dianne, swapped stories and laughed, forming another of those rapid, intense friendships of travel.

The Robb Ranch had also been a crowded trail encampment, and that night Nick and Olive Oyl slept with the bones of the pioneers, out in the tall prairie grasses behind the ranch barns. From my mattress in the wagon I looked out through the wagon cover to a moonlit landscape where the old and the modern trail merged. The South Hills, lustrous and black, were profiled against a lighter sky, and on the summits the rotating beacons from three communications towers flashed red. Coyotes howled from the tree line at Plum Creek and I could hear the rumble of the trucks on Route 80, across the river. I was optimistic about our progress on the trail and pleased about the wagon modifications that Nick had done in Minden. We had come thirty-two miles that day, watered the mules three

times, and arrived at the Robb Ranch with a full day's supply of water still
in our tanks.

The next day, just south of Gothenberg, Nebraska, Nick and I rested the
mules in the shade near another attractive trail remnant, an old log cabin
called the Midway Pony Express Station, which stands near the house
and barns of the historic Lower 96 Ranch. The ancient checked logs and
the cedar-shingled roof of the Civil War–era cabin are protected from
the weather by a modern, three-sided aluminum implement shed, tastefully painted in slate gray and light blue to match the Platte Valley sky
tones. I was touched by the story I learned there about the cabin and the
Lower 96.

Midway Station is a classic example of how an old pioneer encampment and trading post morphed into something new with each phase of
transportation. After the brief, colorful life of the Pony Express ended in
1861, the Midway Station became a stagecoach, freight, and mail stop,
conveniently located along the Platte just a one-day pull by mule from
Plum Creek. The station probably got its name because it was considered
the midway point between Atchison, Kansas, and Denver, Colorado, on
the Overland Mail route, when the stage roads were moved north during the Civil War, to avoid Texas, which had joined the southern Confed-
eracy. But place-names in the West often have multiple origins. Midway
might also have been named because it stands just a few miles from the
fabled 100th meridian at Cozad, Nebraska (100 longitudinal degrees west
of Greenwich, England), the line that roughly bisects the North American
continent running north from Texas to North Dakota.

The spot where I was now carrying buckets to water the mules was
truly saturated with history—the kind of place that makes a book turd feel
light in the knees. In June 1860 a Pony Express rider named Jim Moore
made what is still regarded as one of the great endurance rides of all time.
Receiving a westbound government dispatch marked "Very Important,"
he left Midway Station and galloped all the way to Julesburg, Colorado,
only to discover an important eastbound dispatch for Washington that
had to be carried back to Midway. Changing horses at Pony Express stations every ten to fifteen miles, Moore covered the 235-mile round-trip
in less than fifteen hours, averaging more than fifteen miles per hour. But

legends inevitably get stretched and the distance given in many history books is 280 miles, kiting Moore's average speed up to nineteen miles per hour.

In 1879 the explorer and geologist John Wesley Powell, later the director of the U.S. Geological Survey, established the 100th meridian as the "moisture line," often locally called the "dry line," separating the relatively fertile plains of eastern Nebraska and the arid scrub country to the west. (In Nebraska, an average of twenty-two to twenty-eight inches of rain falls annually east of the 100th meridian; twelve to sixteen inches falls to the west.) Revisions to the Homesteading Act under Theodore Roosevelt— a pro-rancher Republican—allowed settlers west of the 100th meridian to claim a full section of 640 acres instead of the original 160 acres, because the drier land was so much less productive, and this is one reason why eastern Nebraska is cropped, and western Nebraska is mostly cattle country. In nearby Cozad there is a historical marker on Route 30 at the 100th meridian, where the Oregon Trail, the Pony Express route, the transcontinental Union Pacific, the Lincoln Highway, and modern interstate Route 80 intersect. The Concord coaches of the Central California & Pikes Peak Express Company, later the Overland Mail Company, ran nearby.

In the early 1880s, twenty years after its run as a Pony Express station and stagecoach stop, Midway was developed into a successful ranch by a Pennsylvanian, Henry Laurens Williams, whose family eventually expanded it into the Lower 96, a spread along the Platte that included 8,000 acres of cattle range and 1,500 acres of crop ground. More than a century of history is symbolized by the old log cabin station, lovingly preserved by four generations of the Williams family and their in-laws. It is believed that the original log cabin site was a small trading post along the fur caravan routes to the Rockies in the 1820s and 1830s, and the structure itself was built either in the 1850s as a road ranch on the Oregon Trail or in 1860 for the Pony Express. (Some historians question the building's past as a Pony Express stop.) The cabin was in continuous use as the Lower 96's bunkhouse until 1956.

Larry Gill, seventy-one, who married into the Williams family in the 1960s, is the fourth-generation owner-manager of the Lower 96. He was mowing his daughter's lawn on the edge of the ranch when we pulled by with the wagon, and he interrupted this work to follow us up to the

Midway Station in his pickup. Gill is a fit, Hollywood-handsome man who is usually dressed in faded blue denims, pointy packer's boots, and modern nylon shirts that he buttons up to his Adam's apple to protect his chest from the blazing Nebraska sun. Gill reminded me a lot of other ranchers I had met over the years. He is not one of those boastyboy cowboys who tell tall tales, but is instead a modest, gregarious man who exudes a spirit of curiosity about visitors.

Gill told me that, over time, the Williams family has spent at least $100,000 on periodic restorations of the old Midway-Station-cum-bunkhouse—"and that's in old dollars, you know?" An infestation of powderpost beetles in the 1960s required the expert advice of entomologists from the University of Nebraska. The vagaries of Platte Valley weather—heavy rains followed by scorching heat, snow in the winter—caused moisture to wick up from the foundation and sill, rotting the lower logs from the inside. To replace them, Gill and his ranch hands harvested new cedar logs in the South Hills and milled and mortised them by hand. He considered this work the obligation of any ranching family that has inherited a significant vestige of the Oregon Trail, a way of reassuring the public that history could be preserved on private lands.

A few years ago, when Gill began to think about retiring, he faced a problem common among ranch families today. His three children have successful careers and either have moved away or are not interested in ranching. Gill and his wife have been gradually selling off their grazing range to neighboring ranches, but they will retain and farm the most valuable bottomlands along the Platte so that his children can inherit a substantial family asset. He has purchased enough life insurance to cover the estate taxes when he and his wife die. More than 130 years of continuous family management of the Lower 96 will soon come to a well-planned end.

But there was still one more chore to perform, which had just been completed when Nick and I rolled through with the wagon. Gill didn't want to encumber either his children or the eventual owner of the remaining ground on the Lower 96 with the responsibility of perpetual care for the Midway Station log cabin. After making another round of restorations on the old bunkhouse, Gill spent almost $30,000 pouring concrete footings and ordering the attractive, prefabricated implement shed that now shelters the original structure. The big goal was protecting Midway Station from moisture, and the log cabin is now encased in a dry metal barn, with setbacks and space on the sides and in the back designed to encourage a drying circulation of air. The pitched roof extends far enough over the front to protect the facade of the cabin from rain and snow. This side, facing southwest, will remain open, so that the Oregon Trail tourist buses entering the Lower 96 all summer can still enjoy the original prospect of Midway Station. Visitors can stroll inside to see the original floorboards, the old furniture, and the photographs of the ranch in the nineteenth century, when the Oregon Trail ruts were still visible beside the split-rail corrals.

The new metal implement shed that protects the Midway Pony Express station and road ranch, near Gothenburg, Nebraska, is one of the most creative preservation efforts along the trail.

The new implement shed at Midway Station sets off the lines of the original log facade and its window casements like the frame on a valuable print or oil painting. The new roof bathes the cabin in shade, protecting the log-and-adobe structure from direct sunlight, and the space inside is cool. Gill's solution for Midway Station is one of the most sensible historic preservations that I've seen. Government didn't do this; he did it, with his own money.

I stood in front of Midway Station marveling about this while I watered the mules from the ranch spigot. When I put my bucket down to scratch Jake's ears, Olive Oyl dived in headfirst for a drink, overturning the pail and spooking Beck, who reared so high that I could see her shoes above my head and then leaped forward to run away. I was quickly overrun by the team, but managed to pull myself from underneath the hooves by propping one knee against the wagon pole and wrapping my arm around Jake's head. Nick immediately saw what was happening and as I bounced along on the pole desperately hanging on to Jake, he steered the mules toward a cottonwood grove, where they stopped. It was only the brilliant mule handling of Nick that prevented me from becoming one of those wagon travelers who at noon are well and in the enjoyment of good health and in the evening a corpse.

I was winded and rattled by the brief runaway, I was furious at Beck, and my knee was bruised and my shoulder ached from clinging one-armed to Jake. After I helped Nick back the team away from the trees, I walked over to the log cabin and sat at the kitchen table for a few minutes, taking deep breaths as I slowly felt my heartbeat returning to normal.

The experience became another case of fear motivating me to push on, not discouraging me, and at Midway Station Nick and I made a mid-afternoon decision that became habit-forming for the rest of the trip. We had already completed our allotted twenty-five miles for the day, and now we were on a comfortable ranch where we were welcome to camp. But we had made more than thirty miles the day before and could easily bring our total to thirty-five miles today, making our two-day total almost seventy miles, substantially revising my expectations for the trip. There were still four hours of daylight left and the mules weren't spent. My adrenaline drip from the runaway, and then from bouncing along on my ass beside the galloping team, emboldened me. This was mixed with anger at Beck. Fuck you, crazygirl mule. I am going for more miles this afternoon, a lot more miles.

When I asked Gill if there was a ranch farther west where we could camp, he suggested the farm and feedlot of a friend, Jim Hecox, which sat on the bottomlands of the Platte right on the trail.

"Jim won't be there," Gill said. "He'll still be out in the fields cutting alfalfa. But you don't have to worry. He'll pull in tonight when you're asleep and be delighted to see a wagon parked in his yard."

• • •

We clattered off the Lower 96 with a wonderful feeling of being passed from ranch to ranch, and from memorable trail stop to memorable trail stop, by happy Nebraskans. The ranch road curved northwest following the old ruts and delivered us to a large granite Oregon Trail marker out on paved Highway 47. On both sides of the highway, the river was flooded out into large, sandy lakes. Turning in for the Hecox place, we splashed through deep ponds that rose above our wheel hubs and covered the wagon in mud.

That night we were exhausted, filthy, sunburned, and covered with trail grime, and I felt stiff from my runaway drubbing by the mules. But our daily routine was exhilarating. The trail had turned me into an exuberant workaholic. Rise at dawn and carry water and feed for the mules, harness and hitch, walk or ride on a wooden Schuttler seat all day, carry more water, then lug the heavy harness again, wash the mules, cook dinner, and snake a hose across the ranch to refill our barrels at night. Unload and repack the wagon, every day. The endurance required should have been too much for us, but across these Nebraska plains endurance just begat more endurance. Even the smallest decisions seemed momentous now. I was too tired and sore after dinner to wash our dishes and instead collapsed, with my clothes and boots still on, into my wagon bed. Fuck the dishes. Fuck hygiene. We've done seventy miles in two days. The dishes could wait until the morning.

I was too hyped by the day to sleep right away, and the view out the back of the wagon was too beautiful to ignore. The South Hills rose sharply in the distance, with the deep folds of the canyons washed in pastel twilight. As I stared over my boots toward the hills, I realized that I had resolved for myself one of the great debates about the overland years. Some historians, often called "economic determinists," argue that America's frequent cycles of financial collapse and farm failures drove the majority of pioneers to the trail. Other scholars, sometimes called "adventure theorists," postulate that romantic yearnings for exotic travel and for fulfilling manifest destiny were more dominant motives. Reaching middle Nebraska, I decided, had turned me into a diehard economic determinist. Forget adventure. Adventure gets pretty stale after a while and you're not much of a romantic after a month on the trail. No one would do this, day after day, unless he had to.

14

AN APPARITION WAS RIDING WITH me across the trail. At critical moments of the trip I was flooded with memories of my father, and
reflexive comparisons of our adventure now and our covered wagon
trip to Pennsylvania in 1958. There was something pathetic, I thought,
about a sixty-year-old mule skinner remaining so dependent on his past.
I reminded myself of those droll WASPs that you meet at New England
cocktail parties, palavering away about restoring their father's old wooden
boat. But then I experienced an intense moment out past Chimney Rock
that forced me to reconsider the psychic tattoo of paternity.

At North Platte, we laid over for two days at a pleasant house and
pasture just south of town owned by a friendly retired couple who became
our trail family for a couple of days, Don and Sheila Exner. Nick made a
particularly heroic entrance at the Exner place when the mules balked
and reared while he was squeezing the wagon through the narrow space
between two outbuildings, scraping the wheel hubs against a disc harrow
parked near one of the sheds. We used our layover in North Platte to resupply and visit the local museums, the huge Union Pacific rail yards, and
Buffalo Bill Cody's restored mansion north of town.

Don Exner is seventy-three but looks much younger, and he is a brave,
stoic man. He had spent his career managing Woolworth stores in the

Dakotas and Nebraska and then was almost completely paralyzed from the waist down after a thirty-foot fall from a house roof when he was in his early fifties. Doctors told him that he would never walk again, but Don refused to believe it. He hobbles gamely between his house and garage shop on crutches, grimacing with pursed lips as he forces his legs up at every step, and performs his farm chores sitting on a golf cart that is outfitted with conveniently located tool kits.

From the age of eight onward I had watched my father slowly decline from the phantom pain attacks that he suffered from his amputated left leg, and being around someone like Don often reminds me of him. My father struggled around our farm on crutches himself, racked by searing pain, and helping him up from the barn at night or watching him being carried off to the hospital for Demerol shots was part of my childhood routine. The last few years had been particularly edgy in this regard, because I had often written stories about soldiers returning from Iraq and Afghanistan, missing arms and legs. The details about phantom pains still bother me and whenever I wrote an article about injured war veterans, I was likely to be mildly depressed and preoccupied for days. While researching one of these articles, I read a study documenting how modern medical science has made very little progress understanding and alleviating phantom pain and how, for the majority of amputees, the frequency and intensity of attacks will increase with age. That is one consequence of the wars in Iraq and Afghanistan that we don't often read about. Thousands of children of veterans across the country will spend their childhoods as I did, watching their fathers grimace and twitch with severe pain when the unpredictable phantom attacks return. There is probably a family rushing a war veteran to the hospital for morphine or Demerol shots right now.

Don is a lot quieter and more stable than my father was, but there were some similarities that struck me. He has the same clear olive-tone skin, symmetrical oval face, and bald pate, and like my father's his face relaxes with an amused, saturnine expression when he finds something ironic. Dragging his legs around the house, he never complains about his handicap. With our new trail family in North Platte, I woke in the morning feeling that I had just returned home for a long vacation with my parents, and was looking forward to joining them for breakfast. Even the way the light fell across the wainscoting and furniture in the house reminded me of my father's library.

Nick and I had made an important revision of plans back in Minden. We were still determined to make an unassisted crossing without motorized support, but it didn't make sense to leave Nick's pickup all the way back in St. Joe. We would need the pickup to close down the trip once we got to Oregon, and we didn't want to travel two thousand miles on an airliner to retrieve it. If we wrecked the wagon somewhere or our wheels broke, we would need the pickup within a couple of hundred miles. So we landed on the plan of leapfrogging the truck ahead of us once a month. From Minden, Nick had driven with Bill Petersen back to Kansas, and then we had placed the truck forward in North Platte. Now I wanted to place the truck another two hundred miles ahead because I knew that we would have to reshoe the mules and probably make wagon repairs at our next planned layover, somewhere in eastern Wyoming. I had made arrangements with the North Platte Valley Museum in Gering, Nebraska, next door to Scottsbluff, to park the pickup there for a couple of weeks.

The drive west to Scottsbluff would give me a chance to scout the trail ahead and then I would either find a bus or hitchhike back to North Platte. One morning, at breakfast with the Exners, I told Nick about my plans.

"Trail Hand," I said. "You'll have to play tourist without me today. I'm going to drive the Toyota up to Gering."

Don looked up from his plate of bacon and eggs with an amused smile.

"Oh, I'm not sure it's safe for a young man like you to be thumbing rides across Nebraska," he said. "I'll follow you up to Gering and then run you back in our car."

I felt guilty about accepting Don's help, but I could see that he really wanted the excursion, so we agreed to leave after breakfast.

We reached Gering by early afternoon. I parked Nick's pickup in the shade of a pine grove beside the museum and then walked over to Don's car to tell him that I would quickly return—I just needed to tell someone at the museum that I had dropped off the truck.

"All right," Don said. "But don't be long. I can't sit forever in the car."

The museum in Gering is one of those local gems that you can find all over the West. The displays inside include an exquisite collection of Indian arrowheads, a Studebaker prairie schooner, and an Indian bull boat made of buffalo hide. My book turd completely got away from me and I forgot about Don out in the car, and then I wasted more time discussing the pioneer lore of western Nebraska with the museum director.

When I finally stepped toward the glass doors near the museum entrance, I could see Don outside, struggling up the walkway on his crutches. The path was treacherously strewn with large pinecones from the trees. Every time he threw a crutch forward, it landed on a pinecone and threw him sideways, and Don grimaced with each labored step, trying to right himself. *Goddamnit, Rinker. You promised him not to be long. He drove all the way out here for you. Now you've let him down.*

Don stopped to rest in a patch of sunlight along the walk. The survivor's expression on his face was the one my father had worn when he pulled the covered wagon across the bridge to New Hope in 1958. The flesh tones and perspiration on his bald scalp and high cheekbones were also the same.

Suddenly I wasn't in my own moment and my vision of Don had crossed over to a strange junction space. A Niagara of lightness filled my abdomen and chest—whether from a racing heart or just an extreme calmness inside, I couldn't tell. *Oh, I can't believe this. I am way out here in western Nebraska, and my father has come.*

The rest arrived spontaneously. I couldn't prevent the words and the thoughts that welled up.

Dad. I'm sorry that I didn't make it to you that weekend, but you died three days before I could get there. I have detested living all of these years knowing how much I neglected you after I left for college. But I had to get away from you. Can you accept that? I was planning on coming back, I really was. The other thing that I always wanted to tell you so you could feel better about us is that I always remembered what you told me that last time on the phone when you called me in Albany. You said, "Son, you're not going to amount to much until you get an opinion piece in the Sunday New York Times." *Dad, I was fucking twenty-five years old, and a total crazyboy. It's a miracle I got out of bed in the morning. But that article that you wanted me to write, which happened to be a pretty decent piece about prison reform, appeared in the Sunday* Week in Review *nine days after you died. There were many more after that, okay? I just wanted you to know because by your lights I certainly haven't accomplished all that I could have, but I did do that. Late on Saturday night when I knew that the newspaper trucks had arrived I walked in the rain down to the bottom of State Street and bought the paper. I stood at the bottom of the hill reading my story. There's a view of the Hudson from there and I could see the lights on the tugboats pushing oil tenders north and I'm not going to bullshit you and say that I cried but I did spend a very long time down there just regretting and regretting profoundly that you didn't last long enough to see this, but there was nothing I could do but stand there and think about you. I thought about you, then, and a lot later. I just wanted you to know about the article. Dad, I know I let you down, but can't you let me go? I was never worth it in the first place and I would know that you are fine now if you would just let me go. Dad, let me go.*

You never know the real edge of pulling out of a trance like that, but I soon found myself outside on the museum walk, kicking away the pinecones so that Don would have an easier time. I was embarrassed about my rudeness, but he was more pained than annoyed.

"I thought you said you wouldn't be long," Don said, perspiring from the effort of steadying himself on his crutches. "We should get moving."

Don and I had lunch in Gering and then drove back across the plains. Every time I watched him struggle on his crutches to get out of his car, or I noticed him using the hand controls for the accelerator and brakes while he drove, I manically seesawed up and down again—feeling my heart race one minute as I thought about my father, and then afterward experiencing an extreme, chemical calm. It was as if a lifetime of depressive cycles—the dark, gloomy lows, immediately followed by the sharp, ebullient highs— were concentrated inside me as we drove from Scottsbluff to North Platte.

We stopped in Paxton, Nebraska, along the Platte, to meet Nick and Sheila for dinner at a famous old western landmark, Ole's Big Game Steakhouse and Lounge, and Nick and I enjoyed wandering through the rooms looking at the trophies from the founder's safaris in Africa, and the photographs on the walls of Nebraska cattle roundups and jackrabbit-hunting parties.

After dinner, I flashed again out in the parking lot, when the evening light falling on the river caught Don's determined jaw as he struggled back toward his car, reminding me again of my father. I let the moment pass and Don and I drove quietly east together as the darkness gathered on Route 80. I was exhausted and confused by my emotional reckoning with my father and when we got to North Platte I collapsed into my wagon bed with my clothes and boots on.

Over the next few days, I was occasionally moody about my father's reprise, but I enjoyed the therapy of driving mules across the plains. Nick and I had always been able to discuss anything, no matter how personal, and the long, scenic stretches along the trail together had reinforced that. Nick is a veteran of many self-help programs and nothing fazes him. He knows the jargon. When I described what happened with Don Exner in Gering, he tried to be helpful.

"Rink, you're not any more fucked up than the next guy, okay? Nobody really recovers from anything. I'm fucked up. My friends are fucked up. Everyone in the family is totally fucked up. You just happened to see Daddy keel over in the fields too many times. You still feel guilty about it."

"I wish they paid overtime for guilt trips," I said. "I'd be rich by now."

"Look, Daddy was our enabler," Nick said. "That's why I drive team and you are this frickin dreamer. Daddy enabled us for this trip. Why *wouldn't* you think of him on the Oregon Trail?"

"You're probably right," I said. "There's no cure for me."

"There's no fuckin cure for any of us, Rinker. Get into it, dickhead. I'm fucked up, you're fucked up, okay? Fucked up is normal."

Nick was right, I decided. Fucked up is the universal condition of man. We were crossing to Oregon behind a cranky team of mules—the very definition, the apotheosis, the pinnacle, of fucked up. I woke in the morning to harness mules, fucked up, obsessed all day on making more miles, fucked up, and collapsed onto my squalid wagon mattress every night, fucked up. I was having a great time, enjoying the best summer of my life, fucked up. Fucked up is good.

I began to relax about things a lot more. Fathers do not let go, and memories of them condense with age. Nick and I were crossing the trail, fifty-three years after our Pennsylvania trip, thirty-six years after my father had died. Having him along for the ride was as much a part of the journey as the jingling of harness, my afternoon walks, or the hard blue skies against the South Hills.

Twenty miles out of North Platte, along the shores of a modern man-made lake called Sutherland Reservoir, we reached a T in the road near a prominent choke point along the trail, O'Fallon's Bluff. Here, the South Hills abruptly tumbled down to the river, forcing the pioneers either north to ford the river or due west, up the gently rising, sandy slopes of a broad plateau. On the westward route, the wagons would continue to follow the avenue formed by the river and the South Hills out past Alkali Lake and Happy Hollow, to make the "upper ford" at California Hill.

Today, the northern route is blocked by Route 80, which is only a few yards from the old trail, so we couldn't turn that way. The western route would carry us around the lake to a sandy, inferior farm country where I suspected we would have difficulty finding a place to camp. I could tell from my maps that the landscape ahead was the chain of roller-coaster hills that Bill Petersen had warned me about. But I couldn't see very far ahead. It was just a Sahara out there. The prevailing westerly winds rocketing across the plains had churned the bluffs into giant clouds of sand that obscured the roads and sky.

It was late afternoon and I was tired. Beck had been shying a lot all day, and I wasn't sure that the mules could pull our rig, with five hundred extra pounds of water added to the rear of the Trail Pup, over the steep hills of O'Fallon's Bluff. But there was no place nearby to camp, my late-afternoon mania for more miles was quickly turning into an evening mania, and there were still two hours of light left. I decided to push on past a homestead called Dorsey's Road Ranch, another trail waypoint that had enjoyed a second life on the plains as a Pony Express and stage stop.

We could see what kind of trouble we were in as we climbed the first rise after Dorsey's. The western fringe of the bluffs extended as a series of sharply rising hills directly in front of us, with no section roads turning west to allow us to get around the heights. But it wasn't just the climb—the steepest so far of the trip—that we faced. The winds blowing hard from the west had turned the sandy edges of the bluff into an impenetrable gale of sand. We couldn't see how high we would have to climb, or how far the hills stretched, and we were probably going to be driving blind through the sand blasts. In the narrow channel of clear air that we could see to the west, dark, low rain clouds were pushing in.

We were completely boxed in. There was no way we could turn the wagon around on the narrow road. Our only choice was to penetrate uphill through the sand clouds, hoping that we could summit the indiscernible space beyond and then descend into the clear by nightfall.

I was frustrated because I had studied this stretch of trail several times during the winter, and knew that I had to find a way around the high terrain. Now we were headed straight for O'Fallon's Bluff.

"Nick," I said. "I've screwed the pooch on this one."

"Boss, we're on the trail, right? Wasn't that a marker back there?"

"We're on the trail."

"So? Fuck it. Let's go. The trail's the trail. What's the name of this place?"

"O'Fallon's Bluff."

Nick slapped the lines on the rumps of the mules. "Hup, Team! Hup, Hup! C'mon, you odd buggers, it's just a whore called O'Fallon. O'Fallon's Bluff, Team! Bute, Jake, Beck! O'Fallon's Bluff!"

By now we'd learned some things about the team. Bute, a complete laggard for work, nevertheless pulled hard on the hills. It was the procrastinating mule in her. She mostly wanted to lay back all day and let Jake and Beck pull the load. But when there was work to do that couldn't be avoided, she wanted to get it over in a hurry. When she saw a hill coming, Bute leaped into a fast walk-trot, leaned hard into her collar, and somehow lunged her shorter legs ahead of the team. Jake and Beck hated that and never wanted to be left behind by Bute, so they raced forward together as a team, all six tug chains pulled tight. We knew to exploit that now, and Nick yelled to Bute in his best mule-calling baritone and touched her rump with the whip.

"Bute, you odd bugger, up the hill, Bute! We're cutting your weight down for the prom, Bute! Bute! Get up! We're going to the prom. Up O'Fallon's Bluff, Bute!"

The edge of the bluffs rose as a mounded grassland on our right, a little higher than the wagon top, protecting us momentarily from the wind. But then the vegetated ground fell toward a small canyon just ahead. We had another quarter mile of clear air before we reached the high ground obscured by the sandstorm.

As we started uphill, I kept my hand ready for the brake and told Nick that if the summit was obscured by the sandstorm, I'd lock the wheels to reassure the team when we felt the wagon lunge downhill.

"Nick! Here we go! Just see if you can keep them straight on the road."

"Yup, Team! Yup, Team! O'Fallon's Bluff, Bute! Oh, fuck, Rink. Look at this hill. I love this."

It was just a wispy edge of wind and arid soil at first, dust devils on a Nebraska hill. I could feel a sensual pitting of sand on my hands and cheeks. But as we climbed higher the blasting sand stung my skin, even through my clothes. On the exposed ridge below the summit, the wind buffeted us even harder—thirty-five miles per hour, forty-five miles per hour, I couldn't tell. Our hats ripped up against the parade strings under our chins, and I could see Beck's harness rise off her rump.

Farther up the hill, we entered a noiseless zone where the wind racing past our ears was so compressed that there was no sound at all except for a muffled jingling of the tug chains and the groan of the wagon tongue. Nick's voice, calling the mules, reached me as a distant, hoarse whisper. There was nothing to see straight ahead.

Bump. The wagon lurched sideways—hard left. I couldn't see or hear anything in the blinding cloud of sand. I could only sense the wagon by the seat of my pants. Oh, yes. That's three axles back. The Trail Pup is in the ditch, pulling right, jackknifing the main wheels left. Beck had been thrown left by the lurch and was pulling hard right to regain her footing. But Nick, feeling her pull right, was trying to keep her left, thinking that she was leaving the road.

From my position on the right side of the wagon seat, Beck, on the right of the team, was directly in front of me. As she regained the edge of the road I noticed a clear visual reference by staring straight down at her rear hooves—practically the only thing I could see. Her right hind hoof and her right tug chain were about eighteen inches from the fuzzy line of green prairie grass that grew along the road shoulder. Hoof to prairie grass—eighteen inches. That was my distance from the edge of the road.

This was instrument flying, in covered wagon mode. I could almost perfectly assess our position on the road by Beck's distance from the grass line. She needed to get right again to be on the edge of the road, but Nick couldn't see anything from his side of the wagon and kept pulling her left. Bumpety-bump, bump, bump, the right Trail Pup wheel was skidding sideways into the rough off the road and swaying the main wagon off center.

I leaned hard into Nick, yelled into his ear, and grabbed at his knees for the lines.

"Nick! I can see the edge of the road! I'll take the lines. You call."

All of this happened in just a few seconds and now I had the lines firmly in my hands. When I inched Beck back right I picked up the edge of the road and then pulled her even farther into the grass, hoping that I could straighten the wagon and get the Pup wheel out of the rough edge of the trail. I was driving entirely by feel now, steering the rig according to the surface I could sense that the wheels were passing over—bump, bumpety-bump, bump, bump, bump. Then the ride suddenly turned smooth. Yes, I'm back on the grassy edge of the road. Hold it steady on the grass to stabilize the wheels. After twenty yards of that, I coaxed the team left and could see the prairie grass again where it was supposed to be—eighteen inches off Beck's hoof. Good. The ride was smooth and we had six wheels back on solid ground.

It was just a thing of driving beauty after that, with a thrilling sense of danger, competence, instinct, and joy. I was amazed, too, at the wonder of personality. Beck, our Lizzie Borden of a mule, was always acting out when there was nothing to fear. Now, under terrible conditions, she was pulling like the bejesus, and her steps were so consistent that I could drive through a sandstorm by looking at her hooves. For the rest of that blind pull I was one fluid sensation of shoulders and hands coordinating driving lines, mule bits, and wheels dampened by dust. My eyes were bloodshot from the sand and wind but I wouldn't take them off my eighteen inches to the green line of prairie grass. There was still no vision ahead, and not much sound, and I didn't know where the hill ended but somehow I felt secure, neurologically fused to the mules through the lines.

There was a brief clear space of air just below the summit of the first hill where the mounded grasslands returned. I quickly looked west before we reentered the sand plumes and it was an exhilarating sight. For thirty miles the verdant crop fields shone green along the Platte. Directly below us, shafts of sunlight punching through the breaks in the low clouds brilliantly lit the aluminum grain bins on the farms. There were storm clouds farther west. Then we disappeared again into the brown fury of sand.

There must have been something about emerging from the sand plume to see the intense vista below. I was overwhelmed with a single, pellucid sensation. I felt completely free. Nothing existed behind me or ahead of me on the trail.

Uncertainty. Complete, purified uncertainty—that's what I was living for now. I didn't know what lay beyond these hills. There was no place certain to go, no camp that we knew of tonight. What did pushing mules up this sandy hell of hills mean? Beck had been a shying maniac all day and now she was pulling through the sand clouds like a dream girl. My father had appeared to me unannounced in Gering. Our path west carried us toward another thunderstorm. But I didn't want certainty now. I loved living this way and I just wanted three mules, Nick, and the trail. All I could do was continue moving west, west, west, a fanatic for miles. My reward for that was learning to embrace uncertainty.

We were still trapped by the blowing sand when we crested the first hill. I could tell that the wagon was heading downhill again when the pole lifted and the trace chains went slack. I reached over for the brake with my right foot and felt through the lines the mules momentarily panicking and then relaxing when I locked the wheels. We descended in the blowing sand for another minute until we reached a clear spot along the grasslands again, and the next hill was obscured for only about forty yards.

The rest of the hills were lower and the wind began to abate. Over them, we were driving blind for only a minute or less. But I had my mantra now. Uncertainty was a sacrament and the quest for miles meant that we'd never know where or how we'd end the day.

It was nearly dark when we found the first road leading west, away from the hills. Once more we were racing dark clouds over the Platte to find shelter and dodge a runaway before the storm hit. The plains beyond O'Fallon's Bluff were littered with sad, ragtag farms, mostly deserted. These run-down areas, which would become a common sight as we moved west, were produced by the consolidation of farming that has taken place in American agriculture over the past thirty years. Mechanization, chemical fertilizers, and improved seed hybrids have allowed farmers to efficiently till large parcels of several hundred acres, even more than a thousand acres, at once. In the past, a typical one-mile-square parcel of cropland, containing 640 acres and called a "section," supported four family-owned farms of 160 acres each. (Many areas even had "eighth-section" farms of eighty acres apiece.) When these smaller, less efficient farms were abandoned or sold, the larger, prosperous farming outfits that bought the acreage ripped out the old tree lines and irrigation systems to join the neighboring fields into one giant crop factory that could be "plowed through" with huge John Deere or Case tractors for a mile or longer. With typical American indifference to aesthetics and road views, however, many of these new agribusiness firms have simply left the old houses and barns along the road frontages to rot. There are hundreds of clusters of these "ghost farms" throughout the Midwest and West today. While the best ground surrounding the farms shimmers with mile-long furrows of wheat and corn, the sun-bleached old hay barns and wooden houses along the road look abandoned and forlorn, their doors and clapboard siding flapping in the wind.

Just before the storm hit, we finally found a family of renters at one of these run-down farms willing to let us camp, and we stripped the harness off the mules and got them into a corral as it began to rain. Nick wandered off with Olive Oyl to sleep in a dilapidated semitrailer that had been converted into a horse barn, and he would wake in the morning with a beard of manure plastered to the whiskers on one side of his face. I spent my fifth night of the trip sleeping in the wagon during a thunderstorm.

While the rain pounded on the canvas top, I counted the section lines from North Platte on my DeLorme map. We'd covered thirty-two miles that day. The mules weren't even spent, and, at this rate, we could be in Ash Hollow in two days—450 miles from St. Joe in exactly a month.

Pushing on for the hills after we'd already done our twenty miles for the day wasn't a sensible decision. We should have camped before reaching the lake and taken O'Fallon's Bluff early in the morning, when the winds were lighter. It was a mistake. But these mistakes were working for us. After the storm blew over, I fell asleep to the frantic calling of screech owls, who for some reason had decided to dive-bomb the wagon top. I thought back to my sandy epiphany up on the bluffs. Perhaps, on a covered wagon trip, there were no mistakes. Only luck and persistence counted. My father had taken the Delaware that day in 1958 on a guess and a prayer. We had just taken O'Fallon's Bluff, one of several obstacles on the trail I was warned not to cross, driving blind in a sandstorm. Uncertainty and unplanned days were kiting us west well ahead of plan.

15

CALIFORNIA HILL IS ONE OF those places along the trail that Daniel Boorstin was referring to when he described the covered wagon as "plainly a community vehicle: everything about it required traveling in groups." After fording the South Platte channel near present-day Brule, Nebraska, the pioneers crossed twenty miles across a breathtakingly scenic plateau to the North Platte drainage, which they followed northwest into Wyoming and the Rockies. Several fingers of badland ravines, however, coursed through the scrub and brush plains around California Hill, and the only access to the plateau was a smooth, sharp incline between the canyons. The pull to the top involved an elevation change of about three hundred feet in less than a half mile, one of the steepest grades on the trail.

All summer during the trail years, as hundreds of wagons converged above the South Platte, California Hill bustled with purposeful chaos. The white-tops were parked at all angles, spread like dominoes between the canyons. The flour casks and trunks of the pioneers were strewn in piles everywhere. Families camped and cooked as they waited for their turn on the hill. Children earned their keep scurrying uphill, carrying the contents of the wagons piece by piece, and the canyons sang with the sounds of jangling harness and groups of men shouting as the draft teams were doubled and the lightened wagons were pulled upslope.

Studying choke points along the trail like California Hill, I was often struck by the paradoxes of American thinking about the pioneers. We think of them as sojourners in the wilderness, explorers almost, bravely conquering the "Great American Desert." But the many places where the terrain forced the pioneers to gather en masse acted as transient, urban clusters, cities of people in mobile homes traveling to the next big ford or bluff, there to cluster again as an essentially urban unit. The pioneers were mostly rural farmers, but on the trail they had to rely on the negotiating skills and habits of organization demanded of city dwellers. Schoolteachers and historians depict the pioneers as exemplars of that supposed American trait, "rugged individualism." But rugged individualism was wrapped in an envelope of group enterprise.

Even before I left New England, I had known that I wouldn't take California Hill. The old ruts are now preserved by OCTA with a fence line and a narrow gate allowing access to tourists on foot, but preventing damage to the historic swales by teenagers on ATVs and dirt bikes. Nowadays no one wants a team of mules scrambling up there, either. I had planned to divert west to Big Springs on Highway 30 and then climb to the plateau along the steep but graded Day Road.

Most of the Oregon Trail experts, including Bill Petersen, had warned me to resist one temptation. There is now a dusty, steep ranch road that tightly circles the perimeter of the old trail, but this grade is actually *steeper* than the original ruts. Conquering that grade would allow me to say that I had climbed California Hill. But this was considered foolhardy and I would be running the risk of getting stuck or wrecked up there. An unassisted climb up the hill in a loaded wagon, pulling a heavy Trail Pup, would be insane.

We reached California Hill late in the afternoon, tired and hot after a thirty-mile run from O'Fallon's Bluff. Today, there is a pullout and a historical plaque dedicated to California Hill at the base of the rise, along Highway 30. Excited about reaching this milestone of the trail, I stepped from the wagon to read the plaque and to describe to Nick the nineteenth-century bustle of California Hill.

Nick gazed north up the sharp rise with a quiet, faraway expression.

"Rink, I can put these mules up on that ridge."

I didn't want to attempt a difficult ascent like this, risking the whole trip after coming almost five hundred miles.

"No," I said. "It's too dangerous."

"I came out here to do the trail," Nick said. "The real trail. I can put the mules on that ridge."

"Nick. Why do you do this to me?"

"Daddy used to say that. Like it was *my* fault."

"You're crazy," I said.

"We already know that."

The moment condensed our history as brothers. In Maine, Nick was known for fastidiously building mansions and reconstructing burned-out summer camps in record time, but that was when he was working for someone else. On his own time, he sank boats, stripped gears pulling swimming floats from rivers, and wrecked wagons and sleighs. Essentially, crossing the Oregon Trail together, we were a case of collaborating DNA presenting symptoms of incurable bipolar disorder. I proceed with an abundance of caution and prefer not to be dead. Nick is thrilled by danger and proceeds with an abundance of risk.

"Boss?" he said. "Rinker?"

"Let me think," I said.

I leaned against Jake's neck, scratching his ears, and stared down at the river. It was a hazy afternoon and a smudgy pall of moisture rose over the curving channel of the Platte. The wrong move here could end the trip. But without Nick I wouldn't even have been at California Hill. Besides, I was addicted to mileage now. Instead of the twenty miles that I had planned, we were now regularly logging twenty-five miles by late afternoon. Reaching the plateau directly from here would save us an eight-mile detour, once more bumping our daily gain to almost thirty-five miles. There was still light in the sky and I was overwhelmed by my evening mania for distance.

Shit. I simultaneously hated Nick's ass and loved him for asking me to do this.

"Nicholas Buck," I said. "You are a miserable braggart, a shameless daredevil, and a horrible dresser."

"Great, we can do it! Thanks, Boss. Olive Oyl! He said yes!"

"You do know that your ass is grass if we get stuck up there."

"Boss, relax. The mules will climb this hill. Have you ever known me to fuck up?"

"Oh, Christ," I said. "Let's water these mules."

Western hills are deceptive. The ridgeline seen from a hill's base elevation on the flats is often a false summit, but you have to reach it to see the succession of higher rises after that. The sand hill formations of Nebraska are high grassy dune after high grassy dune. As we clambered up the first rise with the team I didn't know what we'd find, except that the ridge that I saw probably hid a few more.

I realized the magnitude of our error when we reached the first summit and stopped beside the OCTA interpretive sign. The fence line protecting the old swales blocked our way, and the original trail disappeared over the green hill on a northwest diagonal. The pioneers had expertly picked their terrain along a narrow corridor of uphill slope between the ravines. But the perimeter road that we would have to follow actually plunged back down into the neighboring canyon, requiring two drops into the hollows and two more steep climbs. The footing on the path was a deep, chalky sand. Steep canyon walls rose on the north and south sides of the last climb, where the soil roadbed was eroded about eight feet below the contour line. The wind had blown onto the roadbed a deep blanket of black, dried tumbleweed, two feet high in some places, and we would have to plow through that to reach the summit.

It was an Everest for mules. I had never attempted to push a team up such steep hills, and we had now inserted our wagon into such a narrow space that there was no turning around. We were committed, but that is far too polite a word for our predicament. We were fucked.

I sighed and took a drink from my canteen, took off my hat, and wiped my brow with my bandanna.

"Jesus," I said to Nick. "Can the mules make that last hill?"

"Boss, chill. When we get into camp tonight?"

"Yeah?"

"You can take your medications."

We plunged down through the first ravine, and then up the rise, without much difficulty. I held just enough pressure on the brake to keep the rig off the mules until the last part of the downhill, and then released two tons of wagon and trailer on the mules to force them nearly to a gallop and gain momentum for the climb. But the next hill presented a new problem. Just before the climb, the road turned sharply west. At the bottom, Nick had to slow the mules to a walk to safely negotiate the turn, denying us a running start for the hard vertical pull ahead.

But the mules looked uphill to the wall of dust and black tumbleweed and wouldn't stop for the turn, pulling right through the brake and fishtailing the wagon around the bend. They dug in their haunches for the pull.

Bute leaped forward and tried to pull the others along with her, as she'd done the night before. I couldn't believe Bute's gumption here—she was the little mule that could. At a moment of excitement like this, herd mentality, the stampede instinct, takes over with mules, and it means a lot. Jake and Beck were now furiously competing for position as the lead.

Oh, mules. Thank you, George Washington of Mount Vernon. Thank you, Royal Gift. These black Andalusians were spectacular beasts. I had never seen such athleticism and drive.

The front hooves of the team pounded the sand, their shoulders were bent low and far forward, and the trace chains against the trees were tense and metallically cracking from the pressure. Twelve hooves pounding sand and threshing tumbleweed created so much dust that I couldn't see the slope ahead of us. The running gear banged and creaked and the mules grunted inside our cosmos of dust.

Nick was pleading with the mules now, begging them, leaning all the way forward on the footboard so that he was out over the team and slapping the lines on their rumps. He was desperate. His bravado terrified him now. His voice cracked as he called the mules.

"Big Team! C'mon, Big Team! Beck! Jake! Bute! Oregon! Oregon, Big Team! We gotta make this hill, Big Team!"

In the swirl of emotion and heart stoppage that our expedition now was, I called the mules too.

"Team! Jake! Beck! We *have* to make this hill. We can't stop! Oregon, Team! Oregon!"

Nick was hoarse now, calling the team in a creaky whisper. Olive Oyl was whimpering and shaking with fear beneath the wagon seat, and I was hanging way off the side of the wagon to look straight down at the wheels, with both hands on the brake, barely able to stay on the seat. If the wheels stopped and began to give even an inch backward, I would have to throw on the brake to prevent four thousand pounds of wagon from pulling the mules backward on top of us.

In the dust, and with the deep bed of black tumbleweed, Nick couldn't see the track ahead. He pulled the team too far to the left, into a beach of sand and tumbleweed that seemed to swallow Bute. She was pumping her legs furiously now, without any traction underfoot. But pulling the team back to the center would have slowed our momentum.

We were just inching forward now. Only Jake in the center position on the pole had any purchase on the hardtack middle of the ruts, and he was still pulling like a monster. Our momentum was stalled, the wagon nearly motionless, seventy feet from the top. We were doomed, a pair of fool-hardy easterners ruined on California Hill, more than a thousand miles from Oregon.

Nick seemed Lilliputian now, his bravado spent, and my confidence in his prowess was evaporating. He was too hoarse to call the team except in a whisper.

But the team, especially Jake, wouldn't stop pulling. We moved forward and uphill, a foot at a time, and near the crest I panicked when I realized that if we stopped too early, before the heavy Trail Pup behind us was off the slope, the wagon would plunge back down in reverse.

I grabbed the lines from Nick and called the mules the last hundred feet.

"Team! To the flats! To the flats, Team! Jake! Beck! You're gorgeous! To the flats!"

With supreme stamina, their mighty chests and bellies heaving, their haunches pushed low to dig in their hooves, the mules grunted us over the top.

On level ground, with the brake set, we sat speechless on the wagon seat, our hearts still pounding. The breeze racing across the broad plateau lifted our shirt collars and hats. The only sound was the heaving of the team. Finally, Nick spoke.

"This is one fuckin awesome team. I cannot believe these animals."

We contemplated that for a while, still chemically high and euphoric from the adrenaline pumped by California Hill. Both of us arrived at the same thought.

"We are going to make Oregon," I said.

"Yeah," Nick said hoarsely. "We're gonna make Oregon this summer."

The plateau surrounding us was uniformly flat and stretched for miles, a heaven of wheat fields in the sky. Once more it was dusk, we had no place to camp, and a new storm with low snarling clouds was bearing down on us from the northwest. We walked the mules west in the fading evening light until we found a farm where the middle-aged couple who owned it welcomed us in, telling us to bed the mules down in their goat pasture and then inviting us into their kitchen for a dinner of pancakes and elk steak.

The storm blew in an hour after dinner. I sat toward the rear of the wagon, propped up by my gear and wrapped in quilts, and wrote notes about the day. To the rituals of wagon travel—prairie dreamscapes all

Our rig on the first slope of California Hill near Brule, Nebraska. The experts said that we could never "take" this obstacle, but Nick was determined to try.

day, Platte River storms at night—I was now adding a new routine. As my white-top rocked with the winds, I debriefed all the mistakes of the day. At the bottom of California Hill, I had known there were probably farms with water and grass for the mules on the plateau. I could have off-loaded all of our hay bales but one, emptied our water barrels, and taken off our grain and returned for it later. Then I should have walked the slope behind the wagon. All told, our wagons could have been lightened by a thousand pounds, immensely increasing our chance of making the steep grade.

But maybe I was changing. As the prairie winds howled, and my womb of oak bows and canvas buffeted and creaked, I put down my notebook and stretched out to sleep, once more luxuriating in the nocturnal romance of sleeping under a white-top in hard rain. I preferred that to a nocturnal cataloging of my errors. Mistake by mistake, haphazard decision by haphazard decision, we were steadily moving west. We had taken California Hill, and I have never slept so well.

16

THE OLD PIONEER CAMP AT Ash Hollow, Nebraska, along the banks of the North Platte, is one of the most scenic and accessible Oregon Trail sites today, and it also typifies what the modern trail has become. The original ruts that plunged off the tableland and dropped for the Platte are too steep for automobile traffic, and the state of Nebraska has mostly protected them by securing conservation easements where the trail crosses private ranches, or by fencing them off on state parklands. But a two-lane state road that descends steeply from the plateau, Highway 26, closely parallels the nineteenth-century pioneer route, and the old ruts themselves crisscross the blacktop several times. Historian Merrill Mattes has described the downhill ride into the fabled pioneer camping grounds seen by contemporary tourists. "Modern highway engineering, ironing rugged topography into gentle declines and curves, makes the automobile descent into the Hollow seem painless." But here Mattes was merely commenting on the relatively sheltered experience of seeing the trail by car.

For more than an hour Nick and I managed the job of guiding two tons of wagons down a steep paved slope. The brakes on the rear wheels of the Schuttler could hold back only part of the load. The downhill gradient was so steep that the mules also had to help hold back the wagons, by leaning backward into the harness breeching straps on their rumps, bracing their weight against the force of the wagon falling downhill. "Putting" a team against its breeching is uncomfortable and awkward for the mules and can be terrifying for the driver because so much depends on the footing underneath the animals. Only Beck on the right, walking the graveled shoulder of the road, had a surface beneath her to grip with her hooves. Jake and Bute were constantly fighting to remain upright as their steel shoes slipped on the slick, hot tar of the roadbed. Every time they stumbled their harness slacked and the wagon lunged forward, threatening to overrun and panic the team.

While Nick drove and called—"Hold back! Hold back!"—I gingerly jockeyed the brakes. But locking the iron wheel rims for too long on the slick asphalt jackknifed the rig, swaying the pole and the team toward the guardrails, and we were burning out the brakes. Our new thresher-belt brake pads billowed smoke, and the acrid smell of burning rubber followed us all the way down to the valley floor.

Still, it was glorious to reach Ash Hollow. From the highway, we stared down the nearly vertical sides of a narrow ravine to the right of the wagon, topped by white cliffs, stretching for four miles down to the North Platte. Natural springs feed a creek that runs the length of the hollow floor to the river. On June and July nights after the late 1840s, this oasis on the North Platte was a busy camp town, with hundreds of wagons parked above picturesque Sioux tepees, U.S. Cavalry detachments, military freight caravans, and parties of buffalo hunters traveling east to St. Louis, their donkey carts piled high with robes.

The mass of humanity wedged into the narrow hollow inevitably created problems—cholera outbreaks, fights over stray cattle, trading disputes with the Sioux—and the pioneers complained in their journals about having to herd their animals several miles down the Platte to find a grassy area that had not been foraged out by earlier trains. During long camps that might last two nights, the pioneers paused to bake pastries from the abundant supply of wild berries in the hollow, and Ash Creek rang with the hammer blows and saw cuts of impromptu wagon-repair shops. Ash Hollow was a nineteenth-century mobile home park, throbbing and noisy, with the lowing of cattle and the caterwauling of whiskey drinkers echoing off the canyon walls all day and night. Here too, however, the noise and confusion of a busy wagon camp didn't prevent the travelers from enjoying the unique landscape. Lingering, powerful memories of the sylvan beauty of the hollow dominated the pioneer journals.

As his eleven-wagon train crossed from the south to the north fork of the Platte in 1849, Israel Hale stumbled on the decaying bodies of four white men who had apparently been scalped by an Indian war party. Hale was incapable of dwelling on that image once he saw the lovely ravine enticing the wagons onto the North Platte.

> Struck Ash Hollow. It is a narrow, sandy valley with low ash trees scattered along its side. We had not driven far when we found considerable underbrush, such as currents, rose bushes and several shrubs that I did not know the name of. The morning was clear, the air was pure and the roses nearly in full bloom, and sent forth a flavor which can better be imagined than described. The air appeared perfectly scented with them and I think if they had named the place the Valley of Roses it would have been a more appropriate name, for there were fifty rose bushes to one ash tree.

Over time, Ash Hollow would also come to symbolize the tragic clash of cultures between the white emigrants and the Native Americans that eventually doomed the Indian tribes. In 1855, a detachment of six hundred U.S. Army soldiers commanded by General William S. Harney surrounded a band of Brule Sioux led by Chief Little Thunder near Blue Water Creek, six miles north of Ash Hollow, slaughtering eighty-six braves and capturing most of their women and children. Harney's expedition was launched in retaliation for an incident the year before, when an inexperienced Army lieutenant, John Grattan, had brashly marched his soldiers into a large Brule Sioux camp outside Fort Laramie, Wyoming, demanding that the chiefs produce the Indian who had shot a Mormon pioneer's cow, even though the Brules had already offered restitution for the cow by giving the pioneer his pick of their sixty-horse herd. The usual army bumbling was involved. Grattan was a recent West Point graduate, unfamiliar with Sioux ways, and his French-Canadian "interpreter" could not speak the Brule dialect and was drunk. After shots were exchanged, Grattan and all thirty of his men were killed. The carnage in both engagements was senseless and produced no results, and historians generally credit the so-called Grattan Massacre and the Battle of Blue Water Creek as the events that set off the disastrous series of Indian wars that racked the west after the Civil War.

The tribes had already been decimated by a silent killer introduced west of the Missouri by the army forts and the overland emigrants. The arrival of diseases such as cholera, measles, and smallpox, to which the Sioux, the Pawnee, and the Osage tribes had never been exposed, began to have a devastating impact after the 1849 Gold Rush. Historians have never been able to accurately estimate how many plains Indians died from the introduction of European diseases in the mid-nineteenth century, but it is clear that it caused widespread panic and disruption in the lives of the tribes.

"Some Indians quickly recognized the consequences of these diseases," John D. Unruh Jr. wrote in *The Plains Across*, "[and] by 1850 a Fort Laramie observer reported that frightened natives were deserting the trails in hopes of avoiding the deadly peril. . . . The demographic impact of cholera alone among the [tribes] was considerable. These population losses had obvious implications for the ability of the western tribes to re sist the American expansionist onslaught."

Captain Howard Stansbury, an army surveyor dispatched across the trail in 1849 to explore new routes and file a report for his unit, the U.S. Corps of Topographical Engineers, poignantly described one scene at Ash Hollow. Stansbury's mounted unit, trailed by five supply wagons, reached the pioneer camp in early July. There, he found a small band of "tall, graceful" Sioux camped at the head of the valley. The Sioux had invited a group of emigrants into their lodges but quickly decamped when cholera broke out. The disease had already spread to the Sioux band, however, and a few days later they returned to Ash Hollow begging for medical help. Then they disappeared again.

The next morning Stansbury saw a small Indian village on a bluff across the Platte.

"The total absence of any living thing about them interested us from curiosity to cross the river, here nearly a mile wide, with a strong rapid current," Stansbury wrote in his journal. After wading across, Stansbury found five tepees with nine dead Sioux inside, their buffalo robes, spears, and camp kettles arrayed around them. He was touched most by the body of a pretty Sioux teenage girl, carefully wrapped and laid out alone in one of the lodges. She was "richly dressed" in scarlet leggings, ornaments, and a pair of new moccasins beautifully embroidered with porcupine quills.

"I learned that they all died with cholera," Stansbury wrote, "and this young girl being considered past recovery had been arranged by her friends in the habiliments of the dead, enclosed in the lodge alive, and abandoned."

There is very little evidence today of the chaotic, crowded wagon cities, or the colorful, scruffy Sioux camps, described by the pioneers. Ash Hollow is now a mostly deserted, well-preserved scenic space operated by the state of Nebraska as a historic park. After resting the mules, Nick and I spent a lazy, pleasant afternoon as tourists, driving the wagon around to the Oregon Trail sites—an old fur trappers' cabin that was probably used as a trading post during the overland years, and a well-appointed visitors' center and museum perched on the ridge above the North Platte. From a parking lot on the west edge of the hollow, an asphalt path climbs Windlass Hill, the sharp, three-hundred-foot drop where the pioneers were forced to lower their wagons with ropes. I was struck several times that afternoon by the irony of visiting preserved space, the contrast between past and present on celebrated ground. The mules clopped from historic marker to historic marker along smooth paved roads, passing neatly mowed picnic grounds, attractive restroom stops, and pullouts commanding spacious views of the Platte. Everything was as orderly and well-appointed as the campus of a wealthy New England college. This is what we so often find when searching for history—emptiness, quiet, acres of mowed grass. Battlefields where hundreds of men died on a single day become vast, pristine lawns, as lovely as a landscape by Constable or van Gogh, and historic birthplaces are so lovingly maintained that it's hard to believe anyone ever lived there. Edith Wharton's cellar becomes a gift shop. In the cemetery quiet of these places, all the clangor and hell of actual history—the smell of manure where horses were bedded, earth scorched from fire pits or cannonball explosions, the stench from bayonets ripping flesh—has been sanitized away. While preserving history, we remove it. There's nothing wrong with this, of course, and I'd rather see a beautifully maintained battlefield than a Wal-Mart parking lot. But that is what we're doing while visiting historic space. It's Versailles without the hideously overdressed and clownish aristocrats, a Potemkin village without the rotting slums behind the facades.

From Windlass Hill, a curving path of wheel ruts, dark against the grassy ridge, meanders south, marking the route that the pioneers followed out of the hollow into the North Platte valley. I was excited about that. After Ash Hollow, we would pick up the trail across several private ranches and the dusty, unpaved Platte River Road, bumping along on original ruts for almost fifty miles. We were just a few days away from some of the most dramatic scenery on the route, the sandstone waypoints of Courthouse Rock, Jail House Rock, Chimney Rock, and Scotts Bluff, which the pioneers knew from their guidebooks were the gateway to the Rockies.

At the bottom of the hollow, a low concrete bridge carries motor traffic across the Platte to Lewellyn, and the summer tourists speed west along the paved highway. We turned left at a small cemetery on the river to remain with the Oregon Trail. The Platte there is moody and dark, with ancient cottonwoods growing out of the black, muddy floodplain, and the sharply rising cliffs to our left narrowed our vision to just the dark tunnel of the trail. We emerged eight miles later in bright sunlight onto a broad grassland plain that swept toward one of the most dramatic escarpments in the west, an old Sioux camp and lookout point, Signal Bluff.

The immaculately restored bunkhouse at the Signal Bluff Ranch felt palatial to us, and the fun-loving ranchers there, John and Nancy Orr, were the best trail family yet. Nick rebuilt the mule bridles and replaced the thresher-belt pads on the brakes, while I wrote letters home and took notes. But there was still more greenhorn revenge for us.

Late in the afternoon during our first day of rest at the ranch, I was sitting on the deck of the bunkhouse, writing letters and enjoying the spacious view down the Platte. When the sun emerged from behind a cloud, I was suddenly blinded by a strobe of light bouncing off the felloe on the front wheel of the Schuttler.

Felloes are the semicircular wooden parts, just below the iron rim of the wheel, into which the tops of the spokes are fitted. But why had a long strip of paint peeled off one of them, revealing underneath what looked like a shiny patch of plastic?

I could see what the problem was as soon as I walked over to investigate. Along about six inches of the felloe, a shiny coating of cheap plastic filler—like auto-body shop "bondo"—had been skimmed over the wood. When I pressed my thumb against the felloe, bits of the brittle plastic fell off and blew away in the wind, revealing a gaping stretch of dry rot underneath. There were more bondo strips on the bottom felloe, and on the other front wheel. Our wheels, the one part that couldn't fail if we were to reach Oregon, were riddled with rot.

"Nick! Have you seen these front wheels? They've been bondoed over. They're rotten underneath."

Nick's Fu Manchu dropped and he stepped over from his chair, where he had been working on the bridles. He looked at my face, sighed, and then stared at the ground.

"Oh, Christ. I've been prayin for weeks that you wouldn't notice these fuckin wheels," he said. "They must have slicked over that rot and then painted the wheels, so they would look fine. It's an old wagon makers' trick—bondo over the rot."

"How bad is this?"

"One rotten felloe won't collapse the whole wheel. Somewhere ahead we'll find a shop and I'll cut out all of the rot and rebuild the wheel."

I suddenly remembered the grimace on Nick's face back in Kansas, after he had given the Trail Pup wheels a hard shake when we were picking up the wagons.

"What about the Trail Pup wheels?" I said.

Nick scowled and limped back to the Trail Pup, pointing a stubby finger at the joint where the bottom of the spokes joined the hub on the left wheel.

When he leaned onto the wheel and gave it a hard shake, a faint creaking rose from the hub and I could see space opening up and closing on the joint.

Nick explained that there was probably dry rot inside the wheel spokes and hubs, which explained the loose fit and the creaking noise they made. That had been painted over as well. If we reached rough terrain where the cart leaned over on one side, the load could shift to the low wheel and lead to "hub failure," breaking the wheel.

"Nick, why didn't you tell me?"

"If we'd stopped way back in Kansas to rebuild all of these wheels, we never would have left. There's at least a fifty-fifty chance these wheels will last all the way to Oregon."

I turned away from the wagon, disgusted with myself for paying so much for a rig with four questionable wheels. Once more, I had been as naive as the pioneers. We had now come 450 miles in exactly a month—spectacular progress. But we still had the Black Hills of Wyoming and then the Rockies to cross, and I didn't even know if my wheels would hold.

Leaving Signal Bluff and riding our first long stretch of original ruts was lyrical. The trail meandered west past towering flattop buttes and golden grasslands that stretched to the horizon. We were now in famous ranch country, where the big herds of longhorn had been driven up from Texas to the Platte after the Union Pacific tracks were laid in 1867. But reaching the cattle lands presented a new problem that I had completely failed to anticipate.

The scrub grasslands of western Nebraska look remote, but the region is heavily fenced. Every mile or so along the trail a long barbed-wire fence line ran down from the South Hills and crossed our path, culminating in an obstacle called a "cattle guard." Cattle guards are welded structures of parallel steel pipes, like prison bars laid flat, placed on top of a deep trench on the trail. Cattle that have wandered off from their herds and broken through fence lines won't cross the guards, because they look straight down through the bars and see the trench, confining them at least relatively close to their intended range. These familiar structures on western roads are also called "auto gates," because they allow a passing car or pickup to rumble over the pipes on top of the trench. Horses and mules won't cross cattle guards either. To let the cattle and horses through for the frequent local cattle drives, however, barbed-wire gates are built adjacent to the guards. The gates are attached to the fence lines with circular loops of wire.

But these gates are maddeningly inconsistent. Depending on the ranch or the age of the fences, some of them were child's play to open, with aged, slack wire holding the gateposts, which were easy to manipulate. But many of the gates were built with new, extremely tight loops of wire. To open the gate, cowboys crouch down low between the strands of barbed wire, push hard against the post with one shoulder, and then move an arm up past the strands of barbed wire to close the attachment. For the tighter gates, most cowboys also carry a large, pliers-type device called a "gate jack," which pulls the posts tightly together, making it easier to close the gate.

Veteran cowboys make this Houdini act look easy. But easterners like me crouch up against the posts, feebly attempting to open and shut the wire attachments, ripping their shirts and drawing blood on the rusty strands of barbed wire.

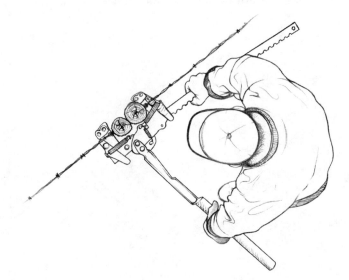

The standard "gate jack" of the West, used by ranchers to open and shut stubborn barbed-wire gates.

There were fourteen cattle guards and gates along the trail after Signal Bluff, and they were particularly frequent after Rush Creek. After opening a gate, we would drive the mules down through the gulch at the edge of the cattle guard and then call them up the steep sides back onto the trail.

The cattle guard gates were a test of our personalities. There probably isn't a barbed-wire gate in the West that Nick can't grunt open, but I struggled with most of them, chastising myself for forgetting to buy a gate jack. By the end of the day we both had been stabbed by barbed wire several times, and the right shoulder of my plaid cowboy shirt was ripped open and stained with blood. Under the blazing Nebraska sun, the blood clotted quickly and hard against my cotton shirt, and the scab reopened and bled every time I jumped off the wagon to push a new gate. I found that pouring water from my canteen on the wound kept it soft and helped it to heal. After a few days of opening gates, my shoulder was calloused with scar tissue and barbecued purple and red where the sun came through the tear in my shirt. For several days, when I woke in the morning, my bloodied shoulder and shirt had matted onto my sheet, and I ripped the wound open getting out of bed. But the fresh blood trickling down my back felt welcome and warm, reminding me of the gratifying soreness I felt at home after a day of logging in the woods.

We encountered more than 250 cattle guards—sometimes twelve or fourteen in a fifteen-mile stretch—across the West.

We made the rodeo corrals at the deserted hamlet of Lisco that night, another camp where the sweet exhaustion of the day, and the poetic sunset over the Platte, seemed joined together as a single sensation. The cowboys from the local spreads, Rush Creek Ranch and Muddy Creek Ranch, had spent the day watching our white-tops cross the rangeland, and many of them drove over in their pickups to see the mules. They brought hay, told us what to expect ahead on the trail, and swapped stories while we sat on our chairs and stared across the river to the Sand Hills.

From the cowboys, we learned that we faced more bad weather ahead. A huge thunderstorm system was forming over the Rockies and was expected to push east the next day, dumping considerable rain, and would probably cause flooding along the low banks of the North Platte near Bridgeport, Nebraska, blocking the trail. Once more we were racing against the storms of the Platte and we had to get past Bridgeport by sunset the next day.

17

NICK'S BRAVURA DRIVING STYLE FINALLY caught up with us the next morning at Lisco. To reach the gate at a cattle guard just above the remote rodeo corral, we had to curve southwest, plunge through a runoff ditch beside the road, and then climb a sharp hill of treacherous soft soil, muddy from the recent rains. Nick loudly called the mules and broke them into a trot to build momentum for the hill, taking the incline on a diagonal, but I was sure we should be going much more slowly.

It became a classic trail clusterfuck. While I was calling "Eas-A, Eas-A, Eas-A" and reaching over toward Nick to restrain the lines, he was slapping the rumps of the mules and calling "Yup there! Big Team! Up the hill!" The team listened to Nick and gamely scrambled up the hill at an angle. When we reached the road we heard a sharp *Bang!* from behind and the mules started digging in their hooves to pull a heavier load, as if we suddenly had a gang plow attached to the rig. Something was wrong.

"Whoa! Whoa, Team. Whoa!"

I pushed home the brake and stood up on the wagon seat to look back over the cover and couldn't believe what I saw. The Trail Pup lay on its left side, mostly intact but smashed in places, like an overturned semitrailer on a highway embankment after a jackknife accident.

"Goddamnit, Nick. We flipped the Trail Pup. The Trail Pup is lying on its side."

"Hold these mules. Let me get back there. I wanna see it! I wanna see it and see if I can fix it."

I was surprised by how calm I felt about our first accident of the trip. I was almost elated about it. The pioneer journals had indoctrinated me that completely. I had always known that there was no way we could cross to Oregon without at least one wagon wreck, and now we had a baptism by disaster that would prove our mettle. We had to be coolly analytical and show ourselves that we could quickly recover and get back on the trail.

I told Nick that we would unhitch the mules from the wagon and drive them over to the corrals before we assessed the damage.

Nick was frantic with worry as he drove the team away, looking back over his shoulder and calling out so that his loud, booming voice echoed over the plains.

"Tell me what's broken! Can I fix it? What's broken?"

It was amusing, in a way, to see my beautiful Trail Pup sprawled sideways on the road. Our external water spigots, equipment hangers, hoses, and ropes had all snapped off and were lying in pieces on the road. Bales of hay, grain sacks, and our camping and cooking gear had spilled through the cover where the oak bows had snapped. Nick's cantilever extension was a testament to overbuilding—the structure had held, but the cooler racks on the side were shattered. The SEE AMERICA SLOWLY sign was pitched up vertically from prairie to sky.

But I could see that we had escaped relatively unscathed. Our mistake hadn't been Nick's racing the team uphill, but negligently taking the incline on the diagonal. The Schuttler, with its four wheels evening out the bumps, had lulled us into a false sense of stability. We had completely forgotten that the two-wheel Pup far behind on the rig was inherently tipsy, especially on sloped terrain. Taking the hill on an angle had transferred the weight of more than a thousand pounds of supplies and water onto the low wheel and, when it all shifted sideways at once, overturned the cart.

But the dumping of the wagon had been so swift that the wheels, miraculously, weren't broken, and the only big part that was damaged was the oak tongue that connected the cart to the main wagon. The tongue was now a mass of twisted splinters. The heavy steel fitting connecting the tongue to the wagon was bent, and we would probably need to heat it with welding torches to hammer it back into shape. The oak bows would have to be replaced.

Flipping our Trail Pup was the first accident of the trip, and held us up along the Platte until we could make repairs.

We were now stranded on a secluded stretch of trail, with no ranches or houses within sight, and we were never going to make it past Bridge-port today. But as I inspected the downed Trail Pup I remembered that the manager of Muddy Creek Ranch, Dan Hanlon, whom I had met at the corrals the night before, lived just four miles west. Hanlon, a joyful, beer-bellied man who rarely shaved, was not a quiet cowpoke. He was one of the boastyboys, dressed in jeans that hadn't been washed in a week, scuffed packer's boots, and a Resistol straw hat browned by the sun, sweat, and grime. But the boastyboys are often the most fun, and some-times the most generous. He had extended the Nebraska welcome as he stepped into his pickup to leave the corrals that night.

"Any old goldarn thang ya want?" he said, wiggling an imaginary cell phone near his ear. "Just give me a jingle on the brain-cancer device and I'll be right there in a jiffy for ya."

I had written Dan's number down in my pocket notebook. Relieved to discover that I had cell phone coverage, I dialed him, and he answered right away. When I told him what had happened, Hanlon said that we could fix the cart in his shop and that he'd be down with a pickup and trailer in fifteen minutes.

While we waited for Dan, Nick made a brief inspection tour around the cart, and I was relieved by his confidence about making repairs. We were both amazed that the overturning had done so little damage to the wheels—maybe the hubs weren't rotten after all.

"I can have this cart back on the trail tonight," he said. "All I'm gonna need is a six-foot section of cured oak, water spigots, and some hardware, and we'll need to figure out somethin to replace those bows. Just get me to a fuckin shop."

Dan roared in a little later in a big rusty King Cab pickup with a bad muffler, pulling a trailer. It took us half an hour to unload the cart, right it, wheel it up onto the trailer with ramps, and then strap it down. We stacked the hay, gear, and broken parts beside it. As Dan drove off with his crazy trailer load of dismembered Trail Pup, he promised to call the lumberyard in Oshkosh to see if it had the oak stock that we needed. I told him that we'd rehitch the mules and be down on his ranch with the main wagon within two hours.

Nick stood with his hands on his hips while the crippled Trail Pup rumbled over the cattle guard and then disappeared west on the muddy trail. He took a deep breath, turned toward me, briefly stared at the ground, and then looked directly into my eyes.

"Rink, just for the record, I apologize about this. This accident was my fault."

I can't account for my feelings just then but I felt terribly guilty for Nick, and I loved him. I wasn't angry about dumping the Trail Pup, but I knew I couldn't explain that to him. But there was something that I could accomplish here. Nick's penchant for reckless driving, his break-it-so-we-can-fix-it style, was a threat to the trip. His insistence that only he knew mules and wagons, that his judgment about driving was always superior to mine, was manifestly wrong. I had to move the conversation to that without making him feel bad for me and blaming himself.

"Nick, I'm not angry, okay? Let's start there. We took the hill on a diagonal. Neither of us saw that."

"Don't be so fuckin polite," he said. "You told me to go easier on the speed, I should have listened. That's what flipped the Trail Pup."

"Nick, I'm actually happy about this. It'll be fun proving that we can quickly get the rig back on the road. It's just . . ."

"My drivin."

"Your driving. I mean, can't you just *listen* to me? You can drive more carefully."

"I should have been listenin. I was drivin too fast. I'm gonna start listenin and this won't happen again. I promise, Boss."

"All right," I said. "We don't need to talk about this again. Just fucking listen to me, okay? C'mon. Let's harness these mules."

Muddy Creek Ranch stood back from the trail about a quarter of a mile and had a ramshackle stucco ranch house buried in a cottonwood grove, lots of barns and corrals in the back, and a yelping pack of furry blue heeler and Australian shepherd puppies scrambling underfoot everywhere we walked. Our afternoon there was another emotional reprise for us. Nick was determined to prove that, having broken a wagon in the morning, he could have it back on the trail by nightfall, and I knew that he would exhaust himself doing that. My job was to pretend that nothing had happened and to run around in the ranch pickup, like an obsequious delivery boy, providing just-on-time delivery of parts. At Muddy Creek, I felt that I had discovered a completely new aspect of management. I had to handle things so discreetly, so invisibly, that there wasn't really a Trail Boss at all.

While Nick hammered away outside the ranch implement shed with an immense ball-peen hammer, to bend the heavy steel fittings back into shape, I ran into Oshkosh with Dan Hanlon and found the last piece of cured oak stock at the lumberyard. I ran it back to the ranch and then raced into Bridgeport for the plumbing supplies we needed to fix the broken water barrel attachments. When I got back from Bridgeport, Nick had already finished building out the new Trail Pup tongue. With his immense strength, he had lifted the heavy Trail Pup by the tongue, single-handedly hauled the cart all the way across the ranch yard, and reattached it to the wagon.

When I drove in, Nick was collapsed against one of the wheels of the main wagon, playing with Olive Oyl and a couple of the blue heeler puppies, who were scrambling around on his lap.

"I can't believe that you've got this much done already," I said to him. "You're a monster for work."

"I told you we could be back on the trail tomorrow."

"You look spent," I said. "Why don't you go into the house and take a nap?"

"I think I will. We can figure out what to do about the bows later."

I knew from my wagon research in the spring that the only source for replacing our broken bows was an Amish wood shop in Ohio—too far away to expect a timely delivery now. Nick wouldn't like it, but I thought that I could somehow shitrig new bows for the covered top of the Trail Pup myself, a good idea to have on a Nebraska ranch, where nothing ever seems to get thrown away. Cruising the scrap piles behind one of the barns, I found several sections of five-eighth-inch plastic conduit pipe that had been used on the pasture irrigators, and could probably be fashioned into bows. In the shop, there was a pile of brackets that I could bend into shape with vise-grips, to hold the plastic pipe to the sides of the cart.

Working frantically so that I would be done before Nick woke up, I cut the conduit down with a hacksaw and drilled holes for the brackets on the sides of the Trail Pup. Then I assembled everything, dusting off the canvas cover before I pulled it over the new bows, and cinched it tight with the pucker ropes.

My solution wasn't elegant. The plastic conduit was much narrower than the original oak bows, and underneath the canvas wagon cover the new plastic bows looked like ribs showing through the loose skin of a starving dog. But the assembly would at least hold the rain and the dust off our feed and gear, and our rig looked like a set of matched white-tops again.

When Nick finally came out, I heard him groan from the corner of the house when he saw the new covered top.

"Oh, shit me," he said. "You didn't fix the bows, did you? I thought you would wait for me on that."

"Nick, it's a good fix. I did all of this myself."

Nick stood on the tongue of the Trail Pup and ran his pudgy hands over the new plastic bows. He leaned his shoulder onto the first bow and gave the whole works a brisk shove.

"All right, Boss. This'll hold in the wind. It looks uglier than a stump post, but it's a decent repair."

I smiled and quietly laughed when Nick said that, and he must have seen the contentment on my face.

"I'm gonna tell everyone at home about this," he said. "You've had a total fuckin personality transplant. You can actually fix somethin now."

"Thanks, Nick. I really appreciate that."

For the rest of the afternoon, while the wind blew dust devils down from the bluffs, Nick and I were a blurred frenzy of hammering and driving in screws, making the rest of the repairs. We were done well before dark, and then we sat beside the wheels on our camp chairs and played with the blue heeler puppies.

The layover for repairs at Muddy Creek stalled us again along the Platte. For the next two days we were stranded at the ranch as the monster storm system we were worried about lashed through western Nebraska, pushing the river over its banks at a giant bend six miles west of the ranch and blocking the trail with an immense lake. We quickly fell into the life of the ranch. Between the worst rain squalls we helped Dan run his cattle to new pastures, splashing on horseback through the sandy mud up on the South Hills, and Nick roamed through the ranch house and barns with his tool kit, replacing leaky hydraulic fittings on tractors and repairing broken light fixtures. I spent the rainy afternoons lounging on a couch in the ranch house, poring over my maps and reading pioneer journals.

The forced stop proved more useful than I expected. With enough time on my hands to calculate our total mileage from St. Joe, I realized that we had made 490 miles in a month, just ten miles shy of my monthly goal. I had always roughly calculated that we would traverse one state per month—Nebraska in June, Wyoming in July, Idaho in August—and we were easily meeting that pace, which would put us near Oregon by September. My furtive instinct about pushing the mules until late in the day seemed to have a logic now. There would always be obstacles along the trail—weather, breakdowns, detours around rough terrain—but we were compensating for the lost time by the extra five or eight miles we made during our evening runs. I even liked being delayed on the Platte, because our adversity seemed so appropriate. Franklin Langworthy, Margaret Frink, Abigail Jane Scott, and Mark Twain had been stalled by the flooding Platte too.

When we finally left, Dan reached into the back of his pickup and gave us a spare gate jack, which we could use at the cattle guards in the rangelands ahead. He decided to ride the wagon with Nick to check the high water on the river ahead, and he gave me his best cow horse, a spirited paint, to ride beside the rig. As we splashed through the puddled sand along the trail where the Platte was dropping back within its banks, I swayed the paint in S-turns behind the wagon and then galloped off to explore a dry stretch of bottomlands along the river. We were past the 100th meridian dry line now, the rains would probably abate, and this was the dream journey by horseback that I had always imagined for myself.

After Bridgeport, Nebraska, the landscape changed dramatically, from grasslands to spare, dry sagebrush country, and the soil turned from sandy brown to pink. We were entering the magic, pastel geology of western Nebraska that was celebrated by the pioneers and became familiar to Americans through the paintings of William Henry Jackson and Albert Bierstadt. Today the only route along the south banks of the Platte is the two-lane Highway 92, a prime example of the Oregon Trail adapted for modern use by paving the ruts with asphalt, but I was delighted to see that the prospect from the wagon seat was virtually unchanged.

The wagons had navigated west through a natural gallery of art. Two adjoining formations, the sand-colored Courthouse Rock and Jail House Rock, were the first in a long string of landmarks composed of sandstone, clay, and volcanic ash that had been eroded by the ceaseless Nebraska winds and over centuries separated from the surrounding formation of bluffs. A profusion of yellow coneflowers and rudbeckia grew at their base and green sagebrush fringed their sides. Then we cleared a rise and, from almost forty miles out, the lavender and pink pinnacle of Chimney Rock came into view.

Chimney Rock, rising almost 350 feet above the sagebrush plain of the North Platte valley, is a pointed sandstone column resting on a conical base. In their diaries and letters home, the pioneers made this landmark as recognizable to Americans as Niagara Falls. Virtually all the trail diarists mentioned it, usually in considerable detail, and the trail annals now contain twenty-one sketches of Chimney Rock, many of them displaying remarkable line-drawing skills, made by the pioneers. Because it could be seen so far away on the horizon, Chimney Rock lingered within sight of the wagons for almost a week, and the pioneers used the pinnacle as both a forward and a reverse waypoint for sixty miles or more. Pioneers who camped and fixed their wagons near the rock learned to judge western distances by eagerly hiking the "few miles" to the curiosity and finding that it was more like five or six miles away. Margaret Frink's husband scrambled up the base of the cone and carved their names into the soft red rock.

Chimney Rock in western Nebraska was among the first of a string of natural waypoints that the pioneers used to steer west.

The diary entries and sketches of Chimney Rock, often reprinted in local newspapers across the country, created additional allure about the trail. The central duality of the land migration—aesthetic wonder trumping hardship—prevailed here. At Chimney Rock, the camps were crowded and cholera occasionally returned. The draft animals were beginning to give out because the sandier soils and sparse rains to the west supported only thin grasses. The trail departed here for about two miles below the Platte, and there were long walks for water. But the beauty of the unfolding western terrain was the predominant theme, as if the pioneers needed a natural wonder reaching for the sky to alleviate—or deny—the hunger, dehydration, and death they saw all around them.

Virgil K. Pringle was a Connecticut native whose family had moved to St. Charles, Missouri, north of St. Louis, in 1826, establishing a lending library and a dry goods store. In 1846, the Pringles decided to follow a brother out to Oregon, and they reached Chimney Rock on June 19.

The dramatic river views and rock formations of the West, like Scotts Bluff on the Nebraska-Wyoming line, astonished pioneers who were used to the more predictable geography of the East.

Passed the chimney in the fore part of the day and the formation of the bluffs have a tendency to fill the mind with awe and grandeur. The chimney might pass for one of the foundries in St. Louis, were it blackened by burning stove coal.

As we dropped the wagon down into the broad valley along the North Platte, the purple beacon of the pioneers glowed against the yellow Nebraska sky, and remained within sight for three days. We found a comfortable, fenced pasture for the mules at the old pioneer camp near the rock, slept through another night of violent thunderstorms beneath the escarpments at Scotts Bluff, and then turned the mules toward Mitchell

Pass, the route through the Wildcat Hills that the pioneers followed after U.S. Army engineers built a military road in 1851. It was a hot day and the mules labored up the eastern slope of the pass, and our brake pads smoked all the way down the other side.

From the summit of the pass we could see the hazy blue dome of Laramie Peak, more than ninety miles away. There were more rain clouds ahead, and once more we would race the storms to shelter. But nothing rattled me now. Our shakedown with adversity—the endless rains, the endless barbed-wire gates of Nebraska—was behind us, and before us lay a mythic stretch of trail, 350 miles of original ruts through the Wyoming Rockies.

18

THE OREGON TRAIL IN WYOMING can be thought of as a giant game of topographic stealth. The emigrant road gracefully curved in a long bend around the Rockies, running northwest and then southwest, following the North Platte and the alluring banks of the Sweetwater for almost five hundred miles across the high desert plains. Because the east face of the Rockies could not be directly crossed with horses and donkeys, over time the Cheyenne and the Shoshone, and then the fur trappers, avoided the impassable mountains by following a meandering route along the lower foothills and the flats. Trailblazers like Marcus Whitman and Jim Bridger, and then the emigrant trains, endlessly refined the route into a system of camps and cutoffs to save traveling time. The result is both ingenious and magnificently beautiful. After Scotts Bluff and Fort Laramie, the pioneers spent a week with the alpine heights of the Laramie Range directly to their left, paid the Mormons to ford them across the Platte at present-day Casper, and then twisted their way down through the dramatic rock formations along the edges of the Rattlesnake Hills and the Granite Range. The snowy, heavenly Wind River Range rose after Casper as a lavender and white mosaic in the sky.

The pioneers could instantly sense that they had entered a vastly changed landscape—the real West. Stands of juniper and ponderosa pine rose steeply on the Rockies and their foothills, darkening the upper views, and the pioneers called eastern Wyoming the Black Hills. (The term was broadly used in the nineteenth century to refer to high ground that was heavily timbered with pine, reflecting the sun as black, and only later formally assigned to the Black Hills region of South Dakota.) The water, dropping from streams with sources twenty or thirty miles away in the mountains, was cleaner now, but sometimes a forced march of a day or more was required to reach it. The soil was dry and brownish red, with a thick overlay of scented sagebrush and scattered clumps of short grass for forage. After the ford at Casper the inclines were mostly gentle and the land underfoot appeared to be flat.

That was the genius of the trail in Wyoming—for that matter, almost all the way across. Appearance vied with reality in a long, gradually staged feat of climbing. From St. Joseph or Independence along the Missouri, the pioneers had now ascended more than three thousand feet in elevation without ever really noticing it, except for the occasional dramatic climbs like California Hill. The base terrain through the Black Hills was more than four thousand feet above sea level. Over the next few weeks, again without ever really noticing it, the wagon trains would climb another 3,500 feet to the 7,500-foot South Pass, as the continent imperceptibly rose toward its divide. In 1860 Sir Richard Burton, the eminent Victorian scholar and explorer, took a celebrated stagecoach ride across the trail to Salt Lake, recording his observations in the bestselling *City of the Saints*, later digested as *The Look of the West 1860*. He called the Platte-Sweetwater route "a line laid down by nature to the foot of the South Pass of the Rocky Mountains."

The high Rocky Mountain country presented other paradoxes. After the Black Hills, the wagon ruts were generally flat, but the ground underfoot was gravelly and bumpy. The constant pounding over the rocky terrain and the dry desert air cracked the wooden running gear parts and wheels, causing frequent breakdowns. In Wyoming, the high mountain country receives thirty-five inches or more of precipitation a year. But just a few miles away, along the Oregon Trail route in the deserts below, annual rainfall rarely exceeds ten inches, in some places less than five inches a year. These stark contrasts of the western high plains were enchanting, but stressful. The reliable winds and the stunning views of the snowcapped Wind Rivers lulled the pioneers into thinking that they were traveling through invigorating, springlike mountain air. In fact, the reduced oxygen level as the elevation rose winded both the draft animals and the pioneers walking beside the wagons, and they were baking all day in the arid terrain.

The wagon trains arrived at the Fort Laramie trading post in eastern Wyoming to find the usual frenzy of discarding and wagon abandonment as the emigrants lightened their loads for the mountains or converted to pack trains. Outside the fort, some of the wagons were even being burned, and they were surrounded by a wasteland of the emigrants' castoff possessions. While parents foraged through another family's ditched goods for what they might use, the children were put to work breaking up the boards of scuttled wagons for cooking fuel. Once more, the trail experience reinforced a natural American bent toward waste, followed by avid recycling. Wagons that six weeks ago had been purchased for top prices along the Missouri, making a considerable dent in a family's savings, were now warming another family's bacon and antelope steaks.

"Wagons are worth nothing," one correspondent wrote back to a Missouri newspaper in 1859. "We frequently cook our supper with the spokes of a better wagon than half the farmers in St. Louis County own."

Pioneers who considered Nebraska dry now realized that they hadn't really seen the Great American Desert yet. On reaching Wyoming, Niles Searls, the 49er from Albany, New York, wrote in *Diary of a Pioneer*, "The country around us presents a dreary desolate appearance, the grass being parched with drought." Kansas pioneer John Boardman lay over for two days at Fort Laramie to attend lively dancing "fandangos" outside the army barracks, but the trail that followed was sobering. "After we left Laramie we came to the Black Hills, the worst of all traveling," Boardman wrote, "[it is] hilly, sandy and full of wild sage—'tis death on a wagon."

For us, the remote country through the Black Hills was our only choice. The segmenting of the western reaches of the trail into a maze of cutoffs and branch routes begins in eastern Wyoming. At Guernsey, the "main ruts" proceeded due west along the south bank of the Platte, through the alkali plains toward Casper. In the 1850s, however, an Oregon Trail cutoff along the north banks was blazed through the Black Hills. This northern detour for Casper was called The Child's Route, after a gold seeker from Wisconsin, Andrew Child, who followed the northern banks and published a map of his eighty-mile route in a guidebook in 1852. The Child's Route was busy with wagon traffic after 1853 and was one of many instances of nineteenth-century cutoffs that, once blazed, proved as popular as the main ruts.

We had to work exceptionally hard transiting the hill country, but I liked being forced onto the cutoff along the north banks by the same kind of problem the pioneers faced—an obstacle, this time a modern one, blocked our way. Interstate 25, the big north-south highway running from Texas to Montana, cut across the main ruts below Glendo, Wyoming, and there were no access roads around the four-lane. One hundred fifty years after the wagons went through, we were experiencing ourselves the multitude of choices offered by the broad associated terrain of the Oregon Trail.

The isolated Child's Route through the Black Hills is now mostly scrub grasslands used to graze cattle, and over the past century the wandering herds have obliterated the wagon ruts. The long fence lines between grazing ranges required time-consuming searches for gates. The ranchers we met in eastern Wyoming said they had heard that there were a few old granite markers for the trail past Wendover Canyon, but they had never seen them. The trail, essentially, had vanished.

After climbing Rifle Pit Hill west of Guernsey in another violent sandstorm, we turned the wagon up a dusty ranch road that my maps showed would lead us to the cutoff over the Black Hills. We were grateful to leave civilization behind for a few days and climbed steeply over the first dusty rise to enter remote, enchanted space. The trail ran up and down through high stands of cedar and ponderosa pine, and the mounded plains were bright with goldenrod, white and purple thistle, and blooming yucca plants. In the morning, the dew drying on the sagebrush released the pungent camphor on the branches, filling the air with a sharp scent, like mothballs mixed with cinnamon and nutmeg.

That night, on the Cundall Ranch, we managed to find the old wagon camp at Cottonwood Creek, which was marked with a plaque, and the next morning I discovered a relatively easy way to make the terrain work for us. The terraced foothills of the Rockies channeled the North Platte into a series of oxbows far below us, a placid navigation beacon that

glowed silver against the pink plains. All I had to do was climb for the
heights on foot ahead of the wagon, and then guesstimate the most pass-
able route that would keep the river in sight while cutting off the extra
miles presented by the oxbows. When the hills were too steep to climb
or blocked my view of the river, I used my compass to follow a course
due northwest over the flats. We found only two Oregon Trail markers in
three days. But the creek washes that we splashed over seemed to be the
same ones marked on the maps, and from the high ground I could see that
we were making steady progress along the North Platte.

I hiked most of the day, scouting a path ahead of us, then signaling
Nick from the heights around the worst gullies and sagebrush thickets.
Up the hills, I carried the heavy gate jack on my shoulder in case I found
another fence and had to search for a gate, and on the descents I walked
slightly ahead of the wagon with a four-foot length of ponderosa pine
on my shoulder, to throw in front of the rear main wheels if the brakes
couldn't hold the wagons. Olive Oyl ran ahead of me in wide circles
through the scrub grass, clearing the trail of prairie dogs and snakes,
which we were afraid would spook the mules. This was one of the places
along the trail where Nick's superlative driving skills proved decisive. He
expertly held the team back through the descents into the creek washes,
or called the mules over the inclines, simultaneously operating the brakes
by depressing his foot on the brake handle. It was arduous work, but I was
exhilarated by conquering this secluded country and making our gritty
way north. The hills rang with purpose each time Nick brought the wagon
up. The pole banged and the canvas top swayed and creaked over the
bumps and sage thickets, and Nick's voice echoed through the canyons.

"Yup, Team! Yup, Jake, Beck! Big Team, Big Team. You're my odd buggers! To the top now, Big Team. To the top."

We emerged from the Black Hills a few miles below Glendo, finding
an improved dirt road marked on the maps that led us to a state highway,
which we followed to the rodeo corrals in town. My shoulder was calloused and sore from three days of carrying the gate jack over the hills,
and our white-top was splattered with mud from the creek washes. I was
relieved about reaching the familiar comforts of the public corrals. Still,
I was wistful about the back country behind us. There are no Oregon Trail
ruts through the Black Hills of eastern Wyoming anymore. But we had

blazed a path of our own and this seemed like a favorable omen for the wilderness we faced ahead.

Escaping the wagon seat for long stretches of the day and scouting up through the ponderosa pines was immensely satisfying, and the Black Hills cleared my head. I had worried all winter about negotiating this blank space on the map around Interstate 25, but now pushing through the foothills of the Rockies required nothing more than walking on two legs and using my eyes to steer by the river. I swelled with simple, un-alloyed feelings of accomplishment and pleasurable fatigue. Walking down from the high timber to signal to Nick, I sat on flat rock ledges with my legs dangling over the edge, taking in the dazzling montage of terrain that dropped to the North Platte and watching the dreamy image of our white-top climbing the ridges.

I was still muddling over my ghost encounter with my father back at Scottsbluff. In the late 1970s, after my father died, I had gone through a similar period of unexpected "visits" from him. I was then a young, struggling writer in New York, anxious about my future, and often found myself in Manhattan neighborhoods where I had spent time with him as a boy. The wedding-cake facade of the old Look Building on Madison Avenue, or the tulip beds in City Hall Park in lower Manhattan, where he had been arrested during an antiwar demonstration, prompted strong memories of him, and then another one of our conversations would begin. Afterward, I felt guilty about not having been able to help my father more while he was still alive, and confused that I harbored such strong resent-ment toward someone I also loved.

I had the emotional intelligence then of a lawn mower. My father's reappearance in my life seemed too macabre and embarrassing to share with anyone else, and my rearing as a Roman Catholic had programmed me to think that if I ignored inner conflict it would simply go away. (My mother and my aunts encouraged me to "think positive," and to pray more often.) Emotional health was not a topic that parents or other adults dis-cussed with the young, and no one ever introduced me to the idea that depression was both common and remediable.

One of my girlfriends, however, could see that I was unhappy and distracted, and she pushed me to see a therapist. I went reluctantly at first but then began to enjoy myself, gradually opening up enough to be steered toward the sensible conclusion that feelings of rage toward a difficult parent like my father were predictable, even normal, and it didn't mean that I had failed to love him. "Why don't you just think of these talks with your father as ordinary conversations?" the therapist asked me. "Many people have imaginary conversations with family and friends. They visit their parents' graves."

This was reassuring advice, but mostly I missed the point. Now that I had been to a therapist, I expected my problems to disappear, and I didn't dig any deeper than that into my complicated feelings about my father. Eventually, as I clicked past the mileposts of life, new prompts— taking out my first mortgage, expecting my first child, getting stalled on a book project—would arrive, and I would tailspin down again into a six-month mire of sleeplessness, depression, and return visits from my father.

One scene from my past returned with annoying frequency. My father had a lot of difficulty letting go of his children once they left home, and his interest in my early career bordered on obsession. He had always been disappointed that the Great Depression in the 1930s and then the responsibilities of raising a large family had forced him into a business career instead of the more romantic, cerebral work he often imagined for himself—writing. The classic, frustrated creative stuck in a "suit" job, he was tortured in old age by a sense that he had wasted his life. Through me, however, he could vicariously enjoy framing the timbers for a writer's life. During college, I made the mistake of telling him that one of my history professors had told me I was already doing "master's level" work on my term papers, after which my father insisted that I send him copies of everything I wrote. When I sent him something, he replied with long, wandering letters with suggestions for making the paper "even better," and he embarrassed me by even contacting my professors with tips for grading me, and steering me in new directions of study. I began to feel a need to push him away, but was still too dependent on his approval to ask him to stop.

The turbulent events of the late 1960s provided ideal social cover for men like my father, who, during the ugly divisions over the war in Vietnam, were becoming disenchanted with traditional politics and toying with new identities. My father experienced a personality shift typical for the time, trading in his old circle of friends—politicians, bishops, newspaper columnists—for his new best friends, antiwar activists. His speaking style, honed by years of AA lecture tours, and his establishment credentials as a successful business executive with eleven children, were ideal for the times. He began making appearances at colleges and demonstrations across the country organized by a prominent antiwar group, Clergy and Laity Concerned. Late in November 1970, he reached me in my dorm room at Bowdoin College in Maine and told me that he would be speaking in Boston in a couple of days at an antiwar forum at Tufts University. He would be sharing the stage with a number of antiwar leaders, including the historian Howard Zinn. He asked me to drive down for the evening so that I could listen to "the old man giving them hell."

"We'll go to dinner afterward at Durgin Park," he said. "It'll be a nice chance for us to get together."

I didn't have the heart to say no, and I was already a fan of Howard Zinn's work and curious about hearing him speak. Bundling up against the brisk November weather in extra sweaters and a leather jacket, I roared off the campus on my motorcycle after my classes were over, determined to enjoy a last dusk ride of the season.

The overflow crowd at the auditorium at Tufts was typical for an early-1970s antiwar event—lots of grungy college students dressed in long scarves and thrift-store coats, with a smattering of prosperous-looking older couples from the western suburbs of Boston. Howard Zinn was already speaking when I got there, delivering a literate and impassioned defense of civil disobedience that brought the audience to its feet with applause and cheers when he was finished. I was immediately worried about my father, who was the next to speak, because there was no way he could match Zinn's erudition and convincing style. But I underestimated him. He began quietly, almost inaudibly, explaining why he called his talk "The Confessions of a Disenchanted American." Patiently, with a lot of humor, he described his difficult personal journey from Depression-era Scranton to starting a family and a successful business career in the 1950s, all of which had made him fiercely loyal to traditional politics and led him to frequently take time off from work to help elect governors, senators, even a president, John F. Kennedy. But the carnage in Vietnam and Washington's refusal to acknowledge the growing unpopularity of the war had turned him against "the system." He spoke about the importance of moral outrage, insisting that protesters were still patriotic Americans. "I have not abandoned my country," he said, raising his voice only at the end. "My country has abandoned me."

It was a very effective piece of conversational storytelling and the crowd cheered with approval. Howard Zinn was the first on his feet, clapping as he walked across the stage to shake my father's hand. I had always been embarrassed by my father's awkward and juvenescent embrace of radical politics, one reason I had turned away from him since my teens, but at that moment I was proud of him, and impressed. I didn't even know this man whom I had barely seen in the past few years, or that he could move a crowd like this.

After the event was over the audience mobbed the speakers near the rear of the auditorium, and I couldn't get close to my father. I waved from a distance near the door and he cheerfully waved back, and I noticed that he was talking animatedly with two older couples, and making arrangements to meet them outside at their car. I drifted outside to wait for him, expecting that I'd have to share him at dinner with these old friends.

I was standing near the curb outside when my father finally emerged and descended the stone steps, tall and elegant in his wool overcoat and tweed cap. The people he was leaving with had just pulled up in their car and he waved and motioned that he would be right over, and then he reached out and shook my hand.

"Your speech was great," I said. "I didn't expect it to be that good."

"Oh, I am sort of getting this one down," he said. "I really appreciate you coming down like this."

"So, dinner?" I said. "Where am I supposed to meet you?"

"Oh, didn't I tell you? I have to run off with these people. But I'll be back again soon. I'll call you. We'll go to dinner at Durgin Park."

What I said then was robotic, just syllables to get through the moment.

"Fine, Dad. I'll see you."

My father tapped me on the shoulder and smiled, giving me a thumbs-up as he pulled his leather gloves from his coat pocket. With that, he disappeared into the night shadows on the edge of the Tufts campus.

A spitting rain had started to fall and, underneath the campus lampposts, the student walking paths glistened with mud. I found my motorcycle a few blocks away, jumped hard on the foot starter, guessed my way through the maze of streets to the interstate, and drove north, a zombie biker in the rain. I bore north through a black landscape on a black motorcycle, so black inside there were no edges, no shapes, no emotional contours to assess as a specific feeling. By the time I reached the Maine Turnpike I was so frozen that I could barely move my arms to steer the bike, and I stopped to warm up at a twenty-four-hour diner in South Portland.

Later, when I thought about that night, I couldn't decide who I was angrier at—him or me. But there was always a solution for this. The Catholic doctrine of silence fixed everything and repression wasn't a fault—it was the only way I could cope. I tried not to remember. My father was a very princely, intriguing man, always changing, always presenting a new side, and I couldn't stay mad at him for much longer than a cold motorcycle ride back to Maine.

After the Black Hills, the Wyoming flats were broad and wide open, mostly cattle country, but there were lovely small towns and views of man-made lakes every fifteen or twenty miles, and the traveling would be easy until we got beyond Casper. We slept at feedlots and at the state fairgrounds in Douglas, where more cowboys pulled into our camp and waited for us to get the mules settled in corrals before taking us out for dinner. Wyoming is a vast state, but everyone in the cattle business seems to know everyone else, and I enjoyed swapping tales with the cowboys. I talked about the ranches and cattle drives I had been on, while they brought me up to date on the antics of hedge fund and media billionaires buying up famous old ranches. Wyoming was my Shangri-la, and I was glad to have reached the high plains this time the way I did, swelling with self-confidence about getting across the Black Hills.

19

WE SPENT THE JULY FOURTH weekend in trail nirvana. A few miles
north of Douglas, Wyoming, as we climbed the hills along the Child's
Route, a local cowboy and Civil War reenactor named Bill Sinnard flagged
us down in his pickup and told us that the Wyoming Division of State
Parks and Historic Sites was inviting us to spend the Independence Day
weekend at the restored Fort Fetterman, just ahead, where the festivities
would include United States Cavalry reenactments, wagon rides for the
tourists, and luncheon and dinner barbecues. The forty acres of the fort
grounds were fenced, and we could turn our mules loose to graze while
we enjoyed the hospitality of the historic site. Two hours later we jacked
open the gate below the fort and called the mules up to a broad plateau
where an immaculately preserved officers' quarters and a munitions barn
commanded a breathtaking vista of the North Platte and the rolling plains
beyond. While I set up camp and ran a hose down from the main buildings to wash six weeks of congealed mud and tumbleweed off the wagon,
Nick entertained the tourists and reenactors with his marvelous palaver
about wagons and mules.

I had read about Fort Fetterman since I was a boy and was delighted
to make this unexpected stop. The fort was built in 1867 and named after
another frontier bounder, Civil War veteran Captain William J. Fetterman.

The winter before, while marching out to protect a wood-gathering detail in the Bighorn Mountains, Fetterman had disobeyed orders and allowed a small decoy party led by Lakota warrior Crazy Horse to lure him over the nearby ridges. Contemporary accounts claimed that Crazy Horse and his braves taunted the soldiers by dismounting their war ponies, pulling down their loincloths, and contemptuously flashing bare-ass moons. Whatever Crazy Horse did, it worked. Fetterman chased the braves over Lodge Trail Ridge, where a mixed ambush party of Cheyenne, Arapaho, and Lakota fighters promptly annihilated his entire command of eighty-one soldiers and civilians. The military disaster quickly became one of those events that typified the lurid distortion of fact during the Indian wars of the late 1860s and 1870s. In the eastern press, Fetterman was lauded as a hero and the outcome of his tactical lunacy was labeled a "massacre." Vengeance would have to be exacted, and the final, genocidal campaign of the Americans against the Indians began. During the subsequent Powder River War the Lakota, Cheyenne, and Arapaho were eventually surrounded, starved out, and forced into the cultural obliteration of reservation life.

At the time, the renewed traffic of covered wagons that began after the Civil War was gradually shifting to the Child's Route along the north banks of the Platte, and the new fort became an important waypoint and resupplying center in eastern Wyoming. Fetterman was also a major stop along the famed Bozeman Trail, which was established in the 1860s to funnel traffic north after gold was discovered in the Dakotas and Montana, and it became the primary route into the Powder River country for cavalry units, miners, and ranchers who were invading Cheyenne and Sioux lands, breaking still more government treaties that had promised the tribes exclusive use of their traditional hunting grounds. After its twenty-year spell as a lonely, frigid gulag for cavalrymen, the fort area was developed into a busy ranching and outfitting center, Fetterman City, which was known throughout the west for its bustling tavern and whorehouse, called the Fetterman Hog Ranch, which drew cowboys, soldiers, and railroad men from miles around. The fort and Hog Ranch eventually fell into disuse after the city of Douglas was founded in the 1880s.

Fetterman was a relaxing hiatus for us, but I was worried about the fencing arrangement around the fort. In addition to a cattle guard near the entrance, a second cattle guard along the distant fencing to the east glimmered in the sunlight as we set up camp. After filling their bellies with grass, the mules would get bored and begin exploring the fence perimeters, and I knew they would be tempted to jump the cattle guards. We were carrying portable electric fencing, which could easily be strung across the cattle guards and, after retrieving it from underneath our gear in the wagon, I headed off across the plateau with the fencing kit cradled in my arms.

Nick was standing nearby with a crowd of cowboys, tourists, and Civil War reenactors gathered around him, yapping away in his booming baritone about our trip. This was not a favorable environment for me. A willing audience brought out Nick's boastyboy, feeding his need to chide the older, more cautious brother, and after six weeks on the trail he was tired of my fastidious attention to detail.

"Nick, would you like to help me fence off the cattle guards?" I said. "The mules might try to jump them."

"Oh, here we go," Nick said to the crowd out past my shoulder. "My brother is the trail boss on the trip, you know? So I have to be the brains of this frickin operation. Rinker, there is no way those mules are goin to jump a cattle guard. I guarantee it."

Everyone laughed at Nick's touching burlesque of family. I was annoyed at him for humiliating me in front of strangers but decided to give up. Forget it. This was just another case of my worrywart nature spoiling the spontaneity of the trip. I stowed the portable fencing back in the wagon and wandered off to explore the fort.

There was a warm breeze up on the plateau and I felt lazy and supremely contented about our trip so far. Back in Nebraska, I had made one of my most useful purchases of the trip—a cheap pair of imitation-suede slippers bought at the Scottsbluff Wal-Mart. After long afternoons scouting ahead of the wagon, my feet were sore and I wanted to get out of my boots once we made camp. But the ground underfoot was prickly with scrub grass and sage, and I needed something at least moderately sturdy against the ground. As the afternoon wore on at Fetterman, I put on my Wal-Mart slippers to relax, sat down in my camp chair, pulled the brim of my hat down against the sun, and fell into a dreamy haze. Fort Fetterman on the Fourth of July. It just doesn't get better than this.

Half an hour later, I was abruptly wakened by the sound of a pickup skidding into the fort parking lot. A cloud of dust blew over the wagon and a voice yelled out through the open window of the truck.

"Hey! Them mules of yours are jumping the cattle guard! They're headed east, back to Missouri!"

Shit. Damnitall, why did I listen to Nick? Running across the fort grounds, I could see the last mule—it looked like Bute—vaulting the cattle guard and galloping uphill. Her shoes glinted in the sunlight as she kicked sideways with joy and then disappeared over the far ridge. The team was already a half mile away.

Nick half ran, half limped over to the pickup, pulled open the door, yanked Olive Oyl in on his lap, and yelled to the rancher at the steering wheel, "Let's go!"

"Nick, no," I said. "Don't chase the mules. They'll just run farther. And your foot. We can't afford to hurt your foot, here."

"Nah. I'll get 'em. Olive Oyl will help me herd."

As the pickup spun gravel leaving the lot, heading southeast toward the mules, I called to Nick to stop at the top of the ridge, where he could keep the mules in sight.

I was all alone at the fort now, but I did have Bill Sinnard's cell phone number. I called and told him what happened, and he said that he'd be back at the fort in fifteen minutes, as soon as he could load his four-wheeler onto a trailer. He knew the country east of the fort and could help us catch the mules. But Sinnard didn't know how far they could run.

"How many miles is it to the next fence?" I asked him. "How far can they get?"

"Oh, hell, we don't do miles in Wyomin," Sinnard said. "That pasture east of the fort is at least a thousand acres."

I ran back to the wagon, scooped some oats into a bucket, and grabbed our three lead chains, carrying them wrapped around my neck. There wasn't time to change into my boots, so I just charged east across the sage in my Wal-Mart slippers.

I have made some pathetic hikes in my life, but my Fort Fetterman mule-recovery recon ranks right up there with Wrong Way Corrigan or Evel Knievel's ride in the Skycycle over the Snake. I was going for the D. B. Cooper Award. I was headed off on a steeply sloped sagebrush plain, with three heavy stainless steel chains around my neck, carrying a full bucket of oats, in my Wal-Mart slippers.

From the window of a car along a highway, a walk through the sage-brush looks like the most attractive thing that a body can do with its legs. But, up close, sagebrush is not very negotiable. First of all, sagebrush is tall—waist-high in some places, more than shoulder-high in others. It grows so irregularly that there is no linear path through it, requiring a mule recon man like me to make several twists and turns around every sagebrush. The cowboy novelists have grievously ignored this aspect of their favorite vegetation. On foot through the sage, at best, there is an overland gain of about thirty yards for every hundred yards walked. I stumbled a lot, dropped my bucket, trying to skirt the sage too close, and then hanging up my Wal-Mart slippers on the clingy branches.

I was winded when I got to the top of the first rise. I could see the mules far off, still more than half a mile ahead of me, with no fence line in sight. They were having a fine time down there, kicking up their heels and galloping together, rolling around in the dirt, free mules again, in the larg-est pasture of their life. The mule that I could tentatively identify as Beck stared back toward me with a sublime look of utter satisfaction, express-ing with her body demeanor and ears exactly how she felt about me.

"Fuck you, Rinker Buck. I've taken seven hundred miles of your shit and now I get to enjoy a real playdate with Jake and Bute."

I didn't want the mules to gain on me so I started running, especially on the descending slopes. But it was too much work darting around a large sagebrush plant every ten or fifteen yards. What the hell, I thought. I have an advantage here without my heavy boots on. Wal-Mart slippers are light. So I started jumping the sage, to maintain a more consistent bearing toward the mules.

Steeplechasing across Wyoming sage in Wal-Mart slippers, however, does present one problem. In Wyoming, wildlife biologists have recently compiled reports showing that the pronghorn antelope population is tem-porarily declining, probably due to drought and energy projects, but there are still thousands of them in every herd. Apparently, antelope die with intense regularity. Carcasses do not decay quickly in the high, arid air, and antelope seem to prefer dying on the east side of sagebrush clusters.

Antelope rib cages are particularly resilient and remain fully deployed, about eighteen inches high, many years after death. Antelope bones are also exquisitely camouflaged a sun-bleached brown and yellow, which perfectly blends in with the desert floor and the sage branches. Unseen, and as dangerous as the tangle-wires of a World War I battle trench, the antelope rib cages lurk behind the sage bushes—not behind every one, but in random sequences that are quite unpredictable to someone making a run like mine.

I was philosophical about this. You learn something new on every trip. It was hard going, but at least I was familiarizing myself with what must have been a common problem for the pioneers—bushwhacking through a hazmat site of camouflaged antelope rib cages.

Every time I encountered a new sagebrush plant in my way, there was a delightful sense of vaulting into the unknown. Leap, reach my apex over the center of the sagebrush plant, phew! No antelope rib cage on the other side. But this was merely temporary relief. The next time it was: leap, reach my apex, oh, shit, there's an antelope rib cage in my way.

When a man in my situation says, *Okay, don't panic now*, it means that he is already panicking. Instinctively, at the first rib cage, I spread my legs to miss the highest ribs, but this just forced me into a very awkward, wheels-up landing, and then a somersault into the next sagebrush plant. I lost a third of my load of oats and two lead chains. After standing up and re-straightening myself and my load, I continued to vault downhill, determined not to make the same mistake twice.

Leap, reach my apex, fuck me, another rib cage. Okay, let's try *tucking* the legs into a cannonball descent this time.

I can now report with authority that a $6.99 pair of imitation-suede Wal-Mart slippers is just a magnet for antelope ribs. You cannot get past your apogee over a sagebrush plant without a Wal-Mart slipper hanging up either on the highest antelope rib, a sage branch, or the other Wal-Mart slipper. The result is severe face-plants on the sandy, abrasive Wyoming soil.

After another quarter mile of this, my cheeks and hands were burnished down to a raspberry luster, the shoulders of my shirt were ripped open again, and there was a sore spot on my right knee where the heavy metal clips on the lead chains banged hard every time I hung up on another antelope rib and cratered into the dust. My new Wal-Mart slippers were tattered and ripped.

But I told myself that I had to retain focus and keep going. I was following the path of the pioneers, and maybe even Winston Churchill. Don't lose sight of the mission, no matter the odds.

For once, Nick had followed instructions. The rancher had dropped him off at the top of the tallest rise, where he could keep the mules in sight. The sagebrush thinned out at the higher elevation and I had an easier time trudging up there. Nick had sat down between two clumps of sage with Olive Oyl sitting on her haunches beside him.

"God, you look uglier than a stump post," he said. "What did you do, fall down?"

"Antelope rib cages, Nick. They're all over the place out here."

"Oh, I wouldn't have known that. In the truck, we just plowed through. By the way, why the fuck did you bring an empty bucket?"

"It wasn't empty when I left the fort, douche bag. The oats spilled out when I fell over."

"Oh, okay. I just figured you were more coordinated than that."

"Thanks, Nick," I said. "How's the foot?"

"I'm on the edge. I shouldn't push it any more. But you can't catch the mules alone."

"Don't worry. Bill Sinnard is coming with his four-wheeler."

I explained my plan to Nick. When Sinnard arrived, I would motion for him to pick up Nick, while I herded the mules toward what had to be a distant fence line. I would hold them against the fence corner from a distance and then, when Nick and Bill got there, we would catch Jake first, because he would walk over expecting us to scratch his ears. Bute would be easy after that. Beck would be her usual pain in the ass but she wasn't going to let Bute out of her sight.

"Okay, but take Olive Oyl," Nick said. "She'll help you hold the team."

Nick stood up and made shooing motions with his arms.

"Olive Oyl," he said. "Help the boss herd the mules. Okay? Listen to him."

Olive Oyl cocked her head and nodded, and then ran off down the hill for the mules.

It was a long march east, but the pasture seemed more heavily grazed on the far side of the rise, with less sagebrush growth, and I could make easier progress in my slippers. On the flats, I frequently lost site of the mules, but I was confident that they would eventually be stopped by a fence line. When Bill Sinnard arrived on his four-wheeler, he skittered off the bottom side of the canyon and braked in a cloud of dust beside me. He was carrying lead lines around his neck and had a bucket of oats clutched on his lap. I told him that I had lost sight of the mules.

"It's all right," Sinnard said. "I could see them from up top. There's a corner in the fence by the wash down there. They're already near it."

"Go back for my brother. He's got a bad ankle and shouldn't be walking anymore. I'll head east and you and Nick can catch up."

Bill roared off on the four-wheeler, taking the hill in a diagonal climb. He motioned for Nick to climb onto the seat behind him, and they bounced back down the rise together, with Nick's big belly bobbing over the bumps against Bill's waist and ass, Brokeback Mountain–style.

Olive Oyl was a real team player that afternoon. Chasing cattle in Nebraska and running interference with the prairie dogs and snakes in the Black Hills had honed her herding skills. When I motioned for her to hold the mules along the south fence, she yapped and leaped up on her hind feet, snarling at the mules and nipping at their legs whenever they tried to break from the fence corner. Meanwhile, I was holding the mules on the other side by running back and forth in an arc northwest.

As we approached the mules in tighter circles, they were trapped in the corner of the fence and knew it. Jake took a few tentative steps toward me, hoping for the eventual payoff of an ear massage. Bute was very curious about the bucket in my hand, which she knew meant sweet oats. Beck was still expressing *Screw you!* with her rump. The mule body language was clear.

Okay, we're done. But we've had our fun. And, Boss, you sure look asinine in those Wal-Mart slippers.

When Nick bounced down with Bill on the four-wheeler, I didn't want him to think that I was angry, so I deferred to his feelings of superiority about managing mules.

"Here, Nick," I said, handing him two lead chains. "You catch the team. But get Jake or Bute first. Don't mess with that goddamn Beck."

Of course, just to prove himself, he caught Beck first, costing us an extra ten minutes while he slowly approached her and then bobbed and wove in the scrub brush as Beck wheeled away from him. But as soon as he had a lead on her, Jake walked over for ear scratches, and Bute for oats, and we had all three on lines.

We were now about two and a half miles from camp, and it was a glum walk back over the hills. Bill puttered off on his four-wheeler, leading Beck with one of the chains. I didn't want Nick to place his weight on his ankle all the way back to the fort, so I clasped my hands together to make a step and hoisted him up onto Jake's back. He led Bute from there while I led Jake. Beside us on the sandy hills, the late-afternoon sun cast tall diagonal shadows of our pathetic little caravan—one beefy brother riding bareback on a mule, the other leading the way on foot, tripping against the sage in his Wal-Mart slippers.

Back at the fort, after we had the mules secured, I wanted to be alone and I grabbed my toilet kit, scrambled down the plateau, and hiked east across the plains to the banks of the North Platte. The sandy oxbow there was shaded by a cottonwood grove, with a flock of American white pelicans swimming in a still pool and snowy egrets wading on the edges. I stripped bare, dived into the river, and washed and shaved.

Under a low, falling sun, the North Platte was bathed in light orange and blue. I swam out across the pelican lagoon and floated on my back, staring at the sky while the feathery river current turned me in circles. I felt so free out there, cast off from the world. It didn't matter to me that our progress toward Oregon was so farcical. The trail was my inebriate against depression, my hedge against boredom with life. I didn't care what happened next on the Child's Route. We would let the mules rest for another day at Fort Fetterman. Then all I wanted to do was wake at dawn in the sage-scented air of the Wyoming plains, call the mules for Casper, and pick up the pink ruts toward Independence Rock and South Pass.

Laying over for an extra day at Fort Fetterman yielded one of the best surprises of the trip. In the early afternoon a living legend of the Oregon Trail showed up. Randy Brown, a trail historian who lived nearby in Douglas, had driven over to Fetterman to enjoy Independence Day at the fort, but he was also curious about the two easterners traveling through in a covered wagon and wondered if we needed help negotiating the cutoffs ahead. I had used Brown's *Graves and Sites on the Oregon and California Trails* all the way across from Missouri and found it an invaluable resource. Grave locations are important waypoints along the trail, comprising a kind of gritty, forensic record of the ground the pioneers actually crossed, offering an infinitely more detailed map than the generalized trail descriptions offered by academic historians. Brown's exacting account of each grave and how it got there, and his biographies of buried pioneers, also provide vital historical and geographic information on the various fords of the Platte or why major cutoff routes were used in certain years. I had not expected to meet Brown, but now I was sitting beside the wagon with him, my maps spread across our knees, absorbing a wealth of detail about the trail ahead.

Unlike such traditional scholars as John D. Unruh Jr. or Merrill Mattes, Brown has never enjoyed the security and prestige of a university professorship or a position with the National Park Service. He began wandering the trail in the late 1970s during his summers off from teaching in rural one-room Wyoming schoolhouses, developing the concept that the hundreds of graves still to be found beside the ruts were time capsules left behind by pioneer families, revealing insights that cannot be found in published histories. Brown doggedly cross-checks information about each grave in emigrant journals, land records, and nineteenth-century newspapers. A lifetime of searching for graves along the Oregon and California trails has also allowed him to create a more complete portrait of nineteenth-century American life, the pageantry of characters thrown west by the great land migration.

One of Brown's best monograph sketches, for example, narrates the tragedy of Charles Stull, a deaf and mute man from Philadelphia who decided to cross the Oregon Trail, alone and on foot, during the peak emigration year of 1852. Stull died of cholera at Castle Creek, just west of Ash Hollow. He was found by the members of a passing wagon train, who examined his body and found $2.75 in his pockets, along with a certificate attesting to his graduation from the Pennsylvania School for the Deaf and Dumb in Philadelphia. I learned from Brown's account how crowded the trail was that year, and new details about the cholera plagues. Brown also portrayed how early-nineteenth-century educators and philanthropists founded schools for the deaf and circulated beautifully illustrated pamphlets on sign language. Stull was an exemplary product of that era. He was one of the first students at the Philadelphia school for the deaf, and he and his brother, an engraver, published one of the first sign-language manuals, an illustrated broadsheet titled *An Alphabet for the Instruction of the Deaf and Dumb.*

The narrative background Brown provided about the grave along Castle Creek tells us something important about nineteenth-century values during the great land migration. The Second Great Awakening, which inspired Narcissa Whitman and thousands of evangelicals like her to venture west, also produced the reformist zeal that was so pronounced in America between the Revolution and the Civil War—a nascent suffrage movement, the antislavery crusade, and socially minded educational reform. Perhaps Stull felt empowered by his success at the Pennsylvania School for the Deaf and Dumb and that is what led him to hazard a dangerous crossing by foot across the trail. His silent journey, however eccentric, evinces the yearnings of a society that was embracing mobility and personal change.

A native of Michigan, Brown moved to Wyoming in 1977 to teach in rural schools, and became interested in the trail before OCTA was founded. At the time, the idea of preserving the trail as a living monument was still in its infancy, following a long period of neglect and then the distractions of the Depression and World War II after Ezra Meeker died in 1928. Brown has long served as the chairman of OCTA's Graves and Sites Committee, and for thirty years has spent most of his free time identifying and reinterring pioneer remains. He has fastidiously restored about forty graves and other important sites along the Oregon Trail alone, and his restoration work stretches some 1,800 miles across the western trails, from eastern Nebraska to California.

Brown had no particular purpose in mind when he began exploring the trail in the late 1970s. "I think I was simply fascinated by the existence of so many long stretches of original ruts more than a hundred years after the trail was actually crossed," Brown told me when I met him for a day of grave tours after we reached Casper. This was about fifteen years before the trail country of Wyoming began to be exploited for gas wells and pipelines, and there was very little concern for preserving the pioneer environment. Even near major landmarks and intersections, the trail was mostly empty and poorly marked. Detailed maps were not available to the public, few modern trail guides had been published, and, Brown says, "It would never have occurred to people to have all of these interpretive museums." Brown is a voracious reader and researcher, and as he discovered more and more evidence of unmarked trail graves, he realized that proper identification of burial sites would not only add to knowledge about trail history but honor the pioneer dead.

In many areas, especially near his home in eastern Wyoming, Brown began to appreciate that vagaries of both the past and the present had combined to preserve critical sections of the trail and pioneer graves. By the time they reached Wyoming, the pioneers were aware that the muddy Platte was not the best source of water. They began to travel in the higher ground of the Rocky foothills to rely on fresh creeks for water, which took them several miles away from the flatter land along the river. Later, these hilly areas were considered agriculturally undesirable because ranchers and farmers knew that they couldn't plant corn or harvest hay there, and eventually these parcels were preserved as public lands controlled by the federal Bureau of Land Management (BLM). "When we got there in the early 1980s," Brown says, "the trail was just waiting for us, mostly undisturbed."

One grave that Brown showed me, along the Child's Route above the North Platte, demonstrates how researching burial sites can reveal important themes about the Oregon Trail migration that are largely forgotten today, and also shows Brown's persistence in preserving trail graves. Brown took me by car to the grave of Quintina Snodderly, a pioneer from Iowa who died in 1852 just west of Glenrock, Wyoming. The grave sat on high land near the entrance road to a ranch, and the site was a mix of the old and the new that typifies Oregon Trail country. A beautifully restored homesteader farm with a log-cabin house and a red Scandinavian barn stood below, and the blades of a new wind-turbine development swayed through the sky in the distance.

"Quintina" was a popular nineteenth-century name, a borrowing from Latin that indicated a fifth-born child. Quintina was a native of Tennessee who moved with her husband, Jacob Snodderly, to Iowa, living there with their eight children for several years before deciding to migrate west once more, this time on the Oregon Trail. The Snodderlys were traveling in a wagon train of evangelical Baptists led by a popular circuit-riding minister, Joab Powell, whose story typifies not only the sweep of American history but an important factor in Oregon Trail migration. Many nineteenth-century Americans, having spent years warring with their neighbors over one doctrinal difference or another, would pull up stakes and move on to seek more religious freedom, frequently migrating by stages all the way across the North American continent.

Joab Powell was a descendant of Tennessee Welshmen who belonged to a unique sect, the "Fighting Quakers," who abandoned the Quaker doctrine of nonviolence during the Revolutionary War, after concluding that resistance to British rule was justified by biblical texts. During the Second Great Awakening in the 1820s, Powell made a common denominational swap of the time, leaving the Society of Friends for the more evangelical Baptists. Powell was a spellbinding speaker and an impressive figure, weighing almost three hundred pounds. Like many converted evangelicals, he was vehemently opposed to slavery, and his small congregation of Providence Baptists was hounded out of Tennessee and moved to Missouri, where Powell homesteaded a 640-acre farm and traveled widely as a circuit preacher. But after twenty years Powell had concluded that Missouri, racked by bloody battles between pro-slavery and antislavery vigilantes, was not hospitable to abolitionists either, and it was time to move on again. In 1852 he led a migration of Baptists to Oregon, in part because he felt called by God to join the political battle to admit Oregon to the Union as a free state, where slavery would not be allowed. The Snodderly family of Iowa apparently decided to join the Baptist wagon train after reaching the jumping-off camps in St. Joseph in the spring of 1852.

Quintina's remains were discovered in 1974, when the owners of the ranch outside Glenrock were building a new driveway and the grave was overturned by a road grader. The gravestone found at the site indicated that the pioneers were in a hurry and didn't have time to finish carving the rock. The inscription was hammered into a flat stone found nearby with what appears to have been either a screwdriver or a wood chisel, by an amateur hand. Its simple text, with the first "N" inscribed backward, read "QUIᴎTINA SNODERLY D J." ("D J" probably signified "Died in June.") In *Graves and Sites on the Oregon and California Trails*, Brown and his coauthor, Reg Duffin, described the condition of the remains when they were found.

> An examination of the skeleton revealed the cause of death. Most of the ribs had been crushed, probably by the heavy wheels of a covered wagon. The skeleton was in otherwise perfect condition, with fragments of a green ribbon bow still around the neck. The Powell wagon train probably crossed the North Platte River at this point and the accident may have occurred as the wagons climbed the river bluffs to enter the north bank [or Child's Route] trail.

The owners of the ranch realized that they had probably unearthed a pioneer grave, and appreciated the importance of preserving the remains, but as yet there was no OCTA to contact, and they didn't know what to do. The family placed Quintina's bones and the headstone underneath the couch in their living room, where they remained, pretty much forgotten, for ten years. At some point Quintina's skull was dispatched for examination by a forensic science team at Colorado State University in Fort Collins. The forensic team wanted to make a facial reconstruction, and then cast it in plaster, to render a fuller portrait of a pioneer woman. But that work was never completed and Quintina's skull remained exiled in Fort Collins for years.

In 1984, the family storing Quintina's headless skeleton underneath their couch contacted Brown, who had now become well known for his reburials of pioneers. They were selling the ranch to move to Washington State, and thought that it was time to properly dispose of the bones. Brown drove up to Glenrock in his Ford Bronco II, and carried Quintina away in a cardboard box. Through OCTA, he raised money to prepare a reburial spot and buy protective fencing, and a friend of Brown's, a handyman in the Douglas school system, built a simple pine coffin for reinterring the remains.

But Brown couldn't proceed with a proper reburial without Quintina's skull, and this proved to be a stumbling block. Despite repeated calls and letters, he got the runaround every time he contacted Colorado State University's forensic science team in Fort Collins. In the meantime, Quintina's skeleton remained in the cardboard box, now in Brown's care.

He put the box of bones in a corner of his computer room at his house in Douglas.

"This was still pretty early in my grave restoration days, and it was a very frustrating period for me," Brown said. "The results of an analysis of Quintina's skull were going to be vague anyway, and it seemed to me that a forensic science team should be more respectful of the need to get her back into a proper grave."

Negotiations with the Fort Collins team went on for months, and finally the university scientists agreed to release the skull, if Brown would drive down there himself and carry it away. On the arranged day, Brown made the 350-mile round-trip to Colorado. On the university grounds at Fort Collins, he found the pathologist with Quintina's skull in his office, and together they packed it in a cardboard box, cushioning it for the ride back to Wyoming with Styrofoam peanuts. Quintina rode Interstate 25 back toward her original resting place in the front passenger seat of the Ford Bronco II.

Brown selected the reburial place with care, choosing ground very near the original burial site on a grassy knoll overlooking the North Platte. Quintina Snodderly's remains, thirteen years after they were unearthed by the road grader, were returned to Wyoming soil in the new pine coffin in the autumn of 1987.

Brown was undecided about what to do with Quintina's headstone, because he was concerned about leaving it outside in the elements, where it might deteriorate over time. Originally, the headstone had probably been laid flat on the ground, not mounted erect. During the century after Quintina's death, the Wyoming winds and rain had covered the headstone with a deposit of sandy soil, which had supported a healthy native growth of grass and wildflowers, preserving it almost intact.

At the time, the city of Casper and the federal BLM were collaborating on plans to build a new museum, now the National Historic Trails Interpretive Center, which Brown thought would be a fitting location to preserve and display the headstone. Working with the new museum staff, Brown arranged for the original headstone to be exactly copied in all-weather plaster by a curatorial shop that also specialized in making precise casts of dinosaur bones. The original headstone is now displayed for museum visitors behind protective glass at the Interpretive Center in

Casper. The attractive facsimile headstone was placed at Quintina's new grave in Glenrock. Brown installed the new cast at the grave with a friend who has helped the Interpretive Center gather pioneer artifacts, and who is also a devout Roman Catholic. When the tombstone cast was reset in the ground, she said a prayer while sprinkling holy water on the grave.

During reburials that occur during the school year, Brown has often recruited the students from his one-room schoolhouses to help rehabilitate grave sites, and they are frequently the only witnesses when the pioneer graves are rededicated with simple ceremonies that include Bible readings and poems written by the students.

"I still remember the students I had with me, each day that we made a reburial," Brown told me. "I taught them to be respectful of human remains, but that a skeleton was not something you should be afraid of, or consider strange. Human remains are part of our education, our appreciation of the past. The kids learned how to use a post-hole digger and to make fence. I explained the history of the trail in each area. I still feel very spiritual about every one of my reburials."

The day I visited the Snodderly grave with Brown, a strong breeze was blowing, swaying the tall grasses, and killdeers and mourning doves were calling nearby. Antelope bounded by on the golden plains. The tasteful pine-pole fencing, and OCTA's practice of mowing the grass both inside and around the border of the preserved grave, make Quintina Snodderly's final resting place look like a lonely but artful outpost on the ruts.

Brown's simple devotion to task and human decency, rare in the America that most of us know, was very moving to me. As we drove off, curious, I asked Brown what he did with the box that for so many years had contained Quintina Snodderly's remains.

"I put it back in the corner of my computer room," he said. "It's still there. I've never thought about it until today. I guess I just don't want to part for good with Quintina Snodderly. Also, it's a good box."

20

NICK AND I HAD OUR first big fight at Casper. We had made excellent time running the mules up from Fort Fetterman and decided to give them another rest before we faced the scorching deserts ahead, and a local taxidermist offered us his large pastures out by Poison Spider Creek, on the western fringes of the city. We had now spent nearly two months on the trail and all of my clothes were ruined from scouting through the sage and gate-jacking fences. We wouldn't hit another city until Pocatello, Idaho, more than five hundred miles away, but we had brought Nick's truck forward to Casper two weeks before, conveniently positioning me for a long, lazy afternoon shop. After I made a morning run to the hardware stores for Nick, getting the rest of the day off was easy.

"Okay, so, Nick. How about I help you with wagon repairs today?"

"Go away. I don't want your college-educated ass anywhere near my wagon."

"Nick, how fair is this to me? You're consigning me to a life of mechanical incompetence."

"Not my problem. Go away."

"I'll hold your grease gun."

"Go away."

After eight hundred miles of wagon travel through rural prairies, indulging the commercial possibilities of a modern, mall-enveloped city like Casper was deeply therapeutic, and it was easy to get carried away. As it happens, downtown Casper has just about the best western wear emporium in the country, Lou Taubert Ranch Outfitters, so I bought a new wardrobe of cowboy shirts there, and then crossed town for Murdoch's Ranch and Home Supply, where I bought new Carhartt jeans, a leather vest, and new work gloves. I needed a haircut, so I got that, found a Japanese restaurant for lunch, and dawdled over a fine daily, the *Casper Star-Tribune*. Nick's pickup needed routine servicing, and I didn't like the way the water pump was screeching, so I stopped at a Lube Express and got an oil change, a coolant system flush, and a new fan belt. At Dog World, I splurged on Pup-Peronis and Milk-Bone minis for Olive Oyl. I couldn't stand the grime in Nick's truck anymore and I pulled into an AutoZone and bought new floor mats, Armorall vinyl shine, and Little Tree hanging car scents. I spent the rest of the day in the shady parking lot of the Fort Caspar Museum, contentedly devouring museum pamphlets and detailing Nick's Toyota.

Back at Poison Spider Creek, as I drove in toward the wagon, I was dismayed to see the debris field of hardware wrappers, tools, wood scraps, KFC chicken bones, and grease rags that Nick had strewn all around the Schuttler. He had emptied out the Trail Pup to make plumbing repairs on the water barrels, but he was too exhausted after his exertions to clean up, and all of our possessions were lying around in haphazard piles or blowing away in the wind. I had enjoyed such a fine afternoon shop. Now I had returned to my home on the plains and it was Fort Laramie, 1852, with the wagons burning. All of my rage about Nick's slovenly ways, after so many weeks of successful repression, exploded in a fireball of anger.

"God fucking damn-it-all to hell anyway, Nick. What is this obdurate mind block of yours about creating a shithole wherever you are? But don't worry. I don't mind! I like being your fucking maid. *I'll* clean up all by myself."

It was just about the most dumbass thing I had ever said, and I immediately regretted it. Nick erupted from his camp chair, disgustedly looked inside the pickup at my bundles of new clothes, and spun around to face me, his sunburned, perspiring face flushed with rage.

"Oh, I see! So I am here all fuckin afternoon in the hot sun making repairs that you fuckin could never do. And you are off doin your fuckin girlyman buying new Carhartt jeans and gettin a haircut. Rinker, you don't know dickshit about life. Fuck your dumb ass."

"Nick, if you don't like the way I am running this expedition, you can get in your fucking truck and drive home. I'm done with your pigsty shit. I've been putting up with your fucking filth for my entire life and I'm done. Understand?"

Men, of course, are eminently rational and astonishingly articulate when they argue. You can never tell from their body cues that they are angry. After I had unloaded my shopping-spree haul from the pickup, Nick decided to use the Toyota to carry some power tools and electrical cords that he had borrowed from the taxidermist back to the ranch implement shed.

Nick made the short run back to the implement shed in the Toyota at thirty miles per hour, in reverse. Engine roaring, spewing up clouds of dust, the Toyota bounced backward down through a gulch and then came partially airborne out the far side, still heading for the barn in reverse. At the big doorways, Nick did not see the two heavy steel posts that had been sunk in concrete near the entrance, to prevent a runaway truck from hitting the barn.

The metallic clang of the Toyota's bumper hitting the posts echoed so loudly that the mules jumped in the pasture. Nick's head banged against the rear window of the cab. I could see from a distance that both the bumper and the tailgate were dented. Nick stormed out of the pickup, throwing his arms in the air.

"See? Fuckin see? This is what you make me do!"

The next fifteen minutes were the worst of the trip. I was furious at myself for initiating a fight, and astounded at the contradictions in my character. Nick flips the Trail Pup in Nebraska, and I am fine. Nick doesn't pick up the wrappers for his wood screws and plumbing tape in Wyoming, and I freak. I was completely in the wrong, detested myself for it, and was terrified that Nick would take me seriously and pack up his tools and his dog and drive home. Brooding and speechless, I wandered around camp picking up and returning gear to the wagon, while Nick, cursing, inspected the damage to his truck, occasionally kicking the fenders and slamming the doors.

It was a standoff to see who would break the silence first, but finally Nick walked over with a melancholy look on his face, Fu Manchu mustache drooped down. He reached over to shake my hand.

"Rink. I'm sorry. I didn't mean what I said. I should have ignored how stupid you are."

"You're right," I said. "I started it. I'm sorry. If I did as much work as you, I wouldn't clean up after myself either."

"We're brothers, Rink. We will always be brothers. Once you're a brother?"

"What?"

"You just can't fuckin undo it."

Among males, conflict resolution requires a rapid return to the basics, preferably sports or automotive mechanics.

"Rink, did you have my pickup serviced?" Nick said. "You got it detailed too. I can't believe that. It looks great."

"I did it myself, Nick. It was fun," I said, handing him the receipts for the oil change, the radiator flush, and the new fan belt.

"Fuckin A. Thanks. I always feel like a new person when I clean out my truck."

I offered to drive Nick over to the Murdoch store to buy new jeans and shirts, but he wasn't interested. He didn't want to blow money on clothes until, he said, he had "greased the last wheel" on the trip.

Nick wanted some time alone and, that night, he drove into Casper, found an AA meeting, and went to the movies. I puttered around the wagon, enjoying the solitude of the plains and the company of Olive Oyl while the coyotes howled out by Emigrant Gap. The next 350 miles across original ruts would be the toughest, most remote stretch of the trip and, as I stared at my maps, I worried about whether we had enough water to make the long runs between the rivers ahead.

Reaching the Oregon Trail in Wyoming and not confronting the Mormon experience would be like reaching Paris and not studying the cathedrals. You cannot understand one without the other, and the Mormon hegira to Salt Lake that began in 1847, and then mightily expanded during the Gold Rush era, is the courageous and violent fable of America itself. Wallace Stegner, the dean of western writers, devoted at least a third of his Pulitzer

Prize–winning career to writing about the Mormons, and he considered the Mormon struggle, and their record of both persecution and grave misdeeds, to epitomize the tortured history of the West. In *The Gathering of Zion: The Story of the Mormon Trail*, Stegner pointed out that the Mormons not only transformed the Oregon Trail but colonized a swath of the West that extended from Utah to the mountains of Idaho, and as far west as the gold fields of California.

"They built a commonwealth, or as they would have put it, a Kingdom," Stegner wrote. "But the story of their migration is more than the story of the founding of Utah. . . . The Mormons were one of the principal forces in the settlement of the West."

Mormon-hating is still one of America's most popular religious sports, and the Roman Catholics, southern evangelicals, and Jews who despise the Mormons have consistently ignored one salient truth. Joseph Smith, the founder of the Latter-day Saints, for all of his bombast, satyriasis, and murderous ways, was the only true prophet of a native denomination birthed on American soil, and he dramatically changed American history. Mormonism is a religion and, like all of them, grossly imperfect, but there has always been a glaring hypocrisy about American attitudes toward the Saints. During the bloody wars in the 1840s over where they would eventually settle in the west—battles mostly conducted in Missouri, Kansas, and Illinois—the Mormons got killed a lot, and they killed a lot of other people. The Mormons are abhorred for harboring many strange beliefs. They believe that we preexist as spirit children, can become divine during postexistence, and that, as the *Book of Mormon* describes, the Angel Moroni revealed to Joseph Smith that one of the twelve tribes of Israel somehow escaped the Mideast and reached North America, to gestate for centuries as an Indian tribe preserving the values of Christianity. The Church of Latter-day Saints practices baptism of the dead, even for non-Mormons.

But the Mormons are strange compared to whom? The biblical heroes of mainline Christianity include a long list of murderers, adulterers, and warmongers, not to mention the philandering popes, genocidal Knights Templar, and Klan-loving Southern Baptists who have led various branches of Christianity since then. Traditional Christians perform some very bizarre mental gymnastics of their own. They believe that Jesus was born to a virgin, and that during Communion His body and blood are transformed into a thin wafer baked in Rhode Island. Which denomination, which doctrine, is more "correct"? None of them are even remotely correct, of course. It's all made up anyway, and dogma is simply another excuse for introducing useless human conflict. Organized religion, mankind's oldest, most exciting adventure, too often comes down to one church accusing another church of heresy. It is the worship of hypocrisy, squared. Mormons have never enjoyed a monopoly at this.

The wonderful story began in the 1820s in Narcissa Whitman country, the Burned-Over District in upstate New York. The Smiths of Palmyra, New York, were the kind of happy family that reliably produces prophets. They were farmers, prone to crop failure and nasty land disputes, who moved around a lot. Young Joseph, born in Vermont in 1805, was crippled as a boy after suffering a bone infection, and walked for many years with crutches. By the time he was a teenager, however, Smith was able to hike unassisted and enjoyed long, solitary walks over the rolling countryside below Lake Ontario. The Smiths were swept up by the evangelistic zeal of the Second Great Awakening, which opened them to many interesting experiences. They had visions, woke up from dreams reporting that they had been visited by God, and practiced a variety of arts common at the time—folk magic, séances, miraculous healing. As a young man Joseph supplemented the skimpy family income by treasure-digging for buried gold and religious artifacts that he believed had been stashed in underground crypts. Smith claimed that placing the right "seer stone" in his hat would help reveal the location of these lost treasures.

The visits by the aptly named Angel Moroni began in 1823, when Joseph was eighteen. Moroni informed Joseph that a book of golden plates, probably containing revealed texts, was buried on a hill near the Smiths' home, but the angel initially prevented his new human friend from finding the plates right away, in much the same way that Moses was extensively tested by God before he climbed Mount Sinai and returned with the Ten Commandments. Over the next several years Smith continued his frustrating search for the buried texts, met and eloped with a Pennsylvania girl, Emma Hale, and, with her help, found the golden plates. Joseph, Emma, and some friends translated the plates, which emerged as the core of the *Book of Mormon*.

The *Book of Mormon* contained everything required in an Abrahamic work of literature—lots of wandering around the deserts by a chosen people, periods of peace followed by periods of intense violence, and wonderfully alluring, made-up events. All of this culminated in the appearance of Jesus Christ in North America a few days after his reported ascension from the Mount of Olives in Jerusalem. Jesus returned later to convert the Nephites, descendants of the group that had wandered to the Americas from biblical lands. This revised travel plan of a resurrected Jesus, now including several North American stops, could not have arrived at a better time. During the Second Great Awakening, the Burned-Over District and other trans-Appalachian regions along the frontier throbbed with resentment over the European and still vaguely papist roots of Christianity, and there was considerable hunger for an indigenous American church. A huge amount of church-shopping was already happening, and the new Mormon faith offered a homegrown, made-in-the-USA doctrinal package not available in the other evangelical denominations. Smith's fusion of mysticism with traditional Christianity proved highly attractive at a time when religious emotionalism had pushed many Americans to dabble in the occult.

Smith promoted to great advantage two other aspects of Mormonism. At the time, during the 1830s, as described so well in W. J. Rorabaugh's *The Alcoholic Republic*, a surplus of corn whiskey—the most efficient way to preserve and market a valuable crop—had made alcoholism rampant in American cities and small towns, even among the young. Another reliable surplus from Virginia and North Carolina, tobacco, had addicted millions more to nicotine. Evangelical moralists were also scandalized by the many whorehouses built along the new water canals to service the men and boys digging the trenches. As reformist zeal swept through churches and political parties, Smith positioned Mormonism as a kind of 12-step program for personal improvement. Converts vowed to abstain from sex outside marriage, and to stop drinking, smoking, and even consuming hot stimulants like coffee and tea. Meanwhile, Smith and his successors, especially the redoubtable Brigham Young, were superb organizers. The Mormons bought up huge tracts of land and homesteaded new areas as religious-agricultural fiefdoms. They sold their crops as a cooperative unit, organized their own dry goods stores and breeding farms, built churches and temples together, and preferred to barter and trade among themselves, forming a clannish economic self-determination that made them not only powerful but resented by non-Mormon neighbors. This blending of abstemiousness and financial drive proved deeply appealing during the 1830s and 1840s, when thousands of Americans were losing their farms and businesses because of the serial panics and bank failures racking a young, unstable country.

Few organized religions, however, can prosper without stunning misbehavior by their leaders. Smith's new faith soon stumbled over his secret endorsement of plural marriage, or polygamy, a practice he justified with a great deal of theological mumbo jumbo designed to conceal his chronic philandering. Smith was an attractive man and a spellbinding speaker, and women swooned during his sermons. He rarely met a follower's pretty wife or teenage daughter whom he didn't covet, and many of them succumbed to his charms without Smith having to make much of an effort. Under an impressive veil of deceit, Smith was eventually "sealed" to forty-five wives, and his successor Brigham Young would go on to build two adjoining mansions in Salt Lake to house his own fifty-one wives and estimated fifty-seven children.

The Mormons were widely despised for all this. By the late 1830s Christian America had settled on a strategy for dealing with them that had already been successfully used against the eastern Indian tribes—violent harassment and containment. The Mormons were hounded out of New York and into Ohio, and then through Kansas, Missouri, Iowa, and then back to Illinois, by late-night vigilante groups marauding through their settlements, shooting cattle, poisoning wells, and engaging in pitched rifle battles with the Saints. The clannish Mormons fought back. Smith organized a secret Mormon militia known as the Danites, for "peacekeeping purposes," he said, but in fact their main business was murdering non-Mormons and apostates.

Religions truly gain the ability to take off when their leaders are martyred, and Smith fell victim to this useful form of departure in 1844. In Nauvoo, Illinois, Mormonism had prospered during an extraordinary period of controversy and temple building when, among other advances, Smith came up with the idea of posthumous baptism. But Smith made the mistake of shutting down and destroying the press of a dissident Mormon newspaper that accused him of polygamy and worshipping multiple gods, and a war broke out between the Mormon factions, forcing the governor of Illinois to intervene. Charges were eventually filed against Smith for inciting a riot and treason, and Smith and his brother Hyrum were held in the jail at Carthage, Illinois. On the night of June 27, 1844, a mob with faces blackened by grease attacked the jail. Hyrum was shot in the face and Joseph was riddled with bullets while attempting to defend himself with a pistol. After calling out his last words to the Lord, the prophet, now quite dead, fell out through a window.

The internecine Mormon battles on the frontier, and the development of the Oregon Trail, occurred more or less simultaneously in the late 1830s and early 1840s, and perhaps it was inevitable that the growth of a powerful nativist religion would coalesce with the great migration westward. Even before Smith's death, the Mormon leaders gathering around Brigham Young had dreamed of making an escape far away from the violent, anti-Mormon frontier in the Midwest, and in 1846 Young began dispatching Mormon exploration parties beyond South Pass in Wyoming along the nascent Oregon Trail. The Mormons eventually decided to colonize the uninhabited desert region around Great Salt Lake in Utah, because it was naturally protected by mountains that would make it difficult for their enemies to harass them there, and the plentiful water falling from the Wasatch range would make it possible to irrigate the land. The Salt Lake basin could be reached relatively easily by blazing a ninety-mile spur off the existing wagon road.

Between 1846 and the early 1870s, more than seventy thousand Mormons would cross the Oregon Trail. Thousands of them were impoverished English and Scandinavian workers who had been displaced by the industrial revolution, and who were ripe for the picking when the Mormons began evangelizing in the European slums. The Mormons were the largest single group to cross the trail and compared their exodus to the Jewish flight from Egypt, which is now an integral part of their faith. This identity has often led the LDS Church to make outsize claims about their right to control the modern trail and the writing of its history, assertiveness that makes Mormons as controversial today as they were in the nineteenth century.

There is no doubt that, with their practiced efficiency and thoroughness, the Mormons accelerated the development of the Oregon Trail.

Brigham Young had the mind and management skills of a military quarter-master, and after 1847 he converted the Mormon resources at his disposal into a bustling covered wagon enterprise. By establishing a series of "winter camps" in Iowa and Nebraska, the Mormon emigrants and their wagons could be ready for early-spring departures. The Mormons replaced the haphazard system of river fords with a network of ferries across the Platte, allowing Mormons to pass for free but charging gentiles $3 per wagon. (In peak years, the traffic jam awaiting the Mormon ferry crossing at Casper stretched back on the trail for twenty miles. One 49er said, "The Mormons have as good a gold mine here as any in California.") The Mormons were the only organized group on the trail to operate west-to-east traffic, so that wagons, supplies, and scouts familiar with the trail could return in the fall and then lead a new group in the spring. The LDS published precise mileage guides, and a Mormon inventor even built a wooden odometer that clacked against the wagon spokes so that the Mormon trains knew their exact distance to the next waypoint. Bad credit? No problem. Young established a Perpetual Emigration Fund to underwrite the travel expenses of impoverished converts and made bulk purchases of wagons from the Peter Schuttler works in Chicago. Mail service, creature comforts such as bathhouses and barbershops at "halfway houses" along the trail, and dairies and vegetable gardens to replenish the wagon pantries of the faithful were among the amenities that Mormons added to the trail.

Because the majority of Mormons departed from Nauvoo, Illinois, and then traveled through Iowa to reach the Missouri, they generally followed the north bank of the Platte through Nebraska. This northern route was also followed by more than 100,000 non-Mormon pioneers and was called at the time the Council Bluffs Road or the Great Platte River Road. There were also plenty of Mormons who followed the south bank of the Platte after disembarking from steamboats along the lower Missouri. At Fort Laramie in eastern Wyoming, the Mormons joined the flow of wagon trains along the main Oregon Trail for five hundred miles to Fort Bridger, and then departed from the main ruts for their ninety-mile run south into Salt Lake.

Less than a hundred miles of the 1,300-mile route the Mormons followed to Salt Lake followed wagon roads that didn't already exist—for the rest, the Saints were simply following the old Indian traces adopted by the fur trappers and then the gentile wagon trains. But politically connected LDS leaders and church historians have long insisted that the Mormons created the "Mormon Pioneer Trail," and they have waged a successful campaign to convince federal agencies to reclassify long portions of the Oregon Trail through Nebraska and Wyoming, and many historic sites, as exclusively Mormon. The renaming of the trail to suit Mormons' needs has even extended to the published maps of the National Park Service and the Bureau of Land Management, angering many trail enthusiasts, western ranchers, and scholars. Promulgating the myth that there was a distinct Mormon trail, writes historian Merrill Mattes, "is not merely inaccurate, it is an injustice to label the entire northern route as exclusively 'The Mormon Trail.' "

Randy Brown, and many other members of the Oregon-California Trails Association, point out that they have many friends in the group who are Mormons. But they are annoyed that political influence by the LDS Church, and what some of them call the activism of a "Mormon mafia" within the Park Service and the Bureau of Land Management, have distorted the historical record to suit the needs of a single religion.

"The Mormons can do whatever they want to out here because the state of Wyoming thinks no one else cares," says Brown. "The rest of us, non-Mormon trail enthusiasts, don't have the money and influence that LDS has."

Recently, the Mormons have become even more controversial along the trail for their efforts to reinterpret Mormonism's darkest hour, the 1856 handcart disasters that left more than two hundred Mormon converts from Europe dead, as one of the most admirable and sacred moments of the flight to Salt Lake.

Brigham Young's vaunted empire-building ability suffered an unusual setback in 1855, when a crop failure in Utah suddenly diminished LDS contributions, reducing the church's ability to continue importing European converts. Young was desperate because by now he knew that Mormon expansion in Utah relied heavily on the annual surge of converts from overseas. Instead of telling the Europeans to wait a year until sufficient funds were available, he devised a strategy of shipping them over from England and having the converts continue their journey from Iowa City with inexpensive handcarts that the immigrants would construct themselves, and then push 1,300 miles to Salt Lake. Just about everything went wrong with Young's handcart scheme. Difficulties in finding enough ships to carry more than 1,800 European Mormons from Liverpool delayed their departures until too late in the spring, the lumber that the church provided the emigrants to build their own handcarts was green and quickly snapped in the Nebraska heat, and herds of buffalo stampeded the oxen pulling the provision wagons, depriving the handcart companies of sufficient food. Many of the European converts were traveling with children and elderly parents, and the agonies of pushing a handcart with all of their possessions and provisions across the arid Oregon Trail were intense. Three of the five handcart companies brought over from Europe in 1856 made a safe passage to Utah. But the breakdown in Mormon discipline doomed the last two groups—the Willie Handcart Company, and the Martin Handcart Company, named after their leaders, James Willie and Edward Martin—which did not leave Iowa until mid-August.

Winter blizzards can begin in the Rockies as early as October, and the Willie and Martin companies were strung out between Casper and South Pass when the first storm struck on October 19, 1856. After holing up in the meager protection offered by the Wyoming bluffs, the handcart companies were found by rescue parties sent out from Salt Lake and encouraged to continue through the heavy snows. Struggling uphill through more than a foot of snow, the holes in their boots wrapped in rags, the hopeless Mormon handcart pioneers began dying by the dozen, especially at a place considered the most arduous climb of the trail, the boulder-strewn Rocky Ridge, a few miles east of South Pass. As many as fifteen members of the Willie Company were buried in a mass grave in a canyon nearby, at Rock Creek Hollow. Meanwhile, members of the Martin Company had begun dying of hypothermia and starvation, but the survivors somehow managed to struggle farther west and reach a somewhat protected cove near another fabled Oregon Trail site, Devil's Gate, where the Sweetwater River cuts through a dramatic three-hundred-foot gorge of the Granite Range. The cove was shaped like a horseshoe against the Granites and the ground inside was a frozen bog. Camping and building fires there were hellish. Fifty-six Mormon converts died and were buried in what became known as Martin's Cove.

At one point in late October, as below-freezing temperatures began to form ice on the Sweetwater, there were almost a thousand shivering Mormons huddled in tents and abandoned log cabins between Devil's Gate and Rocky Ridge. With the help of the Mormon rescue parties, most of the survivors had staggered into the promised land of Utah by early December, but not before a total of 215 had died.

At the time, many Mormons risked censure by their church for criticizing Brigham Young's mismanagement of the handcart emigration, a view that is still privately expressed by some church members today. But during a bellicose Sunday sermon at the Mormon Tabernacle in Salt Lake that November, Young made it clear that dissent was not permitted in his church. For anyone who questioned his decision to bring the emigrants forward so late in the season, he said, "Let the curse of God be on them and blast their substance with mildew and destruction, until their names are forgotten from the earth."

That party line has continued, and even become hardened over time. By the 1870s, the LDS leadership settled on a strategy of repackaging the senseless 1856 dying as a parable of noble suffering, the kind of myth-making that often helps religion grow. The Willie and Martin handcart dead, victims of Brigham Young's overreaching, became martyrs. From the 1870s onward, teams of Mormon researchers and grave hunters have combed the Oregon Trail from the Red Buttes near Casper to beyond South Pass, marking burial sites and landmarks, and elevating the mass grave at Rock Creek Hollow, and the winter refuge at Martin's Cove, to the status of sacred sites. Beginning in the 1990s, the Wyoming and Utah local LDS divisions, called "stakes," have aggressively bought up thousands of acres of deeded ranchland along the trail and now operate these parcels as vast summer camps for Mormon teenagers, who push replica handcarts around Devil's Gate and up toward Rocky Ridge to reenact the struggles of their ancestors. Along the most scenic and famous stretch of the Oregon Trail, the hundred miles between Independence Rock and South Pass, the LDS now operates an ambitious museum-building and evangelization program for summer tourists.

The federal government has stretched the principle of separation of church and state to an amazing degree to assist the Mormon reoccupation of the South Pass segment. In 2003, a clause quietly placed in an appropriations bill signed by President George W. Bush granted the LDS a twenty-five-year lease, automatically renewed, of federal land around the fabled pioneer encampment at Devil's Gate. Since then, under Mormon control, any reference to Devil's Gate—through which more than 600,000 Americans passed from fur-trapping days onward—has been obliterated from the maps and highway signage, and the national landmark has been retitled with the preferred Mormon place-name, Martin's Cove. The LDS now operates Devil's Gate as a religious site for Mormon youth, who every summer travel to Wyoming from all over the world to spend a week or two, attired in "period dress" skirts and pioneer bonnets and hats, pushing wooden handcarts along the renamed Oregon Trail. It is as if the Gettysburg battlefield in Pennsylvania was renamed "Sisters of Charity" or "Mother Ann Seton Hospital" simply because a group of nuns from nearby Maryland traveled to Gettysburg in 1863 to help tend the sick and the wounded after the epic Civil War battle. The LDS estimates that between fifteen thousand and twenty thousand Mormon Youth—in LDS vernacular, they are called MYs—camp in tent cities along the Sweetwater every summer. Today, there are about five times as many Mormons reenacting the trail every year in Wyoming than there were actually traveling it for real in the 1850s.

After Casper, as we followed the trail markers along Poison Spider Creek and then slowly climbed the mules up to the summit of Emigrant Gap, I wasn't worried about what we would face ahead in Mormon land. But from the high ridge of the gap we could see the epic stretch of desert that lay before us. An immensity of pink sand and dirty-white alkali flats, ringed by the parched Rattlesnake Hills, stretched through the mirages. The night before, I had calculated that the mules had been consuming about forty-five gallons of water a day, but they would probably require more like fifty gallons a day across the scorched expanse ahead. We were carrying 105 gallons and would need every drop of it before we reached the Sweetwater at Independence Rock, at least two days away.

That would be our life now for 350 miles, almost a month's travel, during which we would pass only two towns. To reach the Idaho line, we would make a series of river-to-river forced marches, and the earth's most elemental resource—water—would become our ceaseless quest.

21

WE HAD NOW ENTERED WHAT I called the Acropolis stretch of the Oregon Trail. For the next two weeks we would travel over the original wagon ruts, through a series of dramatic sandstone and granite formations—Avenue of the Rocks, Independence Rock, Devil's Gate, Split Rock—that marked our way toward the continental divide at South Pass. After Emigrant Gap, we met no one else along the dusty two-track, County Road 319, also called Oregon Trail Road. The land surrounding us was open and remote, preserving the scenery of the pioneers with a mesmerizing Grecian duality. The powdery sand and shelves of black rock beside the wagon wheels were tangible enough. But hazy mirages obscured the base of the Rockies as the desert receded toward the horizon. The Rattlesnakes and the Wind Rivers in the distance became blurry purple mounds floating in hard blue sky.

The dreamy, vacant sensation induced by the landscape was enhanced by the dry desert heat and rising elevation. After Emigrant Gap we would climb from five thousand to 7,400 feet, and then remain at over seven thousand feet until we reached the Bear River valley in Idaho. The higher altitudes slowed us, calmed us, and winded us and the mules, and the secondary effect of high air is a mild euphoria that lasts all day. Now instead of just becoming sleepy from the monotony of wheel bumps and jingling harness, I was enveloped by the fog of desert hallucination.

Hypoxia, or the oxygen deprivation experienced at high altitudes, causes weariness and sore joints, but the more important symptom is a kind of elevated optimism about life, an impaired judgment not aligned with the reality someone is facing. Short-term memory also begins to fade. We ran into the first instance of this dreamy forgetfulness about a mile after Avenue of the Rocks, when we crossed a long alkali flat that led to the first in a series of barbed-wire gates along the 75,000-acre Rattlesnake Grazing Association ranch. There, after jacking the gate and watering the mules, I jumped back onto the seat and told Nick to call the team, leaving behind one of our water buckets and the stepladder that we used to load and unload the wagon. I didn't discover our loss until that night, when we reached Willow Springs, a small oasis in the desert shaded by ancient willows that was crowded with pioneer camps in the 1850s.

Nick was surprised by my nonchalance when I told him that we had left the bucket and ladder behind us on the trail.

"What the hell," I said, as I began carrying water to the mules. "We don't need three buckets anyway. And we can just buy another ladder somewhere."

"How far is it to the next hardware store?"

"Four hundred miles," I said.

"Are you okay, Boss?" Nick said. "You are usually so anal about possessions."

"Who gives a shit? It's a beautiful Wyoming night. All we have to do tomorrow is get past Horse Creek and then follow the trail to Independence Rock."

Nick was not as affected by the high altitude as I was. The forgetfulness and overconfidence caused by the lower oxygen levels would dog me for the rest of our journey through the Rockies. I should have seen the lost bucket and ladder as a warning sign, but I had already begun to experience the effects of the high elevations and didn't realize that. Later, however, I would understand this as perhaps the most important lesson provided by retracing the trek of the pioneers. Hubris and feelings of invincibility would be required to conquer the many obstacles ahead.

•   •   •

Independence Rock slowly rose as a giant bump on the horizon as we cut across open country to avoid flooding near Pathfinder Reservoir, where the North Platte River is dammed and meets the Sweetwater. I took the lines from Nick and drove the team myself because I wanted to be calling the mules as we approached the famous waypoint, but I didn't say anything to him at first. Nick contentedly daydreamed with Olive Oyl in his lap, staring off across the flats, and it took another mile or two for him to notice the tall, rounded eminence rising off the scrub plains.

"Whoa, is that Individual Rock?" Nick finally said. "That is some big mother stone."

"Independence Rock, Trail Hand. Mile 815 on the trail."

Independence Rock, along the Sweetwater River in Wyoming, became a popular camping ground where thousands of pioneers scrambled up the granite sides to carve their initials and hometown.

From several miles away, it was easy to see why the immense natural wonder ahead, bounded by the Sweetwater River on its southeast side, had sheltered one of the largest campgrounds along the trail. The huge mound of naturally polished granite rises almost 140 feet above the desert floor, covers twenty-eight acres, and is more than a mile in circumference. Pioneers from the East and the Midwest had never seen a freestanding rock of such huge proportions, and they knew that this gigantic signpost in the sky marked their transition from the muddy and diseased drainage of the Platte to the cleaner flow of the Sweetwater. The two-day run down from Fort Casper was desperately dry, and by early summer places like Avenue of the Rocks and Prospect Hill had become animal boneyards, with oxen and mule carcasses scattered across several acres. The morning and afternoon shade provided by the rock created a comfortable layover spot where the pioneers could trade with other wagon trains, refill their barrels, and bathe and wash their clothes in the river.

We arrived at the Sweetwater with our two main barrels empty, and I used a tent pole as a dipstick to measure what was left in our small barrel mounted on the side of the wagon—it came to about three gallons. The area around Independence Rock is now maintained by the state of Wyoming as a rest stop and tourist site along the two-lane highway between Casper and Lander, Highway 220. A paved walk with interpretive signs winds east to the rock and the air-conditioned pavilion of the Division of State Parks and Historic Sites sits at the edge of the highway pull-off. As I refilled our barrels from the water spigot behind the pavilion I could see a dirt access road down the highway with a gate where we could take the wagon through to reach the old pioneer camp. I walked inside the pavilion to tell someone that we'd be camping at the rock tonight.

The uniformed Division of Parks employee inside was sixtyish and bored, wearied by dealing with tourists all day. I cheerfully briefed him about our trip and explained that we'd be pulling the wagon around the back side of the rock for the night.

"You can't do that," he said. "You have to have a permit from the park ranger."

"Okay," I said. "Where's the park ranger?"

"On vacation. He won't be back until Monday."

The Parks man told me that tourists on foot were welcome to walk back to the rock through the narrow gate at the end of the pedestrian trail. But the larger gate down the highway was strictly for state trucks. No "civilian vehicles" were allowed beyond that point. Besides, he said, the mules might damage a historic site.

Fuck this dullard, I thought. For almost a century, hundreds of thousands of fur trappers, cavalrymen, and pioneers had camped here, and their animals had pawed the ground and shit all over the place every night. What damage could we possibly cause?

Still, I felt wonderfully passive about meeting this moron. My Wyoming desert high saved me here. There must be something about oxygen deprivation, not to mention eight hundred miles on the trail, that was turning me into a cupcake. The Oregon Trail was the best anger-management therapy I'd had in years.

"All right, then," I said to the bonehead behind the counter. "We'll be moving on. Happy trails!"

"Happy trails," he said.

Outside, I pulled the gate jack from the back of the wagon and then stopped at the front wheel, below Nick.

"We're good to go, Trail Hand. See that gate up there at the end of the access road? When I jack it, bring the team through."

"Yup, Team! Yup! Big Team! Big Team! Jake! Individual Rock, Jake. Individual Rock."

Nick clattered the rig through the gate and down to the Sweetwater, where, behind twenty-eight acres of Archean granite, we couldn't be seen from the highway or the rest stop pavilion. No one cared, of course, and our camp at Independence Rock was one of the best of the trip. With towels and some rope, Nick rigged the gate jack as a shoulder yoke so that I could carry two buckets of water at once. I walked back and forth to a bend in the Sweetwater where the flow raced around a grassy bank, genuflecting into the shallow water at the edge to fill the pails. Then I carried them back to the wagon, where Nick was shampooing the team, and rinsed each mule with both buckets. It was cool in the shadow of the Granites beside the rushing river and the evening exercise was refreshing. After dinner, I grabbed one of the camp chairs and climbed up Independence Rock, meditating on the dreamy curves of the Sweetwater far below. I tried to imagine what the view must have looked like 160 years ago, when the smoke from dozens of campfires filled the valley with haze, cattle brayed all night, and the oil lamps hung from the hoops made a thousand canvas wagon tops glow like Japanese lanterns.

I would have heard, too, the echoes of hammers against chisels, even past sunset.

During the trail years, reaching Independence Rock aroused a kind of collective, Paleolithic carving gene, a powerful urge among the pioneers to leave behind some evidence of their arrival. While the wagon trains rested for a day or two at the rock, the pioneers found it irresistible to scramble up the curved walls and chisel in the hard granite their names or initials, the year, and their hometowns. There is no way of knowing exactly how many pioneers left their initials or names behind on Independence Rock because erosion by wind and water over the past century has removed thousands of these inscriptions. But perhaps as many as twenty thousand overland emigrants hammered their names or initials onto the rock, turning it into a crowded maze of graffiti. "[The rock] being painted and marked every way, all over, with names, dates, initials, &c," wrote 49er J. Goldsborough Bruff, "it was with difficulty I could find a place to inscribe it."

The signatures left behind on the granite visitors' book at Independence Rock are a vital historical record, and once again the heroic fieldwork of Randy Brown provides the background. His encyclopedic *Historic Inscriptions on Western Emigrant Trails* is one of the most fascinating volumes on the Oregon Trail. For over 450 pages of his illustrated, folio-size book, Brown meticulously records every known inscription on the western trails from Kansas to Arizona. He provides long introductory sections on such celebrated carving sites as Signature Rock and Name Rock in Wyoming, and biographical digests of each pioneer carver who can be established today. Brown's inventory of the inscriptions on Independence Rock alone runs for eighty-two pages.

From Brown we learn many compelling details about the inscriptions. The dated carvings on Independence Rock have allowed historians to confirm when military units and exploration parties reached the Sweetwater, and when the doomed Donner Party of 1846 got there. The stagecoach era that followed the initial pioneer years can also be documented by many signatures. Instead of carving their names into the granite, many pioneers took a shortcut, daubing their inscriptions with a mixture of tar, black paint, and wheel or bacon grease, probably as a message to friends and family in wagon parties behind them that they had safely arrived at Independence Rock. But these seemingly temporary marks actually became permanent, a product of the natural desert chemistry. Over time, the tar mixture was degraded by the desert heat. But enough residual material remained to prevent the growth of desert lichens on the letters, leaving behind a kind of primitive mezzotint image that Brown calls a "shadow inscription." Many of these shadow inscriptions are still legible today and allow chroniclers like Brown to trace the arrival of specific individuals or wagon trains, providing critical cross-checking references against sometimes unreliable pioneer accounts.

Rip-off artists thrived at Independence Rock. The pioneers were entranced by the opportunity to leave a permanent record on the rock, but many of them didn't have the time or the patience to carve their own initials. Stone carvers often camped at Independence Rock for several weeks to help pay the costs of their trip to the California gold fields, and they were notorious for overcharging to inscribe a family's surname up on the rock. The commercially minded Mormons were perhaps the most ambitious. In 1852, Michigan emigrant Thomas Potter found a group of Saints established for business at the large pioneer city around Independence Rock.

> A party of Mormons with stone-cutting tools were located on the spot and did a considerable business in cutting names in the rock at a charge from one to five dollars, according to the location.... Men who passed there a year later said that all the names previously cut in the rock had nearly all been erased and new ones put in their places. So transient is our fame! The scheming Mormons made a nice fortune from the emigrants in a few years by cutting their names in the rock for a fancy price and when they had passed on erasing these names and cutting others in their places.

The accumulated frustrations of the trail after eight hundred miles, and the crowded, competitive conditions in the camps, unleashed another classic American response to stress—murder. In the pioneer journals, homicides suddenly spiked toward crime-wave frequency as the continental divide drew near, almost as if the pioneers were determined to establish a violent legacy for the West and inaugurate clear precedents for frontier justice. At the Mormon ferry crossing at Casper, the traffic backups often stretched east for miles, and armed road rage incidents often led to fatalities. At the confusing Sweetwater fords, it was often difficult to sort out the ownership of cows and calves after several herds commingled while being run across the river at once. Men dueled with rifles and pistols over that. At busy pioneer stops like Devil's Gate, and in the old Green River Rendezvous country ahead, semiretired fur trappers ran frontier saloons inside slapdash log cabins. The alcoholic foreplay produced the usual results. There were gunfights over women, over horses, and competing claims about shot game. In 1852 Virginia pioneer John Clark reported that, at Devil's Gate, a pioneer got into a fight with his wagon driver, shot and killed him, and was "tried and hung on our old waggon at sundown."

The practices at the hastily convened murder trials were fairly consistent, and the pioneers usually tried to imitate the legal venues they remembered from back home. After a murderer was disarmed, either the wagon master, a lawyer, or a minister traveling with the train was appointed judge. The jurors were selected from the men of the company and stood in a semicircle around the accused. A larger crowd formed a human amphitheater behind them. A defendant's chances of acquittal appears to have been about as good as those of accused criminals in czarist Russia. After being found guilty, the murderer was strung up from the nearest tree, but because there often weren't any trees for miles around, a crude gallows was constructed from wagon poles. (The prisoner usually got to watch the construction of the scaffold before the "trial" even began.) There wasn't a lot of time before the wagons had to move on, and digging in the hardtack desert soil was difficult. Account after account describes how the murderer was buried in a shallow grave, shoulder to shoulder with his victim.

Along the ruts between the North Platte and the Sweetwater, accidental death and murder seemed to lurk almost everywhere. In late June 1852, Wisconsin pioneer Polly Coon passed a lone tree along the Sweetwater with an inscription carved on the trunk indicating the graves of a "Man Woman & boy" who were found with their throats cut, the murderer or murderers unknown. The next day her train passed another wagon company mourning the death of two men who had drowned while driving cattle across the river, and then hours later the train arrived at a grove of trees where a man had just been hanged for shooting his brother-in-law.

"It seems that there are some demon spirits near us & the reflection is not very pleasing," Coon wrote. But everything else was fine, for the most part. "Our Co are all well except Ma who is rather unwell."

We entered Mormon country the morning after our camp at Independence Rock, turning west up into the Granites through Rattlesnake Pass. For almost two centuries this scenic area, where the Sweetwater races through a dramatic gorge with vertical walls rising three hundred feet above the water, was called Devil's Gate. From the fur-trapping era in the 1820s to the end of the stagecoach era in the 1890s, as many as 700,000 travelers passed by or camped overnight at these granite portals. On the Sweetwater plain nearby there were log-cabin taverns, mail drops, replacement horse corrals, and encampments of "summer smithies" who operated wagon repair shops. In the 1870s, under the leadership of a canny French-Canadian frontiersman turned cattle baron, Tom Sun, Devil's Gate became the locus of a famous ranch that was declared a National Historic Landmark in 1960.

But that is so yesterday now, so gentile. Since 1997, when the LDS Church took advantage of a disagreement between the Sun Ranch heirs and bought the eastern portion of the ranch around Devil's Gate, the national identity of the Oregon Trail in central Wyoming has disappeared. Martin's Cove, as Devil's Gate is now known, is the first in a string of Mormon sites over the next hundred miles that have transformed the Oregon Trail into a showcase pilgrimage site, a Golgotha for the Mormons.

As we neared the top of the pass, I wasn't sure what we'd see on the other side, but I was determined to reform Nick before we met the Mormons. A lifetime of reporting in the West had familiarized me with the Saints, and I had always enjoyed putting on my Mormon, like an actor going into character for a film shoot. Mormons like a lot of insignia and uniform-type clothing, name badges, just the right black backpacks and shoes, and exacting period dress when reenacting. They are neatness geeks, and I had made sure that both Nick and I shaved that morning before we left Independence Rock. With Mormons, a fondness for corny country and western music, bubblegum pop, and sincerity laid on as thick as meringue also helps a great deal. Family is everything, and the bigger the better. Within ten minutes of meeting a new Mormon I usually try to slip in that I am the fourth of eleven children, information which helps obscure that I am a born drinker, smoker, and curser. I was pretty sure that the American flag fluttering on our wagon and the SEE AMERICA SLOWLY sign would also be real assets for us at Martin's Cove.

As we crested the ridge, I shifted my shoulders, wiggled my ass on the wagon seat, and adjusted my cowboy hat. It was time to go Mormon.

"Okay now, Nick," I said, "you've got to put your Mormon on here, understand?"

"Oh! I can fuckin do Mormon."

"Let's start by eliminating the F-bomb."

"What do I say instead?"

"Fudge is fine, fiddlesticks is also good."

"What about 'shit' and 'goddamnit'?"

"Shit is shucks or shoot, and goddamnit is goshdarnit. Don't forget please and thank you and yes, ma'am, or no, sir. Oh, and, Nick?"

"What?"

"For the rest of this morning, I am 'Brother Rinker' and you are 'Brother Nicholas.' Older men are usually called 'Elder,' okay? It's great. You don't even have to remember the fucking guy's name. Just call him 'Elder.' "

"What about the women?"

"Sister," I said.

"Got it," Nick said. "Just watch. I am goin to be the best fuckin Mormon you ever saw."

We called the mules to the top of the pass and then, cresting, gazed down on a glorious Potemkin village along the Sweetwater plain. For the past fifty miles we had not seen any trace of humanity or habitation—not a single house, a driveway, or even a mailbox. The only cars or trucks we saw were along the brief stretches of highway we had taken where the original trail was flooded. But now, spread out along the oxbows of the Sweetwater, we could see an immense, retro-nineteenth-century jamboree, the extraordinary hustle of Mormon metabolism everywhere.

Down below, at large, graveled parking lots excavated out of the plains in front of the old Sun Ranch cabins, there were Mormon elders greeting tourists stepping out of their RVs. There were acres of yellow school buses from Utah. Satellite pods of Port-o-Potties, disguised by the Mormons as log-cabin structures, but betrayed by PVC vent pipes that stuck out of their roofs, were staged at three-hundred-yard intervals. Brightly colored tent cities swarmed along the bends of the Sweetwater. Large, prominent signs every few yards—NO SMOKING ON ENTIRE SITE, BUSES UNLOAD HERE, MALE URINAL, SISTERS REST ROOM—testified to the Mormon fetish for order. The quaint overtones of nineteenth-century wagon life were reinforced by the presence of replica hand pumps, replica hitching posts, replica log cabins. And, everywhere, parked in neat rows, there were hundreds of replica Mormon handcarts. My first thought as we came over the pass was that the parking lots of replica handcarts in the middle of the Wyoming desert must be visible to the astronauts orbiting in the International Space Station.

Hundreds of Mormon Youth raced around the plain in period dress. They were darting along asphalt and dirt paths pushing Amish-made wooden handcarts freighted down with backpacks, Rubbermaid thermos water jugs, plastic chairs, grocery bags, campfire equipment, and the audio gear for hymn-singing at night. The heartier Mormon boys were pushing teenage Mormon sisters around in their carts, sometimes two or three at once.

At the bottom of Rattlesnake Pass, we rolled the wagon in between the Welcome Area and the Mormon Handcart Visitors' Center, where a gentlemanly elder with a fringe of white hair beneath his cowboy hat greeted us. He was dressed in the practical uniform that the mostly retired "missionaries" from Utah wear while spending six months volunteering at the Mormon shrines—a brown Wyoming Trader canvas vest, nondescript khakis, a plain white shirt, and a large brown plastic nameplate with white type. The elder greeter was hospitable but surprised to see us.

"How come you didn't call?" he said. "We like to know in advance when something special like this is going to happen."

I explained that we were riding the Oregon Trail in a covered wagon and normally didn't call ahead in advance. Besides, we had not had cell phone reception for days.

"Got a point, there," the elder said. "Well, it doesn't matter. All of God's people are welcome here."

The elder could see that I was curious about Martin's Cove and didn't want me to begin my visit with the wrong impression.

"We operate this as a national historic site," he said. "There are thousands of tourists that come through, a hundred thousand a summer. Members of all faiths. We get the Jewish people, Catholics, even followers of the Muslim beliefs. We treat them all the same."

"No evangelization?" I said.

"No evangelization," he said. "Of course, if a visitor asks a question about religion, that's different. We're glad to provide information about the Church of Latter-day Saints. You'd be surprised how many people are driving around on the highways looking for answers."

"Oh, I bet, sir."

While Nick held the mules, I strolled through the log-cabin compound of the old Sun Ranch, which the Mormons have restored to showcase condition. The log sides are aged to perfection and the mortar chinking is freshly whitewashed. Every walkway and patch of grass between the shade trees was immaculately kept.

The Mormons now run a handcart museum in the rambling wings of the Sun Ranch house that, like everything LDS, is exquisitely well designed and tasteful. The typeface on the wall exhibits ("Prelude to Disaster: Mounting Delays & Twists of Fate"), the artwork, maps, and four-color illustrations are of Smithsonian quality. The overall decor of soft, cream white walls and beige trim is so soothing that visitors willingly digest the rewriting of history on the displays.

I fall in love with the Mormons every time. They are divine exhibitors. The antique portable wagon organ for conducting musical services along the trail, the charming old poplar handcart decked out with plates, embroidered cloth napkins, quilts, and gingham bags of flour, the replica odometer, the maple rolling pins and butter churns, the lovely bonnets— oh, just everything Mormon, everything—would make Martha Stewart smile in her sleep. In the museum, the escape to a sanitized world of nineteenth-century covered-wagon travel is enhanced by inspirational music quietly piped in through ceiling speakers—it's a combination of Enya, John Tesh, and Kenny G. The Mormons say that they do not evangelize at this national historic site, but in the handcart museum a whole wing is devoted to "The Gospel of Jesus Christ Restored." It contains hagiographic accounts and portraits of Brigham Young, mural odes to Mormonism, and large displays presenting the handcart disaster of 1856 as a kind of nineteenth-century social welfare state: "HANDCART PLAN: The Poor Welcome Less Expensive Travel."

All of this is presented inoffensively, not urgently. The theme-park feeling inside the handcart museum was quaint, watercolored, and genteel, as if a sedated Walt Disney, after a proper, posthumous baptism, had been rescued from postexistence and brought back to design the space.

The Mormons are effective because they exploit something so basic in the national psyche that most of us have lost the ability to see it. Americans on summer vacation, especially the RVers, are idiots, and haven't read anything in years. Their every cranial neuron has been erased by watching Fox News. The brains of American tourists will accept practically anything as truth because there is nothing else up there to compete with new information. *Just say something, anything*, preferably in bland, thirty-six-point type, and it will stick. And so, "Brigham Young: The American Moses" doesn't have to convert anyone. The Mormons are converting so many people these days in Cambodia and Swaziland they don't even need Americans anymore. They just want to make Mormonism nonthreatening and palatable, chicken soup for the soul.

As I walked up the swept path back toward the wagon, thinking about Mormonism's brilliant fusion with Disneyism, my ears could not believe the words that they were hearing.

At the wagon, Nick was engaged in deep, contemplative conversation with the Mormon elder greeter. Nick was sitting on the wagon seat holding the lines, with Olive Oyl in his lap and his hat pushed up at a jaunty angle. I had never seen Nick quite this earnest, and the Mormon greeter was obviously impressed. He stood with his foot resting on the wheel hub and propping his chin up with his hand.

"Well, you know, Elder," Nick said, "I actually believe that Jesus had me fall off that roof for a reason. I needed to spend eight months on the couch thinkin about my life, takin stock of my values. Then Brother Rinker came along with this mission across the West. It was a callin and I had to respect it."

"Have you figured everything out now?" the elder asked.

"Elder, that's God's work," Nick said. "Let Him figure it out. We're just here on planet Earth to do the best we can."

"Very well said, son," the elder said. "It's important to be humble."

"Humble! Boy, Elder, have I worked on being humble for the last year."

I was afraid that I was losing Nick. I had to get us out of there.

"Brother Nicholas," I said. "That pot of gold for us at the end of the trail won't wait forever. We best be getting on, God willing."

The Mormon elder stepped away from the wagon wheel and reached his hand out to shake mine.

"Be careful out there on the trail, son," he said.

"Oh, I will, Elder. Thank you. And God bless."

I took the lines and ran the mules down past the parking lots and the pastures full of handcarts. When we were out of Mormon earshot, Nick spoke up.

"Hey, Rink, don't you think you were shovelin the shit a little heavy back there? What is this 'God bless you' crap?"

"Oh, and Nick, Jesus kicked your ass off that roof *for a reason*?"

"Rink, you're the one who told me to do Mormon."

Beyond the last Mormon RV park, we turned west through a cattle guard gate to stay with the Sweetwater through the Sun Ranch. Nearby, three teenage Mormon sisters in bonnets and long skirts, exhausted by a long handcart trek, were sitting together against the ersatz log-cabin wall of a Port-o-Pottie, resting. Olive Oyl ran over and jumped into their laps. Behind us, out over the Granites, low cumulus clouds shaded the peaks. With the groups of handcart reenactors pushing up toward Martin's Cove, and the gray and green hues on the misty mountains, the scene reminded me of Thomas Cole's *Travelers in the Swiss Alps.*

22

THE HILLY BUT FEATURELESS SCRUBLANDS of the Sun Ranch presented our biggest challenge yet. For the next thirty-five miles we would disappear into a dry abyss below the Granites with nothing to support us until we reached the next ranch. At Willow Springs and then while we camped at Independence Rock, local cowboys who dropped by the wagon to visit had told us that the raging Sweetwater had washed out the trail ahead, and we probably wouldn't be able to follow the river. Escaping south to the paved highway at Muddy Gap Junction wasn't a good option either, because we would expend all of our water getting there. But my high-altitude euphoria prevented me from registering bad news and, carefree, we pushed on for the foothills bordering the river.

I knew from the pioneer journals that we had to spend most of the day following a consistent bearing slightly north of west, about three hundred degrees on my compass. Within a few miles a large and unmistakable waypoint that the pioneers had relied on, a cleft peak in the Granites called Split Rock, would appear on the opposite side of the Sweetwater, almost due west of our position. "Yesterday from the time we started we steered to this cliff with a steadiness that was astonishing," wrote Kentucky 49er Dr. Joseph Middleton, "never deviating from it more than the needle does from the north pole." Split Rock. We would track this "gun sight" peak for the next twenty-four hours and then when it was abeam proceed due west to the ghost town of Jeffrey City.

For most of the day we bumped west along the range of the Sun Ranch, sometimes on a wagon track, sometimes not, and we saw only one trail marker. By mid-afternoon I began to see the large V-shaped formation at the highest point in the Granites, bearing north-northwest, right where it should be.

"Split Rock," I said to Nick. "All we have to do is keep that rock right there until dark. Then we can camp anywhere and find our way out in the morning."

We steered for the "gun sight" break in the Granite Range, Split Rock, for nearly a day, but even a waypoint as clear as this did not prevent us from getting lost.

But the big split mountain ahead of us was illusory, and I wouldn't realize until the end of the day that I had become a literalist, a strict constructionist of trail literature. Following a giant landmark fifteen miles away was too vague, a century after the main ruts had fissured into a maze of cattle tracks, pickup roads, and breaks in the scrub pines constantly inviting us in every direction over rough, unmarked terrain. Content that I could see Split Rock to our right, I picked a meandering route that climbed the foothills here, and dipped into washes of purple thistles and yellow coneflowers there. At the Sun Ranch watering holes, where there were large, mean-looking herds of longhorn cattle, Beck started dancing in her harness and shying, frothing at the mouth and threatening to run away. We threw Olive Oyl off to chase the cattle away, but Beck was still acting crazy.

In the vast West, the sensation of being lost usually arrives long after you *are* lost, and the limited turning radius of a covered wagon provides almost no opportunity to turn around. You can drive in circles for hours because the moonscape of sand and creek washes always looks the same. By late afternoon we arrived at a very definable fork in the cattle tracks where a right turn would take us almost due north toward the Sweetwater, and a left turn would take us due west into the high country. I hiked both forks for almost a mile but couldn't find any trail markers or much of a route, and when I returned to the wagon I told Nick to proceed on the west fork, because it seemed to follow my compass bearing northwest. Split Rock quickly slipped behind the foothills crowding around us and we wouldn't see it again for hours.

I was supremely oblivious at first to the navigation riddle we faced, the modern danger of riding a covered wagon through the Rockies. There were no clouds of dust from the covered wagons ahead, and no fresh wagon ruts, to follow. My confidence that the trail was well marked was also misplaced. The government surveyors and OCTA volunteers who mark the trail, occasionally, are riding in pickups or on four-wheelers, and turning around and having to retrace their tire tracks back to the last fork is a small inconvenience. The importance of marking forks in the trail has been completely lost. For no other reason except that this is the way it is done, intersections along the Oregon Trail are almost *never* marked today. When you arrive at a fork, the next trail marker, maybe, is a mile or two away—too far to be of any use to a mule skinner.

Finally, when we emerged on a high, cleared plateau, Split Rock was right off our beam again, so large that I felt I might bump into it with my nose.

"There we go, Nick," I said. "We're right on the trail."

"Like hell we are. That's a sheer drop-off ahead of us."

I was irritated that Nick thought he could read terrain better than

I could, and that he was now assuming responsibility for navigation, but I stepped off the wagon and crossed west across the plateau. At the edge, I was staring straight down a cliff, which curved north around the plateau into steep canyons. It looked as though we were trapped.

"You're right, Nick," I said, back at the wagon. "Fuck. We are now officially lost."

"I could have told you that three hours ago."

Lifting Olive Oyl off the wagon so she could run rattlesnake patrols in front of me, I poked through the low ground off to the right. I found a route through the gullies and boulder fields down there, and then walked back to the plateau, signaling to Nick to carefully follow me through the low area by observing my hand signals. It was grueling work, inching the mules over rocks and sage growth that towered over the wagon top, but when we had climbed back to the high ground I picked up an indistinct cattle track.

Traveling by foot, and being able to see the ground more closely, gave me a distinct advantage. I began picking up more cattle tracks—the bigger hoofprints of the mother cows, and the smaller, deer-size prints of the calves—and followed them north. By walking thirty or forty yards out to the sides of the track, I was able to pick up the prints of shod horses. Okay, good, I thought, somebody was moving cattle through here, fairly recently. In Wyoming, late June and early July are often the roundup and calf-branding season, when mothers and their calves are taken off their winter range and pushed up into the higher green pastures in the mountains. Following the roundup tracks would take me somewhere, probably to some high corrals, but I didn't know whether or not we could get the wagon out of there.

After a mile or two of following a narrow rim where canyons fell steeply off on either side, the track ahead opened up into a well-traveled cattle road, and I could make out what looked like barbed-wire corrals ahead. I waited for the wagon and climbed back up.

"Nick, I'm pretty sure we're off the Sun Ranch now," I said. "I think those fences ahead are the spring corrals of the Split Rock Ranch. Sorry about this. I'm supposed to know where we are, but I don't, really."

"Don't worry about me," Nick said. "I love driving team through country like this."

At the corrals, the landscape below us opened to a vast, end-of-the-hills vista where the flats on the Sweetwater ran for miles over to the Granites, and the ground just ahead gradually sloped down toward the river. I still didn't know exactly where we were, but the Sweetwater was right below us, where it was supposed to be.

"It's all trail, Nick," I said. "We're moving west, on the river."

"Rinker, half the time you don't know what the fuck you are doing, but at least you act like you do. We're fine."

There were a couple of other setbacks that night. As we unharnessed, I noticed that we were missing one of our lead chains, and we were now down to two, for three mules. The lost chain was probably another casualty of high-altitude forgetfulness, back at Independence Rock. And the plug on our rear water barrel had popped out, probably when we crossed the boulder fields in the canyons below, and a lot of the water had spilled. The thirty gallons we had left would be just enough to water the mules tonight and in the morning, but then we would be out. After that, I had no idea how far we would have to push the mules without water.

After dinner I called for Olive Oyl to run ahead of me on snake patrol and I followed the cattle path running downhill from the corrals. Years before, on a long cattle drive in the Red Desert country to the south, a legendary western sheriff and range detective, Ed Cantrell, had taught me to read cattle and horse prints, and I was able to pick up most of the telltale marks of a classic spring cattle drive. Most of the cattle had followed a steady southerly course on the higher, smooth range. In the steep draws below, I knelt on one knee in the sand and saw the prints of cow dogs and well-shod horses where the cowboys had galloped down to round up stray steers. There were two distinct tracks from pickup tires pulling trailers—probably a chuck wagon rig and a stock van for the horses. There was a burn mark at the corrals where a branding iron had been used. After calf-branding up at the corrals, the herd must have been driven below for a reason, and I could see from my maps that somewhere down there the highway curved up again for Jeffrey City. I concluded that the herd I was following had been trucked to their summer pastures, and for that there would have to be loading ramps and big gates below, which would only be located on the highway.

As I climbed back to camp, I decided that in the morning we would turn due south instead of northwest along the Sweetwater, following the safety of the herd tracks back to a known road.

I didn't sleep very well that night. My trail navigation had been off all day, and we were down to the bottom of our water barrels. I had performed poorly, just a third of the way across the Acropolis stretch of ruts, and this made me doubt my ability to negotiate what I knew would be even more challenging trail ahead.

I woke up at three in the morning, couldn't get back to sleep, and sat brooding with my legs hanging over the end boards of the wagon, smoking my pipe. I could see the outline of the Granites and stars flickered beside Split Rock. The desert to the west was vast and black, with just a few far-off lights shining weakly from the ranches. My dread hour lasted until dawn and my flagellant impulses carried me in every direction—Nick was losing confidence in me, Beck would run off, we would deplete our water tomorrow before we reached a ranch or creek.

Maybe the Oregon Trail was beyond me. I shouldn't have come west. There wasn't a clear path of ruts ahead of us, just indecipherable space that you got lost in, leading toward more indecipherable space.

We harnessed early the next morning and followed the herd prints down through the draws and, sure enough, there were cattle chutes, an earthen truck ramp, and a big gate opening to the highway. But the elation of having tracked our way out of the maze of Sweetwater canyons soon gave way to anxiety. After several hours of plodding along the lonely highway, there were deep cavities on the haunches of the mules, a sign of dehydration, and our water barrels were empty. We had to get the team to water.

Finally, from a mile off, I saw the large welded-steel letters of a ranch sign, suspended from tall posts of lodgepole pine.

SPLIT ROCK RANCH

As we turned the mules in at the ranch driveway, they broke into a trot and then tried to gallop—they knew that we were making a stop and that they would soon get water. I was intrigued by what we'd find ahead because Split Rock Ranch is one of those Oregon Trail stops that demonstrate how frontier settlement led to boisterous economic development in two directions, east and west, after the initial emigration period ended with the Civil War. From the long gravel entrance, we approached a distant cluster of whitewashed log cabins, barns, and corrals, shaded by cottonwoods and nestled into a break in the folds of the Granites. The 200,000-acre spread typified the immense dimensions of western ranches that we would be crossing now. The ranch's rolling expanse of plains and high country includes twelve miles of riverfront along the Sweetwater, six hundred acres of irrigated alfalfa fields, shaded creek draws, and elk and mountain lion habitat in the mountain forests. The private land and adjoining grazing acreage leased from the government sprawls over the entire valley between two mountain ranges, the Granites and the Greens, and a drive through the ranch, north to south, is thirty-six miles.

Until the 1890s, there were still wagon companies riding through the trail country of central Wyoming, and the homesteaders headed west were joined by military freight convoys, the stage and mail lines, and the long pack-mule caravans of miners. (Gold was discovered in the South Pass hills in 1866.) Cattle herds of 2,500 head or more were driven east against this traffic to railheads in eastern Wyoming and slaughter yards in Nebraska, and were often stopped for two or three days to graze along the Sweetwater. U.S. Army cavalry units, dispatched to maintain order and to provide protection from Indian raids, camped there all summer. The corrals and log cabins at Split Rock became a Pony Express and stagecoach stop, a telegraph station, and a post office, and there were large watering troughs and livery stables for horses. The summer population of one of these busy outposts could number more than a hundred, and there were many settlements like Split Rock—Devil's Gate and Fetterman City behind us, the Ellis Ranch and Burnt Ranch ahead.

After World War I, the mechanization of farming and the transfer of traffic to distant rail lines and highways emptied most of these western ranch towns, turning them into lonely agrarian outposts with just one or two families spread out over several miles of range. It was hard to imagine that the lonely plain we were now crossing once bustled with so much life and commerce. As we approached the ranch, I realized something important about our trip that I had never considered before. For all of my planning and my existing knowledge of the West, I had been stunningly naive about navigating these vast spaces. In the nineteenth century, the Oregon

Trail had been marked with fresh wagon tracks, and there were ranches the size of small towns every fifteen or twenty miles. But the congestion and settlement that had once supported wagon travel had disappeared. Steeping myself in the pioneer journals and history books—literature dating to a time when these plains teemed with human activity—had lured me into thinking that I could easily find my way. But without that naïveté, and without the willingness to tolerate uncertainty, I would never have begun this trip.

Rolling into Split Rock Ranch was also interesting because it was the locale for one of the great fabrications of American life. In the early 1860s a young man with a hardscrabble past, William Frederick Cody, burst out of the Kansas Territory and began to work along the Oregon Trail as a bullwhacker for the freight lines, a U.S. Army scout, and an avid buffalo slaughterer. "Buffalo Bill," as he began to call himself, was a great story-teller, and he went on to become one of the world's greatest showmen, touring America and Europe with his flamboyant circus about western life, "Buffalo Bill's Wild West Show," which made him a fortune and established him as an international celebrity. But very few of Buffalo Bill's stories about himself check out today, and even in his own lifetime he was celebrated more for his flamboyant mendacity than for any actual daring deeds in the West.

While he was still a teenager, it is possible, but far from certain, that Cody worked for the Pony Express, probably building corrals and working as a stable boy. But a true Wild West figure like Cody would not sit at a bar telling everyone that he had mucked out the stalls at the Red Buttes Station. In his various autobiographies Cody alleged that "one day" (he never provided the date) in 1860 or 1861 he raced off on his horse from Red Buttes and galloped across the Sweetwater stretch of the Pony Express route that followed the Oregon Trail. At Split Rock, as the story continued, Cody learned that the rider scheduled to take over at the next station had been killed. So he continued on as a replacement rider and rode all the way out to Rocky Ridge near South Pass and then *back* to Red Buttes. Cody claimed that he had completed the ride, "accomplishing on the round-trip a distance of 322 miles," which was a convenient four miles longer than the real record holder's distance.

Scholars have now concluded that Buffalo Bill's famous ride never happened, and in fact he was not a Pony Express rider at all. ("There seems no point in resisting the inevitable; Bill's pony riding represents another spate of fiction," wrote historian John S. Gray in an influential article in the *Kansas Historical Quarterly* in 1985.) The best that anyone can figure out today is that Buffalo Bill's fabled ride was a "composite" fabricated out of the experiences of several other riders.

But I loved this tale of the frontier and what it meant. The story of Cody's "longest ride in the West," endlessly repeated in puff pieces about him in eastern newspapers, helped build his reputation, and he went on to show how fortunes could be made capitalizing on tall tales of the American West, becoming the spiritual godfather of the Hollywood western. Cody was a classic résumé-bloater, a braggart impresario who prospered by exploiting the gullibility of the American people, most of whom are so poorly read, so bamboozled by religion and the sensationalist, mogul-worshipping press, and so desperate for heroes, that they'll believe almost anything that a grand bullshitter like Cody shovels out. Cody's style of self-promotion is still very much a part of American life today.

When we drove in with the Schuttler, Cooper and Mattie Stevenson, the children of the ranch managers, were dozing on a bench out by the hitching posts. They were kids on summer vacation at a far-off ranch, looking quite bored. Cooper was eleven and his sister Mattie was nine, and they were both tall for their age, with handsome, attractive faces. They were stylishly but practically dressed in jeans with rodeo buckles, plaid western-cut shirts, and pointy stirrup boots. Cooper was snoozing beneath a big buckaroo-style cowboy hat. When we pulled the mules to a stop near the hitching post, the children woke up and looked over at us, cautious but curious.

"Say," I said, "we've been running these mules from St. Joe. Do you think we could fill our barrels and water the team?"

Mattie jumped up from the bench and ran toward the ranch house.

"Mom! Mee-uuuuules, Mom! Mules and a covered wagon!"

"We can water your mules," Cooper said. "But let me just see what my Mom says."

Their mother, Jennifer Stevenson, came out a few minutes later, and she was a take-charge cowgirl with runway model good looks and long blond hair. She was dressed in jeans with a big rodeo belt buckle, a western-cut shirt, and roping boots. Jennifer was glad to see us, but also edgy and tough, and very knowledgeable about western ranching.

Jennifer had grown up on a farm in Wheatland, Wyoming, dreamed of ranching all the way through the University of Wyoming, met her husband, Travis, and together they eventually landed at Split Rock, one of the jewels of the West, where they have built up the herd and improved profitability. Cooper and Mattie began to ride early, and their parents have taught them to rope and cut steers—Cooper is already winning at rodeos and saving money for college. In some ways it's a lonely life. At the Jeffrey City school, there were four students, including Cooper and Mattie, and it's a one-day round-trip to Lander or Rawlins to shop for groceries. But running a spread like Split Rock also provides a lot of romance and variety. In her pickup, Jennifer carries a rifle with a large, long-range scope beside her against the door, for plugging coyotes, which she can hit from several hundred yards away. In the winter, when the Split Rock Ranch makes extra money hosting big-game hunters, Jennifer guides the visitors up into the Granites to shoot mountain lion and elk.

Jennifer was surprised that we had found our way to the ranch through the maze of canyons on the Sweetwater, but was expecting a catch.

"Where's your support vehicles?" she said.

"We don't have any," I said.

"All the way from St. Joe without support trucks? Oh, okay. We haven't seen that before."

It was a sore point with Stevenson, and many other ranchers we met along the South Pass segment. Every summer, when the Pony Express reenactors ride the trail, they roll into the local ranches with as many as forty-five support vehicles—horse vans, RVs, catering trucks—blocking the roads for miles. The Mormon handcarters—several groups of 150 or more can hit the same stretch of trail at once—block the local roads and disrupt cattle drives. It was hard for most ranchers at first to distinguish us from these reenactors. Most of them thought that our trail of support vehicles must be just over the hill.

While Cooper and Mattie helped us water the team, I described to Jennifer our tangled route through the canyons above the ranch.

"How did you know to divert away from the river?" she asked me. "I think the Sweetwater is still flooded up there."

"I didn't," I said. "We got lost up there."

"No you didn't. You got from the Sun Ranch to here, right? It's all trail."

Jennifer explained that cattle grazing in the Sweetwater hills had pretty much eliminated evidence of the Oregon Trail ruts, and that when we had pushed due west instead of north for the river we were actually on a stretch of the associated terrain now attributed to the California Trail. No one can say for sure today why one stretch was called the California Trail and the other the Oregon Trail because wagons destined for both places used either route. The California ruts had lost their definition years ago and had become an endless series of dead ends in the canyons, and the high water along the Sweetwater this year had washed out the northern path along the river. This happens every ten years or so, when the river extensively rechannels itself, forming new oxbows every half mile, and the trail along its banks has continually changed.

"There isn't any consistent trail through there," Jennifer said. "There probably never was. You're probably going to have the same problems getting around Rocky Ridge and finding South Pass."

Jennifer's husband was off cutting alfalfa that day, and he had forgotten to leave a wrangling horse behind in the barn. She and the children were dawdling on a hot day, putting off going into the corrals and wrangling on foot. From Kansas onward, at the ranches and at road intersections where families had stopped to watch us go by with the mules, we had enjoyed giving children and grandchildren wagon rides, and I suggested to Jennifer that Nick take Mattie and Cooper in the wagon into Jeffrey City. Jennifer and I could follow later in her pickup.

"Mom! Don't even think about saying no," Mattie called out. "Sir, just hold on there a minute, okay? I need to get my hat."

When Mattie came out of the ranch house with her big straw hat on, I stood beside the wheel to help her up to the wagon seat, but she raised her hand.

"You think I can't climb into a wagon?"

Mattie nimbly monkeyed up the wheel and sat on the wagon seat next to Nick. Olive Oyl poked her head out from beneath the seat, between Mattie's legs. Cooper climbed up the wheel and sat on the outside of the seat.

"Okay, honey," Nick said to Mattie. "We're just goin to handle this like a real slow mule-drivin lesson. Okay? I'll show you first."

"I don't need showing," Mattie said. "Hand me them lines."

Mattie gathered the lines firmly in her lap and slowly pulled them to her waist, so the team could feel on their bits that she was there, and spoke softly to them at first, just as it should be done. She had already learned their names.

"Bute, Jake, Beck," she said, "we're headed for Jeffrey City."

Then she slapped the lines on their rumps and brightly called the mules.

"Team! Get on there, you *lazy critters*! Get up there Jake! *Buuute!* Get up there, you old mules! Git *movin!*"

The mules pranced with their front hooves and leaped forward into their harness. While the wagon bumped away Nick held his arms high above his head to show that he wasn't handling the mules at all. Mattie was doing all of the driving, and he was just a passenger on the wagon now.

I looked over to Jennifer.

"Has she driven team before?"

"I don't think so," Jennifer said. "Oh, maybe, I don't remember. We have friends with teams. But it doesn't matter. That's Mattie. She usually knows."

I stood there with Jennifer watching the wagon turn west as the noon-time low cumulus rolled in. The sun caught the Schuttler's white-top and green sides, making them shine brightly. Mattie slapped the lines on the mules once more and continued her soprano calling. "Beee-uuuu-ute! I don't see you pulling hard, *muuule*! Get up there, you critters!" Her blond hair blowing back underneath her cowboy hat reminded me of Narcissa Whitman galloping uphill for South Pass, and filled me with happiness about the trip.

23

OUR TIME OF TRIUMPH HALFWAY across the trail—ascending South Pass to cross the continental divide—arrived in mid-July. We rested the mules for an extra day at a magical space along the Sweetwater, the Ellis Ranch, and the young archeologist and ranch manager there, Charles Turquie, briefed me on the best route to follow around Rocky Ridge, the big obstacle that stood between us and the pass. The dramatic scenery along the Sweetwater is virtually unchanged from pioneer days. But the emigrants' many cutoffs to avoid the worst hills, followed by gold mining, stagecoaching, and the modern Mormon reoccupation, has turned the approach to South Pass into a labyrinth of intersecting ruts and tempting wrong turns. In the most dreamlike setting, through exquisite country to savor slowly in a covered wagon, our next week would be hell.

Summiting Rocky Ridge, legendary as one of the most punishing climbs of the Oregon Trail, had never been part of my plan. The gateway to South Pass is a twelve-mile geologic wonderland where the trail twists upward through elaborate formations of dark feldspar and basalt rock striated with pink schist, a giant sculpture park left behind by the collisions of the earth's crusts aeons ago. The route culminates in an abrupt seven-hundred-foot rise over an ascending staircase of gravel and brown shale. On the rounded summit, Rocky Ridge, at an elevation of 7,300 feet, the spines of stone coalesce into two broad boulder fields. It was on this desolate pile of rocks that the handcart Mormons suffered in the snow, and all of the early pioneers struggled. When their draft animals gave out and collapsed onto the rocks, the overland companies lightened their loads and pushed the wagons by hand, easing their axles over the boulders one wheel at a time.

There was no reason for me to tackle Rocky Ridge in the wagon. After 1853 the most popular route to South Pass was the Seminoe Cutoff, a parallel wagon road that followed the south banks of the Sweetwater and avoided the boulder fields above. The wagons also bypassed Rocky Ridge by following the creek beds to the north, and these paths were worn down by heavy traffic after mining began in the late 1860s.

All of these alternative routes around Rocky Ridge are considered the Oregon Trail, but everyone had a different opinion about which ruts to follow. Two ranchers warned me about the narrow bridge at Strawberry Creek, which they didn't think the mules would cross, and others advised me not to follow the old tracks of the Point of Rocks stage road to the Lander Cutoff, which would require crossing difficult terrain at Slaughterhouse Gulch. Nobody really knew, and once more I faced the riddle presented by the multiple cutoffs and the broad, maddening vagueness of the Oregon Trail. There was no single preferred route. We were heading off for the big moment of the trip, crossing the Rocky Mountain divide, into a chasm of doubt.

But the return of the Mormons to the Sweetwater offered some help, and Charles Turquie told us about this as we sat around a campfire at the Ellis Ranch the night before we left. All along the approach to South Pass, the Mormons have staged a series of large, visible camps on BLM land for handcarting Mormon Youth, often at important intersections of the trail. After crossing the river to the north banks out of the ranch, we would follow the most prominent set of ruts west and eventually see a slate marker at the site of the old St. Mary's Pony Express stop. A few miles later we wouldn't be able to miss a large, elaborately designed Mormon monument—fenced in, and marked with a historical plaque—dedicated to the 1856 handcart victims who died on Rocky Ridge. Farther west we would see the colorful tents of a Mormon Youth site, the Sage Creek Camp.

Turquie told us to turn north at the Mormon camp. The road would climb through the canyon and then, at the top of the terrain, branch south again, skirting around Rocky Ridge. We would then follow that serpentine track down through the gulches and back to the main trail.

The country up top would be confusing, Turquie said, but if we missed the turnoff south for the trail we'd end up on the well-marked Fort Stambaugh Road, and along it there would be plenty of tracks south for the trail.

"Just don't try Rocky Ridge at all," Turquie said. "Nobody can get a wagon across that. Rocky Ridge is the only place around here where I've ripped the tires off my truck."

We left the Ellis Ranch for South Pass the next morning in a cheerful, expectant mood. The mules were jaunty after two days of pasture rest and pounded their front hooves into the pink sand of the ruts, perking their long ears forward and asking to trot when we reached the hills.

We found the slate marker for the St. Mary's Station and then the substantial Mormon monument to the handcart victims, on the top of a hilltop to our left. But when we reached a turnoff north that looked a lot like the one for Sage Creek Camp, there was no Mormon camp. A lonely, faux log-cabin Mormon Port-o-Pottie stood up on the hill, its PVC vent pipe glinting in the sun. But the hillside was otherwise deserted and I concluded that our failure to find Sage Creek Camp was just another example of the endlessly confusing directions provided by westerners. The turnoff would probably look just like this one and be a mile or two ahead. We continued to push west on the most obvious ruts.

As we cleared the next rise and began to descend downhill, the climb ahead looked very rocky, with brown and black ledges glinting in the sunlight. The rock formation was stepped and the climb so steep that all we could see beyond it was blue Wyoming sky. By this time, the terrain on either side of us was impassable. To the left the slope fell sharply downhill, and the boulder fields to the right looked like the dump zone of a quarry. The staircase of rock ahead of us looked far too abrupt, and I worried out loud to Nick about climbing the obstacle in the wagon.

"Oh, I can put the mules up through that," Nick said. "It doesn't look that bad."

As we neared the bottom of the small valley before the rock slope, we saw the distant figures of two people easing down the track ahead of us, picking their way over the rock ledges. There wasn't enough room for two-way traffic and we decided to hold the wagon and water the mules while we waited for them to descend. As I watered the mules I looked up-hill at the hikers. They were carrying walking sticks and had water bottles strapped around their waists, and they looked like a married couple out for a day of trekking along the trail.

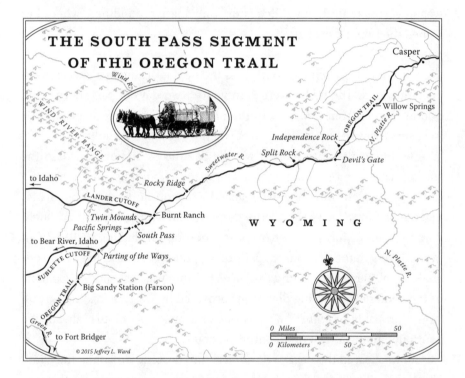

The man looked surprised and was so excited about finding us that he ran the last thirty yards downhill to the wagon.

"I can't believe this," he said. "Who are you? I never expected to see a covered wagon way out here."

His name was Sam Peery and he was a dentist from Logan, Utah. Peery and his wife, LaVora, were descendants of Mormons who joined the trail exodus from Illinois in 1849 and 1851, and they had driven up from Utah for the weekend to make a pilgrimage typical for Mormon couples.

They wanted to see Willie Handcart shrines erected by the LDS and to hike sections of the South Pass segment, and they were particularly interested in exploring Rocky Ridge to learn more about how the heavy wagons of their ancestors had crossed the rocks. Peery told me that he was a horseman himself and owned a draft team and a covered wagon. Like a lot of Mormons who enjoy horses, he had participated in several "Mormon Wagon Trains" along the overland trail routes.

While we waited for his wife to reach us, Peery looked back up the slope and then wiped his brow with his shirtsleeve.

"You do know, by the way, that you're headed straight for Rocky Ridge?"

"That can't be Rocky Ridge," I said. "We haven't reached the Mormon camp yet."

"There is no Mormon camp today," Peery said. "It's Saturday. Those kids cleared out of there yesterday and headed back for Salt Lake. They've got church tomorrow."

He couldn't really mean this. It was impossible, I'd been told, to miss the Mormon camp. My voice was a falsetto now.

"You mean we *missed* it? Missed it? What do we do now?"

I looked off the side of the wagon toward the steeply plummeting ground to our right, and then left, up the boulder fields. The basalt chute surrounding us was only a few feet wider than our wheels. Once more, we were boxed in. We couldn't turn the wagon around and our only choice now was straight ahead, across Rocky Ridge.

I knew that I had to walk ahead to scout the terrain and thought that Sam, a wagon man, might be able to help, and I asked him if he would come along.

"Sure," he said. "It's actually not as bad up there as they say. I think there's a way through."

By this time LaVora had reached us and the Peerys said that they considered our meeting providential. Mormons are wonderfully candid about what they consider the spiritual coincidences of life and don't seem embarrassed about blurting out the mysteries of their faith in front of strangers. God, the Peerys said, had sent them to scout the ridge and lead our wagon across hallowed land.

"LaVora," Sam said. "We are angels today. We were sent for them."

"We are angels today," LaVora said. "There is a reason that we met them like this."

As I climbed the steep, rocky path uphill with the Peerys, I decided that they *were* angels. Ambassadors from God had miraculously appeared to guide us over the notorious Rocky Ridge, and the terrain itself didn't look as bad as all the trail experts had told me it would be. The stepped rock ladder to the ridge wasn't going to be very difficult, at least for a driver like Nick. In many places the ledges were diagonal to the trail, and by angling the pole at the same diagonal we could ease the wheels over axle by axle. Nick would see the same thing. Most of the ledges were eroded from wagon and foot traffic and had either sand or small pebbles on the top, which would give the mules some purchase against their shoes.

The summit seemed navigable—just barely—too. I could instantly see why Rocky Ridge had assumed mythic status during the trail years. The rounded, high ground ahead of us stood alone, separated from the other peaks, and the fierce Wyoming winds prevented soil formation, exposing the bedrock of tall boulders. But the views west were spacious and the ruts below dropped through a green Jordan of grassy meadows along the Sweetwater. Most of the elevation gain toward South Pass had already been made, and the pioneers couldn't resist taking this brutal shortcut to their destination.

Best, we would not have to cross two boulder fields on the top, just one. After the first boulder field, which appeared to be about sixty yards across, there was a red two-track in the sand curving around the second formation of rocks. Modern pickup traffic around the second field of boulders had reduced the challenge of Rocky Ridge by half.

The worn spots on the rocks across the summit showed that the pioneers had simply continued in the southwest direction of the ruts below, taking the hurdles of rocks head-on. The boulders were huge—some of them taller than our hubs. But the rock strata again met the trail at a diagonal, roughly north to south. Between the rock lines, there were jagged but relatively flat intervals marked with sparse green vegetation, where the protection of the rocks had allowed shallow deposits of soil.

When I walked to the south side of the boulder field and stood on top of a large rock, I could see that there was just enough space to squeeze the wagon through these flat intervals. We would take Rocky Ridge at a diagonal, crisscrossing the summit several times along these flat areas. But the only way we could get the wagon swung back around for the next trip between the rocks would be to maneuver the team back and forth in a K-turn, carefully watching to be sure that we didn't jackknife the Trail Pup. It would be tight, but doable.

Before I left the ridge to hike down for Nick and the wagon, I explained my plan to Sam and LaVora. When the wagon got to the ridge, I wanted them to stand at the clearest point at the end of each interval, so that Nick could see through the rocks to his end point each time. When he started K-turning, they could reposition themselves in the best place to show the end point of the next interval.

Sam thought that my route would be difficult. The pioneers had obviously cut straight across the center of the rock field to avoid the clifflike edges of the summit. Maneuvering wagons along the perimeter risked pushing the wheels dangerously close to the edge and falling into the steep canyon below. But we didn't enjoy the advantage of a wagon train with plenty of men available to lift the wheels over the boulders, and our only choice was taking the rock field at a diagonal from edge to edge.

I didn't say much to Nick when I got back to the wagon. By this time I trusted the seamless, terse communication that seemed to come naturally to us when I was leading the way through rough terrain on foot and he was driving the wagon. Our body language together seemed almost spiritual to me now. Just by leaning my shoulder and arm left or right, or placing my foot on a rock, Nick got it.

I explained to Nick that the Peerys would station themselves on the summit to mark the narrow sand avenues between the highest rocks. When we couldn't avoid boulders, go easy on the axles. Baby the wheels.

"Got it," Nick said. "You'll guide me?"

"I'll guide you."

"Let's go," he said. "We're takin Rocky Ridge. I was born for this fucker."

We ascended the ledges climbing to Rocky Ridge axle by axle, pausing at each step, like an old canal boat rising through the locks. The mules adjusted splendidly to the work. Beck's craziness seemed to fade with a challenge like this, as she narrowly focused her attention on remaining the most forward mule on complicated terrain. Jake was athletic and calm. Bute we never even thought about because she was so lazy that all she wanted to do was step up daintily from rock to rock, her loose tug chains trailing behind her like a prom dress. It was fascinating to watch the mules. They all turned their heads sideways at each ledge, to look out past their blinders and take advantage of their wide rear vision, to watch their hind legs on the rocks.

The wagon cover behind him prevented Nick from seeing the two rear axles, but I was standing to the rear of the wagon and giving him advisories all the way up. The team had to be stopped and the wheels gently eased over each new obstruction.

"Rear mains at the ledge."

"Rear mains."

"Trail Pup."

"Trail Pup."

It was an agonizingly slow climb with the pole banging and the tug chains crackling with tension each time we forced an axle over the next ledge. I ran back and forth on the ledges, signaling Nick to angle the pole correctly for the next rock step, then running back behind the wagon to call out the axles reaching the big hoist over the same spot. Several times Jake and Beck stumbled and spun their hooves on slippery, smooth rocks, and the wagon fell backward with a giant groan of pain from the running gear. But Nick stood on the brake and held the team with the lines, calming them in a low, soothing voice.

"Good, Team, good. Rest now. Just rest. Then we'll try again. You're my team."

I was saturated with sweat and my eyes stung from the salty perspiration pouring off my forehead. I was wobbly in the high mountain air and stumbled several times on the ledges, and the sharp edges of rock slit my blue jeans at the knee. In the back of my mind I heard a deep, gravelly voice, Bill Petersen's in Nebraska. "I'm no mule man, but you're not going to get that wagon over Rocky Ridge. Go around." But the gauzy, high Wyoming air drugged me like ether and I felt defiant and inexhaustible. Nobody knows. The experts said that we couldn't do this. But we were climbing Rocky Ridge toward our Mormon angels and we would make it to the other side.

Near the summit, at the edge of the boulder field, we stopped to water the mules, mostly to relax them, and I explained the rock field to Nick. From his high perch on the wagon seat he could see the flat channels between the spines of rock and how we would have to steer through them.

"Boss, I can do this. But it's going to take time."

"We've got all day. We can camp just beyond here if we want."

But it didn't take that long. I stood at the first two boulders in our way and wedged small rocks underneath the wheels and pushed on the spokes to help the wagon over, and Nick entered the first channel, reached LaVora at the end, and pulled wide and due west. Then he backed the team so expertly that he needed only three K-turns in reverse to enter the next channel. Forty yards away, Sam was standing on a tall rock and holding his arms wide to mark the next channel.

The work was exhilarating but stressful. There were a few spots along the channels where I had to run back and either wedge rocks under the wheels or hold back the spokes so the axles rose evenly. At the top of the stones Nick locked the brake and held the team so that the wagon sat perched sideways at a crazy angle on one wheel. Then he gently pumped the brake to let the wheel rim skid down the other side of the rock. He spoke softly to the mules to keep them calm. In a few places, where the channel narrowed to just our hub width, we left skid marks and red paint on the rocks.

Nick tipped the wagon only once, when he misjudged his distance from the rocks on the right side and put both right wheels of the Schuttler on the top of boulders. I could hear the load shifting as the wagon started to lean over on its side, but I didn't have time to call to Nick. He caught the near-spill just in time and calmly pulled the team and the pole even harder right, so that the front wheel pivoted and skidded backward down the rock. Then he eased the rear wheel down by turning left and standing on the brake.

It was a masterly display of driving skills, but the wheels landed hard and the wagon box banged against the running gear as the Schuttler slid off the rocks. We stopped to inspect the spokes and hubs and they seemed fine. I ran back and forth repositioning Sam and LaVora so that Nick could steer for them at each channel, occasionally returning to the wagon to help the wheels over another rock.

The maneuvering at the end of each channel took forever. But Nick was patient for a change and the Oregon Trail had disciplined him into a more cautious driver. Back and forth, back and forth, he expertly steered the mules through the K-turns, turning the wagon one way in reverse, so the Trail Pup angled in the other direction. After forty-five minutes, we were off the rock field and onto the smooth track that skirted the rest of the summit.

We had taken Rocky Ridge diagonally. To gain sixty yards west over a boulder field, we had traversed almost three hundred yards in a series of S-turns. It wasn't the way the pioneers did it but I didn't give a damn because now I could see clear west, through the opening of land between the Wind Rivers and the Red Buttes below. I felt that I could almost touch Oregon from the heights.

The wagon on top of Rocky Ridge. Ascending the rock staircase east of the continental divide was one of the most arduous challenges of the trip.

Before we left for the meadows below, Nick held the mules on the windy summit and our flag snapped in the breeze while I stood near the front wheels and thanked the Peerys. They were excited about their day now. To them, the real-life image of a covered wagon summiting Rocky

Ridge was divinely inspired. God had directed them here to see this and witness it with photographs, so that other Mormons could see too and witness. Utah Mormons live such relatively isolated lives that they don't realize how unusual it is for secular Americans like me to hear people talk so openly and matter-of-factly about their religion. Sam spoke for a few minutes about the stories he had grown up with, the sacrifices the Saints had made to cross to Utah, and the role that pilgrimages to places like Rocky Ridge played in sustaining his personal faith. Now he had seen a wagon cross the fatal Rocky Ridge and the day had sealed him with the Mormon martyrs.

This was all theological ziti to me, but I loved and enjoyed the Peerys, and everything Mormon, that day on Rocky Ridge. Indeed, standing with them on the high rocks, I was a Mormon. My theory about religion is that we should believe in every one of them. Screw doctrine—it's all made up anyway, and too divisive. When I feel like being spiritually revived by great music, I drive over on Sunday to my local Bethel AME church and get a good dose of gospel hymns, and then I'm an AME soul brother for the rest of the day. When I feel like hearing an intelligent sermon, I go to a synagogue, and then I'm a devout Jew. I love Mennonite and Quaker meetings because those faiths are so devoted to social service that I can always rely on an invitation to the next flood-relief mission or the building of a Habitat for Humanity house. That's my dogma. Just borrow any old goddamn religion that happens to be around when you need it and enjoy the pleasure of being with welcoming people. Today, on windy Rocky Ridge beneath a hard blue Wyoming sky, I was Mormon.

Sam and LaVora said again that they thought they were "angels" sent to help us over Rocky Ridge. But Nick and I were their angels too.

"It's a vision that you gave us," LaVora said. "Now we have seen a covered wagon cross Rocky Ridge. We can believe it happened now. It affirms our faith."

"I don't have the same amount of faith as you," I said. "But I guess we can all be angels sometimes."

"That's true," Sam said. "God bless now. We'll never forget today. Can you just be careful out here?"

"Oh, we'll be careful," I said. "You just saw how careful we are."

We all laughed, exchanged contact information, and then Sam and

LaVora turned east to go, holding hands as they stepped high over the first rocks. I walked with them to the edge of the ridge and watched for a minute or two as they descended the ledges, a happy, obliging Mormon couple receding downhill on the old, scuffed ruts.

"Angels, Nick," I said, back at the wagon. "Mormon angels guided us over Rocky Ridge."

"Well, I happen to believe in all that shit," Nick said. "Those people were angels. You don't have to be some Bible-whackin birdbrain from Alabama to believe in angels."

Taking Rocky Ridge infused us with energy. I had studied Rocky Ridge for months the winter before and learned to fear it, and all of the Oregon Trail "experts" had exhorted me not to cross it. But nobody knows. Nobody had taken a wagon over those rocks in a century. Fear was just a deceptive veil obscuring the unknown. But when we got there and saw the terrain, it was just a lot of hard work crossing large rocks.

The wagon box gently bumped over the sandy ruts and the oak bows creaked in the wind as we descended for the bottomlands along the Sweetwater, McLean Meadows. We had saved half a day by crossing Rocky Ridge, and along the boggy edges of the river we saw moose, beaver dams, and sandhill cranes.

24

THE SNOWMELT RAGING DOWN FROM the Wind Rivers had turned Willow Creek, which we had to cross to stay on the main ruts, into a twenty-acre swamp. July is usually the middle of the dry season, but in this record high-water year the channel was almost as broad as a river. Circuiting the mud fields along the banks on foot, I could see a trail marker on dry ground on the far side. But we couldn't reach it across this Euphrates morass, which would have quickly swallowed the wagon and mules. We turned back for the Sweetwater to follow the Riverview Cutoff to the Seminoe Cutoff, which would lead us back west for the pass.

I almost welcomed being forced onto the Seminoe Cutoff. I had always been curious about what it looked like, and the history of this popular shortcut connected the three main periods of trail development in the West. The route was named for Charles "Seminoe" Lajeunesse, a member of a prominent trapping and guiding family from the fur days of the 1820s and 1830s who turned to another line of work after 1850, when European tastes in hats changed from beaver to silk, effectively ending the beaver-trapping era. Lajeunesse saw the new opportunity offered by the growing covered wagon traffic on the Oregon Trail and took over the fort and trading post at Devil's Gate, quickly building it into a busy trail stop. But this business was threatened in 1853 when heavy snowmelt and rains raised the Sweetwater over its banks, causing a traffic jam of wagons all the way back to Independence Rock. To keep the traffic—and his profits—flowing, Lajeunesse blazed a path along the plains south of the river for a hundred miles between Independence Rock and South Pass. The new road eliminated the need for the multiple fords required on the north banks and sidestepped the perilous Rocky Ridge. Over time, especially after the Mormon handcart disaster at Rocky Ridge in 1856, the Seminoe Cutoff became the preferred road and was heavily trafficked by wagon trains, and then by military convoys, mining caravans, and stage lines during the last, busy phase of the trail in the 1880s.

But not every wagon train or stagecoach driver followed exactly the same path along the south banks, and the tangled ruts of the Seminoe road eventually suffered from the neglect that became typical of many other Oregon Trail cutoffs. To trail purists, the exasperating maze of choices made by the pioneers had to be resolved somehow, in order to preserve a single, agreed-upon National Historic Trail. By the late twentieth century, this effort had evolved into a "main ruts" approach to mapping and marking the trail, which allowed many important cutoffs to disappear into the cattle and pickup roads that generally followed the same terrain.

This issue was more than academic to me. Like thousands of wagon travelers before me, I had just been forced off the main ruts at Willow Creek in a high-water year and would need to pick up the far end of the Seminoe Cutoff to continue west to the continental divide. The Seminoe Cutoff *was* the Oregon Trail, but there is no definable, marked Seminoe road anymore. After we crossed a bridge over the Sweetwater, there were several two-track cutoffs bearing southwest across the broad basin between the mountain ridges, all of them unmarked, and any one of them the possible Seminoe route. I eliminated the first two because of hilly terrain and what looked like distant fence lines, and finally asked Nick to turn west on the third track, not because I knew it was the right one, but because we had to start moving toward South Pass somewhere. We were headed straight across open range, and I was pretty sure that we wouldn't see any sign of life or acquire a navigation fix until the next big waypoint, a former trail stop, cavalry fort, and mining town called Burnt Ranch.

By now, I considered myself an Oregon Trail survivor and accepted the imprecise standards of trail navigation. South Pass was about fifteen miles southwest across the hardtack desert, with the gold hills on either side of us wedging us onto level ground. There was no marked road. Any route we followed between Willow Creek and Burnt Ranch was the trail.

As he turned the mules west on the two-track, Nick asked about how I knew we were going the right way.

"Nobody knows, Trail Hand." I said. "We're on the Oregon Trail."

Burnt Ranch, originally called South Pass Station after the U.S. Army fort built there in 1862, was another of those junctions along the trail that once throbbed with the energy of westering Americans. Hundreds of wagons filed through every day to merge at the intersection of the Seminoe Cutoff and the main ruts at the "last crossing" of the Sweetwater. The open prairie outside the fort was the scene of emotional partings as some families elected to proceed due west to Idaho on the mountainous Lander Road, while others continued southwest to the Sublette Cutoff route or followed the main ruts to Fort Bridger. There were separate Mormon and gentile post offices and Mark Twain, Horace Greeley, and Sir Richard Burton passed through on the stage lines, immortalizing the last stop before South Pass in their books. The road ranch got its final name during the Indian wars in the late 1860s when the Sioux, fed up with the continued impact of the emigrant traffic on their traditional lands, and the frequent violations of their treaties with the white man, burned the fort and its outbuildings to the ground.

Burnt Ranch was also an important place in the West that influenced frontier development in ways most Americans forget today. In 1857, to encourage continued settlement of the West, Congress passed the Pacific Wagon Road Act, which among other improvements to the trail called for the surveying of a shorter route to Idaho across the bottom of the Wind Rivers and the forested Bridger-Teton wilderness to the west. Frederick W. Lander, a hotheaded but experienced explorer and engineer, was assigned the job. He made Burnt Ranch the trailhead and main supply depot for the trail-building job, which became one of the largest government-financed projects of the nineteenth century. Lander hired hundreds of workers from the new Mormon settlement at Salt Lake and supplied the enterprise with large mule-team caravans that ferried provisions and equipment from U.S. Army depots in Nebraska and eastern Wyoming. "With crowds of laborers hauling wood, erecting buildings and tending stock," writes historian Todd Guenther, "the area was a beehive of activity."

The engineers, logging crews, and workers quickly hacked out what became known as the Lander Cutoff, which saved more than sixty miles, almost a week's travel, across the mountains. In places, the Lander Cutoff was a steep up-and-down ride, but the route offered cooler, high terrain and plentiful water, an advantage over the scorching desert of the main ruts to the south. Eventually an estimated 100,000 pioneers took this route, and the 230-mile Lander Cutoff was considered an engineering marvel of its time.

This model of government support for a major development project became popular and was accepted as the new norm for western growth. Each new phase of frontier growth—the railroads, ranching, mining—was also supported by either outright government subsidies, land giveaways, or federally supported irrigation and bridge-building projects. That was the tradition established by the Oregon Trail and it has always amused me that the myth of "rugged individualism" still plays such a large role in western folklore and American values. In fact, our vaunted rugged individualism was financed by huge government largesse.

For the past week, looking ahead on my maps, I had assumed that a place as busy and prominent in the history of the West as Burnt Ranch would have to be well marked. But nothing was there when we reached what I concluded was the end of the Seminoe Cutoff, and the spot was as deserted as any we found on the trail. A worn pickup road turned north across the river, probably indicating a ranch above, but the heavy screen of cottonwoods and brush growing along the banks prevented me from seeing very much.

After a long afternoon crossing the unmarked Seminoe Cutoff, I felt that we had to make a certain fix on Burnt Ranch to establish our position before we launched for the pass. My guidebooks and maps showed that a large stone monument—carved and placed by an early trail preservationist, H. G. Nickerson—stood just above the ranch buildings, marking the intersection of the main ruts and the Lander Cutoff. I would have to hike across the river to find the monument and confirm our position.

Nick was anxious to push on for South Pass, and annoyed that I was being so meticulous. We looked at my maps together and he was certain that the creek bed in front of us was Oregon Slough, which we could splash through right now and regain the main ruts over the hill we saw ahead. But there were several piles of rusty water pipe and pumping equipment lying around, and the creek looked so evenly cut that I suspected it had been rechanneled into an irrigation ditch, which might not run in the original direction indicated on the map. This was not the Burnt Ranch I had learned about in my books.

"Boss, it's your readin disease again," Nick said. "You're overthinkin the problem. The trail is right there, over that hill."

"Nick, we have to know. South Pass isn't that easy to find and this is our last fix."

"I bet you the pioneers didn't mess with crap like that. They just went right over the hill."

But my abundance-of-caution gene wouldn't let go. This was our last reliable fix before South Pass. I had to know.

"There were a hundred wagons here every day when the pioneers were coming through," I said to Nick. "They followed the wagons in front of them. I'm hiking in to find the Nickerson marker so we're sure."

I was pleased about the chance to explore Burnt Ranch for another reason. The site was once a famous road ranch and stagecoach stop, and this is what I had come west to see. It was a serious miscalculation, but I had no way of knowing this as I stepped off the wagon and hiked toward the river.

Behind the screen of trees along the river I found a narrow wooden bridge that crossed the Sweetwater. The bridge had no side rails and was barely wide enough for a pickup, but there was a large open field before it, and Nick could always swing the team around there if he decided not to cross. While I hunted for the trail monument, I decided, Nick could bring the mules into the ranch, water them, and let them stand in the shade. I walked out to where he could see me, yelled, and then motioned with my hand for him to come in and cross the river.

While Nick drove in with the mules, I walked beyond a thick grove of trees, which had hidden from my view on the trail an attractive cluster of restored log cabins, an implement shed, and farming equipment parked on the plains. The buildings and farm equipment indicated that Burnt Ranch was probably being used as a cow camp. But the place seemed unoccupied and I assumed that it was like a lot of western ranches now—a lonely outpost for grazing cattle, checked once or twice a week by an absentee owner.

While I began exploring for the Nickerson marker, I heard the clatter of wheels crossing the wooden bridge and Nick frantically screaming at the mules, especially Bute, and at first thought that he might have tumbled the rig into the river when the mules spooked on the narrow span. But as I ran back I saw the wagon emerge through the tree line, apparently unscathed. Nick looked rattled when he pulled up.

"Well, that nearly ended the trip right there, Boss. Frickin Bute wouldn't cross but the other two yanked her along. There's no way we're drivin the team back across that bridge."

"Ah, shit, Nick. I guess I made the wrong decision."

"I'm not commentin on your decision. We're just goin to have to walk the team back across one by one, and then pull the wagons by hand."

Pulling four thousand pounds of wagon across the narrow bridge would be nearly impossible. We were trapped on the wrong side of the Sweetwater. I had blown this one and we both knew it.

While we were standing there thinking about a solution, a pickup truck pulled to an abrupt stop on the hill across the river, blowing off a large cloud of dust. The driver jumped out and crouched on the ground, reading our wagon tracks in the sand. Then he returned to his truck, slammed the door, raced down the hill, and turned in at the gates in a plume of dust, heading straight for us.

"It looks like we've got company," I said. "This must be the rancher who owns the place."

"What does he care?" Nick said. "We're not doin him any damage here."

"From the way he's driving that truck, I think he cares."

I decided to meet the pickup halfway and walked back across the bridge. The pickup driver locked his wheels and skidded sideways to a halt beside me. The thin, angry man inside started screaming out the open window before he had even stopped. He looked sixtyish and was dressed in work clothes and a ball cap, and he had probably driven out to his spread that day to check his cows or irrigation pipe. The woman in the passenger seat beside him, who I assumed was his wife, was glaring past him at me. It was soon clear that nothing I said was going to be of much use.

"Do you realize that you're on private property?" he said. "*My* private property?"

"Sir, I do realize that. I'm sorry if I am inconveniencing you. We're just riding this rig across from St. Joe and . . ."

"Bullshit! Anybody good enough to get a wagon from St. Joe would know this is the last crossing of the Sweetwater and you just crossed it *the wrong way*. How stupid do you think I am?"

I explained that I had crossed the river onto the ranch to find the Nickerson marker. I want to confirm the waypoint of Burnt Ranch as my last fix before South Pass.

"Well I can confirm it's Burnt Ranch! I own it. You're violating private property."

It was immediately clear that after nearly a thousand miles of travel across the trail we had found the one asshole in a hundred who lacked the hospitality we had found everywhere else. The protocols for crossing the vast rangeland across the West are quite flexible, and for a good reason. Most ranches spread out from a relatively small parcel of deeded land along a source of water to the much larger leased grazing parcels owned by the BLM. This patchwork of ownership often makes it impossible for outsiders to recognize the boundaries between private and public land, and the BLM discourages private property owners from denying access between its allotments, which would make them landlocked and thus of little use. This is particularly important along the National Historic Trail route we were following, because the BLM and the park service are also charged with guaranteeing access to valuable historic sites.

With our covered wagon and mules, we hardly represented a threat to the rancher, but I would later learn that he'd had a difficult, erratic relationship with OCTA for years, sometimes flatly denying access to small groups of trail enthusiasts who wanted to see Burnt Ranch and the Nickerson marker, but in other years relenting and allowing groups in. (Ironically, that summer OCTA was giving him a "Friend of the Trail" award in an attempt to placate the landowner of an important trail site.)

Our problem that day was straightforward. To get from the BLM land at the edge of the Burnt Ranch entrance, where we had every right to be, to the historic marker on the main ruts, we had a few private acres to cross. But for reasons we never did understand this had set the rancher off, and anger management did not appear to be his strong suit.

"Sir, now that you've told us this is Burnt Ranch, we'll be on our way," I said. "It will take us some time. We don't think our mules will cross the bridge again, so we'll lead them across and then pull the wagons by hand."

"If they were my goddamn mules they would cross," the rancher said. "What kind of a horseman are you? You know what I'd do if I owned those mules, don't you?"

"No, sir, I don't."

"I'd whip the shit out of them and show them who's boss."

"Well, sir . . ."

"Get in the back of the pickup. I'll run you to the wagon."

Before I could even sit down in the bed of the pickup, he stepped on the gas and bounced off over the bridge, and I was thrown down beside his corgi cow dog.

When we got to the wagon, Nick seemed to sense how bad the situation was but decided that he wasn't going to let that prevent him from being himself. He stepped forward to the truck and reached out his palm to shake the rancher's hand, but he ignored him. Pulling off his cap and throwing it onto the hood of his truck, the rancher reached inside his glove compartment and yanked out a BLM map. Red-faced and angry, he spread the map on the hood of his truck.

"You see these yellow shaded areas here? That's BLM land. You see these blue areas? That's state land. These little white areas are private land. As you can see, you are now on private land. My land."

"Well, sir . . ."

"You don't have to be yes-sirring and no-sirring me to death. I'm just trying to help you here. Do you want an education, or not?"

"I would love an education," I said.

"You mean to tell me you traveled all this way without a BLM map?"

The rancher reminded me of those Emperor Nero state troopers who cannot hand out a routine speeding ticket without pestering a driver with a string of useless and humiliating questions. The cops of America are poster-boys of low self-esteem. Their uniforms, silly hats, and sparkling patent leather girdles freighted down with shiny handcuffs, walkie-talkies, and spray canisters of Mace apparently do not make them feel secure enough, so they always add the hostile interrogation to make sure that the accosted citizens know who is in charge. The owner of Burnt Ranch was that kind of control freak. He loved asking snarling questions that really weren't questions at all.

But it would defeat my purpose to confront him. All I wanted to do now was get the wagon back across the river, hitch the team, and move west on the trail. I would have to swallow my pride and give the rancher the law enforcement treatment. Kiss the trooper's butt and appeal to his low IQ by making him feel that everything he says is profoundly useful.

"I probably should have thought to carry a BLM map," I said to the rancher. "That is a very good suggestion."

At this point, the rancher's spousal unit decided that he wasn't doing a good enough job insulting us. By now she had stepped out of the pickup cab and she started yelling across the truck.

"Honey! Don't listen to him! He's lying! They're not riding the Oregon Trail! They just came out here today to violate our property rights!"

This harridan performance by the rancher's wife aroused their dog, the corgi in the back of the pickup, who apparently was quite influenced by her moods. I had always thought of corgis as harmless lapdogs, ritually placed across Queen Elizabeth's knees when she was photographed for one of her jubilees, more or less just a slightly uglier and beefier cousin of the next most ridiculous canine brat, the Pekinese. But I was misinformed about this. Corgis are vicious little bastards, bred for sheep and cattle herding. They are built low to the ground for snapping at the hooves of cows and sheep, and when that doesn't work, taking a bite out of their snouts.

When the rancher's shrew began to shriek, the corgi jumped off the pickup and attacked Olive Oyl. The corgi's mouth snapped shut into a lock grip on Olive Oyl's rump almost before it landed. Olive Oyl managed to turn her neck enough to get a bite or two out of the corgi, but it really wasn't much of a contest and the corgi wouldn't let go. At my feet, in between me and the rancher, it was just one madass tangle of dogs yelping and blood falling to the sand, and Nick ran over and tried to separate the dogs.

"Just kick the shit out of that little son of a bitch," the rancher yelled. "It's a corgi. You can't hurt him! Kick the living shit out of that stupid bastard."

Nick had the sense not to do that, and the rancher stepped over and did it himself, booting the corgi so hard that it tumbled several times over the patchy brown grass, yelping in pain.

Bending down on one knee, Nick retrieved Olive Oyl, who was now bleeding from the rump with a visible patch of her flesh and hair gone, and cradled her in his arms. Speechless, but trying to comfort Olive Oyl, he turned for the wagon to place her on my bed.

"You've got to kick these sons of bitches to get them to behave," the rancher said. "Corgis don't mind it."

His wife added a quite useful thought of her own.

"You see, even our dog doesn't like your dog! Why did you come onto our land?"

Apparently the rancher was quite used to the splendid non sequiturs of his wife and he ignored her. But the Corgi's attack, and now his shrewish wife, made him feel sorry for us. Suddenly contrite, he motioned me back to the hood of his truck and stabbed with his finger on the map.

"Okay, your only water after you clear the pass is Pacific Springs, but I don't think you're going to make that tonight. You should stop here. You're welcome to camp on our land, or go through the gates and lay over on the BLM land. You'll be comfortable here, and have water. That's what I would have told you if you had called first."

Mood swings this beautiful are ordinarily something to be enjoyed, but the rancher was too angry to be trusted. I didn't want to antagonize him again by rejecting his offer. For now, I would temporize and continue to suck ass.

"Thank you," I said. "That's a generous offer, sir, but maybe we should get the wagon back across the bridge first. Then I'll discuss with my brother where we'll camp."

"Suit yourself. I'm just offering you a nice place to camp."

He stepped to the back of his pickup and grabbed a chain from his hodgepodge of ranch gear.

"Here," he said. "Hook this to your pole and my ball hitch when I back up. We'll get your wagon back across the river."

It was glum work, but I was happy to have the wagon moving in the right direction again. After chaining the wagon to the pickup, I followed it across the bridge, looking back over my shoulder. Nick, downcast and sullen, was walking over to the fence line to get the first mule, and I felt awful for him and for Olive Oyl. I checked on her in the back of the wagon before I turned to go for the other mules myself, and she was lying in a small pool of blood on one of my bed blankets, fast asleep. All of this was my fault, I thought, but I had to remain focused and get us off Burnt Ranch.

Our Burnt Ranch hitch-up was the swiftest in Oregon Trail history. Without saying a word to each other, Nick and I placed the mules abreast, yoked up, and hooked the traces, and Nick scrambled up the wheels and nodded that he was ready.

"Let's get the fuck out of here," he said.

"Go," I said. "I'll walk beside the wagon until we're through the gates. I want to put a blanket on top of Olive Oyl."

"See if she wants any water."

After we cleared the gate, I climbed into the back of the wagon on the run. Olive Oyl woke up and greedily lapped up the water I held for her in my lap, and then began licking my hands and whimpering, begging for sympathy. I shimmied forward in the wagon on my rear to our food bin and found some beef jerky, which she swallowed in a few bites. She licked the wound on her rump a few times and then dozed off underneath the blanket I put over her.

"Nick," I called forward. "I think she's all right. She drank water and I gave her some beef jerky. She just wants to sleep."

"Oh, she'll heal," Nick called back. "Here come the bumps. I'm taking the mules across the creek."

From the back of the wagon I could feel the wheels splash through Oregon Slough, and then I heard the grunting of the mules as they climbed the banks and pulled uphill.

I was humiliated once more when I climbed back onto the wagon seat. At the top of the rise above Oregon Slough, there was a tall concrete trail marker right where the main ruts made the "last crossing" off Burnt Ranch. Nick had been right and we should have just proceeded directly off the Seminoe Cutoff up the most obvious track.

"Nick, I'm sorry. I definitely screwed the poodle back there."

Nick handed me the lines to drive and stared vacantly at the hills to the south, beginning a long brood.

"Don't say nothin, all right?" he said. "I'm not mad at you and I'm not even mad at that motherless asshole back there. I am just worried about Olive Oyl."

The wind pushed against us as we turned back onto the main ruts. We were climbing gently uphill and with the elevation gain the brown hills and sage around us were turning light green. I was morose about my fuckup at Burnt Ranch and rehearsed in my mind all of the things I could have said, should have said, to the malevolent moron back there.

A few minutes later, we had one more bizarre exchange with the mercurial owner of Burnt Ranch. As we bumped along the ruts west of the ranch we heard the whine of a four-wheeler behind us, and he emerged on the crest of the hill.

"Oh, shit," Nick said. "What does that bastard want now?"

"It doesn't matter," I said. "We're back on federal land."

The rancher pulled up beside the wagon.

"Are you sure you don't want to camp on our place?" he said. "There's a big storm coming tonight. My wife sent me back up here because she thinks we might have been too hard on you. Camp here and you can make the pass in the morning, easy."

"Oh, I think we'll push on," I said. "Is this the only two-track to the pass?"

"You'll pass another marker or two. But just stay on these ruts right here. There's some cattle tracks that come in north to south, but stay on this one. Eventually it turns due west."

"Okay, thanks," I said.

He sat on his four-wheeler and watched us go, calling out one more thing.

"Have a safe trip!"

We plodded along the bumpy ruts for a while, not saying anything, but finally Nick spoke up.

"How come they always say that, 'Have a safe trip!'? The biggest ass-holes in the world are always telling you to have a safe trip."

I was too disconsolate to reply.

Ahead, two sandy dimples of land, pink in the afternoon light, began to rise on the horizon. I was pretty sure that they were the Twin Mounds, marking the entrance to South Pass.

25

THE CONTINENTAL DIVIDE AT SOUTH Pass was so featureless and lacking in physical drama that it seemed to have no significance at all. The broad, slightly humped saddle of land beyond the Twin Mounds was indistinguishable from the surrounding terrain and many pioneers had rumbled through with their wagons before they realized they had crossed the divide. "There we saw the far famed south pass, but did not see it until we had passed it," wrote Illinois pioneer Amelia Hadley in 1851. "I was all the time looking for some narrow place that would almost take your breath away to get through but was disappointed." The "visual anticlimax" of South Pass, as one geologist described it, stumped even experts sent out to find it. Captain John Frémont, the "great pathfinder" dispatched by Congress in 1842 to survey the Oregon Trail, identified the summit of South Pass as the land directly in between the Twin Mounds, which was more than two miles east of the true Continental Divide.

But if Frémont missed the exact spot, he did not miss the main point. Crossing South Pass, which by the 1850s had been nicknamed "Uncle Sam's Backbone," required gradual, not extraordinary, effort. Nature had created an easy-to-climb gateway that was ideal for covered wagons. In his report to Congress, *The Exploring Expedition to the Rocky Mountains in the Year 1842*, which was widely reprinted by commercial publishers and became a popular trail guide for the next decade, Frémont's description of the gentle ascent was received as welcome news by a generation of nomadic Americans.

> From the impression on my mind at this time, and subsequently on our return, I should compare the elevation which we surmounted immediately at the pass, to the ascent of the Capitol hill from the avenue, at Washington. . . . It will be seen that in no manner [South Pass] resembles the places to which the term is commonly applied—nothing of the gorge-like character and winding ascents of the Allegany passes in America, nothing of the Great St. Bernard and Simplon passes in Europe. Approaching it from the mouth of the Sweet Water, a sandy plain, one hundred and twenty miles long, conducts, by a gradual and regular ascent, to the summit, about seven thousand feet above the sea; and the traveler, without being reminded of any change by toilsome ascents, suddenly finds himself on the waters which flow to the Pacific ocean.

A natural pathway through the mountains that required no more effort than a lobbyist's stroll onto Capitol Hill was just one of the many dualities of South Pass. Misunderstandings were inevitable because the term "Continental Divide" refers to the division of watersheds and rivers, flowing in opposite directions, and does not necessarily mean that the highest land has been reached. Over time, South Pass would generate a site-specific literature all its own, much of it unintentionally deceptive. Virtually every pioneer journal would mention—simply because the information was repeated in trail guides—that the divide at South Pass separated the drainages of the Mississippi and the Atlantic waters from the Pacific waters. But this grand hydrologic principle was practically worthless. The last rim of mountains in central Wyoming simply separated one desert from another. Finding water could still be maddeningly difficult for the next five hundred miles, and the pioneers would often spend the second half of their journey to Oregon or California making desperate scrambles between the rivers to survive. And by no means did reaching the division of waters at South Pass, at an elevation of 7,400 feet, end the steep wagon climbs for the pioneers. Along the Lander Cutoff there were still nine-thousand-foot peaks to conquer, and the popular Sublette Cutoff wouldn't end until the wagons climbed and then perilously descended an 8,300-foot killer called Dempsey Ridge.

But South Pass was the halfway mark on the wagon journey, and by now the pioneers had survived two months of Platte River storms, the outdoor cholera wards, and the high-altitude weariness of the Rockies. There had to be *something* to say about reaching such an important milestone. For the gifted Margaret Frink, who understood that the small, telling detail is everything, the spare surroundings at South Pass presented few problems. In her *Journal of the Adventures of a Party of California Gold Seekers*, she reported finding the first post office in almost a thousand miles along the trail, and in the distance she heard live music at the summit, but these were incongruities that evoked the long journey she had made from civilization, and the many miles she still had to go.

> We could hardly realize that we were crossing the great backbone of the North American continent at an altitude of 7,490 feet. . . . Near the summit, on each side of the road, was an encampment, at one of which the American flag was flying, to mark the private post-office or express office established by Gen. James Estelle, for the accommodations of emigrants wishing to send letters to friends at home. The last post-office on our way was at St. Joseph, on the Missouri River. West of that stream were neither states, counties, cities, towns, villages, or white man's habitations. The two mud forts we had passed were the only signs of civilization. There was an off-hand celebration of our arrival at the summit. Music from a violin with tin-pan accompaniment, contributed to the general merriment of a grand frolic. In the afternoon we spent some time writing letters to our friends, to be sent back by the express. On each letter we paid the express charge of $1.00.

Another contradiction presented by South Pass—which from afar sounded so mysterious and remote—was that it served as the portal to the nearby campground at Pacific Springs, which was as clamorous and thronged as a walled medieval city. When he reached Pacific Springs at the end of June 1850, Franklin Langworthy camped "amidst thousands of other emigrants." The "splendid carriages" of the commercial passenger trains passing through on their way to the gold fields reminded Langworthy of the busy traffic along the avenues of New York. The braying of cattle and human voices, violin playing, and that favorite pastime of bored Americans—rifle and pistol shooting—kept Langworthy awake all night.

The merriment at Pacific Springs probably had a lot to do with the time of year—most of the wagon trains reached South Pass and the popular camp to the west on or near the Fourth of July. Reaching the Continental Divide on the national holiday was considered a favorable omen and an excuse to celebrate, and the pioneers serenaded the neighboring wagons with bands, shared whiskey and molasses mixed with brandy, and sat up all night watching groups of men igniting fireworks made out of gunpowder, clusters of wood, and rags stuffed into tin cans and water buckets. Perhaps the most memorable of these displays occurred in 1849, when a Missouri pioneer built his fire at Pacific Springs too close to a keg of black powder being carried west for the Gold Rush. A spark from the fire lit some spilled powder nearby and set off the keg, which exploded with a magnificent boom and flash and then barrel-rolled out of sight across the plains.

At the Twin Mounds, I decided to walk the last stretch to the top of South Pass and savor it alone. The dusty ruts curved gently uphill, disappearing above into a metallic overcast sky. It was a lovely hike that revealed the graphic contrasts of nature in the Rockies. The snowfields of the Wind Rivers glittered on the north horizon, the vast alkali flats of the Green River country opened straight ahead, and storm clouds boiled black and gray vapors to the northwest. The westerlies were blowing so hard that I had to lean into the wind to make headway. I was exhausted and filthy after two days without a shower, and my whiskery face itched from sunburn and perspiration, but it was exhilarating to reach the continental divide. In two months we had traveled almost a thousand miles, confirming my estimates from the winter before, and there didn't seem to be anything that could stop us now.

But these were just mathematical calculations, and it felt as though we'd been gone for two years. In the thin air of the Rockies, I had lost all sense of time and the routines of life I knew back east. I couldn't remember the last time I knew what day of the week it was. After Casper the battery in my watch had grown weak, and it was no longer keeping accurate time, but that didn't matter. I woke in the morning, harnessed and hitched the mules, and then rode or walked ahead of a Schuttler white-top until rosy light told me to stop. Finding water was the principal metric of my day. Iterated drudgery—the sound of mules plodding, wheel hubs creaking, and watching Olive Oyl running snake patrols ahead of me on the high desert—was my life now.

A familiar irony of the modern trail greeted me at the summit of South Pass. The preservationists and BLM managers responsible for trail upkeep seem to have thought of everything, except the possibility of a real covered wagon coming through. A large BLM barbed-wire enclosure, to ward off pickups and dirt bikes, had been placed around the Ezra Meeker and H. G. Nickerson monuments at the top, and the fence blocked almost all of the level ground on the crest, forcing Nick and the mules down into the badland gullies and tall sage to the south. After poking around the summit awhile and admiring the monuments—I was particularly impressed with the craftsmanship of Nickerson's monument to Narcissa Whitman and Eliza Spalding—I explored the route south and then walked back and raised my arms to hand-signal Nick. I lost sight of the wagon several times as Nick plunged the Schuttler through the gullies, and the sagebrush crackled and split against the wheels and the wagon cover as he squeezed through the tall vegetation.

When we regained the trail on the west side of the pass, I could see that the situation was still unfavorable for us. The trail toward Pacific Springs, furrowed by thousands of wagons rolling over the same spot, and by pickup traffic later, curved sharply and deeply to the right. The right track sloped sharply downward, about two feet below the high track on the left. This would place most of the weight of the wagons on the right wheels, and I briefly considered emptying our water tanks to relieve the load on the Trail Pup. But this would remove only a couple of hundred pounds from the low wheel and I didn't think we could do without our remaining water at Pacific Springs.

Stumbling through the sagebrush to check the ground ahead, I yelled back to Nick.

"Nick! The slope. Look at the slope! Slow, slow!"

"I know! I can see it."

When I heard the crash, I was just out of sight of the wagon. But I knew what it had to be. A brief, sharp crack of splintering wood was followed by a loud crash as one of the wagons settled onto the trail, the same sound I'd heard when we flipped the Trail Pup in Lisco. Nick was calling "Whoa!" to the mules.

Shouldering back uphill through the sage, I knelt on top of the high wall of the trail, looking almost straight down toward the wagons from above, crestfallen at what I saw. The right wheel of the Trail Pup had shattered, and several of the spokes were scattered on the trail like fallen juggling pins. The impact of the wagon collapsing had snapped both spigots on our tanks and the only water we had for the mules was gushing out in a stream, puddling up on the dust of the trail.

The starkness of that moment took my breath away, and my mind seemed completely empty of solutions. I had never imagined a situation this dire—no worst-case-scenario planning could encompass it. We were forty miles from the nearest help, and the only water we had to support the mules was racing out of our barrels and falling downhill, with a gurgling sound that seemed to mock all of my plans.

Looking down at the shattered wheel, I could easily see what had happened. Inside the broken hub, and in several of the splintered wheel spokes, there was a core of black dry rot.

"Nick, hold those mules! The Trail Pup is down."

Nick was frantic up front, and I knew that he would want to jump off the wagon and rush back to assess the damage.

"Is it hub failure? Tell me! Is it hub failure? Let me get back there!"

"Nick, how do I know? The Trail Pup is down. We've got a shattered wheel. Just wait until I get there."

I slid down the exposed dirt wall of the trail and then inched my way forward against the wagon. I was surprised by how calm I felt. Later, I would conclude that the thin air at 7,400 feet just didn't provide enough oxygen to let me get excited. The altitude slowed me down so that a kind of delayed, deliberative preservation instinct took over.

Think, think, Rinker, don't react. I'd expected all along that our wheels would break somewhere, but I couldn't focus now on the disappointment of that happening just a quarter mile from victory, at South Pass, so far from help. I couldn't dwell either on the overall dimensions of our predicament. Details, a hundred details, crowded my thoughts. But I had to maintain cockpit composure here and concentrate on just the two or three things I needed to do now to beat the storm to Pacific Springs.

At the front of the wagon, I deliberately stood off several steps from the wheels, so Nick couldn't hand me the lines and scramble back to see the damage. I had to calm him down first. I asked for my canteen, which Nick tossed off the wagon.

I also had to work hard at not castigating myself for the broken wheel, because I should have known this would happen. The Trail Pup wheels had sat in the rain in Kansas for years, and the moisture had wicked up through the spokes to the hubs, rotting the wood in several places. With some sanding and fresh paint, the wheels looked fine when we picked the wagon up in May. But after a thousand miles of use and then the heat of the high desert, the undermined oak couldn't take the steeply sloped trail at South Pass.

"Nick, there's dry rot through that whole wheel."

"Fuckin Don Werner."

"Nick. It's really my fault. I bought the wagon in a hurry knowing the history of the wheels. But Don Werner isn't here now. Philip Ropp isn't here. We can't just call Bill Petersen for help. Nobody knows, Nick. Nobody can help us. It's our responsibility to get out of this mess."

"Fuck. I know."

Nick pushed his stubby index finger into his ear and burrowed around for a while, looking off vacantly toward the plains and Oregon Buttes. When he looked back, he was smiling.

"You knew all along this would happen, right?"

"Yeah, sure. We would have to break our wheels somewhere. But not here. Not at South Pass, forty miles from the nearest town."

I looked northwest toward the storm clouds rolling black and gray over each other past the bottom of the Wind Rivers. A misty curtain of rain was falling behind them. We had, at most, a half hour to reach Pacific Springs. When I looked up at Nick on the wagon seat, he was smiling again.

"This is the whole trip, right here," he said. "All I have heard out of you this summer is 'Trail Hand, wait till you see South Pass.' Now we're here, and it's the biggest clusterfuck of my life. I love it. We're still makin Oregon."

The storm clouds were racing in so quickly that we might be forced to unhitch and unharness the mules, letting them go on the plains so they wouldn't panic. We would have to camp in a thunderstorm in open country and then somehow catch the team in the morning. But adversity was my amphetamine now and I loved our journey and Nick.

"We're still making Oregon," I said.

Nick is a lot stronger than I am and I needed him back at the Trail Pup to pull the pin, now twisted in its mount, that held the cart to the main wagon. I told him not to waste a lot of time looking at the wheels because we were abandoning the Trail Pup for now. While I held the mules, he could also transfer two bales of hay from the cart to the main wagon. I did a quick mental inventory of our supplies in the Schuttler and knew that we had our cookstove and fuel, and probably enough food in one of our storage coolers to get us through the night.

We would have to figure out the rest later. Our only priority was reaching Pacific Springs and getting our fencing set up before the storm hit.

I heard a lot of moaning and cursing from behind as Nick examined the shattered wheel, and then a loud thump as he grunted the pin out of the Trail Pup hitch and the cart fell to the ground. The wagon shook as Nick threw the hay on board and then he rejoined me on the wagon seat.

"Fast-walk the mules," I said, nodding toward the storm clouds. "We've got to beat this storm to Pacific Springs."

When we reached the level floor of the valley below the pass, I was annoyed at myself again, surprised by the frailty of my thinking. Back in the crippled Trail Pup, we had left behind several bags of emergency "packing cubes"—a concentrated dry mix of alfalfa and grain used by hunting outfitters for mule treks into the mountains. I had bought them in Casper as a precaution. If we got stranded somewhere in the desert, the cubes would keep the mules alive for a day or two while one of us went for help.

It was a big mistake to have forgotten the cubes. If I went back on foot for them, we would risk getting caught in the storm. But if I didn't go back, we might not get beyond Pacific Springs. I still didn't realize how much the high altitude was affecting me, and I was angry at myself for vacillating over a decision. But I told Nick that he would have to hold the team while I walked back for the packing cubes.

It was the loneliest hike of my life. I ran along the ruts until they began to slope up for the pass and then paced myself to a walk, breathing deeply for air, trying not to think about my mistake of forgetting the cubes. *Just keep going. You don't know where anything leads. Nobody knows. Keep going.* When I reached the Trail Pup it lay crazily on its side, pieces of the platform Nick had built back in Nebraska and our equipment scattered on the ruts. The cart looked so forlorn. I had designed it myself, and all of our hopes for crossing the trail unassisted were invested in that cart, but now it lay crippled between two high dirt walls below South Pass, a symbol of my vanity and naiveté.

Stop thinking, idiot. Move forward.

Rummaging around in the load, I found two bags of packing cubes, hoisted them out, and then genuflected in the mud left behind by our broken water barrels and threw the forty-pound bags onto my shoulders. At first, they didn't feel very heavy. On the slope, I leaned forward slightly to let the eighty pounds on my shoulders push me faster downhill.

I had another interesting flashback to my father right then, and was fascinated about how the mysterious workings of memory could raise an image that had been dormant for fifty years. During our covered wagon trip in 1958, we had stopped somewhere in Pennsylvania just before reaching Lancaster—Morgantown, maybe, or Blue Ball—to buy grain for the horses. One of the Amish men at the grain mill wheeled over a handcart to take the heavy grain sacks to the wagon, but before he could reach us my father picked up both sacks, balanced them on his hips with his hands, carried them over, and threw them onto the wagon.

The Amish there must have known my father from earlier trips. They all laughed, their gray beards shaking, at the man standing there on the loading dock, uselessly, with the handcart.

"Tom Buck!" one of them said. "And he's doing that on a wooden leg yet."

But now I was struggling. When I reached the bottom of the slope, without gravity to help me, I realized that I couldn't make it all the way back to the wagon with two bags. I dropped one bag on the trail, forced myself to make it to the distant wagon without stopping, threw on the bag, and glumly returned for the second bag. All of this was taking too much time. We might not beat the storm to Pacific Springs.

Stop thinking. Just go back for the second bag.

Winded, I reached the wagon a second time and climbed up to the seat, and Nick slapped the lines on the mules, calling them for Pacific Springs. I took a long drink from my canteen. I was amazed by another appearance of my father during the trip, and I told Nick about it.

"Nick, those were hundred-pound bags he was carrying," I said. "I couldn't even get back here with forty-pound bags."

"Rinker, you are so full of shit sometimes that I agonize about you," Nick said. "All Daddy had to do was carry those bags across a parking lot. He wasn't crossin the frickin Wyomin desert. Why exaggerate against yourself?"

"I'm not exaggerating. He made it to the wagon with two bags. I could only handle one."

"Well, good," Nick said. "That's your memory. But Tom Buck isn't here right now. We are. And we're gettin to Pacific Springs before this storm."

We had to travel only two miles to reach Pacific Springs. I used the time to analyze our situation and calculate everything we were up against. We had just dropped our only source of water and feed for the mules behind us on the trail. Our dog was injured, and I had no idea whether we'd find forage or water at Pacific Springs. I was unfamiliar with the maze of trail and fence lines we'd have to cross to reach the highway to Farson, and after that we'd have to travel nearly thirty miles over the scorching alkali flats to our first water on the Little Sandy River. I'd always known Wyoming would be our toughest state, and most horsemen I knew would have given up by now and called for help. But we couldn't even do that. There wasn't cell service out here, and there probably wouldn't be any until we reached Farson.

It started to rain as we pulled into Pacific Springs. The old pioneer encampment had endured the usual transition from the wagon days, briefly housing a post office, a telegraph station, and a stage stop, and then enjoying a few decades of prosperity as a ranching center with corrals, a tavern, and a famous whorehouse. But it was now just a collection of moldering log cabins with fallen roofs and cow manure on the dirt floors. The springs themselves were swampland, trampled into mounds of mud and grass by the cattle, stretching off north toward a shallow creek. A decrepit barbed-wire fence ran above the mud line between two of the cabins.

To the northwest, the black snarling clouds were beginning to drop low.

"This has got to be the fastest unhitching in history," I said to Nick. "I'll unharness the mules. You put the fencing up against that barbed wire."

Nick had the fencing almost done by the time I led over the first mule. The rain was falling harder now, pooling up on his cowboy hat and then dropping as a waterfall off the rim. We were both forcing ourselves to cheer up because at least there was water that we could see, out in the clear creek beyond the swamps. Nick couldn't resist this opportunity to make light of our awful day. Bending low in a bow, he swept his hand toward the fence opening, gesturing me in like a hotel doorman.

"Pacific Springs, Boss," he said. "Welcome to the shithole of the West."

"Ah, c'mon, Nick," I said. "Use your imagination. This was a pioneer encampment. There were hundreds of wagons here every night."

"It's a shithole."

"Nick, they played fiddles by lantern light. They had square dances."

"It's a shithole."

"C'mon. Cheer up. Wait till you see the Big Sandy Station tomorrow, or the Green River Rendezvous. We'll camp at Emigrant Springs on the Sublette Cutoff."

"Shithole, shithole, shithole," Nick said. "You go to sleep every night in a covered wagon. I get to sleep on soggy manure piles. From now on, I'm callin it the Shithole Trail."

When I bent over to laugh, the rain pounded through the holes in the shoulder of my shirt and ran down my back and legs.

"Screw you, Trail Hand. Let's get the other mules."

Pacific Springs wasn't simply the most miserable camp of the trip. It was the most miserable camp of my life. In the middle of one of the most unforgiving deserts in the West there was water everywhere—wind and water lashing us from above, water ponds everywhere we stepped, rainwater seeping through every joint in the wagon—but we could use none of it. The springs themselves, trampled beyond recognition by a century of cattle grazing, stretched for five acres like a giant mud pie across the flats.

The mules hadn't been watered since the middle of the day, back at the Seminoe Cutoff, and I knew that I would have to carry at least fifteen gallons from the springs to get the team through the night. The only route out to the clear water at the edge of the springs was along the patchwork of conical, grassy hummocks that stretched across the swamp. As I started out with a bucket, the grass mounds looked temptingly sylvan and ideally spaced—patio stones crossing to the fabled springs, I thought, placed there for my convenience.

I was even cheerful about it. Disaster had struck, and we were now deprived of our barrels of water and provisions for the team. But this was where crazyass passion and endurance would count the most, and we would define ourselves by lugging enough water for the mules.

Grassy hummocks in Wyoming, however, are a ruse of the landscape. For four or five leaps across the lovely green mounds, the footing was good. But then the sixth and seventh mounds collapsed as soon as I landed on them, pitching me knee-deep into a sludge of black mud mixed with cow urine. Giving up on the hummocks, I sloshed through the winding channels of sewage, dipped into the creek for water, sloshed all the way back, and then at the fence held up the filthy pail for another ungrateful mule. Back and forth I went. I had reached the watershed of the Pacific and it was a bovine septic tank. I didn't so much finish watering the mules as decide that one hour of this revolting therapy was enough.

Back at the wagon, Nick was sitting against a wagon wheel beneath a gray tarp rigged from the spokes to protect him from the rain, with Olive Oyl curled on a blanket on his lap. He was massaging her wounds with mule salve and combing the dried blood off her white coat with a small screwdriver. He asked me what we were having for dinner.

I scrounged around in the back of the wagon, realizing that most of what we needed for dinner was back in the downed Trail Pup. In addition to our cookstove, we had one saucepan, two family-size cans of Hormel chili, no beans, and some leftover Minute Rice. I found plastic spoons, but we had no plates.

I protected the cookstove from the rain with my denim jacket and managed to get a feeble fire going, throwing the chili and rice into the pan together.

"We'll have to eat together out of the pan," I said to Nick. "We don't have any plates."

"Oh, I can find plates," Nick said.

Nick crawled out from underneath the tarp, rearranged Olive Oyl on a blanket, and then disappeared behind one of the log cabins. I heard a prying, crunching sound, demolition noise. When he emerged through the rain, Nick was carrying three cedar shingles that he had ripped from the log cabin roof.

"Boss," Nick said, handing me one of the shingles, "*This* is a plate. And this . . ."

Nick cracked the second shingle in half against his knee.

"Is a spatula."

Our cedar dinner china was tastefully decorated with long green stains where the copper roofing nails had been. With my penknife, I scraped off some dry moss and lichens. Nick wiped off his plate against the sleeve of his hoodie. We crouched in a miserable lake of mud near the rear of the wagon with the tarp stretched between our cowboy hats. When I ladled the chili and rice onto our shingle plates, the copper stain leached up through the rice, turning it green.

"*Bon appétit*," I said, handing Nick his dinner on a shingle.

"*Bon appétit*," Nick said. "Just in case I forget to say so, I'm really glad I stayed with this trip."

I still felt terrible about Olive Oyl, and didn't want her to spend the night outside in the rain. I told Nick that he could sleep with Olive in the wagon until she healed. Nick politely declined the offer. He didn't think that my "college-educated ass" could stand a night in the storm and felt that Olive would feel more secure bundled up with him on the ground underneath the wagon.

Nick and Olive Oyl had a wretched night. They were flooded out underneath the wagon and spent the night migrating in the dark between the log cabins, trying to find one with enough roof for a dry bed of manure.

I didn't sleep very well either. The rain pounded all night against the canvas cover and I could hear thunder far off, rolling across the high plains, but the Schuttler was not the comforting wagon-womb I had enjoyed during earlier storms. Pacific Springs was one long dread hour. We had been on such a high crossing the Sweetwater valley, fording streams, conquering Rocky Ridge, making good time as we saw the most epic and historic stretch of the trail. But now, as we faced the longest desert stretches of the trail, our provisions cart and our water supply lay in wreckage behind us at South Pass. We were sailors, cast adrift off the Horn in a leaky boat without food or water, figures out of Melville or Conrad.

Still, I felt strangely energized by our litany of disasters. Blind endurance was all that we had left for tomorrow. I didn't know if that would be enough to deliver us to Farson, but I didn't feel hemmed in or bored with life's challenges either. Journey was everything and the more difficult it became the more I felt that I was living the life I wanted.

26

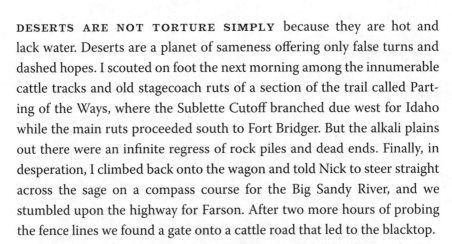

DESERTS ARE NOT TORTURE SIMPLY because they are hot and lack water. Deserts are a planet of sameness offering only false turns and dashed hopes. I scouted on foot the next morning among the innumerable cattle tracks and old stagecoach ruts of a section of the trail called Parting of the Ways, where the Sublette Cutoff branched due west for Idaho while the main ruts proceeded south to Fort Bridger. But the alkali plains out there were an infinite regress of rock piles and dead ends. Finally, in desperation, I climbed back onto the wagon and told Nick to steer straight across the sage on a compass course for the Big Sandy River, and we stumbled upon the highway for Farson. After two more hours of probing the fence lines we found a gate onto a cattle road that led to the blacktop.

Nick was exhausted from not sleeping the night before and spent most of the afternoon flopped on the wagon bed, so I drove alone for hours along the lonely highway to Farson. For four or five miles across the flats the monotony of sage and pink sand was endless but, far off, a rise in the land tempted me with visions of reaching a green, irrigated valley on the other side. But each time I called the mules over the rise, all I could see was the identical monotony of sand and sage, climbing once more through the mirages to another rise. Dreary rise to dreary rise, I spent the day fighting off sleep and worrying about finding water for the mules.

In the late afternoon, a stocky, cheerful trooper from the Wyoming Highway Patrol, Ed Sabourin, stopped on the opposite shoulder of the highway and started taking pictures of the wagon with his iPhone—to show to his wife and children at home. I pulled up the mules to stop and he walked over from his patrol car.

"Whoa, where are you guys from?" Sabourin said. "Nobody told us you were coming."

Sabourin told me that we were still twelve miles from Farson, where we could use the old wagon camp and Pony Express stop, the Big Sandy Station, which had a stable and public corrals for the mules. The town had developed lately as a service area for the big hydrofracked natural gas fields in the dry basins farther north, and we could probably find a mechanic who could run back to South Pass to retrieve our Trail Pup. Sabourin offered to double back for town and make sure that the water was turned on at the Pony Express stables, and arrange for a rancher friend to deliver us some hay.

"Anything else you need?" Sabourin said.

"Water," I said. "We need water for the mules. Maybe twenty gallons?"

Sabourin radioed from his patrol car and twenty minutes later a deputy from the Sweetwater County sheriff's office showed up with three full coolers loaded into the back of his SUV. Nick woke up and held the mules while I emptied the coolers and the mules greedily slurped down several gallons apiece.

After so many hours of riding alone, it was a joy to have Nick on the wagon seat again, and we had only one more rise to clear before we saw the welcome, irrigated lands of the Eden Valley north of Farson. I have never been so happy to see green again. Broad alfalfa fields stretched east and west from the banks of the Little Sandy River and we passed farms, horses grazing in pastures of tall grass, then a school and a Baptist church. A day that had begun with so little hope, with so few resources to rely on, would soon end at the meeting of two sizable rivers, the Little Sandy and the Big Sandy. We had reached water.

But our struggle for water was far from over. After spending several days using Farson as a base for wagon repairs, we would make a series of forty-mile dashes for water across a barren alkali flat called the Little

Colorado Desert. From Farson on the Big Sandy, we would head on a bee-line southwest for the Green River, then to the Hams Fork at Kemmerer. After climbing Dempsey Ridge to a unique, high-country source of water called Emigrant Springs, we would crest the last of the Wyoming Rockies to drop steeply down to the Bear River in Idaho. The parched desert of the cutoff country of western Wyoming would enforce a brutal discipline of travel. We couldn't stop to camp each night until we reached the next source of water.

"River to river, Nick," I said. "Everything else gets eliminated as a worry. But at least we've proved that we can do that."

"I like it when life is that direct," Nick said. "We're just goin for water now."

Farson was a great trail stop for us. We camped at the Big Sandy Pony Express Station, which sat on a hill beside town overlooking a green oasis formed by the flows of the Little Sandy and Big Sandy rivers, with ex-pansive views of the pink desert stretching southwest. The old log-cabin structures and natural pastures along the Big Sandy had evolved in the usual way—from pioneer camp and road ranch along the Oregon Trail to Pony Express and stagecoach stop, then to a livery, blacksmith shop, and telegraph station during the homesteading years, and finally into the public corrals and rodeo grounds serving the northern portions of Sweet-water County today.

We spent our first morning there patching fence and repairing the sta-bles so that the mules would be comfortable during the long stop required to retrieve and repair the Trail Pup. Olive Oyl slowly got better after three days of moping in the wagon and began running around at night, chasing sticks down by the river for children who visited our camp. Nick estab-lished his bedroom on a cushion of dried straw and manure in the stable, near a pile of plastic and wooden toys used to entertain children during the rodeos. I slept in my wagon bed, delighted to be lulled to sleep by the sound of the racing river current below and the comforting ghosts of the past at the Big Sandy Station. It was here, in 1847, that mountain man Jim Bridger gave Brigham Young advice on leading the first Mormon trains into Salt Lake. In the 1860s, Mark Twain, Horace Greeley, and Sir Richard Burton stopped here on their stagecoach trips west.

The whole town of Farson—population 324—became our trail family. In the mornings, I climbed out of the covered wagon and Nick rose from his dirt hovel in the Pony Express stable and we walked over to Mitch's Café for breakfast, falling in naturally with the bachelor ranchers and gas field crews who were the regulars there. They loved Nick and waved him over to their tables as soon as we stepped in, wanting to hear his incomparable yarns about horses or about fishing in Alaska. After breakfast, Nick ran off to a shop near Haystack Butte with a local cowboy and talented mechanic, Tell Brenneman, to chip the rot out of the Schuttler's front wheels and repair them with steel bolts and epoxy glue. I stayed behind to go over my maps with the ranchers, many of whom had worked cattle or wrangled wild horses on the edges of the desert we had to cross. Gradually, I pieced together a route across the cutoffs to Idaho.

The next afternoon, Nick and Tell wound their way up to South Pass by the back trails in a pickup and long trailer, retrieved the Trail Pup, and hauled it back to Farson. When we cut into one spoke on the unbroken wheel of the cart, we found more black rot and concluded that we would have to ship both wheels back east to be rebuilt. That would take at least a month, and I reluctantly decided to leave the Trail Pup behind and transfer our water barrels and provisions to the main wagon. Ditching the Trail Pup and admitting that my prized design for crossing the West was now more trouble than it was worth would be difficult, but I was philosophical about it. Like the pioneers, I was trimming down and abandoning excess weight for the punishing crossing of the deserts ahead.

But wagon master Ben Kern, a veteran trail explorer and booster whom we had met in Casper, saved us. When I called him and told him about our accident at South Pass, he offered his own "kooster" half-cart for the rest of our trip. It had been sitting in a friend's barnyard since his last big wagon trip and, within a day or two, he could run it down to Farson for us.

I was frantic for the next two days, making arrangements to ship the broken wheel hubs to Don Werner in Kansas for rebuilding, and arranging for the bed of the Trail Pup to be shipped ahead of us to Idaho where, later, we could have the new wheels shipped and rebuild the cart. I was dubious about using Don Werner again, but Nick and I concluded that we had no choice. Sending the wheels all the way back to Ohio or Pennsylvania to an unfamiliar Amish wheel shop would take too long.

Nick was furious that I was considering paying for new wheels. But I resorted once more to appreciation of the pioneers. Many of them had problems with their Missouri River outfitters too, but what could they do about it, a thousand miles away, out beyond South Pass? Their only choice had been to ditch their wagons, or cut them into carts, and continue moving west. There was a harsh determinism about it, a defiance of modernity that I liked. Taking on a covered wagon trip in 2011 wasn't any different from taking one on in 1850.

The next morning, when I called him in Kansas, Don Werner was defensive. After we flipped the Trail Pup in Nebraska, I had sent him a picture of the downed cart with a note of thanks for building such a strong vehicle. I now realized that this was a mistake.

"Well, when you flipped that cart in Nebraska, you damaged the wheels," Werner said. "Everything on that rig was prefect when it left here."

"Don, we found rot in both wheels. There's dry rot on the Schuttler wheels too, which we're repairing right now."

"Not from my shop, there wasn't any rot," Werner said. "You didn't know what you were doing. You've abused that wagon too much."

I told Werner that I had already shipped the wheel hubs back to him, and gave him a month to rebuild the wheels and ship them to us in Idaho. When we were done with the trip, I would settle up with him for the cost of rebuilding the wheels.

When I got back to the wagon after my call, Nick was disgusted with me for agreeing to pay Werner for the wheel repairs.

"You're *payin* him to fix those wheels?" he said before stalking off. "This was all his fault."

I sighed, and stared down at the Big Sandy, which was racing at flood stage around the corners of the old trail stop, carrying logs and debris underneath the highway bridge. It was early August and we were halfway to Oregon. We had survived peril after peril and I knew we could make it the rest of the way by the fall. It didn't matter anymore how many mistakes I made. It didn't matter that, to Nick, almost every decision I made defined me as a college-educated jackass with nonexistent mechanical skills. The whole trip was just one long collection of mistakes, and, to put mule shoes in Oregon, I had to be willing to make them.

• • •

At night, at the Big Sandy Station, as we sat around the wagon cooking Hormel chili, no beans, and brewing coffee, the oil field mechanics and ranchers who were helping us make repairs dropped down the hill to visit. Ed Sabourin came over after finishing his highway patrols and drove Nick back to his house for a shower. Wildlife officers from the BLM wanted to sit down with me and my maps, offering tips about how to get across the Little Colorado Desert. Everybody wanted to be a part of our ride and to help. We had enjoyed the same kind of hospitality at the public corrals since Marysville, Kansas, a thousand miles away. This was more than a lesson in how spontaneity and unplanned days are still so richly rewarded in the American West. On the Big Sandy, I found the soul of my country.

The Americans today who like to whine all the time because they say that taxes are too high and that government costs too much should leave their television sets behind for a while and go out and see the country they live in. For a change in their lives they could educate themselves about America by reading a book. They would learn by such activities that nothing happens by accident, and that the cordiality of the American West exists because real Americans with real problems willed over more than a century that it be so.

During the homesteading years that began after the Civil War, the recurrent financial panics of a very primitive American economy sent successive waves of displaced farming families west on the overland trails. There was still free land out west, available through a variety of federal programs, but mostly through the Donation Land Act of 1850 and then three separate Homestead Acts passed by Congress in 1862, 1909, and 1916. The essentially homeless, rootless American farming families who took advantage of this sensible government largesse often departed for the West not knowing where they would end up.

Many of these families didn't find land right away, and the small settlements and nascent towns of the West discovered that they had a problem. When the homesteading families arrived, they needed a place to camp for a few weeks while they waited for their land claims to be approved. The families camped beside their wagons near the edge of town, or sometimes on vacant prairie lots surrounded by the new houses and general stores that were shooting up, and gradually improvements were made to make the newcomers more comfortable while they waited for their land. Barrels mounted on wooden stands were set up for water, wells were dug, and outhouses and platform lean-to shelters were built.

These temporary settlements were called "camp towns," a term that was carried west after the similar shantytowns that had always formed on the outskirts of rapidly developing cities like Pittsburgh, Cincinnati, and Chicago. Stephen Foster's popular minstrel song of 1850, "Camptown Races" ("Gwine to run all night! Gwine to run all day! Doo-dah! Doo-dah!"), evoked the transient camps of African-Americans, where betting on horse races was common. These camps sprouted up around the rail yards in his own native western Pennsylvania and in any given year, there were dozens of similar camp towns all across America. In the nineteenth century, America was a developing country with an emerging town grid ringed by boisterous, haphazardly organized camp towns. That's where people lived.

The need for these camp towns never went away. America throbbed with financial panics through the 1890s, and during World War I thousands of U.S. Army recruits were stalled in small western towns because of traffic snarls on the railroads. The Great Depression and the Dust Bowl of the 1930s flung millions more out onto the roads. We think of the American West as a boundless, scenic space where city dwellers and tourists roam for a few weeks in the summer, vacationing and visiting the national parks. In fact, more often than not, the old frontier lands beyond the Missouri River have been a place where a lot of people at once needed a place to camp.

Franklin Roosevelt's New Deal had an enormous impact on all of this, and permanently changed not only the face of the American landscape but our national character. The millions of men dispatched across the countryside to work in such New Deal programs as the Civilian Conservation Corps, the Works Progress Administration, and the Public Works Administration built the access roads, lodges, bridges, and campsites at the national parks. There was no national park system to speak of before the Depression. The millions of acres preserved a quarter century earlier during the Progressive Era were mostly just forests and empty open lands, with no entrance roads or campgrounds to accommodate people. (The original progressive ideal had been to preserve forests and wildlife habitats as pristine natural spaces, not necessarily places that the public would actually visit.) But creating better access and facilities for federal lands was only the beginning. The CCC also built, in all fifty states, an extensive system of state parks—more than eight hundred in all between 1933 and 1941—and developed more than fifty thousand acres of state campgrounds.

Many of these new parks were built right on top of the old camp towns. During the Great Depression, when millions of people were on the move again, the New Deal built them parks with clean bathrooms, showers, cooking pavilions, and fire pits. The government effort to build national and state parks—a legacy as important as Social Security or stock market regulation—was so extensive that a whole new architectural look was needed to systematize what was happening. CCC forestry projects and the excavations for road building produced a lot of logs and stones. The CCC also built an impressive network of sawmills, to produce planking and cedar shingles for park rangers' houses and picnic pavilions, and the agency helped support itself by selling finished timber to the commercial lumber market. These basic materials were put to use creating the "government rustic" style, a look that merged features from the Adirondack, "arts and crafts," and log-cabin designs with the distinctive poled porches, shingle siding, and intersecting eaves and dormers that still dominate park architecture today. This look proved attractive, and the contingencies of an economic depression had an interesting and lasting impact on American design. Today, the mansion districts of Vail and Beaver Creek, Colorado, Jackson Hole, Wyoming, and Lake Tahoe, California, are heavily influenced by this lodge-style "parkitecture."

During the 1950s and early 1960s, when the interstate highway system was built, America was on the move again. Touring the national parks created during the Depression was the only vacation many families could afford, gasoline was cheap, and many working-class families from the Midwest owned small pop-up camping trailers that auto and steel industry workers used for hunting and fishing trips. Families drove out to Yellowstone or Glacier National Park for a couple of weeks, camping at the CCC facilities along the way. State tourist agencies considered free or modestly priced camping facilities an important asset, both for establishing a reputation for hospitality and capturing tourist dollars for nearby towns. During the postwar years the states spent considerable sums adding free showers, recreation pavilions, and ball fields to the summer campgrounds. On public lands along the North Platte River in Nebraska and eastern

Wyoming, and the Snake River in Idaho, a network of fishing access points with campgrounds was also built. The public pump-priming helped build the recreational hunting and fishing industry into the $150 billion sector it is today, and once more the echoes of nineteeth-century pioneer life influenced the look and economic prosperity of the country. West of the Missouri, many of these campgrounds and public amenities were built not just near the Oregon Trail, but *on* the Oregon Trail.

The ranching system that evolved in the West after the 1880s developed another kind of facility that can be found in virtually every western town. Large herds of cattle have to be moved twice a year, in the late spring and early fall, between summer grazing areas in the mountains and the winter rangelands below on the sagebrush flats. Ranches aren't so much a single place as a collection of grazing areas, some privately owned by the rancher, some government "allotments" on Bureau of Land Management (BLM) parcels, interconnected by cattle paths, feedlots, and highways. Nationwide, about 35 million calves are born every year, usually in February, requiring a mass movement of cowboys and horses to tend the herds every winter. But winter winds and storms often force the closure of highways, trapping cowboys and their stock trailers overnight, or for a few nights, in small towns. In sparsely populated Wyoming, at the approach of a large storm, the state highways are locked shut with heavy metal gates, so that motorists can't get stranded on a lonely section of road drifted with snow.

As a result, for more than a century now, most western towns have maintained "public corrals" with good access to the highways, so that the ranchers can turn their horses loose in a safe place and then camp in their trailers or find a nearby motel for themselves. Today, many of these public corrals also serve as the local rodeo grounds. Before that, they were Pony Express stables, stagecoach stops, and military bivouacs. Along the Oregon Trail, many of these public spaces began their existence as overnight camping spots for the wagon trains.

Today, the West is still full of such places, creating an interesting political irony. Some of the most conservative, red-state bastions in America—Nebraska, Wyoming, Idaho—are the most park-rich states of all, with rodeo corrals, state fairgrounds, and free or inexpensive municipal campgrounds nearly everywhere. Untold millions in tax dollars were spent to build these national assets, and millions of dollars of public funds are spent every year to maintain them. The public corrals and parks measurably improve the quality of life and the local economies. But this region is also the Tea Party belt, where the central ideological pretense of the day is that government is the enemy and that every penny of taxes collected is a political crime.

The picture in Wyoming is typical of most western states. In Wyoming, travel and tourism—a sector heavily subsidized by government—is a $3 billion annual business. In Casper alone, there are two large Oregon Trail museums, one maintained by the city, the other by the BLM, and the tourists flock to them on the way to Yellowstone National Park or Fossil Butte National Monument. The federal government pours roughly $6 billion into Wyoming every year, more than $4 billion of that for assorted BLM, forestry, tourism, and road projects, making Wyoming one of the most federally dependent states in the country. According to federal statistics compiled by the news service WyoFile.com, in 2011 Wyoming residents paid an average of $6,795 in federal taxes, but the state collected more than $11,000 per capita in federal funds. In Wyoming, there are twice as many federal employees—thirteen thousand—as state employees. Federal dollars flow into the state and private coffers of Wyoming as plentifully as water spilling over the North Platte dams. Tea Party antitax activism isn't just hypocrisy. It is total bunk.

Over the summer, we camped at small-town public parks and the public corrals dozens of times, across two thousand miles of America. We lived on the public space established by the pioneers. Rugged individualism and manifest destiny, for which the West is still celebrated, are fine things to believe in, but they never existed as abstractions. People were desperate and they needed free land and free places to camp, which government decided to supply, and still does. This national legacy was one of the best discoveries of crossing the Oregon Trail, but we never would have found it without detaching ourselves from the umbilical cord of the interstates and the motel chains, forcing ourselves to forage every night for a place to stay.

We left Farson early in the morning after a five-day camp. Ed Sabourin met us on the hill above the public corrals, his cruiser lights flashing, so that he could "escort" us up the highway until we made the turn onto the dusty Farson Cutoff. Just before Mitch's Café, he gave his siren a squeal and the ranchers and waitresses poured out of the café and stood in the parking lot with their cups of coffee, cheering and urging us on.

"Go get 'em, boys! We're rootin for ya!"

"Yo, Nick! Don't let a mule sit on you!"

One of the ranchers who had helped me with the maps had scrawled a motto on the back of a paper place mat with his pen.

OREGON OR BUST!

Nick and I spent the next fifteen hours bouncing and rattling across the draws of the Little Colorado Desert, swapping driving duties while one of us sought relief from the sun and dust in the back of the wagon. We had just one mission to accomplish by nightfall, or even after dark if it came to that. We had to reach the Green River, more than forty miles away across the scorching sands. We had just enough water in our barrels to keep the mules hydrated for twenty-four hours. But we would probably be empty by the morning, and would have to water the mules and refill the barrels from the Green before we took on an even longer forced march for water—more than fifty miles to the Hams Fork River on the western edge of Wyoming. There was no stopping until we made camp within sight of the Green. I discovered, however, that I could just barely tolerate the tedium of sand and black rock by noticing the minute patterns of life in the desert environment. There was a fascinating connection, too, between observing the wildlife and navigating over the sands.

The desert actually teemed with wildlife, which I could easily see by keeping track of the geologic formations we were passing in the wagon. Spiny, exposed skeletons of rock beside the trail usually announced the approach of a dry creek wash, where there were often prairie dog colonies drawn to the underground flows of water. Because the prairie dogs were there, prairie falcons and red-tailed hawks were circling low for prey. The creek washes were unnamed but marked on my topographic maps, and by looking ahead through the mirages for the raptor birds, I could roughly gauge our progress across the endless flats.

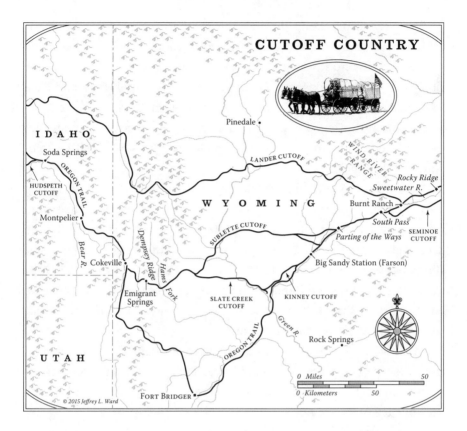

Observing the wild horse herds also provided occasional waypoints, and relief from the boredom and heat of crossing the desert. Piles of stallion manure beside the trail—dropped by the dominant males to mark their breeding area and to protect their mare harems—gradually increased in height as we neared the center of a herd. Near the tallest manure piles, worn, single-file horse paths dipped south as the land fell to an occasional watered draw or mud hole. The mares and their foals linger all summer as close as they can to the water draws, and we often saw small herds there, browsing on the richer grass near moisture. "Bachelor herds" of young studs driven away by the dominant stallion wandered closer to the trail, nibbling on the short, sparse grass away from the draws. They were scrawny and looked lonely and lost, and they pointed their ears and galloped over from the hills nearby, curious about the mules. The taller the manure piles, the closer we were to the draws to the south, many of which were also marked on the maps.

We were also passing through the southern edge of the Jonah gas fields, one of two vast hydraulic fracturing zones that stretched north almost to the Wind Rivers and the Tetons. The old cutoff country to the Green River Rendezvous was just one long "Energy Trail" now, and Nick and I started counting the gas pads we could see in the distance from the wagon seat. By the end of the day, we had passed forty-six wells. These too were marked on the maps—Little Colorado Well Number 5, Little Colorado Well Number 13.

That was our life until nightfall, watching the wildlife, and navigating across the ruts, according to the wealth of detail available from the seat of a covered wagon. We watched for hawks, assessed the height of stallion piles, and counted fracked wells, cross-checking these fixes on our maps. When battling sleep became too much, but I couldn't nap in the bumpy wagon bed, I climbed off and walked. Several times we thought that we saw the Green River, but these were false sightings caused by the low afternoon light slanting through the mirages.

At dusk, the land suddenly dropped off to our right and we could see a large, S-shaped lake, gray-blue in the weak light, and then a ribbon of ox-bows falling to the south. It was the big reservoir where the river was held back by the Fontenelle Dam.

"The Green, Nick. That's the Green River."

We pushed on through the dark for two miles, occasionally losing the ruts as we steered for the river. We stopped on a high rise a quarter of a mile from the Green, stumbling around in the dark as we unharnessed and built fencing for the mules. I carried the last of our water to the team while Nick made dinner with just the light from the burners of the gas stove. The views down to the river and the flats beyond were spectacular and we were too tired to say very much.

"Forty-two miles in one day," I said to Nick. "The Big Sandy to the Green."

"It feels like Farson was a month ago."

"It was a month ago. There is no time out here."

"I don't ever want to go back home," Nick said. "I want to live out here in the wagon for the rest of my life."

The desert cooled rapidly after the sun set. I wrapped myself in an extra blanket and stared down from the wagon at the silvery band of the river. Deserts are supposedly barren spaces but I had navigated all day by the clues of the terrain and the richness of wildlife. The black expanse of the cutoff country to the west seemed inviting and I would find a way through there too.

27

WE MADE OUR LAST CAMP in Wyoming at 8,300 feet on the top of
Dempsey Ridge. From the alpine heights we looked across an immense
gorge to the sandstone palisades of Fossil Butte National Monument.
For two days we had climbed the mules up the steep ruts of the Sublette Cutoff, emerging every few hours onto a series of stepped plateaus
that were brilliant with yellow rudbeckia and purple thistles. We filled
our water barrels at the Hams Fork River and, almost at the top of the
ridge, at the old wagon campground at Emigrant Springs. We saw no one
and at night the only sounds we heard were the wind whistling through
the wagon cover and the mules placidly grinding their molars on high
mountain grass, which filled me with a sense of complete isolation and
freedom. River to river and pasturage to pasturage we had followed the
old pioneer road, living as they did, simply, off the land. But we still faced
an inescapable irony of the Oregon Trail. Reaching these beautiful places
also required escaping them. Our only route down to the safety of the
Bear River valley in Idaho was a two-thousand-foot plunge through Rock
Creek Ridge.

The trail we patched together across the old pioneer shortcuts—we
followed portions of the Farson, Slate Creek, and Sublette cutoffs—
was about seventy miles shorter than following the main ruts south to

Fort Bridger, and it delivered us to high country that one 1849 pioneer called a "perfect oasis in the desert." In the early days of the trail, the last mountain barrier before the Bear River sheltered exotic remnants of the fur-trapping era, a mid-nineteenth-century melting pot high above the neighboring desert. Small bands of Shoshone and Snake Indians were camped on the ridges above Hams Fork, and these were interspersed with colorful "Frenchmen" camps of mixed-marriage fur trappers and Indian squaws. As fur trapping waned and the big summer rendezvous along the Green River ended, these Indian and French traders drifted north to resupply the emigrant trains by selling crafts, equipment salvaged from abandoned wagons, and preserved food. The pioneers would encounter these trading camps—each a sort of mixed-race flea market, bake sale, and entertainment center—all the way west to the Columbia River, as the crude merchant system originally formed to service the fur trappers evolved into spontaneous road ranches supporting the white migration.

In 1849, mapmaker and artist J. Goldsborough Bruff met one trader above the Hams Fork who had counted more than three thousand wagons that passed though during the month of June alone. "Here was a mixture, white women, and squaws & children, of every age and hue," Bruff wrote, and they were camped in a mixed settlement of tepees, covered wagons, and temporary summer houses made of brush and sticks. The traders were dressed in deerskin shirts and pants, and the camps were filled with crude log booths displaying Indian goods and provisions—moccasins, skin water jugs, dried fish, and smoked muskrat. "Fat ponies and horses" for sale browsed in the meadows.

For the covered wagon travelers who had diverted due west and missed Fort Bridger, the mixed-race camp below Emigrant Springs was the first opportunity to trade in more than 250 miles, and they were fascinated by these mountain nomads. One night Bruff and a party of musicians from his covered wagon train, carrying violins, a bugle, and an accordion, walked over to the traders' camp nearby and were invited inside one of the skin lodges.

Our party of a dozen, and the Frenchmen & squaws, all crowded around the interior of the lodge. . . . They performed several lively airs, such as "Dan Tucker," "Carry me back to old Virginia," "Zip Coon," Etc. accompanied by singing, which delighted the traders much, and particularly the Indians.

Another "pleasant divertissement of the mind and eye," as one pioneer called it, greeted the wagon travelers as they climbed above Emigrant Springs at seven thousand feet. Thick stands of mature whitebark pine and aspen swayed in the mountain breezes, the first extensive shade that the pioneers had found since Ash Hollow in Nebraska, 650 miles behind them. The surprise of finding carving surfaces as inviting as these trees had the same effect on the pioneers as Independence Rock or Devil's Gate. By 1850 the lower trunks of what was variously called Pine Grove or Aspen Grove were so covered with names that the pioneers had to climb to the high branches to find a place in the bark to leave their initials. Pioneers and their children shinnied up the trees as high as they could to see if they could discover the names of friends or relatives who they knew were crossing the trail in front of them.

Wisconsin pioneer Jared Fox established a near record for a speedy crossing in 1852 when, relentlessly lightening his load and passing fifty to a hundred wagons a day, he reached Oregon City by the remarkable date of August 17. Fox is also appreciated by trail historians as a meticulous recorder of detail. Hurrying over the top of the Sublette Cutoff, he paused long enough to describe the elaborate forest of initials at Aspen Grove.

Passed through a grove of some 20 rods shade, the most timber we have seen in a thousand miles & in this grove there is I suppose 5 or 10 thousand, for aught I know, names cut in the trees. Some printed with chalk or waggon grease, red paint & anything and everything. Dates from 1845 to the present, but most 1850 & many of them are 10 to 15 feet from the ground.

But there was a price to be paid for these scenic pauses, and the time saved by cutting straight across the deserts. Dempsey Ridge dropped to the Bear River valley as a straight defile west with precipitously high canyon walls, which limited the pioneers' ability to maneuver around cliffs and formations of slate ledges that fell in steps to the grassy bottomlands below. The two thousand feet in elevation that the pioneers had gained in fifteen miles of climbing from the Hams Fork would now have to be shed in less than two miles of descent. It was a wagon driver's nightmare, and negotiating it was made possible only by the advantage of traveling in wagon trains, which provided enough human labor and restraining equipment to hold back the wagons with ropes after the rear wheels had been chained. The wagons were also lowered by roping fallen logs or large rocks to the rear axle, adding drag for the slope.

There were two routes down this covered wagon chute. The first trended northwest over milder terrain to the top of Dempsey Ridge and then dropped through a series of excavated switchbacks to the Bear River just a few miles from present-day Cokeville, Wyoming. But this route has gradually disappeared over time through neglect and reforestation. The second route plunged due west down to a secondary elevation, Rock Creek Ridge. In high-water years, the Rock Creek descent was notorious for gullies and washed-out trail where fast-running creeks crossed the ruts. The Rock Creek ruts are a classic example of how solving one problem of wagon travel often created a new one. In the early 1850s this route had been relocated away from steep fifty-foot cliffs that were hidden in the tree groves and required an emptying of the wagons and then a difficult belaying of the wagon boxes and running gear with ropes. But the new route was prone to washouts and difficult creek fords.

In her 1852 diary, Abigail Jane Scott reported that she walked ten miles the day her wagon train crested Dempsey Ridge, probably because of the need to lighten the wagons for the steep slopes, and because the experience of sitting on a wagon pitched straight downhill was both frightening and dangerous. "We traveled two miles without unlocking the wagon wheels," Scott wrote, "and in many places the men held back the wagon in addition to having both back wheels locked." The dread associated with the final drop into Idaho's Bear River valley was expressed by the name the pioneers gave this stretch of trail. The exit from the Sublette Cutoff was called the "Rock Slide."

I didn't deliberately choose the Rock Slide because I preferred a last, perilous descent out of Wyoming. We could have followed the main ruts south toward Rock Springs and Fort Bridger, and then picked our way along the ranch roads and highways that curled in a long loop around

Fossil Butte and then north onto the Bear River. However, the paved Route 30, portions of which we would have to follow to remain with the main ruts, is busy with semitruck traffic. This notoriously accident-prone two-lane highway is curved and drops precipitously through canyons with almost no road shoulders, and several truckers and ranchers I'd spoken with in Farson warned me to stay off the highway. Besides, water would be difficult to find in the parched butte country to the south. Emigrant Springs below Dempsey Ridge was our last chance to refill our barrels for the final assault on the Rockies. The end of the Sublette Cutoff was our only modern wagon route to the Bear.

During our torpid days in the deserts, and then while we climbed up through the rock outcrops and pine groves of Dempsey Ridge, Nick took long afternoon naps on the mattress behind me and I spent a lot of time alone on the wagon seat. The mules were peaceful and easy to handle and softly tugged the lines in my hands. The wildflower fields were lyrical gardens in the sky. I fell into the combined melancholia and joyful romance that comes with rigorous travel and I felt meditative about my past, winsome. I was completely at home on the covered wagon, at rest with myself, and was finally beginning to understand the forces that had driven me west and compelled me to prove myself.

When I was in college, my friends and my professors occasionally chastised me for complaining about my father and his meddling ways. "You need to accept that families are always difficult," my favorite professor, James Bland, said to me once. "At least your father cares. He has goaded you to do good work."

When I graduated from college in 1973, I won the history prize and was selected as a commencement speaker, but my father was not there to share this with me. He had retired and moved to rural Pennsylvania two years earlier and his health had rapidly declined. There were some weeks when he was fine and could remain active, and he sounded on the phone as if his old exuberance had returned, but there were other weeks when his phantom pains were so severe that his doctors worried about the impact on his heart. The month that I graduated was not a good one and he couldn't travel north to Maine. My closest friends from New Jersey drove up instead and became my surrogate family for the weekend.

But there was one last favor that he could provide. On a motorcycle trip south that spring, I had talked my way into my first writing job, at the respected *Berkshire Eagle* in western Massachusetts, a "feeder paper" for talent hoping to move on to big-name publications in New York. My responsibilities would include taking photographs for the stories I wrote. I was knowledgeable about photography but completely unskilled at using a camera, but this was exactly the kind of challenge I enjoyed. I had three months to give myself a crash course in taking pictures before the job began. I rented a cheap room in a boardinghouse in Great Barrington and found work at an all-night truck stop out on the turnpike, but I still couldn't afford to buy a camera. When my father learned about that he offered me his best 35-millimeter camera, a Nikkormat, and several expensive lenses. They just happened to be in New York, he said, getting serviced and cleaned at "the best photo shop in Manhattan." I could start my first job with the finest photo equipment available.

"Why don't we meet in the city next week?" he said. "I can give you the camera and show you how to use it, and we'll go to lunch."

The details about our luncheon date seemed a bit off. In the past I had usually met my father at publishing industry haunts where he felt comfortable and would run into old friends, fashionable midtown restaurants like Sardi's or the 21 Club, but this time he asked me to meet him at a seedy Irish pub way over on Tenth Avenue, because that would be closer to his parking lot. I got there on time and chained my motorcycle to a parking meter between a Puerto Rican bodega and a used furniture store on Forty-Sixth Street, feeling out of place while I waited for my father at the bar, which was mostly filled with idlers and a few construction workers drinking beer with their lunch.

My father arrived late, carrying a small travel bag and a brown manila shopping bag with paper handles, and I tried not to show my reaction to his appearance. He looked jaunty in his crisp white shirt and a summer-weight Irish tweed jacket that I recognized from years before, but it no longer fit him. He had lost a lot of weight and the thinned curvature of his cheeks reminded me of an old picture of him that my mother had kept on her dresser for years, taken when he was in his mid-thirties and underweight, still recovering from his air crash in 1946. But he was sprightly in that photo and his face beamed with optimism about the small magazine he had just founded. Now, the sadness in his eyes and the defensive inflection in his voice were things I had not noticed before.

We moved to a table away from the bar and my father asked me if I wanted a beer, and said that he was ordering one for himself too. This was the first time I had ever seen him order a drink. He had been sober for twenty-five years and his identity as an AA disciple was so complete that I considered it an inseparable part of his personality. I must have looked surprised.

"Well, son," he said. "Sometimes after a life of successful sobriety a man like me decides that it's safe to drink again. Just a little. I can handle it now."

After we ordered a simple lunch of hamburgers and french fries, my father started emptying the camera and lenses from the paper bag. He had also brought me a new camera bag with separate storage compartments for film, lenses, cleanser, and the like. He thought that I would look "real smart," "a young reporter on the make," with the camera bag slung over my shoulder as I chased around the Berkshires for my stories. He explained a few things about f-stops and exposure speeds that I already knew and regaled me with stories about the famous *Life* and *Look* photographers he'd known over the years. I loved my father most for this trait. The stores of information and trivia that were hidden in his memory, and then presented later as conversational surprises, had always impressed me, and I enjoyed myself at lunch. There were glimmers, lasting just a few moments, of his old brio and appeal.

When my father had arrived at the bar I was overwhelmed by a sense that he had been wandering the streets for a while, almost secretively. This wasn't an impression that I could grasp very well and I forgot about it. But then, I knew. As I played with the lenses that he had given me, experimenting with inserting them into the aperture ring of the camera and then twisting the lens shut with a snap, I noticed that they were all labeled with fresh, shiny stickers. CASH FOR GOLD, the stickers read, above an address on Forty-Seventh Street. The camera box itself had the same shiny stickers, one on each side.

I probably wouldn't have figured this out, except that two of my best friends from college were photography majors, and they often made trips to New York to buy the best camera boxes and lenses—Nikons, Leicas, and Minoltas—at the steep discounts offered in the Forty-Seventh Street pawnshop district.

Oh, I thought, my father had been artful about smoothing this over, but not quite artful enough. His best camera had not spent the last few weeks in a photo shop for cleaning. He had hocked it for cash on his previous trip to New York and had just retrieved it, for me, from a pawnshop. Along with everything else that day, the discreet way that he had fished the pawnshop receipt out of the bottom of the shopping bag, and then stuffed it into a side pocket of his sport coat, made it all fall into place. It was that bad for him now. He was pawning his possessions to get through the month. His gifts for me, his buying habits, had always been so extravagant that I'd taken his carefree life for granted. Now I tried not to think about where he'd found the cash to spring his camera for me, let alone to buy gas for the long drive from Pennsylvania to New York.

The welter of emotions that coursed through me then—guilt, love, empathy, fatalism about his future, and pining for the past—felt like a turbulent ocean inside. I couldn't even attempt to disguise my feelings because there were too many feelings colliding at once.

Oh, fuck me, Dad. Fuck me, fuck me, fuck me. You're such a great person, so blindly altruistic and beguiling, and look at the trouble you're in now.

By the time he finished his second beer, with a bourbon chaser—"just to give the brew some taste"—he was slurring his words. I had already told him that I had to leave by early afternoon to get back in time for my evening shift at the truck stop. I didn't like the way he was fumbling for money in his pockets so I spent most of what I had in my wallet to pay the bill, which at least gave me something to feel good about.

Out on the street, my father wished me well at my first job, encouraged me to work hard, and said that he was planning on taking out a subscription to the *Eagle*, so he could follow my progress as a reporter. If it was all right, he would call once in a while to make suggestions about making my copy better.

"Okay, Dad," I said. "But just go easy. You've got your own stuff to worry about."

We shook hands and, before he turned to go, I thanked him for the camera and threw my new camera case over my shoulder at a rakish angle. I wanted him to have an image of me dashing off to report my first story. He smiled at that, winked, laughed quietly, and started down Tenth Avenue. I noticed again how thin he was. He walked with a stoop, his neck and his wrists were no longer buffalo-brown and brawny, and he didn't try to hide the limp from his wooden leg anymore. Ah, shit, Dad. Shit. Watching him walk away and then disappear around the next corner felt like the loneliest moment of my life and I worried that I would never see him again.

There were broken cumulus clouds over northern Manhattan as I drove up the West Side Highway, and I liked the way that the sunlight pushing through the holes in the overcast made glittering patterns on the Hudson. Instinct told me to be greedy and not sad about the day, and I was manically happy about my new camera. Don't concentrate on him, I thought. Don't think about him. It will kill you to worry about him. Throw yourself into learning to take pictures. I decided to find a photo shop on the way north, buy some film, and start taking pictures at work that night. The sky opened up north of Peekskill and I wanted to put as much distance as possible between me and New York. I pushed the bike hard and reached my new refuge in the mountains in under three hours.

We stopped the mules at a lovely spot high on the ridge where the ruts curved into the shade of an aspen grove. This was probably one of the spots where the pioneers had scrambled up the trees with carving knives in their teeth to leave behind their initials or names, but of course time had erased any evidence of their inscriptions. As I stepped down from the wagon to explore the route off the ridge, the darkness of the white bark pine groves below looked spooky and treacherous. This was another place, like California Hill or Rocky Ridge, where the difficulties of a modern crossing seemed condensed at a single obstacle. Once we started downhill, the steep canyon walls below would prevent us from turning back. I wouldn't enjoy the advantage of a large wagon train and its labor pool of men to restrain my wagon. Nick would have to trust me to have made the right decision, even though there wasn't really a choice at all, and I would have to trust him to drive us out of the certain hazards we faced below.

"The Rock Slide, Nick. It's our only way down."

"Do we know what's there?"

"A two-thousand-foot drop to the Bear River."

"Fuck, let's go. I can't wait to do this."

At first, dropping down through the shade of the whitebark groves was refreshingly cool and peaceful. But as soon as we were off the summit and rounding the first corner of the trail downhill, a canyon wall of loose sandstone and rock rose to our right, higher than the wagon top. The spring rains had distributed a thick scree of gravel on the ledge in front of us. The rear legs of the mules slipped out from underneath them and they couldn't hold the wagon back along the ledge. But by pushing the brake back and forth and judging the distance ahead to the slippery gravel beds, I found that I could jolt the wagon back against the mules and pull them upright at just the right moment, forcing them to pull the load downhill and gain their footing.

I was grateful then for a lifetime of fear about moving wagons downhill. It was like driving a heavy truck over hills. Never coast. Never let the gravity of the load apply on the team. Pivot the weight of the wagons *against* the mules, pulling them aft, so that they will be held upright by the load and can enjoy the stabilizing effect of the harness pulling backward on their shoulders.

Coordinating our descent was difficult for Nick and me, but it was also very athletic—this was distracting and helped a lot. There were places where the trail curved downhill at a 20 percent or 30 percent slope and we were looking almost straight down at the mules. When I locked the wheels, we were both thrown forward and fought with our thighs and our feet, wedging against each other to remain on the wagon seat. Each time, Nick could feel my hips tensing for stability before I threw the brake.

When he felt me tense for the next push of the brake, Nick called the mules.

"Yup, Team. Yup. Pull!"

But I corrected him.

"Don't call the team," I said. "Don't slap the lines. No excitement at all. Hands. Talk to them with your hands. Calm, calm."

Nick looked annoyed but he was willing to give up his vestigial driving self.

"Fuck. You're giving *me* a driving lesson? But you're probably right."

We reached a place then driving mules that was beyond all experience or training. Wordless intuition and shared physicality joined us. Reach right with my arm for the brake and tense left against Nick on the narrow wagon seat. The mules felt the brake retard the wagon and gently lowered their necks into their collars and pulled downhill. Nick held the lines sharply back and then slightly released pressure to move the team forward. The communication passed from my brake arm through my hip to Nick and then down the lines to the mules, five minds fused to manage the load down the steep pitch.

We were out of the wind now and there was no breeze to cool us or carry away the sound of the wheels. The iron rims screeched against the rocks while the harness chains cracked against the load. The high wall on our right held in the acrid smell of the smoking brakes.

We were just a descending cauldron of shrieking brakes and burning thresher belt now. When the mules felt the brakes land hard they held their legs rigid, skimming along on the gravel for a few feet. The dust raised by their hooves billowed up past their bellies and spread sideways, completely obscuring our view. There was no terra firma now. I could feel how the wagon was doing only through the muscles of my brake arm. It was a magic carpet ride behind mules gliding through clouds of dust.

When we reached Rock Creek Ridge, the trail curved sharply to the west and then disappeared around the cliffs, and we couldn't believe what we saw. The grade plunged steeply down across a slick rock face of brown slate that would be a children's slide for the mules. I could imagine holding the main wagon off the mules—perhaps just barely—but the heavy cart behind us would probably jackknife across the slate and overwhelm us, pulling us backward into the canyon below.

But Nick had an idea.

"Hold these mules for a minute," he said. "I know what to do here."

Nick reached underneath the seat for a heavy chain, threw it onto his shoulder, and then slid down the wheel and disappeared behind the wagon. I heard the rattling of the chain back there for a minute or two and then he climbed back on and took the lines.

"What did you do?" I said.

"I roughlocked the cart wheels. It'll work fine."

I had heard about roughlocking, but would never have thought to do it here. By wrapping the chain around the spokes of the wheels on both sides of the cart and then hooking the ends onto the running gear, Nick had locked the wheels so they wouldn't turn. Now the one-ton cart acted as a drag on the rig, to which I would add the braking power of the main wheels. We had converted our provisions cart into an anchor.

Still, I didn't like the look of the slick table of slate plunging downhill and around the corner of the cliffs. There was no way of knowing from above how much longer the ledge was, or if it got steeper.

"Jesus, Nick. I don't know."

Nick looked at me, grimaced, shrugged his shoulders, and then gently elbowed me in the ribs.

"I'm glad you're afraid," he said. "At least I'm doin the trail with someone who knows this can be dangerous. Are you ready?"

I took a deep breath and exhaled.

"Let's do it."

"Ease-A, Team," Nick said, quietly, slightly pulling the lines. "Team, slow. Hold 'em back, Jake. Hold 'em back. Team, slow."

I released the brake handle and quickly adjusted to the rhythm of sledging downhill. The roughlocked cart provided tremendous drag on the rig, but the Schuttler still wanted to race ahead as soon as the brakes were released. Brake, then release, let the wheels roll a quarter rotation. Brake again. Release. Gravity has never impressed me so much. My shoulder was already thrown out and aching from the braking above but I was fixated on the tug chains, keeping them tight so the team was always pulling downhill. The iron rims screeched over the slate, the brake pads smoked, and the pole banged between Jake and Beck every time the front wheels hit a bump on the ledge.

The mules were even farther below us now, but I didn't dare look forward to judge the slope. I had to lean way out on the brake handle to see the tug chains, and then look straight back for the cart. Brake and release. From nowhere, aspen branches suddenly appeared, whipping my face. I felt a bump from behind and quickly looked back. I had jackknifed the rig with the brake and the right wheel hub of the cart was scraping the cliffs. But this was good, providing more drag on the load. I jockeyed the brake to keep the right wheel slightly hung up on the rocks and we left a deep gash where the hub dug into the shale cliff.

It seemed to take forever. Release, lock the wheels. Release, lock the wheels. Keep those tug chains tight. Skid the cart up against the cliff embankment. I didn't know that we had reached the bottom of the ledge until the screeching of the wheels over rock stopped and we began to push up dust. We were level again and I could see the backs of the mules.

Nick was smiling broadly on the wagon seat, ecstatic to have roughlocked his wheels and managed a team down a Wyoming mountain like this. It was a moment of supreme triumph. Wordlessly, never really expressing to each other what we had to do, we had lowered several tons of mule and wagon down one of the steepest wagon slopes in the West.

"Jesus," I said. "Roughlocking. It really worked. How many times have you done that before?"

"Oh, this is the first time."

"Jesus. Why didn't you tell me?"

"Rink, think about that. If I had told you, you would have shit your pants."

The trail disappeared uphill as a switchback that curved northwest again, around even higher cliffs. Nick took the chain off the wheels of the cart but when we reached the top my heart stopped again. The pitch down over gravel and dust was almost as severe as the slate tables above and the trail had now dramatically narrowed. The canyon gradually coming in from behind us had grown into a deep gorge and, off Nick's side of the wagon, we were looking down at the tops of mature pine and aspen trees that were a hundred feet below us. It was a sheer drop-off, and the width of the trail provided just enough clearance for the wagon.

I was terrified about staying on the wagon and briefly tempted to climb down the wheel, squeeze between the team and the cliffs, walk down to scout, and see if the trail became even more narrow. My excuse would be that if one wheel went over the edge and pulled the whole rig into the gorge, one of us needed to be alive to go for help. Nick could sense my fear and offered me an out.

"You should be off the wagon here," he said. "We need you on foot to check if the trail is wide enough. I can manage the lines and brake with my foot."

It was an act of will—where the determination came from, I don't know—to turn down his offer.

"Shit, I really do want off this wagon," I said. "But I'm not doing that. I've got this brake routine now with the mules."

We both looked forward to study the trail again, and the physics of our descent were clear. There were curves ahead where the gorge beside us dropped more than a hundred feet straight down. One mule jumping to the left, one bad jackknife of the cart, and we would be pulled over the edge. We both realized that if the wagon started to fall, I would probably be able to get off in time on my side. But Nick would plunge with the rig into the gorge.

"Shit," Nick said. "This is goin to be fuckin great."

As we started to inch down, I wasn't really aware of my surroundings, and I didn't have time to be afraid. All I could do was lean out over the side of the wagon with my hand on the brake, staring ahead at the tug chains to make sure they were tight, and then quickly looking back at the cart to make sure it wasn't jackknifing. The instant the cart wheels started to jackknife out of sight I released brake pressure, waited a second for them to straighten out, and then faced forward again to reapply the brake.

Brake, release. Brake, release. Our American flag scraped against the cliffs and Nick held the team so tight against the wall that I couldn't see any space between the rocks and the hubs. My face passed just inches from the boulders on the ledge and my cheeks were whipped again by aspen saplings growing out of the rocks.

There were moments of panic. Two or three times as we descended Jake and Beck reached high with their necks to snag an aspen leaf from the scrub growth hanging from the cliffs. This pushed the pole almost into the rocks. We passed several cone-shaped piles of elk scat on Beck's side and I knew that if she got a strong whiff of unfamiliar wildlife she might bolt and try to run away. But Beck quietly sidestepped each pile and I could tell that the team sensed how hard I was working to keep the weight of the wagons off their shoulders and backs.

I was nervous, too, about the trail suddenly narrowing, or the left side of the ground suddenly giving way from the weight of the wagons. But

I was still looking backward to keep the cart straight and couldn't see for myself. Almost involuntarily, I begged Nick for resassurance.

"Nick, the trail. How wide?"

"Wider. We're good."

I tried to discipline myself not to ask again, but then I did.

"Still wide," Nick said. "We're almost to the bottom."

When I felt Nick pull up the team and call "Whoa" I could hear water running. I slowly turned around to face forward and waited for the dust from our descent to clear.

We had reached the bottom of the elevation, but ahead of us the creek had washed out the trail. There was a two-foot drop to reach the creek bed, then a natural corduroy of driftwood and logs. In the middle of the creek there was a deep pool of moving water, and then a steep climb through river rock and mud to regain the trail. It was the kind of obstacle that would have worried me five hundred miles ago, but not now.

My arms were shaking and my heart was still racing but I needed something to do. I took the lines myself, eased the team one axle at a time into the creek bed and across the logs, and then slapped the mules' rumps through the water and up through the muddy banks to the trail. Moving uphill again and being able to call the team felt like salvation.

We stopped in the shade slightly uphill of the creek and sat for a long while, speechless, drinking from our canteens. I was still shaking several minutes later.

From our uphill position I looked back and saw our fresh wagon tracks on the trail. There were spots where I could see that we hadn't had more than a foot of clearance. We were that close to falling sideways into the gorge.

"Nick, you told me the trail got wider. But look at that spot, where the cliff juts out. We were almost over the edge."

"Okay, so I was lyin. Big fuckin deal. I knew I could thread us through that needle and get us down here alive. Besides, if I was wrong?"

"What?"

"We'd be dead. We wouldn't give a shit."

After the gorges, the trail rose and fell across two sets of foothills, but there were wide, grassy meadows in between and I knew that we had reached the bottomlands of the Bear River. Overcome by my exertions all day in the thin air, I stumbled several times carrying water for the team, but I steadied myself by clinging to Jake's bridle and then asking him to raise his head to hold me up. We were still hours away from Cokeville and I had to leave the wagon a few times to track us on foot through the cattle ranches, once more experiencing the strange effects of hypoxia. As I scouted ahead through the gulches, I looked back at Nick on the wagon seat. He seemed miniaturized and far away, and I was afraid that he wouldn't be there the next time I looked. My arms seemed grotesquely long and bent, as if I were looking at myself in a fun house mirror.

But these moments passed quickly and the oxygen deprivation helped too. With even the slightest exertion on foot, I felt light-headed and weak, disconnected from the ground underfoot and even from my arms and legs. Nothing worried me and my brain wouldn't engage with my old obsession for detail and following maps. At sunset, we finally found the BLM dirt road that followed the final stretch of the Sublette Cutoff ruts.

It was dark when we reached the asphalt road along Spring Creek, and the valley leading to Cokeville was grassy and cool. The evening inversion of colder air replenished our oxygen supply, and I felt better. The mule shoes clopping on tar soothingly mixed in the air with the splashing of the creek as it raced through the oxbows below the road. Water sprinklers hissed back and forth on the lawns of the horse farms, catching the light from the barns as thin, silvery fans.

Cokeville was quiet, except for the occasional rumble of a diesel semi or a freight train. The Union Pacific line running up from southern Wyoming rejoined our route on the west banks of the Bear River and, on the east banks, the shortcut between the big interstates of Wyoming and Idaho, Highway 30/89, had been paved right over the main ruts. After 350 miles of the desolate, original ruts, we had returned to the sandwiched transportation corridor of the modern trail.

Ahead of us, the only thing I could see was a familiar lit sign, the purple and orange logo of a Flying J truck stop. It was the only place we could camp and we pulled in, fenced the mules inside a dry, brown-grass field behind the truck parking lot, and then went inside to feast on hot dogs and fried chicken.

Exhausted, I climbed over the end boards of the wagon, flopped onto my mattress, and untied my bootlaces lying down. Behind me I could hear the humming of the truck stop and, now, instead of rivers flowing, I listened to the low rattling of air conditioners cooling the sleeper berths in the parked trucks. Through the wagon cover I could make out the high purple-black rim of Dempsey Ridge and the profound blackness of Rock Creek gorge. It still didn't seem possible that we'd come down through there. My stumblebum performance while watering the mules, and my bizarre longing for Nick when I hiked away from the wagon, seemed like mental lapses that had happened to someone else. That is the nocturnal Oregon Trail, just before welcome sleep. Time and distance seem implausibly stretched, and the day just experienced seems a long time ago.

O, Wyoming. I have always given my all to you, but you have paid back even more. But this time, Wyoming, you took everything I had.

A Union Pacific whistle shrieked at the Cokeville crossing and I listened as the clacking of the iron wheels faded north behind me. The whistle sounded at a few more road crossings, a receding, meditative wail that evoked space, the passages between mountains and rivers, the enormous energy and drive unleashed by the trail. Persistence is a drug that delivers strength, but it also dulls our sense of reality. My last thought before falling asleep was that we are all a lot more capable of conquering obstacles and fears than we think.

28

IDAHO BECAME OUR DAYS OF heaven stretch of the trail. The balsam vastness of the Bear River valley and then the Martian emptiness of the Snake River Gorge entranced us as the breezy afternoons of August passed by. There was nothing left to prove after five hundred miles of original ruts, and Nick and I happily rode along the two-lane highways and dusty back roads that crossed the surreal corridor of beauty that the pioneers saw. The old covered wagon stops—Register Rock, Three Island Crossing, Bruneau Dunes—were now comfortable state parks with barbecue pits, water hydrants, and horse corrals that conveniently appeared ahead in the early evening when we needed to camp. Oregon was just a month's ride away and now we wanted to live spontaneously and enjoy what the modern trail had come to be. At Soda Springs, we camped behind the ninth hole of the Oregon Trail Country Club. At Grand View, we hosed down the mules inside the car wash at Gus's Gas. In Lava Hot Springs, we rolled the wagon into the parking lot of Riverwalk Thai and I bought us a take-out lunch of drunken noodles and beef satay.

We could see right away how Idaho's spectacular geology had bedeviled the pioneers. At the end of the last ice age, fifteen thousand years ago, much of Utah and southern Idaho had been a vast inland body of water, Bonneville Lake. But the lake had suddenly breached above American

Falls and sent millions of cubic feet of water crashing over the volcanic landscape at seventy miles an hour, carving the dramatic basalt gorges along the Snake River. The breakage from the gorges was carried away by the racing water like shattered china and distributed as thick debris fields of lava rock that extended for miles along the riverbanks. The pioneers, dependent on the river both for navigation and for water, were trapped inside this volcanic skillet, just as they had been trapped by the cholera swamps along the Platte. Following the rock fields along the Snake exhausted the pioneers and their draft animals, and after just a few miles mule shoes and iron wheel rims were reduced to slivers. The river itself was close, but maddeningly inaccessible—the only route to the water was straight down perpendicular cliffs.

The pioneers struggled during the hot weeks of August over the lava-rock fields and steep mountain buttes along the gorges of the Snake River in Idaho.

In peak migration years like 1852, when sixty thousand pioneers crossed to California and Oregon, the calamities of overland travel were multiplied by the sheer number of wagons occupying the same narrow space along the river. By August the animal boneyards along the Snake exceeded what the pioneers had already seen on the alkali flats of Wyoming.

Esther Bell Hanna was a Pennsylvanian who crossed that year, and her narrative is considered important because she typified the thousands of ardent Christians who migrated in wagon trains strictly segregated by denomination, motivated more by religious zeal than financial necessity. At the age of eighteen Esther married a Presbyterian minister and left for the frontier the same day, joining a wagon train group planning a "Presbyterian Colony" that would populate the Pacific Northwest before rival Baptists and Methodists could establish too strong a foothold. (The more pious, the more schismatic, and the Hannas left the Presbyterian wagon train when the other families refused to stop their wagons all day to observe the Sabbath.) But there was no dispensation for the faithful from conditions on the trail. In her narrative *Canvas Caravans*, Hanna described the combined carrion field and invalid ward that stretched for three hundred miles after the wagon trains left the Bear and climbed for the Snake.

> I do not think I ever shall forget the sight of so many dead animals seen along the trail. It is like something out of Dante's Inferno—this barren waste of lava peopled with the skeletons of animals. . . . Lost two more oxen today out of our train, one drowned in the river, another died from fatigue. A camp near us at noon had 12 sick in it, all the same disease, some of them very low. . . . O for more patience to endure it all.

Every draft animal or head of beef that dropped represented a privation for the owner, either in terms of additional possessions that had to be jettisoned from the wagons, or lowered expectations of establishing a herd in the Northwest. In *Hard Road West*, historian and geologist Keith Heyer Meldahl describes how, by the time the travelers reached Idaho, "the accretion of hardships inevitably wore down spirits and civility." Meldahl quotes one particularly colorful 49er, Illinois pioneer Israel S. P. Lord, whose trail account was patched together from articles he sent back to Illinois for the *Western Christian* newspaper. Lord was one of the first pioneers to travel the Hudspeth Cutoff, a popular shortcut to the California Trail blazed in 1849 between Soda Springs and City of Rocks in southern Idaho. Lord described his fellow travelers as "cross, peevish, sullen, boisterous, giddy, profane, dirty, vulgar, ragged, mustachioed, bewhiskered, idle, petulant, quarrelsome, unfaithful, disobedient, refractory, careless, contrary, stubborn, hungry and without the fear of God and hardly of man before their eyes."

The Hudspeth Cutoff that we followed ourselves before picking up the main route along the Snake had been considerably softened over time, mostly by the extensive irrigation projects built during the homesteading years, and then by the paving of roads after World War I. Occasionally, cattle fences forced us up onto the plateau near the river and we spent long afternoons easing our wheels over fields of pumpkin-shaped lava rock. At the higher elevations along the Portneuf Range, the mules struggled through the passes and I was forced to empty our water barrels and walk behind the wagon to lighten our load. But by the evening the trail always seemed to deliver us to the hospitality of a Mormon ranch or a riverside park with spacious views toward the mountains. We were inured to the hard work and long days by now, and our passage along the Snake felt like a vacation.

The pleasant night sounds of our wagon camps in Idaho—mules eating, water spraying through irrigation sprinklers in the fields, our whitetop creaking in the wind—made me feel dreamy, contemplative, more willing to accept my motivations for making this trip. I was reminded of the same kind of overnight stops that I had made as a boy with my father. In the orange embers of our charcoal grill I could see the flames of my father's fires at Valley Forge or along the Delaware Canal. That was a half century ago, thousands of miles away, but the joyful vagabonding I had shared with him that summer felt here, now, joined, shared across elastic time. Maybe the Mormons are right about the living actively communicating with the dead and I was united forever with my father on an eternal covered wagon trip. I didn't understand now why I had spent the last few years worrying about turning out like him. Night after night in camp, while the sun fell as an orange disc against the distant Sawtooths, I was filled with acceptance, a soothing accommodation with aging and the passage of time. I was camping beside my covered wagon in Idaho, once more sealed with my father, enjoying the sunset in Pennsylvania along the Snake.

•   •   •

In Idaho, our tempo also changed. We had visitors, and we quickly acquired modern trappings of the "community vehicle" that Daniel Boorstin
had described. I was grateful all summer about my decision not to include
family members and friends on our ride, mostly because I quickly realized that very few of them could endure the regimen of filth and drudgery
that Nick and I by now embraced, and I was too obsessed with reaching
Oregon to want anyone along who might slow us down. But I made one
exception, knowing that by central Idaho I would feel more relaxed and
willing to make compromises, curbing my mile-Nazi tendencies now that
Oregon was almost in sight.

Two of my closest friends, George and Cindy Rousseau, a flying
couple from the eastern shore of Maryland, had begged to come along on
the wagon ride as soon as they heard about my plans. I temporized at first,
but still I considered them excellent candidates for covered wagon travel.
George is a mechanical ace and nonstop tinkerer, and he could take a lot
of the burden of wagon repairs off Nick. Cindy, a trim, brown-faced brain-
iac out of the Jewish suburbs of Baltimore, has fabulous life skills. She
harvests wild mushrooms and berries, hunts rabbits with hawks, and her
favorite hobby is collecting and restoring fucked-up friends. In the woods,
her map reading and scrappy, sarcastic banter are top-notch.

When we talked on the phone one night, about a month before they
were going to come, however, Cindy told me that George couldn't get
vacation time in August. She had decided to bring along a friend of ours,
her current project, Donna Moran, who was in the middle of a divorce
and, Cindy said, could use the "covered wagon cure." We agreed that they
would fly to Salt Lake in mid-August, find a rental car, and track us down
on the trail.

We were up early to hitch the wagon the day Cindy and Donna
were scheduled to arrive and I was happy about the timing. We would
be spending most of the day climbing up and down the foothills west of
Lava Hot Springs, on a section of original trail called Old Oregon Trail
Road, and so our guests' first impressions would be formed by the kind of
authentic surroundings we'd seen all summer. But as I pushed the mules
through the canyons behind town to reach the trail, Nick's Forward Sens-
ing Olfactory Radar picked up a strong signal below. He pointed two

fingers south, toward the Sunnyside Sinclair and Deli along the highway, where the rooftop fan was discharging a big lardy cloud of cooking exhaust.

"They're cookin fried chicken down there," he said. "It's real good fried chicken too. I can tell."

I was disgusted because I wanted Cindy and Donna to see us first on real trail, but Nick insisted that he needed a "healthy breakfast."

So, we took the Fried Chicken Cutoff for Nick. As we clattered down the hill and crunched across the gravel parking lot of the Sinclair, we saw Cindy and Donna leaning against the hood of their rental car—they had seen our white-top from the highway. They had left Salt Lake very early and they both looked eager for trail. Cindy, dressed in camouflage cargo shorts and a rimmed sun hat, had water bottles dangling from her belt loops, and she was testing a new solar charger that she had bought for the trip, so she could charge her smartphone and track our progress across the trail via GPS. Donna, the ultimate tall, skinny blonde, was applying suntan oil to her long, thin legs. Stereoscopic images of the mules reflected in the lenses of their sunglasses as we approached.

Cindy started flashing away with her smartphone camera.

"Oh, look at you guys!" she said. "This is so cool! I'm posting these pictures, right away. No one believes that I'm really going on a covered wagon trip."

Having visitors along was fun right away. Nick and I couldn't believe how quickly Cindy and Donna were able to identify each mule, just from the descriptions I'd sent in my occasional emails. Olive Oyl, ecstatic to have girlfriends around, was dancing on her hind legs and begging for scratches. Nick loved the company and was wonderfully hospitable. The arrival of two upmarket women from the east coast naturally drew out his Wagon Professor Buck. He patiently gave them mule-driving lessons, explained every piece of harness, and regaled them all day with his fishing and sleigh-driving yarns.

Cindy was aware of my worrywart reservations about having company and determined to fulfill one vow she had made about the trip.

"Okay, what's our goal for the day?" she said. "I promised you, Rinker. We are *not* slowing your ass down."

"I'd like to make the rodeo corrals at McCammon by late afternoon,"

I said. "Most of it is original trail along the Portneuf River, and then we follow that to the Snake."

"Okay. I'll GPS it," Cindy said.

"Fine, Cindy, but we have maps. That solar charger is going to conk out within an hour and then you won't have GPS. Chill. We have maps."

"Luddite. Just because we're on a covered wagon trip doesn't mean we can't use GPS. I really don't want to put up with your technophobia all week."

"Cindy, I'm the one who just came fifteen hundred miles with this rig, but now I need your GPS?"

"Dickhead."

"Cindy, you just got here, and you're already calling me 'dickhead.' That's probably a record."

"Oh, look, I've got it," she said, waving her index finger to move the GPS map forward on her phone. "Old Oregon Trail Road to East Sublette Road, and then we turn north for the river. This is going to be fun!"

We decided to divide into teams. Nick would take Donna in the wagon for a long mule-calling lesson in the morning while Cindy and I scouted ahead in the rental car. Then Cindy and I would run the team the rest of the way up the Portneuf in the afternoon while Nick and Donna took the rental car and shopped for dinner.

It was a delightful day, not simply because I enjoyed the reunion with an old friend and Nick and I needed time away from each other. Cindy had always been skeptical about my claims about the West and thought that I exaggerated the *Riders of the Purple Sage* splendor of my surroundings, but that was just the kind of day we had. In the afternoon, as Cindy and I climbed the old wagon road toward McCammon, low cottony cumulus clouds raked the peaks and a cowboy herding steers on a gorgeous dapple-gray horse galloped over, asked about our trip, and gave us directions for a shortcut around the interstate into McCammon. Children on bikes circled the wagon as we pulled into the outskirts of town and I borrowed a barbecue grill from a couple sitting on their porch, stowing it in the back of the provision cart.

When we reached the rodeo corrals, Cindy and Donna were great about falling into the routines of camp. They helped us unharness the team and cooed at the mules and babied them during washes, giving them extra-long shampoos. Olive Oyl had completely transferred her loyalty to the girls and wouldn't leave their side. It was great, introducing some femininity to our wagon trip. But we nearly had a trail mutiny when we started unloading the wagon.

Back in Annapolis, Donna is a marathon entertainer and chef, and the kitchen in her McMansion sparkles like the glass counters at an Apple Store. Cindy had warned me about that—Donna needed a covered wagon trip, she said, to cure her neat freak—but I had forgotten what she said. When I handed out the plastic dairy cases that we kept our kitchen gear in, Donna looked at our pots and pans and dishes and stood straight up with one hand on her hip and the other pinching her nose.

"This is disgusting," she said. "I am *not* cooking on top of filth like this."

Cindy came over for a look herself.

"This is revolting," she said. "Rinker, you used to be so clean and neat."

I didn't think our kitchen gear looked that bad. A few of our dishes were stuck together because the night before we had accidentally spilled some harness oil on them after dinner, and clusters of dog hair, hayseed, and oats had stuck to our fingerprints. I had scraped most of the scorched Minute Rice, Wesson Oil, and Hormel chili, no beans, off of the pots and pans. Yes, our food coolers were shiny with cooking oil and axle grease and slipped out of our hands on a rainy day. But this was normal. Everything was shipshape, exactly as it should be on a covered wagon trip.

I explained to Cindy that I washed the dishes myself every morning.

"What did you wash them with?" Cindy said. "Motor oil?"

"A caveman wouldn't eat on these plates," Donna said. "Get out of here while we do a rescue clean."

Nick walked over to see what the fuss was about. He pulled an undershirt out of our laundry bag and began rubbing the grime off the frying pan.

"Ladies, ladies, ladies," he said. "Let's not panic here. I've got some Grease Monkey Scrub in my tool kit and I'll shine these pots right up for ya."

Donna raised her voice now.

"Go. Both of you. Out of this camp for an hour."

Perhaps I could smooth things over by offering to help.

"Cindy," I said. "While you wash, I can dry, okay?"

"Did you hear her, dickhead?" Cindy shrieked. "Out! Out of this camp! Why don't you go somewhere and take a shower!"

"There's detergent and Scotch Brite in the bottom of the green cooler," I said. "I'll get it for you."

"Go! Out of this camp!"

I looked over my shoulder as Nick and I meekly walked toward town, and what I saw is still one of my favorite images of the trip. Cindy and Donna were bent over a plastic washbasin with our kitchen equipment spread out on the grass. Olive Oyl snoozed in the shade of the wagon behind them. The pressure nozzle on the hose was spraying a rainbow-colored fan of water, and the wind picked up the foamy detergent along Cindy and Donna's tanned arms and blew it away in bubbles.

When we got back an hour later the whole camp smelled like Brillo pads and Palmolive cleanser. Cindy and Donna had even washed the mule buckets, our camp chairs, and the wagon seat.

Cindy didn't believe my claims about western nightlife either. After my trips herding cattle or covering wildfires in Wyoming or Arizona, I often described to her how I would drive every night to the nearest set of public corrals and camp, enjoying the carefree, bumptious company that I found at the local rodeo grounds. The rodeo corrals of the West, like the Dairy Queens in the Midwest, are major dating sites. The fun, wisecracking cowgirls and their hunky boyfriends all start rolling into the corrals together around six o'clock in the evening, in pickups towing horse trailers, four or five teenagers sitting on each other's laps in the cab. For the rest of the night they goof off and flirt, cook hot dogs and steaks on barbecue grills, smoke and sneak beers, and then saddle up and chase around the ring for a couple of hours, practicing their roping or barrel-race turns for the summer rodeos. There's always an extra horse and I loved those nights in the West, cantering around the rings with a pack of young riders.

"You're such an exaggerator—nobody lives that way anymore," Cindy said a couple of times when I told her about my latest trip. "You just go to the corrals to look at pretty girls."

But, sure enough, the teenagers in their pickups and horse trailers started to arrive about an hour after we got to the McCammon corrals.

While Donna cooked up a shish kebob feast on the grill, Cindy and I helped the rodeo kids unload and saddle their horses. They were an attractive group, mostly just fifteen or sixteen, but seeming much older because they were so experienced with their mounts.

Cindy and I sat high on the rodeo bleachers, sharing some wine, watching the riders circle on their horses.

"Okay, so I'm sorry," Cindy said. "I never should have doubted what you said about life out here. Will it be like this every night?"

"Pretty much. All you have to do is roll in with the rig, and the fun begins. Everyone wants to be a part of your trip."

"Nobody cares where you camp?"

"Nobody cares. Just live."

"Okay, so how are you doing? You look so trim."

"Yeah, thanks. From Ash Hollow in Nebraska to here, I've probably walked four hundred miles ahead of the wagon, jacking fences. I must have lost twenty-five pounds."

"Drinking? What about drinking? You're only getting one more wine tonight, by the way."

"Cindy, I got drunk one night in early July in a cowboy bar in Glenrock, Wyoming. The ranchers were buying, okay? But that was seven hundred miles ago. No drinking. There's no time to drink when you're running mules and scouting trail."

"Okay, sleeping. What about sleeping? Maybe you actually sleep now?"

"Like an old dog. There's no insomnia on the Oregon Trail."

"Okay, reading. What about the reading?"

"Cindy, you're not going to believe this one, but nothing. I've read exactly two pages of Wallace Stegner since we left. What is reading, anyway? I don't even remember that person. I don't have time for reading."

"Oh, boy," Cindy said. "Where are we? What state are we in, again?"

"Idaho."

"Idaho. But they have doctors, right? They must have doctors in Idaho. We can get you checked."

"Ha, ha, ha. Let's eat dinner, and then we'll put up your tent."

The McCammon corrals swelled with sociability that night. Two draft-horse couples from nearby ranches, towing along their grandchildren, dropped by to inspect the Schuttler and our mules, and they gave us several bales of alfalfa hay. More teenagers pulled in with their horse vans, and the rodeo grounds began to fill up with young families and children as an amateur-league softball game began on the diamond nearby. The town maintenance man dropped over to visit and tell us that he had relocated the lawn sprinklers so that they wouldn't spray on Cindy and Donna's tent. He would leave the door to the restrooms near the ball field unlocked for the night.

After dinner we borrowed a couple of horses and took turns galloping around the rodeo ring, and I was surprised by how well Donna rode. Cindy and I stood with our arms resting on the top rail of the arena fence, watching her circuit on a buckskin mare. Donna leaned in almost perfectly with the gait of the horse, signaling a turn more with her body than the reins, and then pulled up in front of us in a wisp of dust.

"Go, girl," I said. "How come you didn't tell us you could ride so well?"

"It's only my third or fourth time on a horse," Donna said. "I love this out here!"

Then she galloped off again.

"See, what did I tell you?" Cindy said. "This is so good for her. It's the covered wagon cure."

Nick and I felt joyfully reunited as a wagon pair after Cindy and Donna left. West of American Falls the contrasts in the landscape passed like a lyrical microcosm of America. Out past Dietrich and Gooding, where the ground is irrigated, there is a green Eden of dairy farms that looks like Minnesota. Other stretches along the Snake, where the land is not watered, could pass for Death Valley. Along the Owyhee Mountains south of Boise, the August potato and onion harvest was under way, and the open trucks racing by with several tons of pungent onions made the mules sneeze. We camped several times at state fishing pullouts along the Snake. In the morning I loved waking early, stuffing our dishes and pots from the night before into my knapsack, hiking down to a quiet cove along the river, stripping bare, and stepping into the water up to my chest. I floated the dishes and a bottle of detergent out behind me to wash them, and then held them farther out to rinse in the current. While I shaved, by looking at the reflection of my face in the river, iridescent circles of soap and dish detergent eddied downstream.

By Homedale, at the western edge of Idaho, the long stretches of lava-rock fields and concrete highways had worn the mule shoes down to thin, shiny shards of steel. We stopped for two days and camped at the fairgrounds in town to find blacksmiths and to grease the wheels. Nick hitched a ride with a rancher back to American Falls to retrieve his pickup. Homedale was an enjoyable, civilized respite for us in a quintessential American small town, and we ate breakfast and dinner at the Owyhee Lanes and Restaurant, bowling after dinner before we returned to camp.

Still, our domicile at the fairgrounds and the pleasant routines of Homedale made me feel hemmed in, stalled. More than three months of obsessing for miles had turned me into a feral, nomadic creature who couldn't stop moving, and life was no longer life for me when the wagon wasn't pushing west all day. At dawn, I shivered through an hour of anxiety while I fed and watered the mules. I could almost smell Oregon now, but we weren't *there* yet. It was only eight miles away and I couldn't stand the suspense.

The morning when it was time to go, Nick helped me harness the mules and then leaned against the metal gate of the fairground corrals, looking down and gently toeing the dust with one boot. He pushed his cowboy hat back on his head and looked up.

"Boss, I'm headin into town for hardware parts, and then I think I'm goin to do some clothes at the Laundromat. Okay?"

"Nick, *now*?" I said. "Now?"

"Rinker, I think you should drive this last stretch into Oregon by yourself. This is your trip. You decided to do it. I really like the idea of getting back to Maine and telling everyone that you drove the mules into Oregon alone."

"You think I should do that?"

"I think you should do that."

And so, solo with the mules, I drove the last, dream stretch into Oregon. It was a beautiful, cool morning to be alone on a wagon, and the harness jingled and the iron rims sang as I passed the alfalfa farms and the irrigated orchards along the quiet road west. The country in western Idaho is hilly, and from the tops of the rises I could see the golden folds of the Owyhee Mountains ahead. I passed a mobile home with lovely gardens and my heart started to race when we reached the Stateline Store: GAS—BEER—POP. At Deer Flat I saw the large green sign ahead and started to sing to the mules.

WELCOME TO OREGON

I wanted to cry but couldn't, I wished Nick were there to share this with me, and I was proud of my mules. There was a nice breeze on my face as I talked to the team and I thought again of my father and what I would tell him now. *Thank you, Dad, for raising us so crazyass, because that was the reason I could not only imagine this trip, but do it too.* Right then, I didn't mind at all being just who I was—a loopy, anachronistic, dreaming jackass who had crossed to Oregon in a covered wagon. That was the journey I dreamed for myself and now we were there.

At the large green WELCOME TO OREGON sign I pulled the team onto the sandy shoulder of the road and tapped the sign with my hand as we passed by.

"Twelve shoes in Oregon, Team! Big Team! Big Team! Jake! Beck! Bute! Big Team! Twelve shoes in Oregon, Team."

The road into Oregon from there twists beautifully down into an agricultural valley along North Alkali Creek. Irrigated alfalfa and soybean fields are planted like wall-to-wall carpeting across the bottomlands and, to the west, brown grasslands rise to the Owyhee Range. I passed several horse farms, and, at one of them, a buckaroo wearing a wide sombrero straw hat was saddling a chesty palomino-paint at a hitching post beside a red barn. He waved, quickly finished cinching his saddle girth, and galloped out to meet the wagon. The cowboy was named Clyde and he was training the paint for a client up in Prairie City. He rode beside me for an hour and we talked, and the spontaneous trail companionship seemed like something I had dreamed for myself about arriving in Oregon.

A few miles ahead, the road joined some low grassy banks along the Snake. Clyde tied his horse to the rear wheel of the Schuttler, climbed onto the wagon seat, and held the lines while I watered the mules from the river.

Clyde galloped off after that, a friendly cowboy on a pretty paint disappearing into the green bottomlands. On the road ahead, the wheels rhythmically sounded on the pavement joints, and my blue jeans were refreshingly wet and cool from watering the team. The scent of freshly mowed alfalfa was hypnotic. I was in Oregon now, alone with my mules on the road toward Keeney Pass, and I didn't think that I would ever again enjoy such a perfect day.

29

PROBABLY VERY FEW NINETEENTH-CENTURY OVERLANDERS believed the exaggerated claims about pigs fattening to the size of cows and turnips growing as big as pumpkins in the fertile Pacific Northwest, but nevertheless there was a widely shared assumption that Oregon would be grassy and arboreal. Disillusionment was the reward for getting there. The long "rain shadow" cast by the distant Cascades limited precipitation to eight inches or less a year on the lee side of the mountains. Eastern Oregon is the far edge of the Great American Desert and the pioneers and their failing draft animals would struggle across another three hundred miles of salt flats and yellowish-brown ravines before they reached the green Willamette Valley.

For the wagons, eastern Oregon became one long breakdown lane. After banging over every rock and dry creek bed along 1,700 miles of river frontage, and drying out and cracking in the desert heat, the Schuttlers and the Studebakers were falling apart faster than the pioneers could repair them. Many pioneers, following the example of Marcus and Narcissa Whitman, cut their disintegrating wagons into one-axle carts and continued on with a single draft animal. When those broke down too, they walked or rode the rest of the way to the Columbia River and then boated down to the Pacific coast.

There was no single way to reach the end of the trail and a lively atmosphere of experimentation prevailed, turning the last stretch to the Pacific into a busy jalopy and boat works. As far back as the middle Snake, many pioneers decided to leave their wheels and running gear behind. Then they caulked the wagon boxes and floated them downriver, making long, difficult portages between the Snake and the smaller rivers ahead, following a meandering northwest course to the Columbia. In high-water years, these unwieldy wagon scows capsized in the rapids, and in low-water years they ran aground, and the rivers continued to exact sizable death tolls. Accurately calculating the percentage of wagons that made it all the way across is impossible today, but probably no more than half of the white-tops that left the jumping-off grounds along the Missouri finally made it past the Cascades intact.

The scuttled wagons and parts along the linear junkyard of eastern Oregon rarely sat for very long on the desert floor. Milled lumber was a valuable asset in frontier America and it was aggressively recycled, often more than once. During the flatboat and canal era in the 1830s and 1840s, coal, grain, and livestock from Pennsylvania, Ohio, and the upper Midwest were floated to markets in New Orleans and beyond along the Mississippi river system. After the cargo was unloaded, some of these flatboats were poled back upriver, but that was arduous work and few river men enjoyed taking on the Mississippi's powerful southern flow. Import-export towns like New Orleans were rapidly expanding at the time and needed lumber. On the Louisiana waterfront, the flatboats were carefully disassembled and the deck planking and framing timber were sold to be planed for houses, furniture, and wagons. The salvage value of Wisconsin or Illinois lumber carried downriver as a flatboat often delivered a large share of the profits for a cargo trip, and hundreds of boats were built every year with the explicit idea of quick resale on the New Orleans waterfront.

In the 1850s, the same kind of industry was built up at the Dalles and other settlements along the Columbia River. For a fee, teams of carpenters would take apart a wagon and use the parts to fashion a raft or a keelboat, sometimes even building a crude sleeping shanty on deck, and the pioneers continued toward the Willamette Valley on these marine contraptions. Commercial boat operators also hauled paying passengers downstream, many of them accepting payment in the form of wagons and teams. At Portland and Oregon City, most of these vessels were converted to fishing boats or river ferries, or taken apart and sold by the board foot as housing or furniture lumber. In most years, of course, the majority of wagons that reached Oregon managed to struggle over the Blue Mountains ahead and then follow the Barlow Road Cutoff around the Cascades. But hundreds of thousands of board feet of milled lumber also reached the west coast as wagon salvage, providing building material for mining camps, farms, and the burgeoning cities of northern California and Oregon.

It's interesting to speculate just how far a single board from a covered wagon might have traveled, and how many uses it served before ending up as tavern flooring or siding on a livery barn in Portland or Sacramento. Certainly the leftovers from the estimated 150,000 wagons that crossed the western trail system was a lot of wood. At antique stores in Oregon and California, I've seen plenty of blanket chests and old hutches with handwritten placards stating that they have been "expertly" appraised by antique furniture specialists and labeled "19th Century, Real Wagon Boards." It's a great sales pitch and, in many cases, probably true. Given the hand-me-down nature of the nineteenth century's rural economy, it's not far-fetched to conceive of the greatest land migration in history as something more than a removal of needy families and religious zealots to cheap Western lands. The iconic covered wagons churning up dust on their way toward Oregon were also a massive transfer of valuable resources from the forested East to the drier West.

Oregon flummoxed us in the same way that it flummoxed the pioneers. The alkali flats stretching up from the Snake microwaved with dry heat, and, as I knelt in the sand to open cattle gates, dust devils blew down from the Owyhee hills. In Nyssa, we passed an outdoor bank clock registering 102 degrees, and I noticed that night that the metal frames of my sunglasses had left barbecue marks on my face. Our cart wheels got hung up on a gatepost at Keeney Pass above Vale, and we spent half an hour on the scorching summit grunting and heaving the wheels back onto the trail. Oh, sumptuous, verdant Oregon, the land of my dreams! Rinker, you may be the first wagon traveler in a century to cross the trail, but you are also that century's most gullible dunce.

Nick spent two days fixated on wagon repair while we camped at the rodeo corrals along the Malheur River in Vale. A few days before, I had spoken by cell phone with Don Werner in Kansas. Our Trail Pup wheels had been rebuilt and I had him ship them to Idaho, where I had found a trucker to haul the Trail Pup and new wheels to Oregon and then return our borrowed cart to Wyoming. Keeping the wagons moving across the trail was getting expensive—all told, I had now spent over $5,000 on Trail Pup repairs and shipping.

When I scouted the trail ahead, my expectations about enjoying a leisurely run down the home stretch were dashed. The ruts north of Vale up through Alkali Gulch were as authentic and beautiful as the Acropolis stretch in Wyoming, but we were blocked again by an interstate. When the interstate highway system was built in the 1950s, the Oregon Department of Transportation solved the problem of routing traffic through the narrow canyons and over mountain ridges of the state by selecting the proven terrain of the pioneers. U.S. Highway 84—today called the "Old Oregon Trail Highway"—covers long stretches of the original Oregon Trail ruts throughout the state. Searching for a route around the interstate on the seven-thousand-acre Birch Creek Ranch, I found a prominent stone trail marker high up in the Owyhee foothills, but the trail route below became a morass of muddy cattle tracks that disappeared into a man-made lake, Love Reservoir, which was built early in the twentieth century to sustain a large cattle operation.

Dejected and sunburned, my water canteen empty after a long afternoon of hiking the Owyhee foothills, I sat on a rock near the muddy fringes of Love Reservoir, once again stymied by trail interruptus. This was the story of our trip, the conundrum of the modern trail. My beloved ruts had just vanished under a lake and ahead, behind a screen of craggy badlands, they were paved over by a four-lane highway.

As I glumly climbed back up the foothills, I found a NO TRESPASSING sign at a barbed-wire gate, with a phone number for a land management company back in Idaho. I called that night when I had cell reception in Vale. Rancher Vince Holtz was excited to hear from me. Holtz ran a typical western agricultural operation—crop farming and a large seed-growing business in western Idaho, and rangeland for cattle at the Birch Creek Ranch in Oregon, seventy miles away. He had heard about our trip when we passed just a few miles from his farm near Marsing, Idaho, and was thrilled that someone was making an authentic crossing of the trail. He had spent the week worried that we would get lost when we reached the last trail marker on his ranch at Willow Creek. But he had no way of contacting us and was happy when I called.

"Oh, a guy can easily get lost up there," he told me on the phone. "But there's a way through on original trail around the lake. I'll come up there tomorrow and lead you through."

I didn't like the idea of inconveniencing the proprietor of a substantial ranch, but Holtz insisted on driving up from Idaho the next day and guiding us. He turned out to be one of the best finds of the trip. But our struggle was far from over and I would soon learn why the pioneers considered eastern Oregon unremitting hell.

The Trail Pup was my Gettysburg, my Gallipoli, my perpetual Pearl Harbor and Dien Bien Phu. The invention that I was so proud of, and which had made our trip possible, just wouldn't stop boomeranging back to torture me. It was my Watergate on wheels, my $13,000 boondoggle of the trail.

Nick and I decided that, because we were now only a camp or two from Farewell Bend, we might as well keep the pickup with us until we decided where to end the trip. So, while he lingered behind in Vale for a healthy breakfast of fried chicken and tater tots, I pushed north out of town in the wagon alone, singing to the mules as the irrigated alfalfa country went by, then turning north a few miles above town for the marked trail up through the salt flats of Alkali Gulch.

Everything was running well and I loved pushing mules up the mountains through classic trail country, alone on the wagon. Antelope bounded by on the scrub-grass hills and prairie falcons swooped low over the range. The salt flats were as hard as pavement and it was a joy looking back over the rig and seeing my jaunty Trail Pup, freshly rebuilt by Nick, bouncing along behind the main wagon with its American flag dancing in the wind.

Nick was delayed when a part of his bumper fell off as he bounced through Alkali Gulch. He circled back to look for the missing part, which put him out of cell phone contact, when I dropped behind a tall, rounded peak beside the trail, Tub Mountain. I was in the middle of singing one of my favorite songs, "I'm a Ramblin' Wreck from Georgia Tech," to the mules when I heard a loud *bang!* from the rear. The mules started digging in to pull a suddenly heavier load.

"Team, whoa! Whoa! Jake. Just relax now. Jake, hold them."

I didn't have to look back to know what had happened—it was the Lisco sound that I heard, the South Pass sound of splintering wood and then a heavy cart collapsing and dragging on the sand. The Trail Pup was down.

When I did stand up and look back over the white-top, I could see that both of the shiny new cart wheels were intact, but angled in and resting against the box, collapsed from the center. It was axle failure this time. Now I would have to wait in hundred-degree heat for Nick to catch up, and once more pause and reorganize for repairs.

I should have been crying, but I could only laugh at myself. We were twelve miles from Vale, twenty-four hours after Nick had completed a $5,000 rebuild on the cart. It was not even noon yet. It took only that long for the Trail Pup to once more shit the bed. Everything on the trip had gone so well so far, except for this one small problem of staffing that I had overlooked. Yes, Rinker Buck, the twenty-first-century trail boss and wagon architect, had undeniably designed one of the most attractive Trail Pups since the fur-trading days. It complemented the Schuttler as adorably as a shiny Airstream Bambi following an SUV down the highway. For reliability, however, the Rinker Buck Trail Pup was the Chernobyl of the Oregon Trail.

For some odd reason that I still can't figure out—except that memory does work in strange and amusing ways—I was reminded that moment of sitting in a movie theater as a boy and listening to the lyrics of a popular Rodgers and Hammerstein number from *South Pacific*. While taking baths on a palm-fringed Hawaiian beach, Mitzi Gaynor and the rest of the female cast spontaneously broke into song, lamenting the state of their boyfriend relationships. I've always loved the tune and, now that it was so appropriate, I began singing it to the mules, improvising my own lyrics.

I'm gonna wash that man right outa my hair
And send him on his way.

I'm gonna throw that Trail Pup into the Snake
I'm gonna throw that Trail Pup into the Snake
I'm gonna throw that Trail Pup into the Snake
Deep-six that fucker today.

The song therapy felt good and I was at one with my life, my mules, and my wagon. Desert meadowlarks sang along with me from the hills and the mules contentedly munched on wild sunflowers growing beside the trail. I had screwed the poodle again. Big fucking deal. Littering the trail once more with broken wagon parts and freshly splintered wood just made me a better pioneer.

As he came over the rise in his pickup, Nick excitedly honked his horn and skidded to a stop behind the crippled Trail Pup.

"This Trail Pup is like a bad girlfriend," he said. "She never goes away."

"We're throwing that fucker into the Snake as soon as we get to Farewell Bend," I said.

Wagon Professor Buck quickly diagnosed what had happened. The cast-iron hub skeins on the wheels were connected to the wooden axle on either side with a big lag bolt extending several inches into the oak. The lag bolt hadn't failed, but the oak axle had, probably from sitting out in the open in Don Werner's Kansas pasture for years, then drying out after bouncing across a thousand miles of desert.

"Running gear failure," Nick said. "Metal to wood is your weak point in every rig."

I quickly decided that we would again abandon the Trail Pup beside the trail. We could always find a cowboy ahead who would help us retrieve it later. Nick yanked the drop-pin attaching the Trail Pup to the main wagon and I heard the tongue drop to the trail with an ignominious plop. While he unloaded the water barrels and provisions in the cart into his pickup, I would drive ahead to meet Vince Holtz at Willow Creek.

And so, cheerfully singing "I'm Gonna Wash That Man Right Outa My Hair" to the mules, I climbed the wagon up through the sunny Owyhees. Calamities seemed to suit me and I was filled with a lightness of being. The skin on my hands was stretched tight and baked translucent by the sun, and I was now so thin that my belt hung loose on my waist. Abandoning the Trail Pup had reduced our load by a ton and the mules were giddy about pulling the lightened rig. In country as golden as the wheat hills of Montana, my wagon was light, the lines were feathery in my hands, and the wheels padded gently over a cushion of dust. I wanted to ride my Schuttler forever.

In the West, you can always tell the working ranchers from the rich-boy hobbyists out of Jackson and Palo Alto—the real deal could easily be mistaken for the service manager at the local John Deere dealership. As I climbed the rises through Birch Creek Ranch, I could see Vince Holtz far ahead, leaning against the fender of his battered pickup and photographing the wagon and the mules as I approached. He was tall, rangy, and white-haired, with a boyish face and hands that were calloused and smudged from turning a lot of wrenches. He wore a Carhartt T-shirt, ratty jeans, and scuffed black work shoes.

I apologized for being late and explained that we'd just dumped our provision cart behind us on the trail. Nick was still back there loading our hay and oats into his pickup.

"Oh, you don't have to leave your wagon on the trail," Vince said. "How big is it?"

"Half the size of this wagon here."

"I'm going back to help your brother. We can easily fit the cart in my truck and I know a shop in Huntington where we can fix it."

Vince handed me bottles of chilled Gatorade and spring water from a cooler in the back of his pickup and told me to wait for him at the next cattle gate. When I reached it, I steered the mules into another large bloom of sunflowers and sat in the bright sunlight singing some more tunes to them.

When Nick and Vince finally came up, we formed a jaunty, shitrig caravan of vehicles, bobbing up and down the hills. The Trail Pup and its wheels hung off the back of Vince's pickup and bales of hay and our gear were stacked high on Nick's Toyota. Vince led the way through his ranch, turning northeast for Love Reservoir at the Oregon Trail marker below Willow Springs Camp. I followed with the wagon and Nick brought up the rear. I could relax and just enjoy driving through lovely country now. For the rest of the day Vince would guide us through Birch Creek Ranch, and he knew the way to Farewell Bend on the original trail.

We had lost a lot of time monkeying around with the Trail Pup and our trip through Birch Creek Ranch would be the longest day all summer. After he guided us around the lake and over the steep dam embankment on the far side, Vince stopped several times to explain how the first homesteaders had built their aqueduct down from the hills, and then fenced in the old Oregon Trail country for cattle range. He showed us the deep wagon swales that still exist on his lower ranch. All of this took time and we didn't stop the wagon and fence in the mules until eleven o'clock that night. It was after midnight when we finally dumped the remains of the Trail Pup at the Snake River Garage in Huntington.

The mules had been in harness for fifteen hours, but I was elated. For four months now, from St. Joe, I had carried on the back of the wagon the SEE AMERICA SLOWLY sign that identified Farewell Bend as our destination, our end-of-the-trail goal. We were now camped just a mile away from the old pioneer stop on the Snake.

I thanked Vince for a great day and told him that I was worried that he still had an hour's drive to get back to his farm in Idaho.

"Oh, it's no big deal," he said. "If a guy decides to make a trip like this?"

"Right."

"Things work out. I'm just lucky I met you."

I thanked him again and he rolled down his window after stepping into his pickup.

"I'll see you soon. My wife really wants to meet your mules."

Fantails of welding sparks sprayed through the air as Nick and the owner of the Snake River Garage, Steve Stacy, rebuilt the Trail Pup axle. It was another repair interlude that morphed into a covered wagon party for us. Merri Melde, a photographer and endurance rider whom we had met back in Idaho, drove up for the weekend to share camp and shoot pictures of us riding the trail. Vince Holtz and his wife, Sue, drove back to Huntington with a large shopping bag full of apples for the mules and seemed to be very taken with the team. We all sat around on lawn chairs in the shade of the cottonwood trees at the garage, drinking coffee and eating take-out breakfast burritos while we watched the axle being rebuilt.

We faced one more peril ahead. To get around another stretch of the interstate, we would have to follow the original ruts that climbed a notorious wagon graveyard in the ravines above the town of Lime, the Burnt River Canyon. The fifth-generation owners of the mountaintop ranch that the ruts crossed were excited about guiding us through the area, and they were certain that no wagon had been over the original trail there in more than a hundred years.

But there was a big hazard at the end, along the Burnt River below the canyons. When the first railroads were introduced to eastern Oregon in the 1880s, the surveyors were so intent on following the favorable Oregon Trail terrain along the river that they laid the rails adjacent to the ruts. Freight trains ran through this section of track several times a day, after emerging through the tunnel on the north face of Lookout Mountain. If a locomotive roared through we would have no warning until the train was almost on top of us. Then we would be sharing the trail with a mile-long freight train, separated by only a few feet.

Steve Stacy offered to round up enough pickup trucks and trailers to ferry the mules and wagons north along the interstate. But I was entranced by the opportunity to cover another fifteen miles of original ruts, and I didn't want to truck the mules after 1,800 miles of unassisted wagon travel. I would take my chances with the trains.

On our second day in Huntington, I was anxious to put the Burnt River Canyon ruts behind us, but Nick and Steve were still finishing the repairs on the Trail Pup. I decided to forge ahead over the canyons with Merri Melde, and Nick and Steve would catch up with us late in the day, bringing the repaired cart forward on a trailer.

It was a fun, rigorous day, with some of the toughest driving of the whole trip. Merri clicked away with her camera while I threaded the team through the ravines, and by late in the afternoon we had splashed across the last creek and reached the bottom of the canyon. I pulled the mules up to water them, a few feet away from the Union Pacific tracks.

I stared down the track, which disappeared into the foothills along the narrow river plain. Our graveled route literally abutted the tracks to the left, and there was a steep embankment sloping down to the right where the ground had been built up to lay the elevated track bed. We faced a classic runaway scenario if a train rumbled out of the Lookout Mountain tunnel behind us and spooked the mules. They would probably protect themselves by not turning left onto the tracks, or right over the embankment, but instead galloping straight ahead to escape the sound of the train.

I told Merri that if a train arrived and the team took off, I would let the mules run themselves out. Once they realized that the rushing sound behind them was a train—something they recognized by now—they would tire and slow down.

"I read somewhere that if a team takes off, it's better to stay on the wagon instead of jumping off," Merri said. "Is that true?"

"I don't know," I said. "But stay with the wagon. I may need you to hold one line and help me control the team."

Of course, just a minute or two after we turned down the access road and were committed, I heard the metallic echoing of wheels against rails and the muffled roar of turbine exhaust funneling out of the Lookout Mountain tunnel behind us. I knew that the freight train would be a big one—more than a mile long—and that it would clatter and bang over the rails for almost fifteen minutes, less than three feet from the mules.

But I was also counting on one thing. All the way across from Missouri we'd met Union Pacific trains along the trail, though never as close as this, and the engineers had always waved and slowed down the trains as they passed. In June, we had met several engineers at the big Union Pacific yards in North Platte and they told us that they were all exchanging information about our crossing, keeping up with our progress across the West. The fraternity of trainmen knew that the Union Pacific tracks hugged the Oregon Trail across the continent, and this was the first time they had encountered a covered wagon. They loved seeing our white-tops and fluttering American flag from a distance. This engineer would have to know about us. My luck across the plains had been good so far. I hadn't reached the Burnt River Canyon in Oregon just to meet the one engineer in a hundred who didn't recognize the Schuttler with the American flag along his tracks. The mules might not spook if I could just get the engineer to slow down and ease past us with his turbines at an idle.

When the locomotive was a hundred yards off, I gave the lines to Merri and stood up on the seat, waving my hat first and then dramatically raising and lowering my arms—*slow, slow*—to signal the engineer.

Good. This guy was swift. Instead of signaling me back with a blast of his whistle, which might frighten the mules, he waved his ball cap out through the cab window and then flashed his big grimy center light several times. Black exhaust billowed from the engine vents as the engineer flooded his turbines to make them inefficient, to slow the train down without applying his screeching brakes.

The train was coming, but I felt composed, resigned to fate. The diffused history of the Oregon Trail felt spiritual now. The path of purpose and hope that spanned the plains had joined everything—tracks that followed the wagon ruts, churches rebelling, fur trappers and dreamy adventurers, wagon millionaires, new irrigation ditches, the magnificent folly and stoic sacrifice of a land joined by a route through South Pass. And now, line hand to throttle hand, mind to mind, I was joined with that engineer like the bonds of man celebrated by a Walt Whitman poem.

The rumble of the train was louder now, with the echoes of the rear cars thundering out of the tunnel. The tracks beside us vibrated and groaned from the approaching load. I took the lines back from Merri and spoke to the mules above the roar just behind us. They had to know that I was aware of the hazard coming, and that I would protect them.

"Just a train, Team. Just a train. Jake! Be my boy, Jake! Be my boy. Hold them back, Jake. Hold them back."

A whoosh of noise, turbine exhaust, and compressed hot air blew past as the grimy yellow engine approached. Beck started to dance in her harness, lowering her neck to leap into a run, but I caught her as hard as I could with the right line, double-wrapping the leather against my hands. Jake turned his head to quickly look back at me and then leaned sideways and nipped Beck hard just behind her ears.

"Thataboy, Jake. Eas-A, Eas-A, Team. Jake, that's my boy. Just a train, Team. Just a train. Eas-A. Eas-A."

As the locomotive went by my left cheek I gave the engineer the "A-Okay" with one hand while still holding the lines, and the engineer looked down and smiled from his open window. Two thumbs up in a red Carhartt T-shirt. Whooooosh, harrumph, harrumph, harrumph, metal to metal clanging, the long freighter began to pass. The boxcar doors just a few feet from my face rattled on their mounts.

"Just a train, Team. Just a train. Jake, Beck. Eas-A, Eas-A. Hold them back, Jake. Walk, Team. Walk."

Beck danced in her harness a few more times and threatened to bolt, but Jake was sick of her shit by now and arched over with his neck and planted a big feral bite on her neck. Once she could see more train ahead of her and realized it wasn't a threat, Beck calmed down, and Bute looked so relaxed that I thought she might fall asleep in harness. Jake had one ear flopped backward to listen to me and one ear forward following the train. He was pulling backward against the yoke with his massive neck and chest to keep the team at a walk.

"You're my boy, Jake. You're my boy."

Ka-plunk-ka-plunk-ka-plunk, for more than ten minutes, the train rumbled by.

I was still guarded about a runaway, but thrilled by the sight of the narrow canyon walls, the plodding mules, and the long curving outline of the train, sound and image merging against the orange triangle of light where the canyon ended ahead. While the locomotive and the front cars disappeared around the end of the canyon, the rear cars were still screeching and lurching beside us. The tracks cracked loudly with iron tension.

The train was gone by the time we reached the end of the Union Pacific access road, leaving behind the rail yard smell of brake fluid, grease on rust, and bleached paint. The canyon seemed strangely quiet as we reached Sisley Creek and then turned northeast to follow the Oregon Trail up onto the ridges again, toward Gold Hill.

"Good team! Good team! Jake! Beck! Bute! You're my team! I love you, Jake!"

We rose through hills striated with basalt rock ledges, and then green short-grass pastures—the fairyland contrasts of the trail. Far away, the train moving north across the plains blew three short blasts of its whistle, probably at a road crossing. But I told myself that the engineer knew that his caboose was safely past the wagon now and happy about it. He was shrieking his whistle as a good-bye to the mules and me.

30

THE OREGON TRAIL WAS MY home now, and the rhythmic sights and smells of the trail country were comforting and familiar. Through the first weeks of September we harnessed and hitched the mules early every morning, drinking coffee and pulling on extra shirts against the cold. Nick had his pickup now and often drove ahead to scout our routes and make fried chicken stops, and I enjoyed the solitude of driving the mules alone up through the old mining district of Sutton Creek and Quartz. Drawing deeply on brisk autumn air scented with sage, I sang to the mules and gave wagon rides to children waiting by their mailboxes to wave.

I didn't want my wagon journey to end and deluded myself into thinking that if I procrastinated about it, I wouldn't have to make a decision about stopping. But as we approached Baker City, the nights were getting colder and it was often raining, and new snow had fallen overnight on the Elkhorn peaks to the west. I knew that I would have to stop by October to avoid getting trapped by winter weather in the mountains. The trail from here was mostly on heavily fenced small farms where we would never get through, or paved over by Interstate 84. I had proved my point by reaching Oregon and couldn't push the trip much farther.

Besides, as far back as Idaho, I had been tortured about what to do with the mules when the trip was over and often lay awake at night in the wagon worrying about it. Closing up the trip and finding a decent home for the mules required stopping somewhere long enough to think about it and make calls, and I berated myself for lack of planning. But that's what the trip was all about. We'd done quite well all summer living spontaneously day by day, allowing events and the surprises of the trail to guide us. I had no plans. I lived in a covered wagon. I relied on the generosity of trail family and slept like a hobo in public parks and rodeo arenas. It was too addictive and satisfying a life to toss away for domestic habits like planning.

At Baker City, Nick had driven ahead in his pickup along the Powder River to find the ranch belonging to Vince Holtz's brother-in-law, where we had been told we could camp. But he got lost in the maze of ranch roads up there and didn't return. As I pushed the mules north on Highway 30, I realized that I had badly miscalculated the sunset. The Elkhorn Mountains rise abruptly to the west after Baker City, blocking the evening light, and the road was pitch-black by seven o'clock. As I pushed north in the darkness of the highway, the only thing lighting my way were the headlamps of passing cars.

But I wasn't driving completely blind. Pickup trucks and minivans started pulling over ahead of me, and everyone had a suggestion about where I could stop and camp—a sister's place here, the parking lot of a church there. As I passed a very sweet-looking ranch on the right, the rancher was pulling out of his drive in a four-wheeler with the lights on. I asked him if I could camp there and explained that I might need to stay for a few nights to rest the mules and resupply in Baker City.

"My other place just north is better," the rancher, Mike Williams, said. "I've got four acres of fenced grass for the mules, and a big watering trough. If it rains you can sleep in the barns."

I yelled ahead to a minivan driver to ride in front of the wagon slowly with her emergency flashers on. A pickup was parked right beside me, and I asked that driver to follow me with his flashers going and high beams on, to light my way from behind. My rear LED strobes were flashing too.

That is how I arrived at our final camp, in the middle of a mixed transportation parade of wagons and cars, with three sets of flashers bouncing light off the yellow divider line on the highway. The purple-black rim of the Elkhorns was etched in the sky to the west as I turned up the ranch road. My trail family escort of ranchers in pickups and mothers with children in minivans followed the wagon in.

The Williams ranch was ideal, if spongy underfoot from heavy irrigation. I pulled the team up against a corral fence to unharness in the dark and gave a few of the trail family kids rides around the corral on Jake. When Nick finally found me we used his pickup lights for illumination to bathe the team. One by one, when their baths were done, the mules happily galloped off into the broad green pasture.

It was cold that night in the Elkhorns, and when I stepped from the wagon in the morning Nick and Olive Oyl were huddled together on a wet patch of grass, shivering with a soaked blanket wrapped around them. God. I still couldn't believe that they had slept outdoors this way, no matter the conditions, for four months. I had to get them under shelter soon.

"Yo, Sidekick," I yelled. "Coffee coming right up. We're out of bacon and eggs. How about Hormel chili, no beans, for breakfast?"

"Great. Put on an extra can for Olive Oyl."

Both of us loved Baker City, which reminded me of a miniature Eugene, Oregon, or maybe Leadville or Telluride in Colorado. It was a graceful and gentrified old mining town that had been built a few miles from the trail during a precious metals boom after the Civil War. There was a palatial robber baron–era hotel, the Geiser Grand, and a trail museum run by the BLM, the National Historic Oregon Trail Interpretive Center, built on a high bluff above the ruts three miles out of town. The breakfast joints were great and there was a wine bar, and a good bookstore, on Main Street.

I couldn't stand the thought of another layover on the trip with Nick and Olive Oyl sleeping outside in the cold, on wet irrigated ground no less, so I rented him a room at the Oregon Trail Motel and told him to splurge on meals across the street at the Oregon Trail Restaurant. I found a laundromat, washed our clothes, and then wandered into the spacious library a block off Main Street to check my email.

One of the first emails in my inbox had no subject heading but it was from Sue Holtz, back on her farm in Idaho:

Hi Rinker,

*Vince and I have been talking, and we would be honored if the
wagons and mules remained here and a part of the ranch.*

*We would love for you to let us know what your plans are for them,
and we'd like to have the opportunity to talk with you about them.*

We were really touched by what you have done.

Please contact us, we'd appreciate it.

Thank you!

Sue Holtz

My heart raced and I had almost no interest in answering the other emails that had accumulated in my box. Sue's language—"a part of our ranch"—indicated that she wanted to keep the team together, and since I knew that the Holtzes were not experienced horse people, the only thing Sue could mean was that she essentially wanted to buy the team and treat her ranch as an equine retirement farm. But I had no idea what they were willing to pay for the wagons and team or even if they had the right pastures, barns, and the wherewithal to care for the mules.

Sue's email jolted me back to reality. After four months of the trail with my Amish mules, I was philosophical about them and pragmatic about what I had to do with the team. Yes, Beck was a phobic mess who had given me *nervosa extremis* all the way across the trail, and she hated me so much that Nick always had to harness her. Bute had bad feet and was chronically allergic to work. I loved only Jake, and passionately. But together they were a great team of Andalusians, the first mules in a century to cross the Oregon Trail, and I had watched them as a threesome for four months now, huddling together against storms, affectionately nipping at each other when competing for feed, kicking up their hind legs with joy when they were let free in the high pastures at Signal Bluff or Poison Spider Creek. They had pulled like the bejesus and never given up over California Hill and Rocky Ridge.

Mules are very social and fraternal, they often bond together for life, and I had heard stories about an animal completely breaking down and spiraling off into prolonged mule depression when a partner died or a team was broken up and sold. Beck and Bute had been together all of their lives. Jake was a blessed soul of the earth and loved his mollies. I owed it to the mules to find them a decent home, together. I would be the cad of the century to break up this team.

It had never been my plan to keep the mules. Shipping them back east would cost almost as much as I paid for them, and my relatively small spread in New England wouldn't support a big draft team. Philip Ropp was so enamored of Jake that he had offered to buy him back after our trip was over, but he had shown no interest in reacquiring Beck and Bute. I was determined to keep the team together but knew that it might be difficult. In Idaho, pictures of us driving the team across the trail had appeared on the front pages of several newspapers, and the television stations in Pocatello and Boise had broadcast stories about us. Two mule brokers from the northern part of the state had tracked me down through the TV reporters, and they were anxious to buy the team. One of them offered to meet us anywhere I wanted in Oregon to buy the team and the wagon and said that he would bring $25,000 in cash. Not including the expensive Trail Pup repairs, this was pretty much what I had invested in the wagon and team, and I was tempted. But both brokers acknowledged that they would probably break up the team, saving Jake for the big fall mule auctions in northern Idaho, where they expected him to fetch a very high price, and selling off Beck and Bute to outfitters, who would use them as pack animals for the fall hunting season into the Rockies.

The team was attractive to the brokers because the mules were obviously in prime condition. After four months of thirty-mile days, they were muscular but not at all underweight, with shiny black coats and plenty of energy. All of the horsemen we passed on the trail were surprised at how athletic and healthy the mules looked after almost two thousand miles of hard work.

Nick deserved all of the credit for this. From his sleigh business days in New Hampshire, he knew how to work a team hard all day and then baby the mules at night with high-quality feed and fastidious care. Nick was usually worried about how much money I was blowing on the trip, but not when it came to the best raw grain and expensive vitamin supplements for the mules. He bought them boxes of gelatin mix at supermarkets because gelatin is known to promote nail growth in humans, and it would help keep the mules' hooves firm. To ward off the muscle soreness and mild inflammation caused by her bad feet, he kept Bute comfortable by administering two doses a day of liquid equine aspirin. The mules ate the best alfalfa hay we could find, and we bought them apples and carrots whenever we could so that their diet was balanced with vegetables and fruit. We ate like shit every day, subsisting on Hormel chili, no beans, Slim Jims, and canned chocolate pudding, and never took showers. The mules ate like royalty and got a long relaxing bath every night. All of this showed when we reached Oregon. The team was as buff as race horses at a track.

I was enjoying myself in Baker City, and even went on a date with a saleswoman I met at the D&B Ranch Supply store. But my joint obligations to Nick and the mules weighed heavily on me, and I knew that I couldn't enjoy the satisfaction of finishing the trip until I made the right decision about the mules. Nick was reluctant to discuss selling the team, because he knew the pressure I was under and didn't want to crowd a decision that involved my ability to recover some costs from the trip. But I knew that he was particularly fond of Beck and would worry about her if the team was broken up. We talked about the situation one afternoon outside the implement shed at the Williams ranch, where Nick was helping Mike repair his disc harrow.

"It bothers me that I still don't know what to do," I said. "I should have planned better than this."

"Stop worryin, Boss," Nick said. "The thing I've always said to people is that Rinker is completely fucked up. But things work out for him."

I walked over to the wagon to sit on a camp chair and think about things. The mules were browsing comfortably in the grass of the pasture and I stared west beyond them to the white peaks of the Elkhorns.

I called the Holtz Ranch in Idaho from a bench under a tall shade tree at Geiser-Pollman Park in Baker City, which overlooked a winding stretch of the Powder River. I reached Vince, who told me that he had dozens of acres of fenced pasture at his Oregon ranch, where he and Sue lived for long stretches during the winter to protect their land from elk poachers. He and Sue would love to buy a work sleigh and use the team on their winter patrols protecting the elk herds. If I sold him the team, he would also build fences for a seven-acre summer pasture, and walk-in barns, on his Idaho farm. His brother-in-law on the Powder River had a stock van and equipment trailers to haul the team and rig down to Idaho, more or less right away. When I told Vince what I had invested in the wagons and mules, he offered me $21,000 for the whole package. He could wire the money to my bank account right away.

"Sue has always wanted a team of mules," Vince told me. "When we saw you ride across the trail on our ranch, we were very moved by what you've done. It just seems to us that mules that have crossed the trail all the way from Missouri deserve a good home."

Vince and Sue were also attracted to the symbolism of owning the team. Both of their spreads, in Idaho and Oregon, sat on the Oregon Trail, and they had always enjoyed this pioneer legacy. Nick and I, Vince said, could visit Idaho anytime we wanted to drive the team, and he had already moved one of his RVs down to the spot on his farm where the mule pasture would be built. He was hoping that we'd visit for as long as we wanted on the way home.

Trail family doesn't get much better than this, and I knew that I had just been handed a turnkey package. I would not have to break up the team.

I told Vince that I would give him an answer by the end of the day, explaining that I didn't want Nick to feel I'd been hasty about a decision or failed to consult him. On the way back to the Williams ranch in Nick's pickup, I received calls from both of the mule brokers, who gave me big sales pitches about why they were the best ones to buy the team. "Hell, the only mules to cross the Oregon Trail in a hundred years?" one of the brokers said. "Everybody will want to buy that." They were anxious to drive down to Oregon to haul away the wagons and mules.

I found Nick back in camp, leading Bute across the pasture to chain her to the fence while he administered her afternoon dose of liquid aspirin. I helped him with that and then we sat on the edge of the watering trough to talk, and I explained the offer from Vince and Sue Holtz, and what the brokers wanted to do.

"It's a brain-dead decision," Nick said. "The Holtzes are great people.

They're just goin to put Bute here on chocolate bars and alfalfa for the rest of her life. But, hey, it's your call. You're still the wagon boss."

"I'm going to sell the mules to Vince and Sue," I said. "It's the right decision. I guess you know what this means."

"I know what it means."

"The trip stops here."

"Yeah, but not really," Nick said. "I'll be bullshittin about this fucker for the rest of my life."

It started to rain and I went over to the wagon to call Vince Holtz back and close the sale. Nick decided to drive into town and visit the Oregon Trail museum. When I was done speaking with Vince, I pulled on a rain slicker and walked over to the mules in the pasture. Beck and Bute kicked up their rear hoofs and ran away, but Jake came right over, bowing his head and burying it under my arm. I scratched behind his ears, and his dandruff mixed with the rain reminded me of the smell of freshly trimmed hooves in the blacksmith shops of Pennsylvania.

"Ah, shit, Jake," I said. "Shit, shit, shit. You're my boy. But I am going to have to say good-bye soon."

Jake smelled the apple that I had bought for him in Baker City and started to nuzzle hard for it in the pocket of my rain slicker. I held it out for him on the flat of my hand. I patted him some more and enjoyed the sensation of his warm saliva mixing with the cold rain on my hand, and then I turned back to the wagon to sit in the rain and brood.

By selling the mules to Vince and Sue, I had landed on an emotionally sensible plan. Nick and I wanted to gypsy around the West for a while before returning home, taking in the rodeos and mule-driving competitions that we hadn't had time for while crossing the trail, and the Holtzes wanted us to use their place in Idaho as a base. They invited us to stay there as long as we wanted. This would allow us to gradually decompress from the trip, commuting around for a few weeks via pickup and remaining close to the trail. We could part with the mules in stages.

The morning that the trucks arrived to trailer the mules and wagon down to Idaho, Nick and I were up early at the Williams ranch, brushing and bathing the team, labeling the harness, and sweeping out the wagon. I had bought myself a used Chevy pickup for transporting the gear I wanted to keep back east, and I used it to cruise around Baker City off-loading my filthy mattress and blankets in dumpsters and distributing our other excess gear to thrift stores. Closing down the trip had gone well, and everything was shipshape for the drive down to Idaho to deliver the Schuttler and mules.

Settling in with our newest trail family in Idaho was seamless, and a lot of fun. All of the pressures of the trip were behind us now and the Holtz place sat on the rolling hills of a vineyard district, a little Napa in Idaho overlooking the Snake River and a trail landmark, Lizard Butte. Nick left after a couple of days to head up to a big mule event, Hells Canyon Mule Days in Enterprise, Oregon, while I stayed behind in the comfortable camping trailer parked beside the new mule pasture. Vince had already purchased a beautiful one-horse victoria, and a team fore cart, from a wagon dealer in Oregon, and I taught them how to hook Jake. Vince and I bounced around between his farm and his seed-drying sheds with Beck and Bute hitched to the fore cart, pulling trailers loaded with equipment and seed bags. I quickly fell into the life of Marsing, the small agricultural town on the river near the farm, and we often drove Jake down for breakfast at the Whitehouse Drive-In, or dinner at a Mexican restaurant, tying him to fence posts while we dined inside.

Nick thrived back in Oregon. Before heading home by a circuitous route through the Dakotas and then parts of the South, to visit wagon shops, he wanted to take in not only Mule Days in Enterprise but the largest rodeo and wagon parade in the West, the Pendleton Round-Up in Pendleton, Oregon. By this time everyone in the horse world had heard about our trip, and Nick's arrival at Mule Days was classic. Within a few minutes of pulling into Enterprise he had announced in his best Radio Free Europe baritone, in response to an event organizer's question, "Oh, yeah! I'm the one that just finished drivin mules across the Oregon Trail!" He was mobbed by all the mule skinners, their wives and their grandchildren, and offered a free place to sleep in town. He showed up at the corrals early every morning to help the mule owners harness their teams for competition events. Nick entered the toughest event, team log-pulling, with a borrowed pair of mules and won first place.

Nick did just as well at Pendleton, where I caught up with him a week

later. One of the biggest attractions at the weeklong Pendleton Round-Up
is an evening entertainment, Happy Canyon Night, when more than
five thousand spectators crowd the rodeo bleachers to watch a kind of
western-themed outdoor vaudeville show. When another actor backed
out, Nick agreed to play a burlesque part that called for a man dressed as a
frontier woman to drive across the stage in a buggy pulled by a mule. The
cowboy in drag, furious about catching "her" husband visiting a whorehouse, breaks into song. Nick was outfitted in a full-figure gingham dress,
a blond wig, and a large bra stuffed with straw. In the middle of Nick's performance, the wig fell off and the dress parted at the back seams, spilling
the straw from his falsies across the stage. Undeterred, Nick finished his
song as the rest of his costume disintegrated around him, and the crowd
went wild. He was a celebrity for the rest of the week at Pendleton.

At breakfast and lunch in town, Nick frequently interrupted our
meals to sign autographs for tourists on their Happy Canyon playbills, and
cute cowgirls blew him air kisses across the café.

"I still can't believe you kept singing after your bra bit the dust," I said.

"Rink, the thing you've got to understand about me is that I am a professional actor," Nick said. "I had a wardrobe malfunction. The same thing
happened to Janet Jackson at the Super Bowl. Big fuckin deal."

Nick dreads change, and I can always tell when he is approaching it. Because his days are often frantic and out of control, he clings to the routines
he can rely on—sitting with Olive Oyl at night, feeding his horses, wandering off after dinner to visit friends. When these routines are interrupted,
or are about to be interrupted, he gets moody and curt and his sense of
humor disappears. After we got back to Baker City and moved into the
Oregon Trail Motel for a few days, he was edgy and preoccupied. The Oregon Trail was his home now too, and our wagon-tramp life all summer
was his routine. He was jumpy about knowing that it was time to leave.

One morning while we ate breakfast, Nick sat quietly with his head
buried in a newspaper, acting as if I weren't there. Neither of us wanted
to say good-bye, and there was a dark cloud of silence between us. But
I knew that I had to speak up.

"Nick, it's time for you to leave for home, you know? What about your
tour of the wagon shops?"

Nick's Fu Manchu dropped and he looked up with a surprised look, but then a resigned one, shrugging his shoulders.

"You're right," he said. "But can't we just spend one more day together? We can drop my truck off for new tires, and then go visit museums."

"Good," I said. "I would like that."

I had already spent an afternoon wandering around Baker City, looking for presents for Nick. At the ranch supply store, I found the exact model and brand of an American-forged set of fence pliers that Nick had covetously eyed back in Wyoming. I found the last ball cap in town silkscreened with OREGON TRAIL on the front, as well as an illustrated guide to nineteenth-century farm implements. The clerk behind the counter at the bookstore helped me wrap the gifts in attractive paper and ribbon. I knew that Nick wouldn't take any money from me, but I stopped at an ATM just in case and stuffed my pockets with cash.

The next morning, after breakfast, we drove up to the large Oregon Trail monument near the center of town, where there was enough space to park our trucks bumper to bumper. As we sat together in the cab of Nick's Toyota, I cradled Olive Oyl in my lap and Nick opened his presents. He loved the fence pliers and eagerly began thumbing through the farm equipment book as we spoke.

"How did you know I wanted these fence pliers?" Nick said. "I can't believe that. Thanks. These are really great."

"I saw you looking at them that day we went into Douglas for parts. The Fort Fetterman camp."

"Oh, yeah," he said. "You may not know how to *use* tools, but you sure as fuck can *buy* them."

"Thank you, Nick."

Nick spoke for a while about how the trip had made him feel like "turning over a new leaf" when he got home. He was going to clean up all the piles of used lumber and farm machinery in his yard and rebuild his sagging porch. He always felt better, he said, after he cleaned out his pickup, and sprucing up his place would feel like that, a "major lifestyle improvement."

He was also looking forward to his monthlong tour of wagon shops around the country.

"Okay now look," I said. "On the way home? No buying any more wagons. You've got enough wagons in your barn."

"Oh, Jesus," he said. "I just told Mother on the phone last night that you've finally gotten control of your control freak. That's not controlling your control freak."

"Shit," I said. "You're right. I'm sorry. But look, about Mother. Just keep bullshitting her, okay? Tell her I'm great so she's happy."

"I'm goin to bullshit that lady till the moon goes down on that one. 'Mom, Rinky lost his control freak on the Oregon Trail, and now he can't find it again.' But to everybody else?"

"Shit."

"Rinky's a frickin control freak."

"Okay, that's fair," I said. "But it's not really true. I didn't freak when you flipped the Trail Pup."

"Oh, see? You're goin to be remindin me about that one forever."

"No. I'm going to be reminding you about California Hill and Rocky Ridge. You were so great on those days."

Nick was fidgeting with his fingers, drumming them on the Toyota steering wheel.

"Oh, fuck, Rinker. I hate saying good-bye to you. Can I just say that I'll never forget this trip? I mean, I'll always be the guy that drove team all the way across the Oregon Trail. Thank you. Ah, shit, I don't even know what I'm sayin here. What am I sayin here? Thank you, Rinker. I would be dead right now if I was home in Maine and you hadn't let me come along."

My heart was skipping with roller-coaster emotions and I could feel my eyes fill with moisture. I hated it when Nick ignored his own contribution and heaped all of the praise on me.

"Nick. I'm going to say just one thing. You stayed with me at Shickley. I'll never forget that and I couldn't have crossed the trail without you."

Nick sighed, turned the key in his ignition, and reached over and hugged me shoulder to shoulder.

"Go, Rink. I love you but we have to do this."

"Okay, me too," I said. "Do you have maps? Did you buy maps?"

"You don't think I can find my ass back across the country by now?"

"Money? I've got cash."

"Don't need money either."

"Cell phone?"

Nick slapped all of his pockets, pawed around the pickup for his cell phone, and then asked to borrow mine.

On my phone, Nick dialed his own number and we heard the muffled ring of his cell coming from a brown paper bag full of candy bars and Slim Jims behind the seat.

"See? I told you," Nick said. "That's where I put my cell phone."

I gave Olive Oyl one last hug and handed her to Nick. I stepped out of the passenger side of Nick's cab and walked around to his side, shook his hand through the open window, and we both smiled and laughed.

"I love you, Wagon Master," Nick said.

"We did this together," I said. "Together."

Nick's muffler roared and he pushed his RPMs high through the gears as he turned south toward the interstate. Olive Oyl was sitting on Nick's lap with her snout pushed forward out the window, and the wind flattened her ears. As the white pickup disappeared I swelled with regret about parting with him, but then a cloud raced off from the sun and the Oregon Trail monument was illuminated in brightness, with deep shadows cast into the engraved words, and I felt light inside.

Now I knew what it was like to be part of a team that was broken up and for several days I was lonely and misplaced when I woke in the morning.

31

I SPENT THE NEXT FEW days alone in Baker City, treating the effects of wagon withdrawal by clinging to a town that felt like home. Everyone seemed to know me as "the covered wagon guy." The manager of the laundromat on Campbell Street was considering chucking everything in Oregon and moving with her husband and children to a log cabin in Alaska, and wanted my advice on that. Betty's Books gave me the bulk discount when I bought a stack of pioneer journals. Waking up to motel showers every morning was luxurious, and at the restaurant across the street the Trail Boss Burger, with jalapeños and provolone, was the best helping of protein I'd had all summer. I was loitering, reluctant to part with the hobo life.

Vince and Sue Holtz were expecting me back in Idaho, where we were planning on hitching Jake to their new carriage and making an all-day tour of the vineyards. After that, I would ride with Merri Melde up in the Owyhees and then enjoy several trail family reunions on my leisurely drive home. But there was still one more trail pilgrimage that I wanted to make.

In the early 1840s, the main ruts of the emigrant road after the Blue Mountains in northeast Oregon proceeded north to a place called Waiilatpu on the Walla Walla River, in what would become Washington

State. Marcus and Narcissa Whitman had spent eleven years there with the Cayuse tribe after their historic crossing in 1836. The Whitman Mission served as a vital frontier outpost in the early days of the trail, resupplying weary pioneers on their way to the Columbia River and offering medical care provided by Dr. Whitman. I had heard that the restored mission and visitors' center there, run by the National Park Service, was a moving and peaceful site. I couldn't end the summer of my dreams without saying good-bye to Narcissa.

I drove up through the Umatilla National Forest in late September, enjoying the solitude of the long pickup ride. In the Cayuse language, *Waiilatpu* referred to the flat plains that stretch for dozens of miles along the Walla Walla and meant "place of the people of the rye grass." The Whitman Mission there is windswept and serene, beautifully maintained by the park service. Beneath a tall, rounded hill, topped by a granite obelisk commemorating the Whitmans, Doan Creek winds through cottonwood groves that border broad green pastures and old trail ruts. Most of the buildings at the mission have collapsed or were burned during Indian raids in the late nineteenth century, but their foundations have been identified and carefully marked, and the attractive visitors' center contains a small but interesting museum on the Whitmans and the early trail years. With a couple who had just completed a transcontinental bicycle trip from New York City to Astoria, Oregon, I went along on the afternoon tour and lecture delivered by a young, earnest park service historian.

Even the kindest of biographers have concluded that Narcissa and Marcus Whitman were miscast as missionaries, completely unsuited by temperament and ill-prepared by nineteenth-century cultural mores to minister to the small Cayuse band. After settling at Waiilatpu in the late autumn of 1836 and building their first house, the Whitmans spent the next decade living as *refuseniks* in the host Cayuse society. Initially, Marcus Whitman was too busy building fences, a blacksmith shop, and barns to spend much time with the Cayuse, and Narcissa was perpetually frustrated by tribal conventions as she began Bible classes for the natives. She never learned Cayuse and expected the native people to understand when she explained the difficult concepts of reform Christianity in their broken English. The Cayuse saw no need to strictly observe the Sabbath when they had already spent several days of the week learning about

Christianity, they interrupted their Christian education every summer to travel to the mountains to harvest berries, and they treated the Whitman house as just another one of their lodges, strolling through at all hours, sitting on the floor to talk, and helping themselves to whatever food they saw on the counter. Eventually the Whitmans built a new, larger house with a separate "Indian great room" walled off from the family quarters. Visitors to the mission were surprised by Narcissa's condescending treatment of tribal members and often described her as "haughty." The word the Cayuse used when referring to her meant "very proud."

With Narcissa refusing to change and adapt to Cayuse ways, and Marcus frequently absent to organize a territorial government or lead wagon trains, the Whitmans came to symbolize the unbridgeable gap between the white settlers and the native tribes. There were many other problems and even tragedy. At the age of two, the Whitmans' daughter, Alice Clarissa, drowned after wandering off to play in the creek, and Narcissa fell into a long, deep depression that didn't lift until she adopted a family of pioneer orphans. The wagon trains now flowing through the mission every summer decimated the local Indian tribes by introducing European diseases for which the natives had no immunity, and the Cayuse suspected Marcus Whitman of treachery because he seemed able to cure measles and smallpox among the white travelers but not in the tribe. The Whitmans' evangelical work with the Indians eventually collapsed amid bitter recriminations, which included ugly spats with rival Catholic and Methodist missionaries plying the frontier for converts.

But the Whitmans were still celebrated as founding pioneers, especially after Marcus successfully led the first large wagon train west in 1843. They were road ranchers now, planting large vegetable gardens and wheat for the summer pioneers and running a thriving blacksmith shop for the passing wagon trains. By the mid-1840s, the mission for the tribes had evolved into a bustling, whites-only trail stop with a school, a trading post, and a transient population of fur trappers, traders, and pioneers often numbering in the hundreds.

Marcus Whitman's identity as both a missionary and a medical doctor had imperiled his position among the Cayuse from the start. By the fall of 1847, the frontier clash of cultures along the Columbia River plateau had led to a complete social collapse. The Cayuse and many neighboring tribes were beginning to resent the endless stream of wagon trains along the Oregon Trail every summer, and a harsh winter in 1846–1847 had decimated the wildlife, contributing to a belief among the tribes that the white man was taking too much game. The Cayuse and the Umatilla had traditionally served more migratory tribes as traders and berry pickers. But now, in a market swelling with passing pioneers, they had been displaced as traders by the Whitmans. Factions within both tribes, abetted by a group of mixed-race trappers, resented the evident wealth that the Whitmans had amassed by serving the wagon trains.

As tensions rose among the Cayuse and sporadic violence broke out, the Whitmans were warned by fur traders and tribal chiefs to abandon their mission and move to the safety of the Willamette Valley. But Marcus was proud of the role that the Whitman Mission now played for the pioneers along a strategic stretch of the Oregon Trail and refused to move on. In October 1847, as the last of the wagon trains disappeared over the horizon for the Columbia River, an epidemic of measles and dysentery broke out, and as usual most of the white children at the mission recovered while the Cayuse children died in great numbers. In late November, enraged by the death of their children and convinced that the Whitmans had contributed to the epidemic, a small band of angry Cayuse made an all-day assault on the mission, killing fourteen whites, including Narcissa, Marcus, and several of their adopted children.

News of what became known as the "Whitman Massacre" did not reach Washington, D.C., until the early spring of 1848, but it had a lasting impact on the territorial drive of America. For the next twenty years, politicians, army generals, and freelance Indian fighters would use the "slaughter" of the Whitmans as a rationale for escalating the campaign against the western tribes. In the summer of 1848, amid a popular outcry about Indian attacks, Congress created the Oregon Territory, the first territorial government west of the Rockies, and appropriated funds to build army forts to protect the pioneers. The Civil War would interrupt efforts to empty the plains of the wandering tribes, but the war against the Indians would resume in earnest once the whites tired of killing each other.

In the meantime, the Oregon Trail was rerouted away from the gruesome remnants of the Whitman Mission. Instead of going north to the Walla Walla, pioneers now pushed due west for the Columbia. The Whitmans left behind a tragic statement about missionary zeal, and a dark stain on American history. Over eleven years on the Walla Walla, the Whitmans had evolved from benevolent missionaries to the Cayuse to commercial proprietors who prospered from a continued influx of white settlers. Their deaths became a rallying cry for ethnic cleansing. Few Americans at the time, of course, perceived this as a classic corruption of values.

The common grave of the Whitman Massacre victims, called the "Great Grave," stands today in a small open area of mowed grass along a bend in Doan Creek. Pheasants call and tree frogs sound from the nearby marshes, and cattails and willow branches bend in the breeze. I felt there the mixed spirituality and melancholy that I often experience when visiting historic graves. After the other members of the tour group had left for their cars, I sat on a bench and meditated about Narcissa Whitman.

History almost everywhere is tragic and ironic, but in America the contrasts are more stark because we set such high ideals. Fortified by stirring Enlightenment appeals to the rights of man, we fought a war of liberation from the British crown and then decided to constitutionally protect the enslavement of our African laborers. The great evangelical pulsation of the 1820s spread religion and inspired useful social reform, while also unleashing decades of denominational squabbling, even murder, in the name of Christianity. We fought the Civil War over slavery that cost more than 600,000 deaths but still sugarcoat what happened by describing it as an unresolved conflict over "states' rights." I try not to even think anymore about the serial idiocy of leadership during my own lifetime, when sixty thousand American lives were squandered in Vietnam, Afghanistan, and Iraq. Perhaps someday we'll begin teaching our children the full, demythologized truth about ourselves, but I doubt it.

Narcissa Whitman lived this national irony to the fullest. Propelled by missionary zeal and visions of a frontier utopia where "heathen" pupils would patiently consume Christianity, she was then unwilling to change according to the conditions she actually found in the West. Her ultimate mission was unsuccessful, but her journey getting there, and writing about it, was epic and changed her times, opening the gate for women and families to join the largest land migration in history. Which one do we remember? Who was the real Narcissa Whitman—the proud, self-important evangelist from the Finger Lakes, incapable of getting along with the Cayuse, or the brave, adventurous woman galloping sidesaddle up South Pass? The inconsistencies of history and character don't require us to choose between these identities. Narcissa Whitman was both.

Still, sitting beside her grave, I felt settled about making Narcissa Whitman my heroine as I crossed the trail. I was comfortable about my own western quest. The wrong outcome, or no outcome at all, is often the only result of a journey. Walkabouts and odysseys have always been common, and we needn't search too hard for tangible returns. Journey for journey's sake is enough. For weeks or months of a climb or a trek, we are forced to be in the moment. For Narcissa Whitman, this meant a lot. Behind her, the trapped energy of a country exploded west for two thousand miles.

I didn't accomplish that much calling mules for nearly two thousand miles across the plains, and I wouldn't be returning home a changed person. The benefits of the trip related mostly to journeying itself. I had proven to myself that I could scout for vanished trail on modern terrain, and I drove team a lot better now. My habitual impatience was suspended to deal with frustration after frustration on the trail. I'm not worried anymore about my father's reappearances in my life, because they're just something to live with and accept. I know a great deal more now about a seminal time in my country's history. But, mostly, I had indulged in a wonderful summer of romance and grit.

The sun was falling against the distant wheat fields, it was time to go, and I drove south enjoying the anvil-black peak lines of the mountains and the lights of the combines in the fields as I passed the scattered farm communities on the way back to Baker City.

In Idaho, Vince, Sue, and I enjoyed our vineyard tour behind Jake in the new carriage, getting a little boozy by nightfall after sampling our share of local chardonnay and merlot. In the evenings, from a fire pit overlooking the Snake, we watched the sun drop while Sue taught me to cook stew in Dutch Oven pots. Vince and I cannibalized parts from an old disc harrow and welded them into a portable barbecue hearth that I could use on the way home. I ran the farm errands into town with Jake and the carriage, dropping down past the faux-Tuscan villas to cross the old trail ford at Lizard Butte.

I left for home early in the afternoon on a warm October day, after taking Jake out for a last carriage drive. Beck and Bute were way off among the trees in their new pasture and weren't going to come down to say good-bye to me, so I savored my time with Jake. I grained him as a reward for our pleasant ride, cleaned his hooves, and gave him a long bath with a hose strung up from Sue's dog kennels.

"Ah, screw it anyway, Jake, I'm leaving today but I'll be back, I promise."

When I massaged his withers and lower legs with shampoo and a brush, Jake's eyelids began to flutter and he dropped his head and began to snore. I told Jake that it was fine for him to take a snooze. I just wanted him to know how thankful I was for the way he held me up that day when I nearly passed out at the bottom of Dempsey Ridge. I thanked him for holding the mollies back and being the calm center of the team so many times.

Jake woke up when a black fly landed on his rump and he swished at it with his tail, showering me with bubbly shampoo.

"I'll miss you, Jake," I said. "I wish I could bring you home. But you belong here with the girls."

I hosed Jake down with the spray nozzle on full just the way he liked it. At the fence gate, I pulled an apple from the feed box, held it for him, scratched behind his ears one last time, and then watched him canter off to join Beck and Bute.

My truck was right there, packed and ready to go. I had said good-bye to Vince and Sue at breakfast. I took one last look at the mules, browsing on grass and swishing flies under the trees, and then I started my truck and drove down past Lizard Butte.

I turned left after the bridge over the Snake and headed east along the trail country. The basalt cliffs along the river gleamed in the sunlight, and the austerity of landscape reminded me of the austerity of mission. Journey is all, and we did it, we made it, we got there. We had followed the Platte to the Sweetwater, the Sweetwater to South Pass, and then we slid the wagon down Dempsey Ridge to the indescribable beauty along the Bear. Broken wheels and a thousand miles of fences couldn't stop us. The impossible is doable as long as you have a great brother and good trail friends. Uncertainty is all. Crazyass passion is the staple of life and persistence its nourishing force. Without them, you cannot cross the trail.

ACKNOWLEDGMENTS

CROSSING THE OREGON TRAIL AND then spending more than two years writing about it constantly reminded me of Daniel Boorstin's description of the covered wagon as "plainly a community vehicle" that required working in groups. Even while lost in the remote Wyoming desert, or struggling over the lava-rock abyss of Idaho, I was always confident that I could find help ahead. In this way our covered wagon trip was not so much an adventure shared by two brothers but a display of the communal ingenuity and hospitality still to be found in the American West. The reassuring feeling of being handed off every day from rancher to rancher, and from trail expert to trail expert, remains my strongest impression of the trip. Likewise, my research into the history of the trail was built upon the heroic scholarship of many who came before me.

My brother Nick deserves most of the credit for the success of our trip. His outstanding horsemanship, mechanical and harness-making skills, alacrity at making friends, and ability to get by with limited resources almost anywhere made the trip possible. The difficulty of finding friends and family members who can rise at dawn and then sustain physical activity on a project all day has been a major inconvenience in my life, but Nick made an ideal partner. I am especially grateful for his decision in Schickley, Nebraska, to remain with the trip. It is rare for two brothers to share a journey as unique as this, and I will always remember his gift to me.

The Oregon-California Trails Association (OCTA) of Independence, Missouri, struggles with a small staff and budget against such modern threats to the trail as mining and energy projects, housing developers, and hordes of dirt-biking enthusiasts. Chapter presidents and volunteers in the eight states through which the trails pass perform the largely un-rewarded functions of marking the trail, applying for preservation grants, and testifying at court and federal agency hearings when the trail is threatened with new developments or road-building. OCTA also main-tains an invaluable website devoted to the history of major trail stops and pioneer histories and publishes the *Overland Journal*, an excellent quar-terly on selected trail topics and research that I often used while compil-ing the history sections of my book. Before we left on our trip, association manager Travis Boley and headquarters manager Kathryn Conway shared with us maps, insights on the trail, and a complete list of OCTA contacts in each state. This help proved invaluable during our four-month journey.

OCTA also published Randy Brown and Reg Duffin's *Graves and Sites on the Oregon and California Trails*, and Brown's *Historic Inscrip-tions on Western Emigrant Trails*, which were immensely useful toward understanding the history we were passing and provided exact directions to trail sites. The compendium of geodetic maps on the trail originally compiled by OCTA founder Gregory Franzwa, *Maps of the Oregon Trail*, published by the Patrice Press in St. Louis, was indispensable for finding our way in the backcountry and narrow canyons of Wyoming and Idaho.

Philip Ropp of Ropp's Mule Farm in Jamesport, Missouri, fulfilled the one essential requirement I placed before him: selling me a team that could make it to Oregon. Yes, Bute was a laggard with pigeon-toed hooves, and Beck was our Lizzie Borden of the trip, but Jake's imperturb-ability and good sense made up for this. Buying a team as quickly as I did and then realizing where I had erred only enriched the pioneer experience for me. Ropp and his neighbor, machinist and blacksmith Ivan Schrock, made it possible for us to get all our wagon modifications done on time.

Elmer Beechy and the leatherworkers at the Jamesport Harness Shop quickly made all the adjustments and fabricated the extra parts I needed for our rig. Beechy taught me a valuable lesson in jumping off economics by quickly flipping my trade-in saddle at a profit. God bless the Amish for their industriousness and fun.

Don and Connie Werner at the Werner Wagon Works in Horton, Kansas, maintain one of the best wagon restoration shops in the country and produced a serviceable rig under a tight deadline. I realize now that the problems we later had with the wheels and brakes on our Peter Schuttler wagon were mostly the result of my unyielding ambition to reach Oregon clashing with modern-restoration standards. The Meader Supply Corporation of Rochester, New Hampshire, promptly filled our orders for harness replacements and shipped them ahead of us on the trail. Dan Hathaway of Illusion Farm in Fryeburg, Maine, was always available when Nick called for advice on the veterinary care and shoeing of the mules, and indeed deserves a great deal of credit for the excellent shape they were in when we reached Oregon. Ripley and Susan Swan of Hallelujah Farm in Lisbon, Maine, also provided much needed equine and human help.

In Kansas, I want to thank muleman Doyle Prawl of Troy for helping us haul the wagon and mules across the Missouri River and then building wagon parts. The groundskeepers at the Brown County Agriculture Museum in Hiawatha and the Four Mile Corner Rest Area in Sabetha maintain beautiful camping facilities for transients like us. Pony Express reenactor Frank Wessel and his wife, Cheryl, welcomed us to their farm in Axtell for an overnight camp. In Marysville, Ken and Arleta Martin of the Oregon-California Trails Association graciously interrupted their schedules to escort us around the many trail sites in the area. More than a dozen people in town dropped down to our camp at the fairgrounds to offer help and gifts of food and free hay. The volunteers at the Habitat Thrift Shop in Marysville left the door of their shop open at night so that we could curl an extension cord outside to recharge our cell phones. The staff at the Hollenberg Ranch State Park graciously allowed us to use the restored Pony Express station there when we needed shelter from heavy rains.

Riding across Nebraska in a covered wagon was a monthlong

immersion therapy in kindness, a reminder of the essential decency of my country. When thunderstorms surrounded us just after we crossed the Kansas line, Norman Rupprecht of Odell, Nebraska, flagged us down at a rainy crossroads and led us to safety nearby at an abandoned farm, then returned the next morning to help us with chores and run errands while we were stranded for another day. A couple camping next to us at the Rock Creek Station equine park drove me to the Fairbury Sale Barn so I could buy replacement harness parts for the team. At Shickley, when we were again trapped by storms, Don and Shirley Kempf and Will and Margie Swartzendruber allowed us to camp at their farm for two nights, take showers, and borrow their pickup, and even took us along to their church supper. My concept of "trail family" began to form at Shickley with the Kempfs and Swartzendrubers. I have already visited them twice since, and they will be lifelong friends. Also at Shickley, retired cowboy Bill Eich of Geneva, Nebraska, adopted us as his "trail project" and followed our wagon tracks for three nights to visit us in camp, running down the harness parts, camping equipment, and plumbing supplies we needed to add an additional water barrel. I still wear the silk cowboy bandanna that Bill gave me to protect my face and neck against the dust and sun. I have lost count of the number of happy Nebraskans who dropped into our camp in the evening and brought us food, water, and free bales of hay.

At Minden, Nebraska, where we paused just below the Platte River to reoutfit and make wagon repairs, Bill and Nancy Petersen, and their son Jim, were gracious and fun-loving hosts who fed us, welcomed us to sleep in their backyard camper, and charted the rest of the trail in Nebraska for us. Bill, the president of the OCTA chapter in Nebraska, has an encyclopedic grasp of the trail and frequently helped me track down obscure references on trail history. The way that the original fur-trapping route across the Rockies followed by the pioneers eventually grew into a cattle-driving road, a military freight route, the Pony Express, telegraph, the stagecoach road, the railroad tracks West, and then even the Lincoln Highway and the interstate highways, is essential toward understanding the trail's role in American history. Petersen intimately knows the history of each phase of development and was instrumental in helping me understand the organic nature of the trail. His knowledge of the major cutoffs in Nebraska and Wyoming also helped me realize that what today is known as a "trail" was in fact a broad landscape supporting migration and settlement across the West.

In Minden and nearby, woodworking hobbyist Ross Wright built us a new right brake out of oak stock when our original brake disintegrated after just 250 miles. Farmer and horseman Kevin Christensen gave us a spool of thresher belt that we could cut into brake pads and also lent us a second wagon seat for the rest of the trip. Tom and Theresa Delaet let us pasture the mules at their farm, and Tom opened up his shop while Nick was repairing the wagon and building a platform for an additional water barrel. Gene Hunt, the superintendent of the Fort Kearny State Historical Park, welcomed us to the Platte River country with a barbecue and a shady spot to rest the mules. Gene also provided us with a map of Nebraska state parks and public corrals and told us that we were welcome to camp at any of these facilities, even if we arrived too late in the day to find any staff.

We also made camp and enjoyed the hospitality of "cowboy poet" Joe Jeffrey and his wife, Dianne, at the Robb Ranch near Plum Creek, Nebraska. John and Nancy Orr at the spectacularly beautiful Signal Bluff Ranch near Ash Hollow lent us their bunkhouse while we rested the mules for two days, and Nancy found us new collar pads at the Haythorn ranch in Arthur. John Orr's tour of the high country around Signal Bluff allowed me to see how the pioneer trail along the Platte, and the big encampment nearby at Ash Hollow, intruded on traditional Sioux lands and eventually led to one of the earliest conflicts of the Indian Wars, the Battle of Blue Water Creek. Dan Hanlon at the Muddy Creek Ranch near Lisco rescued us with a pickup and trailer when we flipped our Trail Pup, opened his shop while we fixed it, took us on a short cattle drive, and suggested routes around the flooding of the Platte. The cowboys at the Rush Creek and Sun ranches near Oshkosh were kind enough not to laugh when they attempted to teach me how to open barbed-wire gates.

Larry Gill at the Lower 96 Ranch and Jim Hecox in Gothenburg were also wonderfully hospitable, and Gill later made time for a long interview about his preservation of the Midway Pony Express Station. Ann Smith of Cozad, Nebraska, took wonderful pictures of Nick and me with the mules, and she and her husband, Tony, gave me an informative historical tour of the 100th Meridian area, and their family's historic homestead farm, when

I passed through on the way back from Oregon. I have described in the book how grateful I am for the hospitality and instant friendship of Don and Sheila Exner in North Platte.

In western Nebraska, Barb Netherland, then the director of the North Platte Valley Museum in Gering, arranged for us to camp on a nearby horse farm, let us drop Nick's truck on the museum grounds, and took me on a tour of the original Oregon Trail route, pioneer graves, and the fur-trading station at the scenic Robidoux Pass in the Wildcat Hills. Barb also provided introductions to a number of Mormon and western Nebraska trail historians.

The park rangers and staff at the U.S. National Park Service's Scotts Bluff National Monument invited us onto the site to deliver a covered wagon lecture, and I am particularly grateful to Robert Manasek, the resource management specialist at Scotts Bluff, who gave me a tour of the park's archives and showed me many pioneer artifacts and the original watercolors in the William Henry Jackson collection there. It is a shame that I couldn't find room in the book to write more about the remarkable career of Jackson as an expedition photographer, artist, and adventurer. Readers interested in how the trail looked at the height of the nineteenth-century migration can find his pictures on the web or in such excellent coffee-table books as *An Eye for History: The Paintings of William Henry Jackson*.

In eastern Wyoming, Dr. Charles Cawiezell and his wife, Luanne, opened the grounds of their equine clinic and spacious house, and fed us wonderful meals when we stopped for vet checks, shoeing, and teeth-filing for the mules. Cawiezell also read and offered comments on the cholera section of my book. Rancher Bill Reffalt of Fort Laramie let us keep the mules overnight in his corrals and lent me a pickup to scout the trail ahead.

Wagon master Ben Kern of Evansville, Wyoming, who has made assisted crossings of virtually every major trail in the West, caught up with us within a few days of our reaching the state, found us camping spots in Glenrock and Casper, scouted the trail with me as far as Independence Rock, and then drove all the way to Farson with a replacement provisions-cart after we broke our wheels at South Pass.

Randy Brown, chairman of the Graves and Sites Committee of OCTA, probably has done more than anyone else alive to preserve the original

Oregon and California trails, and his work identifying and preserving graves and other sites has added considerable information to our knowledge of routes, pioneer camps, and river fords. Brown was kind enough to spend two days showing me sites along the trail in Wyoming, and we exchanged dozens of emails fact-checking points, place names, and pioneer histories. I often relied on Brown's monograph sketches when describing the major cutoffs and sites of the West. Brown also read my manuscript and made several useful suggestions for improvement.

Modern Wyoming homesteaders Polly Hinds and Lynda German run one of America's most unique retailing locations, Mad Dog & The Pilgrim Booksellers in lonely Sweetwater Station—the sign outside reads OLD BOOKS, FRESH EGGS FOR SALE—and Polly was generous with her time, explaining the impact of the recent Mormon developments along the South Pass stretch of the trail. Jeanne Maher and her grandson, Charles Turquie, have done an extraordinary job protecting the wildlife corridor along the Sweetwater River at their Ellis Ranch near Sweetwater Station, and Charles was most helpful in showing us the various routes through South Pass. Tyler Cundall of the Cundall Ranch near Guernsey, Wyoming, Bill Sinnard at Fort Fetterman, Bill Larsen of the Rattlesnake Grazing Association in Casper, Jennifer Stevenson at the Split Rock Ranch, and Tena Sun of the Sun Ranch allowed us to cross the trail on their land and helped with directions and support. Vikki Correll and her daughter Crystianna Crawford of the Split Rock Café in Jeffrey City allowed us to camp on their grounds and rose early to feed us breakfast.

I have described how Sam and LaVora Peery of Logan, Utah, interrupted their day to climb back up Rocky Ridge and assist us across some of the most difficult terrain of the trip, and I was moved by their religious faith and their dedication to strangers. Elder Doug Ellett and his wife, Beth, of St. George, Utah, welcomed us into Rock Creek Hollow and made us dinner when we camped beside the Willie Handcart burial site, and drove us ahead on the trail to scout our route to South Pass. In Idaho, several Mormon ranchers and their wives extended us similar courtesies. While I disagree with many policies of the Church of Jesus Christ of Latter-day Saints along the modern trail, particularly the renaming of Devil's Gate along the Sweetwater, the individual Saints I met were unfailingly helpful and devoted followers of the Good Samaritan rule.

The residents of Farson, Wyoming, particularly Wyoming Highway Patrol trooper Ed Sabourin, cowboy and mechanic Tell Brenneman, and farmer and pilot Allen Stout, were lifesavers when we limped into the old Big Sandy Station after breaking our wheels at South Pass. My old friend Joe Cantrell of Rock Springs, now a district engineer with the Bureau of Land Management, met us in Farson and offered good advice on the routes through the cutoff country of western Wyoming.

In Idaho and Oregon, ranchers Justin Smith, Gordon Thompson, Tony Clapier, Joe and Glenda Adams, John and Steph Teeter, Chip and Leila Lockett, and Wade Harris allowed us to use their corrals. Steve Stacy of the Snake River Garage in Huntington, Oregon, helped Nick rebuild the axle of our Trail Pup and arranged for us to climb twelve miles of original trail through the Langley Ranch above Burnt River Canyon. Photographer Merri Melde of Oreana, Idaho, who writes the Equestrian Vagabond blog, was wonderful company and made many contributions to our trip. Mike Williams of Baker City, Oregon, welcomed us onto his ranch for our last long camp. Wagon collectors and reenactors Lloyd and Julie Jeffrey of Glenns Ferry, Idaho, who have plunged into the Snake River at Three Island Crossing more than thirty times with their covered wagon and draft horses, spent an afternoon with me explaining the perils of river fords with horses and wagons.

I will never be able to thank Vince and Sue Holtz of Caldwell, Idaho, and Farewell Bend, Oregon, enough for offering a permanent home to our mules and for their wonderful hospitality afterward. Their brother-in-law, Curt Jacobs, hauled Jake, Beck, and Bute and our wagons to their new home in Idaho.

The staffs of the following museums and interpretive centers generously shared their archives and answered my queries while I was writing the book: the National Frontier Trails Museum in Independence, Missouri; the Great Platte River Road Archway Monument and the Museum of Nebraska Art in Kearney, Nebraska; the Fort Caspar Museum and the National Historic Trails Interpretive Center in Casper; the National Oregon/California Trail Center in Montpelier, Idaho; and the National Historic Oregon Trail Interpretive Center in Baker City, Oregon. At the trail center in Montpelier, executive director Becky Smith and mountain man reenactor Kurt Morrison helped make arrangements to receive our rebuilt Trail Pup wheels.

I read nearly one hundred general-interest histories on the West and the emigrant trails, from Bernard DeVoto's *The Year of Decision, 1846*, to Richard Slotkin's brilliant and exhaustive series on the mythology of the frontier, *Regeneration Through Violence*, *The Fatal Environment*, and *Gunfighter Nation*, and relied on reference books like Robert Frazer's *Forts of the West* and Nick Eggenhofer's *Wagons, Mules and Men: How the Frontier Moved West*. For readers interested in more detailed histories of the trail, John D. Unruh Jr.'s *The Plains Across* and Merrill J. Mattes's *The Great Platte River Road* are monuments of scholarship, dense-packed with information and statistics on the commercial scams of the jumping off towns, Indian and pioneer cooperation and conflict, cutoffs and alternate routes, the cholera epidemics, and religious strife. Mattes, a cofounder of OCTA and a former National Parks Service historian, worked from the 1930s to the 1990s, and is credited with rescuing Western trail scholarship from the "main ruts" mentality to a more sophisticated approach that appreciated, as he put it, "that the various routes and trails were all simply components of one big natural and providential travel corridor, the Platte River Valley." Mattes spent almost three decades compiling what has to be considered one of the most triumphant volumes in American history, the *Platte River Road Narratives* (University of Illinois Press), a six hundred-page bibliography of more than two thousand pioneer journals, with biographical sketches, journal excerpts, and manuscript locations for each one. Marathon readers willing to spend a few months with Mattes's research opus will learn more about trail history than by reading several other books combined. I paid $160 for my copy and feasted on it for three years, relying heavily on Mattes's precise entries when quoting from the pioneer journals.

Keith Heyer Meldahl's *Hard Road West: History and Geology along the Gold Rush Trail* vividly mixes pioneer accounts with scientific descriptions of the terrain they were crossing. Will Bagley's excellent series on the western trails—*So Rugged and Mountainous*, *With Golden Visions Bright Before Them*, and *South Pass*—offers new research and additional pioneer voices not heard in earlier histories. The monographs and articles of Todd

Guenther, a history and archeology professor at Central Wyoming College, were useful when I was writing about the South Pass segment of the trail, and Guenther was kind enough to help me straighten out some details about the cutoffs in the area of Burnt Ranch and the Ellis Ranch.

The best and liveliest sources about the trail, of course, are the original trail journals and travel guides written after 1843. I read more than thirty original pioneer and Gold Rush journals, and excerpts of many more, which I identified in my text when quoting from them. I followed the practice of always trying to obtain an original copy of the manuscript or the published journal on the web or at antiquarian bookstores, but in cases where these were not available I attributed my source to the history book where I found it. For readers interested in reading the best journals I would recommend either used or republished volumes of Franklin Langworthy's *Scenery of the Plains, Mountains and Mines*, or *Gold Rush: The Journals, Drawings and Other Papers of J. Goldsborough Bruff*. Kenneth L. Holmes and Dale Morgan have done an excellent job editing the multivolume pioneer journal collections published by the University of Nebraska Press, *Covered Wagon Women* and *Overland in 1846*.

For my chapter on Narcissa and Marcus Whitman, I relied mostly on Narcissa's own published letters and the comprehensive, two-volume biography written by Clifford M. Drury. Richard Slotkin read and commented on sections of that chapter and I cross-checked information with other published histories, including an essay by Todd Guenther, Erin Hammer, and Fred Chaney, which included a very useful map of the Whitman route after South Pass, in the Winter 2002/2003 issue of the *Overland Journal*.

I was able to cobble together my history of the American mule from pioneer accounts, and the excellent web databases and histories offered by the American Mule Museum in Bishop, California; *Western Mule Magazine*; the North American Saddle Mule Association; and *Rural Heritage* magazine. The state of Missouri, which after the 1840s became the mule-breeding capital of America, has funded extensive studies on mules, and I relied on the publications of the State Historical Society of Missouri; the Missouri Agricultural History Series; and the University of Missouri College of Veterinary Medicine. In 1994, Melvin Bradley, a University of Missouri professor of animal science and mule lover who was also known as "the mule's best friend," published his six hundred-page opus, *The Missouri Mule: His Origin and Times*, a copy of which I managed to locate at a used book store in Kentucky. Susan Orlean's excellent article on modern mules in the February 15, 2010, issue of the *New Yorker*, "Riding High: Mules in the Military," confirmed many details that I originally learned from special forces veterans of the war in Afghanistan. Betsy Hutchins in *Rural Heritage* and Steve Edwards in *Cowboy Showcase* have written superb articles titled "How to Buy a Mule." These included vital tips about making detailed inquiries about a mule's bad habits, carefully checking their legs and hooves, and "[taking] your time while mule shopping," advice I completely forgot when buying my own team of Missouri mules.

I considered the evolution of the Pennsylvania Conestoga and the common farm wagon that eventually became the prairie schooner of the plains—in particular, its role in developing the American economy and manufacturing technology—an important aspect of my tale. I was able to pull the many strands together with the help of Jack Day of Monkton, Maryland, the former secretary of the Carriage Association of America and a vice president of the Carriage Museum of America in Lexington, Kentucky, and the preeminent builder of wagons and stagecoaches today, Doug Hansen of the Hansen Wheel and Wagon Shop of Letcher, South Dakota. Histories and articles that I was able to obtain on the internet included Dan R. Manning's "The Challenger," about the Springfield Wagon Company; "Wagons of the West" by Jerry Adams; the *Wheels that Won the West* website; and "Wagon Makers & the Wheels of History" by John Knarr, published by the North Manchester (Indiana) Historical Society in May 2010. On eBay, I obtained original nineteenth-century wagon manuals and sales pamphlets with detailed specifications and company histories from the Peter Schuttler Wagon Co. in Chicago, the Studebaker Brothers Manufacturing Co. in South Bend, Indiana, and the J. Murphy & Sons wagon factory in St. Louis. I was able to follow the development of the larger Conestoga into the smaller, more streamlined mover's wagon of the 1830s—paticularly the development of the fitted bolster—by examining the wagon collections at the Mercer Museum in Doylestown, Pennsylvania; the Cornwall Iron Furnace in Cornwall, Pennsylvania; and the Pioneer Village museum in Minden, Nebraska. The photographs and displays at the Erie Canal Museum in Syracuse, New York, and the National

Park Service's Roebling Bridge Tollhouse at Minisink Ford, New York, provided several examples of farm wagons at work on the canals. Merrill Mattes's *The Great Platte River Road* and Will Bagley's *So Rugged and Mountainous* have long sections about wagon parts, wagon-cover inscriptions, and how the wagons were purchased and put together on the frontier. Peter Schuttler Company histories, the *Encyclopedia of Chicago*, and John Carbutt's *Biographical Sketches of the Leading Men of Chicago* contain extensive material on the Schuttler family and their house-building spree after the Civil War. Communications manager Julia Tunis Bernard and museum director Beverly Smith at the Wells Fargo & Co. in San Francisco confirmed information about the company's early stagecoaches.

I am happy to have written a book that contains a long section expressing ambivalence about the Mormons, because I feel the same way about my own "birth religion," Roman Catholicism. I know so many wonderful, accomplished, and open people within the Saints that I am tempted to ignore the often clumsy administration and public relations of the official LDS Church. Lately, there have been encouraging signs that LDS leaders and scholars are promoting a more tolerant approach to issues like minority membership, the role of women and gay rights, and a more honest assessment of the controversial roles played by Joseph Smith and Brigham Young, polygamy, and the Church's violent history on the frontier. But a book about the Oregon Trail and what it has become today cannot ignore the Church's efforts to control important historic sites and retell frontier history to its own advantage.

Wallace Stegner's *The Gathering of Zion: The Story of the Mormon Trail* remains the single best book about the Mormons and a classic work of history. Fawn M. Brodie's biography of Joseph Smith, *No Man Knows My History*, is also excellent, and I also relied on John G. Turner's *Brigham Young, Pioneer Prophet*, and *The Mormon Experience* by Leonard J. Arrington and Davis Bitton. David Roberts's *Devil's Gate: Brigham Young and the Great Mormon Handcart Tragedy*, and Tom Rea's *Devil's Gate: Owning the Land, Owning the Story*, document the 1856 Mormon handcart tragedy and its repercussions today.

The LDS Church maintains an extensive web archive on the Mormon crossing to Utah after 1847 that includes individual pioneer journals, histories of each year's crossing, descriptions of the Mormons' impressive network of road ranches and trail markers, and documents on the 1856 handcart crisis. I found the work of Chad M. Orton, an archivist with the Family and Church History Division of the Church of Jesus Christ of Latter-day Saints, especially informative. LDS publications such as "Willie Handcart Historic Sites Information" and the "Handbook for Trek Leaders" at the Mormon historic sites in Wyoming were also very helpful. I obtained the May 2006 agreement between the Bureau of Land Management, the LDS Church, and the American Civil Liberties Union, which essentially converted a national landmark along the Oregon Trail in Wyoming, Devil's Gate, into a Mormon-controlled site, and renamed it by the preferred LDS place name, Martin's Cove. Attorney Megan Hayes of Laramie, Wyoming, who was hired to represent the ACLU in its action against the BLM and the LDS Church, explained during a phone interview the reasons for settling the case. Eric Hawkins, the print and broadcast media representative of the LDS Church in Salt Lake, answered my questions and confirmed details of my account. The Mormon takeover of Devil's Gate was extensively covered in the Wyoming press, and occasionally by national newspapers, and I consulted articles published by the *Billings Gazette*, the *Green River Star*, the *Deseret News*, the *Casper Star-Tribune*, the *New York Times*, and the *LDS News* operated by the Church.

My lifelong association with the Amish and Mennonite communities of Lancaster and Snyder counties in Pennsylvania, and the Old Order settlements now spread throughout the Midwest, helps me greatly whenever I purchase horses, wagons, or harness. I received help from many Old Order friends while preparing for my trip across the Oregon Trail, particularly John R. Martin of Ephrata, Pennsylvania, Lamar Martin of Leola, Pennsylvania, Aaron Martin of Versailles, Missouri, and Rufus and Alice Martin in Vandalia, Illinois.

My agent, Sloan Harris of ICM, performed his usual miracles of remaining in touch, arranging for more time for me to finish writing, reading and commenting on my manuscript, and encouraging me during a long writing process. Heather Karpas, Josie Freedman, and Heather Bushong at ICM are unfailingly helpful and prompt.

Illustrator Michael Gellatly, whose work has graced my earlier books, surpassed himself with line drawings, and I am grateful to mapmaker Jeffrey Ward for responding to my specific requests for each map.

Writers who complain that they don't receive enough editing, or can't get their editors to return phone calls, should try and place a book with Jofie Ferrari-Adler at Simon & Schuster. Over three years, working with a manuscript that at one point had ballooned to over 250,000 words, Jofie never lost his focus or interest, and his suggestion that I dig deeper into family memories to explain my reasons for crossing the Oregon Trail greatly improved the book. Jofie has a steel trap mind for details, an excellent BS detector, no pause button, and a touching and rare humility. The support of publisher Jon Karp and associate publisher Richard Rhorer has been heartening, and I am grateful for the hard work of Julianna Haubner and Jonathan Evans. Cary Goldstein, Anne Tate Pearce, Dana Trocker, and Jackie Seow were also wonderfully supportive.

I am blessed with many friends who understand the loneliness of writing and reach out to support me with dinner invitations, moral support, and weekend junkets, especially George and Cindy Rousseau and the entire Rousseau family, Bob and Judy Spiering, Scott Asen, Kirt and Kerri-Lee Mayland, Eileen Fitzgibbons, Danielle Mailer, Peter McEachern, Cynthia Oneglia, Dan Whalen, Tony Bill, and Helen Bartlett. Billy Richards and Tracy Bartells are the most steadfast of friends and have often given me a quiet place to write at their Blue Sky Ranch establishment in Gardiner, New York. My brother Adrian Buck offers me the refuge of his quiet place in Maine.

My sisters Bridget Buck and Ferriss Donham, and their husbands, Ralph Moore and Will Donham, are always exceptionally supportive, and my children, Paper Buck and Charlotte Buck, are loving and loyal beyond reason.

INDEX

Images are referred to in **boldface**.

ABOUT THE AUTHOR

RINKER BUCK began his career in journalism at the *Berkshire Eagle* and was a longtime staff writer for the *Hartford Courant*. He has written for *Vanity Fair, New York, Life,* and many other publications, and his stories have won the Eugene S. Pulliam National Journalism Writing Award and the Society of Professional Journalists Sigma Delta Chi Award. He is the author of the memoirs *Flight of Passage* and *First Job*. He lives in northwest Connecticut.